Reforming Public Management and Governance

The book is dedicated to Peter Aucoin and Christopher Pollitt, pioneers in the field of comparative public management who are no longer with us, both of whom are sorely missed as valued friends and exemplary scholars.

Reforming Public Management and Governance

Impact and Lessons from Anglophone Countries

John Halligan

Emeritus Professor of Public Administration and Governance, Institute for Governance and Policy Analysis, University of Canberra, Australia

Edward Elgar
PUBLISHING

Cheltenham, UK • Northampton, MA, USA

Published by
Edward Elgar Publishing Limited
The Lypiatts
15 Lansdown Road
Cheltenham
Glos GL50 2JA
UK

Edward Elgar Publishing, Inc.
William Pratt House
9 Dewey Court
Northampton
Massachusetts 01060
USA

Paperback edition 2021

A catalogue record for this book
is available from the British Library

Library of Congress Control Number: 2009941234

This book is available electronically in the **Elgar**online
Social and Political Science subject collection
http://dx.doi.org/10.4337/9781839107498

ISBN 978 1 84844 643 4 (cased)
ISBN 978 1 83910 749 8 (eBook)
ISBN 978 1 80220 835 1 (paperback)

Printed and bound by CPI Group (UK) Ltd, Croydon, CR0 4YY

Contents

List of tables   vi
Preface and acknowledgements   viii
Glossary, acronyms and abbreviations   x

1   Reforming Anglophone public management and governance   1

2   Administrative tradition and Westminster in reform-era
        governance   22

3   Politicising the executive branch: changing roles,
        resources, relationships   38

4   Ministers and mandarins under political management   66

5   Management dilemmas   90

6   Contradictions in implementing performance management   113

7   Management and bureaucracy in a political milieu   136

8   Coordination and collaboration   156

9   Long-term reform and public management systems   186

10   Postscript: directions for change   211

Appendix 1   Reform programmes and judgements in the 2010s   222
Appendix 2   Country chronologies   227
Appendix 3   Dynamic of change: centring and decentring   236
Bibliography   244
Index   290

Tables

1.1	Instruments for expanding ministerial influence	10
3.1	Political and policy roles and instruments	40
3.2	Ministers' increasing influence in policy and management roles	44
3.3	Ministerial staff in Australia, Canada, New Zealand, and the United Kingdom	54
4.1	Politicisation impacts on senior public servants	78
5.1	Management results and status of dilemmas	107
6.1	Dimensions of frameworks	131
6.2	Performance 'system' by country and performance instrument ownership	132
7.1	Changing environments and types of accountability for Australia	146
7.2	Effect of demands inside government	148
8.1	Vertical coordination: political and administrative instruments	159
8.2	Instruments of horizontal coordination	170
9.1	Major functions affected by politicisation	188
9.2	Use of political instruments in Anglophone systems	189
9.3	Types of relationship between ministers and public servants	190
9.4	Managerialism: long-term results for components	196
9.5	Twenty-first-century components of public management systems	201

10.1 Public management system: scenarios for the twenty-first
century 215

A2.1 Timeline Australia 228

A2.2 Timeline Canada 230

A2.3 Timeline New Zealand 232

A2.4 Timeline United Kingdom 234

A3.1 Recentring and centralising in the twenty-first century 239

Preface and acknowledgements

This study commenced with two fundamental propositions. The first was that public sector reform had either failed in some respects or was not achieving traction despite the efforts of reformers. Secondly, relations centred on governance had been repeatedly ruptured and not reconstituted. This was reflected in the fluctuating gaps between principles and practice. In particular, conventions that had restrained behaviour and discretionary power applied less. Throughout what is called the reform era (from the 1980s on) that governments have variously been both less in control and more controlling (and sometimes out of control) has been apparent with new heights being attained in the twenty-first century. The book analyses the core dimensions of the two strands of managerialism and politicisation and the interconnections between them. Some chapters are devoted to either, but the majority cover both to varying extents. The cutoff for the book was late 2019.

Many debts have been accumulated over several decades of comparative research on Anglophone countries, and while drafting this book in the late 2010s. The earliest work dates from collaborative research conducted with Colin Campbell and John Power and has continued since, most intensively in recent years, including that with Jonathan Craft. Many former and current public servants have spoken to me off the record in all four countries. Their insights are greatly appreciated.

A large debt is owed to the many authors and official and think tank reports that I have made extensive use of. Comparative book projects initiated by Geert Bouckaert, Tom Christensen, Per Lægreid, Guy Peters, Jon Pierre and Donald Savoie (and the comparative civil service systems group centred on Leiden University: Frits van der Meer, Jos Raadschelders and Theo Toonen) contributed to my understanding of comparative public management and governance. Some of the analysis has appeared in edited books, as acknowledged.

The Governance of Public Sector Organizations Permanent Study Group of the European Group of Public Administration was a sounding board for ideas, even though the Anglophone focus may have sometimes been bewildering. More generally, meetings and members of the SOG (Structure and Organization of Government) group, Research Committee 27 of the International Political Science Association provided a constant source of advice and inspiration.

The book has benefited from the erudite observations of Michael di Francisco, who read and commented on the manuscript. His deep understanding of both the managerial and political dimensions of the Australian and New Zealand systems (and more generally) has been much appreciated.

At the country level, many Canadians provided insights and facilitated the research, most particularly Peter Aucoin, Jacque Bourgault, Margaret Biggs, Colin Campbell, Amanda Clarke, Jonathan Craft, OP Dwivedi, David Gow, Ralph Heintzman, Jim Lahey, Evert Lindquist, Luc Juillet, Rob Shepherd and David Zussman. Jacques Bourgault allowed me to sight his manuscript based on a survey of Canadian deputy ministers. The former Canadian Centre for Management Development and the Canadian School of Public Service hosted me as I learnt about the Canadian system.

On the United Kingdom, the study has benefited from the advice of Gavin Drewry, Patrick Dunleavy, Catherine Haddon, Peter Hennessy, Martin Laffin, Martin Lodge, Julian McCrae, Christopher Pollitt and Jill Rutter, and more generally the unrivalled expertise and analysis undertaken by the Institute for Government and the National Audit Office. Many insights about the New Zealand case were acquired from Jonathan Boston, Chris Eichbaum, Elizabeth Eppel, Derek Gill, Bob Gregory, Colin James, Karl Lofgren, Graham Scott, Richard Shaw, and from the State Services Commission. Canberra colleagues who contributed to my understanding of Australia (and beyond) are Mark Evans, Paul Fawcett, Lewis Hawke, Maria Maley, Dave Marsh, Ian Marsh, Andrew Podger, Graham Smith, Roger Wettenhall and John Wanna.

An Australian Research Council grant on Whole of Government stimulated work on horizontal governance. The University of Canberra and Institute for Public Administration Australia Trust Fund provided support for comparative analysis. The Institute for Governance and Policy Analysis at the University of Canberra provided a stimulating environment for finalising the study.

I appreciate the patience of Edward Elgar, and in particular the support of Alex Pettifer, the Editorial Director, and the comments of the anonymous person commissioned to review the book.

Finally, my thanks go to my wife, Penelope St Clair, who deserves the highest credit for her immense support, wise advice and incisive editorial contributions to this book.

Glossary, acronyms and abbreviations

accounting officer	senior civil servant responsible to the UK parliament for the stewardship of resources. Canada also uses a variation on the concept
agencification	creation of semi-autonomous agencies as part of a disaggregation process
agency	used as an alternative to 'department' and in other contexts might encompass departments and non-departmental organisations
AO	accounting officer
APS(C)	Australian Public Service (Commission)
AU	Australia (abbreviation)
Barber, M.	architect of UK's implementation unit and advisor to governments
BASS	Administrative and Support Services Benchmarking (NZ)
BPS	Better Public Services, a priority-driven reform initiative originating in the NZ Better Public Services review (BPSAG 2011)
bureaucratisation	reliance on controls, rules and regulation, and processes and procedures
CA	Canada (abbreviation)
CAG	Comptroller and Auditor General (UK)
central agency	cross-government agencies at the centre
CEO	chief executive officer
civil service	used in the UK. The preferred term elsewhere is 'public service'
core executive	components of government and their relationships; narrow and broader versions in use (UK)
CPA	Committee of Public Accounts (UK)
CSC	Civil Service Commission (UK)

DBP	departmental business plan (UK)
delegation	assignment of responsibilities from one level to another
department head	generic term for chief executive officers (NZ), departmental secretaries (AU), deputy ministers (CA), and permanent secretaries (UK)
dept	department
deputy minister	head of department in Canada
devolution	used by reformers in Australia and New Zealand: 'the transfer of decision-making capacity from higher levels in the organisation to lower levels' (TFM1 1992, p. 89), and was applied to transfers from central agencies to departments and within departments
DoF	Dept of Finance (AU)
DPMC	Department of the Prime Minister and Cabinet (AU, NZ)
exempt staff	Canadian term for staff appointed by a minister
Finance	Department of Finance (AU)
FMI	Financial Management Initiative (UK)
FMIP	Financial Management Improvement Program (AU)
GFC	global financial crisis
Gomery Commission	Inquiry into 'sponsorship scandal', with accountability focus (CA)
HC	House of Commons
IDC	interdepartmental committee
IMAA	Increased Ministerial Authority and Accountability (CA)
KPI	key performance indicator
MAC	Management Advisory Committee (AU)
MAF	Management Accountability Framework (CA)
Manzoni, J.	CEO of the UK civil service
Maude, F.	Minister for the Cabinet Office in the Cameron government (UK)

ministry	The term co-exists with departments in NZ and for some agencies in the UK. The term department covers both
MRRS	Management, Resources and Results Structure (CA)
NAO	National Audit Office (see CAG)
No. 10	Downing Street, Prime Minister's Office (UK)
NPG	new political governance
NPM	new public management. A slippery concept because of loose applications. It is mainly used here in the narrower sense of a reform programme emphasising boundaries and external actors
NZ	New Zealand (abbreviation)
OAG	Office of the Auditor General (CA)
OPA	Output and Performance Analysis (UK)
PBE	policy-based evidence (as opposed to EBP: evidence-based policy)
PCO	Privy Council Office (CA)
PF2	Private Finance 2 (UK)
PFI	Public Finance Initiative (UK)
PGPA	Public Governance, Performance and Accountability Act 2013 (AU)
PI	performance information
PIF	performance improvement framework (NZ)
PMD	prime minister's department. A generic term that covers the Australian and New Zealand Department of the Prime Minister and the Cabinet (DPMC), the Canadian Privy Council Office (PCO), and the UK Cabinet Office (CO)
PMDU	prime minister's delivery unit (UK)
PMO	prime minister's office, a term in standard use across the four
PMS	public management system
PPP	public–private partnership (UK)
PRAS	Planning, Reporting and Accountability Structure (CA)

PSA	Public Service Agreement (UK)
PSC	Public Service Commission
red tape	excessive reliance on regulations and bureaucracy
reform era	early 1980s until the present
SCS	senior civil service (UK)
SDP	single departmental plan (UK)
SES	senior executive service
SOA	special operating agencies (CA)
SOI	statement of intent
spad	special adviser (UK)
Spending Review	a process run by the UK Treasury every few years for setting expenditure limits and planning
SSC	State Services Commission, a leading central agency in New Zealand
TBS	Treasury Board of Canada Secretariat
TPA	traditional public administration
UK	United Kingdom (abbreviation)

1. Reforming Anglophone public management and governance

The starting point is a conundrum: why in the fourth decade of reform to public management and governance have major transformations being sought in Anglophone countries raised the same basic questions that engaged reformers in the 1980s? There are two parts to the problem.

First, major reform has occurred to public sectors, yet official reports suggest that the public service has not changed in significant respects, and new reform agendas keep being launched (see Appendix 1), but generally with mixed results. A number of factors can be advanced for this, but it may be because the conditions for effective implementation of reform are missing or that the public management systems have become irreformable in many respects. Other than hard-edged, structural changes, and blunt-instrument resource cuts other types of innovative reform are often dissipated. The lack of progress in key areas suggests the unlikelihood of durable reform in public management systems which have showed signs of ossification and gridlock for some time.

The second point of departure is the consistently strong indications that governance systems are out of kilter because of the lack of fit and balance between the parts, relationships and capacities. This is displayed in many ways. There is the seeming inability of political executives to get traction on the public service, to handle relationships effectively, and to obtain a results-focus and implement their priorities. Ministers and their advisers continue to exclaim about the public service and the need for reform, yet their own performance and leadership have been wanting and the handling of governance and public policy often ineffectual. There has continued to be rancorous debate about fundamentals that signals lack of agreement between principal actors. The plunging public perceptions of central governments reflect this.

The four systems are prone, to varying degrees to lurch towards instability. This judgement is supported by independent analyses in the four countries that have intensified the level of critique in the 2010s and diagnoses of the dire consequences for good governance of this neglect.

There are a number of factors in play which cannot all be addressed in one book, but which have to be recognised as disrupters to government and reform. There is the moving feast of national and international crises, the implosions of party government and coalitions, ever increasing environmental complexity and turbulence, and the impact of technological change and the rise of social media.

This chapter frames the book's approach in terms of the two dominant reform agendas of Australia, Canada, New Zealand and the United Kingdom: managerialism and politicisation. These agenda have different implications for the role and functioning of public management and governance and are in conflict in important respects. The chapter develops an approach to comparing jurisdictions that have been managerialised and politicised and asks why unintended consequences such as bureaucratisation need to be taken into account. It addresses chronic discordant elements and sources of friction as a basis for exploring the consequences of the contradictions and shortfalls in performance.

The longevity of the reform era allows for the examination of the experience of four countries spanning several decades of reforming the system of public management and governance by exploring the results of an extended period of management reform and political change; the consequences, including the long-term impact of political and managerial reform; and what accounts for the results, including the role of the Anglophone model and approach to reform. To engage with the fundamental issues, it is necessary to interrogate fundamental relationships and the reprogramming of politicians' roles, the experiments with managerialism, and the connections between the two.

QUESTIONS ABOUT LONG-TERM REFORM AND GOVERNANCE

The reform era (commencing around 1980) presented unparalleled opportunities for reformers to learn about what worked and to choose between an ever-increasing range of instruments for pursuing government objectives. Yet there have been continuing questions about experiments (and misadventures) with managerialism and politicisation, what was accomplished, and the lessons to be learned from the experience. Central to this book is an analysis of key dimensions of political and managerial change with an emphasis on the twenty-first century.

The modern era of public sector reform was instigated around four decades ago when Margaret Thatcher enforced political and operational transformation in the United Kingdom. The political dynamics of reform were highly significant as the origins of the reform era were identified with politicians with conviction who aimed to deal with the civil service (Savoie 1994). However, broader questions about the capacity of the centre of government had already emerged and been debated. Management ideas had originated earlier (e.g. Canada, via the United States, in the early 1960s) but no reform initiatives bit into the fabric of public administration in the way that Thatcherism did

(Campbell and Wilson 1995). The Australian reform agenda surfaced next, but the subsequent entry of New Zealand transfixed thinking about public management internationally (Boston et al. 1996). New theories about organising the state and key relationships flourished, often with an economic basis. These developments produced the realisation that major reform was possible, overturning conventional wisdom about reform failure (Caiden 1991), but was it sustainable and effective?

What has Changed because of Managerial and Political Reform?

The first dominant change concerns the political executive. Observers in the early 1980s would have difficulty recognising the relationship between the public service and politicians in the 2010s. Basic tenets of the relationship were transformed and often existed in a contested and fragile environment. In the decades between these periods, debate heightened as political executives exploited previously unused powers to direct and influence public management. Their main motives for reform were to assert their authority within the executive branch, to determine what levers targeted political priorities and extract better results from the public service. To achieve these ends a range of political controls and instruments were used. The expansion of executive power led to recurrent questions as to how effective their choices were and with what impact, including whether these actions shattered the existing institutions and foreshadowed the end of Whitehall (e.g. Campbell and Wilson 1995; Page 2010; Diamond 2019b). Similarly, Aucoin's (2008, 2012) diagnosis of 'new political governance' was emblematic of an advanced stage of politicisation in the context of the environmental pressures of the twenty-first century.

A management approach was injected rapidly during the 1980s. By the end of the first decade of the reform era, managerialism had been recognised (Pollitt 1990), an Anglophone triumvirate had been identified (Hood 1990) and new public management (NPM) was distinguished (Hood 1991). For another decade, the experiences of and myths about the Anglophone group were highly influential for reform internationally (OECD 1995). Fast forward beyond the NPM variant and the fallout it produced, and the post-global financial crisis (GFC) scrambling to either re-inject NPM elements or renew flagging systems with ailing managerial capability and performance. Governments had to review their public management systems in the 2010s because they were performing poorly in important respects. Repeated attempts at reform had a direct impact when they were rule-based, structural and hard-edged (e.g. privatisation, resource cutbacks), but other management measures were more susceptible to the vagaries of reform contexts, relapses and unintended consequences from pendulum swings and cyclical changes (Pollitt 2008). Consequently, management and political change occurred but not necessarily as expected and hard evidence of the results was often scant (Pollitt 2013b).

What are the Results and Consequences of Sustained Reform?

The components of executive branches were out of kilter by the 1960s and 1970s. These imbalances encompassed fundamental and unresolved questions about the roles of ministers and public servants, the relative importance of policy and implementation, the mix of centralised control and decentralisation, the roles of administration and management, and the level and form of external engagement; all of which had direct implications for the public management system. A succession of official reports in all four countries produced diagnoses, critiques and recommendations during two decades of review (1960s and 1970s). They were followed by the reform era in the 1980s in which public sectors were redesigned and reconstituted. These diagnoses of the condition of the four systems are a useful counterpoint to the ideological drive of neo-liberalism and new public management. Despite what was claimed, fundamental principles of organisation and public administration were not superseded by the advent of managerialism as some analysts pointed out after the first tranche of reforms (Pollitt 1990; Hood 1998; Gregory 2001).

A central question to ask is, what has become of the public management system over the long term? In the early years the Anglophone countries were acclaimed for the relative ease with which they initiated reforms; however, they subsequently had difficulties sustaining many of them over time. Consider the official reports in Appendix 1, which include references to fundamental issues thought to have been addressed in the 1980s. An outstanding example is the constant search across four decades for methods and techniques that deliver *results*. Moving from diagnosis to effective and sustained implementation proved to be challenging (twentieth-century implementation issues have been identified in, e.g. Pollitt and Bouckaert 2011; Zifcak 1994). The relapses often signalled a return to confronting the big issues addressed earlier in the reform era: the need to increase control over permanent bureaucrats because they were perceived to be too powerful; and the need to modernise and incentivise bureaucratic decision-making (discussed in the next section).

This apparent loss of the reform achievements and momentum of the 1980s and 1990s can be attributed both to inattention to the governance of the public management system and undue attention as reform agendas swung in diverse directions, the turnover of reforms resulting from new leaders and governments. External factors have also played a part: inter alia economic and political contexts, technological change and management fashions (Pollitt and Bouckaert 2017). The need to adjust and realign with environmental change offered one powerful argument about progressively redefining the state's role:

'What was critical and possible in . . . 1990 is not necessarily vital or possible in 2011' (BPSAG 2011, p. 2; Ryan and Gill 2011; Canada, Clerk of the Privy Council 2013; APS Review 2019).

This leads to a core question of how to account for the mixed results of change over the longer term. At one level, questions can be asked about the relative impacts of managerialism and politicisation. How is it that the gains and potential of the reform era were apparently dissipated by dysfunctions and unintended consequences? Three fundamental tensions exist: how to balance the political executive's demands for responsiveness with inconsistent support for public service competence and capability; how to balance the managerialist ability to utilise a range of instruments with the retention of public service effectiveness; and how to reconcile the contradictions that derive from the interaction of politicisation and managerialism.

This chapter later addresses several factors that can vitiate relationships and the functioning of public management systems. At another level, there are fundamental questions that echo through the history of systemic reform about finding appropriate mixes in the redesign of public management, and balance in the relationships integral to effective governance and policy delivery. Of increasing importance has been whether there has been an understanding of and interest in the condition and sustainability of the public management system.

What is the Role and Continuing Significance of the Anglophone Approach?

The Anglophone approach refers to both the relationships and conventions of an administrative tradition and a public management model. The four Anglophone countries have been regarded as constituting a coherent group because of their common tradition grounded in the Westminster model, and historical associations and interactions. It has long been maintained that there was an 'Anglo-Saxon' administrative tradition, the term favoured in Europe, that differed from traditions on the Continent and elsewhere (Peters 2003; Rhodes et al. 2009; Painter and Peters 2010a).[1]

The coherence of the tradition appeared to be reaffirmed once the reform era was underway as few other countries could respond so directly and quickly. The emergence of a distinctive pattern of public management reforms and the commonalities between the countries confirmed a connection between the administrative tradition and an Anglophone reform model. Australia, New Zealand and the United Kingdom were the countries most identified with major change in the initial decades of the reform era, and they acquired a rep-utation for being significant reformers and leaders of the public management movement (Pollitt 1993; OECD 1995), and a source of reform experience that was diffused internationally (Halligan 2015c). Questions about the efficacy and sustainability of reform in these countries point to the need to examine the role of the tradition, and its associated model.

First is the question of how well features of the Anglophone reform model relate to the tradition. The Anglophone reformist agenda has been comprehensive, continual and iterative, and reliant on using a range of public and private instruments, enabled by managerialism. The administrative tradition plays a role in reform because it is both facilitative, enabling instrumentalism while also constraining reform in some respects. The logics of rational action and appropriateness can be seen to be in play here (March and Olsen 1989).

Secondly, the assumption that the four countries are part of one tradition suggests the need to demonstrate the extent to which they operate within and engage with it through comparisons across political, managerial and governance dimensions. There are distinctive elements to their historic pathways (see Chapter 2), which might suggest divergence and a loosely coupled tradition, but the strength of the core principles and reform dynamics might still produce adherence to a common tradition. Other state traditions have exhibited variations between countries (cf. Veggeland 2007; Ongaro 2009; Lægreid and Rykkja 2015), the implications being that if the influence of country contexts is strong, several public management models could be apparent.

Thirdly, there is the question of whether the tradition has been 'reconstituted' or modified (Richards 2008; Rhodes et al. 2009). Given the level of changes, to what extent has reform remained true to Westminster principles and maintained something distinctively Anglophonic? The internationalisation of reform has led to commonalities in approaches to public management, which suggests the need to compare countries operating under different traditions to establish whether traditions retain distinctiveness.

Finally, there is the question of the significance of the Anglophone model and its public management approach over the long term. It has long been apparent that Anglophone countries are not necessarily at the forefront of international reform as their performance is less prominent in international rankings (e.g. the UK is no longer the model: King and Crewe 2014, p. ix). Other, usually small, often northern European countries have acquired that status in international benchmarking exercises.

FRAMING THE ANALYSIS

Three big ideas dominated the outset of public sector reform: traditional bureaucracy had failed because it was no longer suitable for the current environment; managerialism was the alternative, the new paradigm for achieving public purposes; and elected politicians were responsible and should lead, direct and control. The latter two ideas are fundamental to reconfiguring the public management system.

The lack of frameworks for analysing reform led observers to draw on general analyses of public administration that delineated major components that were subject to change. Several arenas of 'behaviour and belief' have been distinguished, each associated with an agenda (Self 1978, pp. 313–14; Pierre 1995). Categories for demarcating the analysis of major changes to public sectors include the bureaucratic, political, social and private sectors. The latter two focus on external relationships between a bureaucracy and its environment; the first two are fundamental to a system of government. The two internal agendas reconstitute the bureaucracy and redefine the political executive's role, both of which are the focus of this study.

These types of analysis were salient to the traditional model of public administration and its modern successor in so far as the latter was a response to the limitations of the former. Traditional public administration (TPA) held sway in Anglo-American countries from the nineteenth century to after the Second World War and was grounded in explicit distinctions between the public and private sectors, and between politicians and civil servants (Garvey 1993; Hood 1994), the latter being delegated responsibilities for implementation as per the classic conception and accorded discretion to use their expertise (Garvey 1993). The bureaucratic agency was a largely bounded organisation that operated according to principles that in many material respects reflected Weber's depiction of an ideal bureaucratic type, in particular specialisation, hierarchy and formal rules.

In an era of unprecedented reforms since the 1980s, two fundamental questions of public management and governance have featured and emphatically shaped the design of the public management system. These questions are interconnected in that they both represent an assault on existing notions of bureaucracy and relationships within the executive branch and challenge the Westminster system. The first question centres on the role of executive government in the state, and how it operates in terms of Westminster principles in Anglophone countries and institutionalised understandings about the roles of politicians and bureaucrats. A central dimension is the relationship between democracy and bureaucracy and the complexities that this entailed (Etzioni-Halevy 1983). The lineage of how this relationship should be redefined was articulated through 'responsiveness' and the assertion of the authority of representative government and received expression through rational choice theory. These ideas represented a swing away from the conventional wisdom of the 'administrative state', and from trustee perspectives on bureaucratic roles. The second set of ideas is about moving beyond bureaucracy as it had been experienced (Barzelay 1992; Halligan and Power 1992), and its associated features. At its core was the promotion of managerial over administrative principles associated with TPA as advocated by proponents of generic management. A set of features associated with traditional bureaucracy (e.g. the focus on process) were replaced by a new set (e.g. the focus on results). A strong underpinning was offered by private sector experience, which was echoed in the erosion of the differentiation between the two sectors.

Each approach pointed to distinctive ways for developing the public management system. The first reinforced hierarchy by substituting one form of control for another – a top-down political direction for bureaucratic processes. The second sought to release the system from the constraints, boundaries and operational modes of traditional bureaucracy, but subjected it to management precepts as well as the mania of managerialism. Both opened the system by freeing it from the limitations of traditional principles and boundaries and exposing it more directly to a range of environmental influences, the fashions of generic and private management, and the dogma and vicissitudes of politics. In several respects the public management system was now the obverse of its predecessor, presenting both perennial and new tensions and dilemmas.

The focus of this book is the analysis of the longer-term impact of managerialism and politicisation and the consequences of a political management approach based on the combination of the two (Halligan and Power 1992). The literature has addressed the initial impact of reform, but much less so the second half of the reform era (with the turn of the century serving as an approximate transition point). The issues emerging from the changes have continued to reverberate in the twenty-first century, questioning the purpose of a public management system once seen as the stable element that supported the dynamism of politicians; and asking whether an appropriate balance and fit could be developed and sustained through roles and relationships.

Politicising the Executive Branch

Under the Westminster model, relations between politicians and bureaucrats traditionally centred on the co-existence of the neutral public service and responsible government (Aucoin 1995). The embedded tension between the two elements was kept in balance by applying well-established principles, but their enactment had become dependent upon the overarching role acquired by permanent secretaries (i.e. heads of public service departments). By the beginning of the reform era, this type of relationship could no longer be assumed and was being challenged.

During the last 40 years, a new imbalance became characteristic as politicians expanded their authority over the previously ascendant officials. The relationship between the political executive and the public service changed independently of management reform, although the two were interlinked. The origins of the revolt against an entrenched public service long predated the reform era and was foreshadowed in the United States with the move away from progressive values by more assertive political executives and political appointments to the civil service following the Second World War. Canada's Prime Minister Trudeau initiated changes to the core executive that presaged the 'new political governance' (Aucoin 2006).

There has been extensive discussion of what constitutes politicisation (e.g. Mulgan 1998; Peters and Pierre 2004a, 2004b). In this study, politicisation refers to extensions to the political executive's influence and control within the executive branch. The usage here has been chosen for its simplicity and its inclusiveness (cf. Kemp 1986). It focuses on the use of ministerial levers for increasing political influence, and resources and changing relationships. The expansion and contraction of political roles are normal in governance over time, and ministers are constitutionally empowered to exercise authority.

The modes of demarcating politics and administration range from a model that firmly separates political and public service careers to that in which the careers intermingle and boundaries are weak (Pierre 1995, p. 207). The relative independence of the political and bureaucratic spheres has meant that the apolitical British model could once be represented as being at one end of an international spectrum that envisaged a heavily 'politicised' system (mainly political appointments) at the opposite end. A set of issues for the reform era was whether, to what extent and in what respects, systems were moving along this spectrum, and what the impact was on effectiveness of relationships and the performance of the public management system.

A traditional relationship is based on well-understood norms: a neutral public service that serves the political executive regardless of party, and a political executive that in turn respects the integrity of the civil service by supporting its apolitical and professional character. Specific features are the career public servant, a permanent official who survives successive governments; senior appointments drawn from the ranks of professional careerists; and the ministerial department as the repository of expert knowledge and primary policy adviser to government (Roberts 1987; Aucoin 1995; Campbell and Wilson 1995; Halligan 2001). The contrasting features of the responsiveness model have important implications for the operation of the political-administrative system because it is no longer a relatively closed and stable system underpinned by a general understanding of roles. Instead, the political executive seeks to secure and sustain its control over the public service. There are various interpretations of the direction of the relationships internationally with generic 'politicisation' being favoured by observers (Peters and Pierre 2001, 2004a).

How can politicisation be conceptualised and analysed? Principal–agent theory provides a distinct alternative to traditional formulations emphasising the administrative state and guardian roles. The shift from a trustee to an agency conception is one basis for analysing changes to the relationship.

Table 1.1   Instruments for expanding ministerial influence

PM/Minister's levers	Potential extension
• Prime minister	Prime minister's office.
• Ministers' roles	PM's dept centralising role. PMD delivery/results unit.
	Principal–agent: range of roles, authority, responsiveness.
• Ministers' offices; partisan staff	Roles in policy processes and management.
• Policy advice	Pluralisation of roles in policy development.
• Management roles	Implementation.
• Appointments	Senior appointments; performance assessment of officials.

Agency theory is of value for drawing attention to ministers' attempts to reduce information asymmetries and to seek control of the public service and the results of its work (Laffin 1997). For the political executive, the means of changing the basis of the relationship is through managing the incentives faced by public servants. Under a rational choice approach, the incentive structure for an actor involves the costs and benefits in making choices (Ritchie 2014). For a politicising agenda, the question is how public servants' incentives can be reshaped to suit ministers.

The incentives for public servants to respond derive from ministers exercising ministerial authority (and through partisan agents operating as extensions to that authority). The analysis of politicisation is based on the extent to, and ways in, which political instruments are employed (Table 1.1). The relative use of these instruments in different countries provides a means for making comparisons about modes of politicisation. The expanded bevy of instruments applies also to a range of processes, such as coordination, performance and implementation examined in later chapters.[2]

Managerialism

The conception of managerialism used in this book assumes a set of core features that are present in some form. Managerialism is favoured over NPM because it is a more focused concept and does not carry the same baggage. It was in fact a forerunner of NPM (Pollitt 1990, 1993), and an older and more diverse movement (Painter 2011). It was the preferred term in Australia (Considine and Painter 1997; Halligan 2007b; Painter 2011); and Canada (Aucoin 1990).[3] The position here is that NPM is a variant of managerialism (Pollitt 2016).

Management evolution occurs because of the ability to incorporate new approaches, and to refine old ones, although they may be vulnerable to transient fashions and agendas. Specific components may be elaborated (performance, agencification), or externalised (e.g. outsourcing), recalibrated internally (horizontal management), or invested with specific meanings (values management), but the managerial centrepiece provides the continuity. For most authors previously mentioned, managerialism is the core concept, and rather than being distracted by NPM (or new public governance), all iterations are depicted as variations on managerialism.

The conception of managerialism has several components, not all of which can be addressed in this study. Prominent features, such as efficiency and resource use, are central objectives (and prevail over other objectives when austerity is prominent) but have been examined (by e.g. Hood and Dixon 2015). The attributes most relevant to this study are:

1. Management processes are central to the functioning of the public management system but depend on improved managerial capacity for delivering results and services,[4] and this is contingent on allowing managers to manage.
2. Improved performance and results are fundamental and underscore expectations of managers.
3. Discretion via forms of decentralisation: 'devolution' of responsibilities to departments; delegation to managers allowing them line authority over resources; and disaggregation of departmental responsibilities through agencification. It addresses one of two principles of TPA, generalised rules, and their replacement by managerial discretion (or flexibility and freedom to manage) (Dunleavy and Hood 1994; Hood 1994).
4. Change and reform. Managerialism emphasises change because of its receptivity to new techniques and responsiveness to environmental change, a distinguishing feature being 'flexibility . . . in absorbing or generating new ideas and models' (Painter 2011, p. 238). Change management and management improvement are priorities because of the acceptance of the ethos of continuous change. System design and reform are constant features.
5. Managerialism was conceived in terms of debureaucratisation (Savoie 1994), the removal of features associated with rigid forms of organisation. To what extent bureaucratic features were reinvented as part of the controls of a new management system (Gregory 2001) for the imperatives of managerialism required measuring, evaluating and rationalising (Hoggett 1997).

Managerialism was also superimposed on an existing TPA system and the extent to which the old was replaced by the new was an open question (Halligan and Power 1992) and depended on whether functional specialisation, hierarchy and the reliance on rules could be addressed. There was extensive choice and flexibility in steering, which encompassed a range of instruments for organising and controlling public management, including structures, delivery options, performance and coordinating.[5]

In addition to managerialism (about changing internal operations) and politicisation (about changing relationships and authority), there have been two contenders for greater attention that highlight external relationships: NPM has focused on transferring responsibilities to external agents, and is closely associated with reducing the role of the state; and new public governance relies on networks that extend (or exist) beyond the boundaries of government. Both cover activity outside the scope of this study at least in terms of systematic analysis, although externalising agendas have had major effects on internal competence and can be touched on by drawing on a recent study (Craft and Halligan 2020).

New public management (NPM) has of course been influential. Several features distinguish it from managerialism, most importantly a mainstream view that NPM, 'fundamentally espouses economic values and objectives' (Christensen and Lægreid 2011a, p. 3; Halligan 2011b) and the minimisation of public–private distinctions. At the time it was coined, NPM was informed more by developments in New Zealand and the United Kingdom than Australia (Hood 1990). An NPM approach entails inter alia externalisation, marketisation, privatisation and competition, as well as disaggregation (e.g. Hood 1991; Lane 2000), but many applications of NPM inflated it to be a catch-all that encompassed anything that happened. These features remain as options rather than core operating principles of the public management system.

Another set of ideas, variously known as 'new public governance', 'governance' or 'network governance', has been recognised as addressing the limitations of other models (Osborne 2010; Pollitt and Bouckaert 2017). A further approach, also hailed as a likely successor of NPM, is 'public value governance' (Bryson et al. 2015), which has the advantage of encapsulating public governance dimensions while bringing into relief public value. The emphasis on engaging non-government actors and networks is arguably most relevant to the sub-national level, although the pressures on central governments to engage externally have been increasing (Prince 2018). But note the contrary argument that traditional governance has decreased at the centre in Britain with less consultation and an 'impositional policy style' (Richardson 2018). The centrality of the state continues (Bell and Hindmoor 2009) and may increase under governments exploiting the plenitude of power. Nevertheless, the underlying principles have resonance: a focus on the horizontal rather than the vertical, and incorporation of a broader range of actors and voices in the policy process. Much of the twenty-first century reform agenda was rotated to address joining and coordinating increasingly fragmented government. Public governance complements and extends the repertoire of management (cf. Hyndman and Liguori 2016). Public governance is employed here in the sense of governing the public management system and specifically horizontal collaboration and networks within the system.

Where is managerialism located in the overall approaches and models that have proliferated? One response is to use hybridity as a means of capturing the 'layers' or contradictory dimensions of public management systems (Christensen and Lægreid 2011c). There are several reasons for adopting a different approach if hybridity applies to broad brush approaches. First, at their core the public management systems of Anglophone countries adhere to managerialist principles. Secondly, the argument that there is a progression through models, which naturally leads to new public governance, has yet to be established (although it is more apparent at the delivery end where substantial interaction with third parties is required). Specifically, there is a lack of evidence for NPM being transitional between TPA and new public governance (Hyndman and Liguori 2016). In addition, the significance of the new digital era is unmistakable (Dunleavy et al. 2006), but less as a successor to public management than a major overlay. Thirdly, a neo-Weberian option is advanced (Pollitt and Bouckaert 2011, 2017), because of its relevance to European countries, but is normally grounded in a different administrative tradition and adaptation of Weberian principles.

The position here is that public management systems in Anglophone systems are anchored in managerialism as defined, but to varying degrees other nominal (quasi-) paradigms are either absorbed or constitute periodically prominent elements with the potential to influence its character. Public management became the mainstream with variations (notably TPA, NPM, digital governance and public value governance) encompassed by it. Other tropes can also be subsumed within a public management approach, and in that sense the public management model is more complex and hybrid (Allen and Eppel 2017). It is important to emphasise at this point that the incorporation and significance of managerial and other dimensions varies among the four country systems.

INTERPRETING LONG-TERM IMPACTS

Just as policy reversal is a product of internal decay and external pressures (changes in ideas, interests and environments), it can be represented as a hybrid of these factors (Hood 1994, pp. 4, 16). In seeking to interpret the condition of Anglophone systems in the long term four questions are addressed. Apart from the effects of managerialism and politicisation, their co-existence has consequences which are incompatible. A second focus is the impact of the changing environment on the behaviour of political executives, a syndrome christened 'new political governance' (NPG) by Aucoin (2012), and which reverberates within the public management system. Thirdly, an administrative tradition interpretation examines the tensions between the precept of enabling change (arguably more salient than countries from other traditions) and constraining departures from conventions. Finally, constant change can be a result of internal dynamics (the managerialist's compulsion to change and the politicians' inclination to press against boundaries and conventions) and movement in the external environment, but there is a broader literature on the role of cycles, which offers insights on long-term patterns (Pollitt 2008).

Managerialism and Politicisation: Complementary and Competing

Managerialism and politicisation derive from different sets of ideas. The combination of the two has had powerful and far-reaching implications for the public management system. Operating together they may be mutually reinforcing. But they are also susceptible to intractable tensions for they reflect different sets of principles, one primarily about political control, the other about management autonomy. This is explicit in Aucoin's argument about two strongly etched paradigms (reflecting public choice theory and managerialism) that support different organisational principles based on incompatible premises (Aucoin 1990; cf. Pollitt and Bouckaert 2017). One is essentially about centralisation and political authority, the other about decentralisation and management authority and autonomy. Because of the internal contradictions of managerialism these two are often in competition or conflict.

This representation needs to be qualified because applications are mediated by the administrative tradition and country contexts. Centralisation is not the sole preserve of the political executive, and decentralisation may aid ministerial roles. Managerialism is a fusion of ideas that has continued to evolve (Pollitt 1993) and which is not necessarily consistent in practice (Gregory 2001). The point to be underscored here is that there are contradictions within managerialism, the internal inconsistencies meaning that central control and management autonomy must somehow co-exist.

Four dilemmas that arise in government organisation are control and autonomy, contrasting role conceptions, internal and external capacity and structures, and stability and change. In each case the dilemma arises from how to reconcile the arguments of opposed positions.

Control and autonomy
The question of control within the public management system and the discretionary provisions covered are central to a range of issues. One articulation of the 'bureaucracy problem' points to potentially irreconcilable conflicts between two paradigms where they co-exist because public servants are unclear about how to operate due to different perceptions of the problem. Politicians seek to tame bureaucrats by concentrating power in the political

executive. In contrast, under the managerialist paradigm excessive controls over bureaucratic behaviour are unacceptable because they reflect the incentives under traditional bureaucracy that produce administration by rules and regulations rather than by results (Aucoin 1990). How is control handled under the combination of managerialism and politicisation? What do politicians' controls mean for managerial autonomy?

There is a broader question about the exercise of discretion and how it is constrained, which applies to both politicians and public servants (Garvey 1993). The dilemma derives from levels of discretion and how they might be counterbalanced. Bureaucracy produces a dilemma for democracy if it becomes too independent and powerful, thereby posing a threat to the political executive. However, bureaucratic independence is indispensable for preventing political malfeasance and safeguarding democratic procedures (Etzioni-Halevy, 1983).[6]

Agency, stewardship and trustee perspectives

The role conceptions adopted by political executives in their relationships with public servants are central. The dominance of principal–agent theory has meant a huge investment in agents who are responsive to political executives and a reinterpretation of the role of the public service. The primary objective is securing this responsiveness by employing incentives (Knott and Miller 2008). Contrariwise trustee theory envisages that the public interest is best ensured over the long term through insulating specified responsibilities from the short-term interests of politicians by assigning them to public agencies. The problem is determining constraints on bureaucratic discretion.

Two alternative perspectives have gained currency. A refocus on the virtues of bureaucratic discretion is based in part on the argument that the main organisation problem is not the moral hazard of the agent but that of the principal. This can be seen as a re-statement of the argument for delegating responsibilities to trustees, which is argued to be a factor in democratic success (Miller and Whitford 2016). The alternative stewardship perspective entails demarcating responsibilities for senior public servants with a focus on the public interest and the long term. Central questions are whether to and how to incorporate these perspectives in the public management system.

How are spheres of responsibility delineated for policy and management? If the 'public choice paradigm' is integral then the emphasis is on the top-down role of political executives. If ministers function as policy managers, those who serve them operate as agents and cannot 'function as independent "experts" with discretion to counter the will of their political "managers or "masters"' (Aucoin 1990, p. 127). Partisan actors may pervade policy and management, which either dissipates a division of roles between politicians and bureaucrats other than command and control or imbues it with ambiguity.

There have been predictions for three decades of the potentially negative effects of the assertion of ministerial authority and the expansion of the political realm (Campbell and Wilson 1995), particularly where ministers' actions are unbridled and arbitrary and political controls relentless. Increasing politicisation has challenging implications for the institutions of government if the constraints on excessive discretion are relaxed or ignored.

Capacity of the state
Managerialism allows flexibility and choice in ways for achieving objectives, which can be wide-ranging. Capabilities may be sourced from internal and external actors. The use of third parties for the provision of services is a significant thread of debureaucratisation. Politicians may regard the private sector as the first choice where it has the capacity to provide services, thus reducing the role of the state. The twentieth-century use of contracting out and using external agents for service delivery are beyond the scope of this study but are related to the five features identified above. However, where the provision of capacity relies on extensive use of different actors because of the loss of expertise, the externalisation of management capacity impacts on internal capacity as anticipated earlier. The department is expected to be able to respond to ministers' needs and priorities as required but confronts the problem of maintaining internal capability where externalisation is prominent. The dilemma centres therefore on the question of balance between external and internal capacity.

Stability and change
An accepted principle of government has been the provision for both stability and change. Three questions are significant. The first concerns the dominant ethos of managerialism: the commitment to change and responsiveness. The second concerns the standing of the public service and whether it is owned by a government or is an institution in its own right that serves a succession of governments. This is the crux of a set of tensions that have bedevilled Westminster systems, which have a constitutional basis, and arise in the next chapter and subsequently. The third dimension relates to the roles of politicians and bureaucracy. Under the traditional system, a distinction has been drawn between the dynamic element (politicians subject to turnover) and the stable component (the permanent bureaucracy) (Aberbach et al. 1981). Traditional bureaucracy, which was relatively pragmatic and instrumental following the Anglophone tradition, had the ability to change, but boundaries insulated it from external and internal influences and the ethos was not one of responsiveness and continuous improvement. In contrast, managerialism is attuned to change, adjusting techniques as appropriate, and the intensely instrumental focus offers flexibilities and options. But this dynamism aligns it with the political cycle rather than offering a counterbalance.

Change and Cycles

Patterns of change over time can be analysed through different reform stages, and there is a substantial literature that adopts that format (e.g. Christensen and Lægreid 2006; Dunleavy et al. 2006; Richards and Smith 2006; Halligan 2007b). Rather less attention has been given to twenty-first-century stages because the patterns appeared to fade with less distinct indicators that can be linked to reform models. A sense of progression was also lost with the recycling of reform types (e.g. NPM) and layering and sedimentation offered an alternative interpretation (Christensen and Lægreid 2011c).

The role of cycles in public management provides one type of interpretation of change dynamics (Pollitt 2008). Public organisations are dynamic and undergo constant changes, particularly where a premium is placed on environmental responsiveness. Organisations must attend to a range of problems, which can be defined in basic terms, such as technical, political, and cultural (Tichy 1980). These problems are ongoing and require adjustments at different points, which can be conceptualised in cyclical terms producing separate cycles (i.e. technical, political and cultural adjustment). However, organisations vary in their investments in undertaking adjustments in each cycle (Tichy 1980, p. 165; Pollitt 2008). The several types of management addressed in Chapter 4 can be associated with separate cycles. Most importantly for this study, political and managerial agendas operate on parallel cycles that can often be in sync, but frequently are not. Recognition of the role of pendulums, e.g. centralisation and decentralisation pre-date the reform era (Spann 1981), but radical reforms that are highly centralised (rigid and impervious), decentralised (problems with coordination and steering) or politicised can be expected to produce a response of similar intensity.

A second view is of the longer term and the role of institutional aging both of the political realm, and managerialism. An exploration of the middle age of managerialism at the mid-point in the reform era inquired whether there was movement into an age of paradox (Hood and Peters 2004). In the twenty-first century what indicators are available on the condition of public management systems? The ossification of traditional public administration and excessive bureaucratisation were well established (Caiden 1991), yet unintended effects were apparent in the early decades of managerialism (Hood and Peters 2004). Other indicators of the aging process are also available: aversion to risk taking, rule encrustation, routinisation and burgeoning procedural rules and 'mutation-based discretion' (Garvey 1993, pp. 188–92). Regardless of an ageist judgement, the key point to note is that evidence of systemic changes in the use of rules, regulation and red tape is likely to signify some broader condition of the public management system.

THE ARGUMENT AND APPROACH OF THE BOOK

The condition of Anglophone public management and reforms has been closely observed, but there are few systematic and comparative treatments of them in the twenty-first century. European countries have been the subject of comparative studies (e.g. Ongaro 2009 on Napoleonic countries; Greve et al. 2016 on Nordic countries; Van der Meer et al. 2015 and Hammerschmid et al. 2016 on reforms in Europe). OECD countries are covered in editions of Pollitt and Bouckaert (2011, 2017). There have also been individual country studies that illuminate public management in Australia (Edwards et al. 2012); Canada (Aucoin et al. 2013; Thomas 2014; Savoie 2015a); New Zealand (Boston 2017); the United Kingdom (e.g. Campbell and Wilson 1995; Richards 2008; Rhodes 2011; Dunleavy and Carrera 2013; Diamond 2014, 2019b; Hood and Dixon 2015). Analyses of major issues are also relevant: coordination (Bouckaert et al. 2010), new public management (Christensen and Lægreid 2011a), digital era governance (Dunleavy et al. 2006; Clarke 2019), new political governance (Aucoin 2012), political system reform (Raadschelders and Bemelmans-Videc 2015), governing for the future (Boston 2016, 2017), and comparing Westminster systems more generally (Rhodes et al. 2009; Weller 2018).

Overall, the literature on Anglophone countries as a group is incomplete, lacks a comparative dimension (but see Maor 1999; Rhodes et al. 2009), and does not engage with major issues over the long term. More specifically, the separate and combined effects of managerialism and politicisation have been neglected (but see Pollitt and Bouckaert 2017). The limitations in the treatment of topics central to this study may derive from sub-disciplinary specialisations and too few attempts to incorporate separate literatures. This book draws on both public management and the executive politics literature (e.g. Lodge and Wegrich 2012; Pollitt and Bouckaert 2017) and recognises that the 'partisan-political' dimensions of policy-making exposed in the recent advisory literature has been insufficiently addressed in mainstream studies (Craft 2015).

The book covers the central governments of Australia, Canada, New Zealand and the United Kingdom, and how political executives in these countries, particularly in the second half of the reform era, have sought to rework their public management systems to suit political agendas and environmental pressures. This focus means that neither the Australian states and Canadian provinces nor the 'four-nation governance' (Burnham and Horton 2013) of the United Kingdom feature in discussion. The choice of countries derives from their common adherence to an Anglophone tradition and their early and continuing commitment to public management reform. There are several striking differences among them, reflecting contexts and responses to pressures for change: the type of early engagement with managerialism, and the nature of the enthronement of the political executive, being prominent.

The study is both comparative and historical. Several dimensions of executive branches are examined over time and across the four countries. The comparative analysis focuses on politicisation and managerialism and elements thereof. It is informed by historical institutionalism because of the emphasis on long-term patterns and the role of traditions, structures and institutions (Pollitt 2008, 2013b). The relationship between stability and change is central, as is how the patterns are frequently punctuated by reforms. The role of political leaders in initiating and driving change in the executive branch is a strong current, although the study does not systematically explore the interaction of structure and agency.

The study draws on extensive interviews with public servants, present and former, in central agencies and departments, and with think tanks, overseas agencies and academic observers. These occurred over a decade or more in the capital cities of the four countries but were concentrated in 2016–18. Secondary sources encompass public documents, both official reviews and reports (which can be candid, if circumspect, with regard to details) about the state of public management – and independent analyses by audit offices, parliamentary committees and other government agencies, as well as think tanks and other experts. The rationale for the extensive use of document analysis in qualitative research has been made (Bowen 2009) and used with good effect in relevant studies (Pollitt 2012). The consilience method involves combining evidence from numerous different sources, which together provide a strong evidential basis for the analysis (Hood and Dixon 2015; Matthews 2016). The main characterisations are not tied to a specific time or government.[7] This is a late 2010s study with analysis focusing on the twenty-first century but extending back to the early reform era as appropriate.

Argument and Structure

The fundamental issues about the constitution and operation of a public management system comprise core questions of traditional public administration, and new questions that arise from the results of extensive political and managerial reform. First, the analysis of the political-administrative relationship addresses the changing roles of both the political executive and the public service, and how their relationships are now conceived and operate. The impact of politicisation features in all chapters. The second dimension focuses on management processes as a means of tracking through managerialism. These processes are examined in terms of the devolution of responsibilities, capability and capacity, core components of managerialism, such as performance management, and the continuing focus on results. The third dimension is the governance of the public management system, which considers institutions integral to the executive and the maintenance of understandings about the Westminster model and coordination within the public management system.

Recurrent themes within the book are the meaning of these reforms for the Anglophone administrative tradition; how the tradition constrains initiatives and facilitates reform; and the extent to which the tradition can accommodate variations and still remain distinctive. Diversity within the tradition and the associated public management model means that generalisations about trends and patterns apply more clearly to some countries. In terms of comparing public management systems, the working assumption is that similarities will be pronounced because of the shared administrative tradition. However, the differences will provide explanations for variations among countries, such as structures (e.g. the federal/unitary distinction) or in context choices (e.g. level of managerialism and the use of political controls). The four countries are compared across indicators for managerialism and politicisation, and the relative importance of instruments for specific purposes.

The structure of the book moves from the contexts of cultural and historical reform to the political and managerial dimensions with a macro-level focus on coordinating the public management system, then providing more holistic perspectives on the public management system. The framework for the book is centred on managerialism and politicisation, the two separate but often interdependent agenda that launched the reform era.

The examination of the Anglophone administrative tradition (Chapter 2) addresses its distinctive features, and how it is differentiated from other traditions. The question of how a distinctive model(s) of public management has become identified with countries in this tradition, and how it compares, is also addressed. Country patterns of change in the reform era are outlined in Appendices 2 and 3.

The following two chapters analyse the redistribution of roles and power between the political executive and the public service. Chapter 3 explores the expansion and strengthening of the political executive in all four systems. Chapter 4 examines the effect on senior appointments in the public service of the changing dynamics of the relationship between politicians and senior bureaucrats.

Managerialism is addressed in Chapters 5 and 6. Chapter 5 examines the fluctuating fortunes of key management processes and precepts, and the implications for capability and management improvement. The central question of performance and results is considered in Chapter 6. The redux of bureaucracy in a management and political milieu is the subject of Chapter 7, and the impact of excessive regulation on attaining objectives. Different forms of coordination are examined in Chapter 8, focusing on how instruments have changed, and the relative importance of political control, the vertical and horizontal axes and collaboration.

Chapter 9 pulls together the strands of the book, revisits the core questions and addresses the implications, including unresolved issues, which are fundamental to the functioning and condition of the public management system. These include the implacable problems that arise unless there is careful attention to system imbalances that inevitably become endemic where political priorities dominate. The long-term impact of reform over more than three decades is analysed by examining the condition of public management in the 2010s, the impact of managerialism and politicisation, the lessons and implications of the reform era, and the condition of the Anglophone tradition. Chapter 10 (a postscript) addresses agendas and scenarios for the four systems.

NOTES

1. The term Anglophone tradition is preferred to the broader Westminster model (see Marsh's 2011 formulation), although the latter is used where appropriate. 'Anglo-American' is a broader conception of the Anglophone group (Halligan 2003a).
2. Other politicising instruments are available, including board appointments of statutory authorities, and pressures on agencies normally thought to be beyond political interference.
3. A variation was managerialism as one of four models of NPM (Barzelay 2002). Definitions of managerialism also vary (e.g. Barzelay 2001, pp. 183–4). Compare 'neo-liberal managerialism' and the clumsy 'post-NPM managerialism' (Painter 2011, p. 248).
4. Delivery failure was a primary driver of original reform in Australia. It later become more prominent across the systems (1990s), and UK-inspired deliverology became a fad in Canada in 2016.
5. One expression, 'mix and match', suggests how ministers (and public managers) could make calculations that include internal and external options. For an expression of this, see Taylor (2008). Market design and related ideas extended the external options, although the focus here is internal instruments.
6. The broader complexities are captured through Etzioni-Halevy's second dilemma. Democracy creates a dilemma for bureaucracy because the 'rules are self-contradictory and put bureaucracy in a double bind . . . to be both independent and subservient, both responsible for its own actions and subject to ministerial responsibility, both politicised and non-politicised' (Etzioni-Halevy 1983, p. 87).
7. The transience of political leadership in the 2010s meant that relating the study to specific governments would have been problematic, e.g. Abbott, Gillard, Rudd and Turnbull (Australia); Martin, Harper and Trudeau (Canada); English (New Zealand); and Brown and May (United Kingdom).

2. Administrative tradition and Westminster in reform-era governance

Administrative traditions reflect those values and principles that are influential in shaping structures, behaviours and cultures (cf. Painter and Peters 2010a). The distinctive quality of the Anglophone tradition is that it both facilitates and constrains change, a combination that contrasts with other traditions, and which has played an important role in the modernisation process.

There are several questions to be addressed, beginning with the relationship between the administrative tradition and reform: i.e. the extent to which the tradition affects reform, and the effect of reform on the tradition. How are the principles and conventions a vehicle for continuity and change? In what ways do they facilitate and/or constrain? Another question concerns the continuing distinctiveness of the Anglophone tradition given the level of change, and the emergence of a reform model featuring managerialism (Pollitt 1990). This raises the question of identity in two respects: whether countries continue to share enough common characteristics to be grouped together; and how durable is a tradition when there are conflicting indicators of both continuities in and erosion of basic principles. Does the ability to facilitate change override the constraints? Finally, is the tradition to be employed either a flexible framework that can be adjusted to suit the needs of leaders of the day (Weller and Haddon 2016) or a set of principles against which to evaluate the system and the limits of action (Campbell and Wilson 1995)?

SPECIFYING THE ANGLOPHONE TRADITION AND THE ROLE OF THE WESTMINSTER MODEL

Four features of administrative traditions provide a basis for differentiating them: the relative significance of the state and society, the importance of management and law, political and administrative roles, and variations in law and administration that make for diversity (or uniformity) (Peters 2003; Painter and Peters 2010a, 2010b). The use of these categories defines an administrative tradition, such as the Anglophone, in part by what it is (e.g. instrumental), and partly by what it is not (e.g. a rule of law system with a developed concept of the state).[1] What is important is how elements of the tradition interact: the conception of the state, the role of administration and the nature of political and administrative relationships (Halligan 2015c).

The Anglophone administrative tradition is enabled to both facilitate change and to constrain change where it departs significantly from accepted understandings. The constraints derive from the Westminster model as well as routines and conventions that emerge from experiential learning, while the pragmatism has its origins in British administrative style. They can be seen to correspond to the logic of appropriateness and the logic of consequences (March and Olsen 2006). In both cases the application of these roles is tempered (and reinforced) by country contexts.

Westminster Model as a Source of Core Principles and Constraints

The Westminster model is integral to the four Anglophone systems, although several components do not directly impact on either administrative tradition or public management. An administrative tradition focus speaks to the culture of the countries' systems (Pollitt and Bouckaert 2017). The starting point for establishing the basis of the tradition is therefore the Westminster model, which provides a framework for the constitutional and governance attributes of the state.[2] The constituent features of Westminster are centred on responsible government as defined by the fusion of the executive and parliament. English writers articulate at great length the centrality of Westminster (Richards 2008; Diamond 2014). In Rhodes' (2011) formulation the Westminster narrative comprises beliefs (strong cabinet government, constitutional bureaucracy, etc.) and practices (hierarchy, specialisation, rules and commands, etc.). The notion of the administrative tradition is located there. Westminster can also be depicted as an alternative (or counterpoint) to managerialism (and governance) and as offering contending narratives (Richards and Smith 2006; Rhodes 2011).

The significance and meaning of elements of the Westminster model have varied over time and between countries. Public service leaders have accorded different emphases (Weller and Haddon 2016), reflecting contexts and issues of the day. Competing interpretations of dimensions of Westminster, such as the role of public servants, have long existed (Di Francesco 2012a). This has meant that the beliefs and practices are quite contingent. Nevertheless, there have continued to be shared core beliefs about a public service that is permanent even if the most senior appointments are not; the separation from the political executive even if the boundaries are porous and shifting; and a reliance on professional and internal appointments even if political influence is substantial.

There is general agreement that the bureaucracy is neutral, non-partisan and professional. There is also the sense of permanence in roles, careers and continuity of office-holding (Campbell and Wilson 1995). In support of this professional role public servants have been insulated from, although responsible to, the political executive as envisaged by the 'constitutional bureaucracy' (Parris 1968). How this works in practice has been the subject of high tensions in the reform era. Mounting pressures on the professional standing of public servants have produced requirements for them to be variously 'frank and fearless' but also responsive to ministers.

A core element is the ministerial department in which the minister has constitutionally derived responsibilities, and where the concept of ministerial responsibility prevails as an operational principle. The role of the public service is to serve the government of the day, but in order to insulate public servants the emphasis has been on their separation from politicians.

The combination of the British tradition and the circumstances that emerged in old and new world settings produced a set of shared components in this administrative tradition. These can be identified in terms of the relationship between public servants and politicians and two aspects of administrative and political culture and style: instrumentalism and pragmatism. The combination of the two is distinctive and has had significant implications for the machinery of government, processes of change and relations with society.

Administrative Tradition as a Facilitator

The identification of an instrumental administration with Britain resonates with the experience of other Anglophone countries (e.g. Goodin and Wilenski 1984).[3] Instrumentalism is recognised at one level as part of the government tradition, and importantly provides the 'significant *potential* to transform administrative structures and practices' (Knill 1999, p. 127). This interpretation is illustrated by a comparison between countries from different traditions. Examining autonomous and instrumental administrations indicates significant factors that differentiate them (Knill 1999). For reform capacity defined in terms of executive leadership, administrative entrenchment and the influence of the civil service, Germany and the United Kingdom reflected respectively low and high administrative capacities to reform, but high and low influence of the civil service.

The concern here is with the application of instrumentalism to the operation of the public management system, although it has been applied more broadly to government's roles.[4] The public service's primary role was to execute the will of the government of the day. In return the public service was protected in certain respects from arbitrary decisions at the individual level. Organisational change is fair game for political executives seeking to implement their policies with potential options for levering reform (e.g. appointments and the use of the public service); however, politicians did not avail themselves of these opportunities beyond piecemeal changes. These countries' administrative histories like most others up until the 1980s were littered with unimplemented reform initiatives (Caiden 1991). Accumulated discretionary responsibilities, the powers of public officials and agencies, and under-empowered political executives, historically placed brakes on meaningful change.

The related attribute of administrative and political style, pragmatism, featured in the country literature as a characteristic of government in practice. The Anglo-American systems were identified with the 'pragmatic and incremental nature of governing' (Peters 2003, pp. 21–2). This had its origins both in traditions inherited from Britain and the colonial development experience where conditions (e.g. lack of political parties with strong ideologies) reinforced it. For its part the British tradition was seen as atheoretical and dominated by experience and working through problems. Many qualities of the civil service were 'achieved piecemeal, over long periods of time. They were not the result of major statutes or great constitutional landmarks' (Chapman 1996, p. 188). A standard explanation was that this reflected a system of government that lacked a written constitution (Baker 1972), a feature also of New Zealand.

Australian and Canadian governance traditions have also been represented as pragmatic. In Australia's case, there has been a tendency to blend various ideologies, as was expressed in nation building. The administrators were 'utilitarian and pragmatic – and pragmatism triumphed as a creed and ideological position' (Wanna and Weller 2003, p. 67). Canada has also been depicted as having a tradition of pragmatism and moderation that applied to political and public service leaders: its 'public service culture is pragmatic, little driven by theory' (Gow 2004, pp. 9, 21; Lindquist 2006).

Pragmatism is not of course exclusive to this tradition (compare the Nordic style: Lægreid and Rykkja 2015), but it has been important for how the conception of the state has evolved. What has distinguished pragmatism in this tradition is that it can be readily employed as part of the change agenda to serve the requirements of the government of the day whether under conditions of modern reform or traditional incrementalism. By adopting a pragmatic approach, a change-oriented government accepts the malleability of governance and management and allows major reforms to be readily implemented.

The implications of these features are important in two areas here. First, under the Westminster model, relations between politicians and bureaucrats have traditionally centred on the co-existence of a neutral public service and responsible government (Aucoin 1995). The embedded tension between the two elements has been kept in balance by applying well-established but typically uncodified principles. The relationship was traditionally based on a neutral public service serving the political executive, regardless of party. The political executive in turn respected the integrity of the civil service by maintaining its apolitical and professional character. Specific features – the career public servant as a permanent official, senior appointments drawn from the ranks of careerists, and the ministerial department as the repository of policy knowledge and primary adviser to government – were affected when a more assertive political executive was seeking to implement its policies.

The second area centres on the external boundaries differentiating the state from the non-state parts of society (i.e. the private sector). These have often been imprecise and blurred (for New Zealand, see Mulgan 1997) and have varied over time. Australia has differed by having relied more historically on private (or at least non-state provision) in education and health services. Yet there was acceptance across the Anglophone systems that the public and private realms were distinct, and this was reflected in explicit boundaries around the public services in terms of careers and identity. The breaching of boundaries occurred selectively long before the reform era, but not extensive externalisation and use of third parties.

The question of management's place in the system is more problematic because these countries had not traditionally accorded it primacy. In terms of how questions were posed and resolved, the focus was on organisational administration to achieve policy objectives rather than their legal character as in Europe (Peters 2003). Under the influence of US thinking, Canada's engagement with management came earliest with the Glassco Commission (RCGO 1962), but for the other countries, administration was the dominant concept until it was displaced by management within the reform era (for Australia, see Halligan and Power 1992).

CLARIFYING THE IDENTITY OF THE ANGLOPHONE GROUP AND THE ROLE OF CONTEXT

These countries constitute a coherent set not only because of their common tradition but because of the concomitant historical and continuing close associations and interactions. The 'Westminster democracies' have formed a natural group of industrialised countries with institutional roots in the British tradition. The group is regarded as reasonably homogeneous for analytical and comparative purposes. The assumption is that this comparability results from a shared heritage, even though the countries are in some respects heterogeneous (Peters 1998a).

Continental Europeans who are sensitive to the existence of different state traditions recognise 'Anglo-Saxon' as a distinct and meaningful category differentiated in part by the lack of a well-developed concept of the state, whereas others simply address the Westminster system or model (Lijphart 1984; Aucoin 1995). This would normally include Australia, Canada, New Zealand and the United Kingdom, plus Ireland, specifically the fusion of the executive and the legislature under responsible government.

From the outside, the commonalities look strong, but within this group variations are apparent in governmental institutions, such as federal or unitary structures. The central governments of unitary systems have a different purview for some purposes, including proximity to citizens, more options for choice (e.g. with utilities), large delivery systems, responsibility for local government, and high-profile policy fields (e.g. policing) that are not undertaken by federal governments. This distinction carried over into reform with unitary countries disaggregating extensively (i.e. executive agencies) while federal systems were restrained. They also have public sectors of different sizes: Australia's has been smaller over several decades, the rest falling closer to the middle range for the OECD. Intra-country traditions may be relevant. Competing intellectual traditions may exert influence at different points in time. A multiplicity of traditions has been reported for the UK and Australia that may either coexist or evolve sequentially (e.g. Bevir and Rhodes 2003; Wanna and Weller 2003).

The differences between the countries were observed at an early stage through using a pragmatism–apriorism dimension and a Taylorism–public choice dimension. Australia and the United Kingdom were distinguished as having a modern variant of Taylorism and a reasoned pragmatism while New Zealand combined new institutional economics and aprioristic NPM (Hood 1990, p. 210). While this categorisation was subsequently less relevant it served to indicate significant variations.

The UK and New Zealand were regarded as 'NPM countries', because of distinctive initiatives, although NZ has spent decades trying to modify original features. The four were classified in terms of openness to NPM change: UK and NZ – 1, Australia – 0.75, and Canada – 0.25 (Dunleavy et al. 2006, p. 102). Even if absolute differences may be ruled out, the relative positioning is suggestive although subject to variation over time. This estimate puts Canada on the margins of NPM (cf. Savoie 2008), a more selective, discrete and incremental variant of managerialism (Shepherd and Stoney 2018). The Canadian public service did not develop 'along the UK "business process" or New Zealand "accountability" lines, instead retaining its historically well entrenched and consensual public service ethos and traditions' (Dunleavy et al. 2006, pp. 103–104). Australia has displayed NPM features, but in a less intense way than the UK or New Zealand, although Australia and the UK provided stronger NPM inclinations under austerity in the 2010s.

Variations within the Group

The notion of 'exceptionalism' is most usually associated with the United States because its governmental institutions and structure are idiosyncratic, although there are still debates about whether it is different but not comprehensively unique (Wilson 1998), or if exceptionalism continues to prevail (Kelemen 2015). However, its North American country neighbour, Canada, also stands out within the Anglophone group in terms of its trajectory and mix of characteristics. But does it pass the 'Rogers rule', which requires a rule that can systematically explain differences (Dowding 2017, p.167)? Canadian public administration has presented a set of features that is familiar as well as elusive in some respects (Halligan 2009). Many characteristics place it in the Anglophone family, but the influence of the United States was highly significant because academics and practitioners lacked political and academic traditions and looked elsewhere for relevant debates, and especially to the United States (Dwivedi and Gow 1999). Prior to the First World War, administrative ideas in Canada came mainly from Britain, but after that influences were largely American, with Canada following the US progression in management ideas and practice (Dwivedi and Gow 1999), and the Civil Service Act of 1918–19 (Hodgetts et al. 1972; Roberts 1996). Similarly, Frederick Taylor influenced personnel administration at the federal level: 'Scientific management and the classification movement, both American in origin, were decisive influences on Canadian ideas' (Hodgetts et al. 1972, p. 65). Later, the Glassco Royal Commission on Government Organization (RCGO 1962), to which the origins of modern Canadian management can be traced, was regarded as the Canadian counterpart of the US Hoover commissions (Dwivedi and Halligan 2003). Of significant innovations introduced between 1960 and 1990, two-thirds were directly based on US influences (Gow 1994).[5]

Is it appropriate, therefore, to contrast the North American country with the others? The countries that pursued comprehensive programmes of public management reform – the United Kingdom, Australia, and New Zealand – were clear cases, whereas Canada fitted the category of a partially reformed system until the 2000s produced more explicit agendas at the centre. Consequently, for some purposes, patterns of convergence and divergence can be illustrated by looking at the North American and the other Westminster countries separately (Halligan 2003a; 2003b). Despite this North American context, the Anglophone tradition shines through the work of Canadians who have wrestled with the ideas and relationships derived from the fundamentals of Westminster and responsible government. These include constitutional conventions, conflicts between values, ministerial responsibility, and the relationships between the political executive and the public service (Sutherland 1993; Aucoin 1995; Savoie 2003; Aucoin et al. 2004). The complexities of accountability in Anglophone countries also displayed common features (Thomas 1998; Savoie 2003; Aucoin and Jarvis 2005). In these areas, the core Canadian issues resonate with other Anglophone countries.

Canada has actively operated within an Anglophone tradition, although tempered more directly by the influence of the USA. As Hodgetts (1983, p.

x) observed, Canadian administrative culture comprises 'the British heritage of institutions and conventions mingled with American ideas and practices, with adaptations of both to meet the indigenous features of a federal state, overlaid by regional and cultural factors'. There is also something definably Canadian about these other factors in the mix that reflect differences from other Anglophone systems (Heintzman 1997), such as the accommodations of a plural society reflecting major minority concentrations in specific jurisdictions (i.e. principally Francophone Quebec). The state in Westminster systems has become more complex, but is this complexity greater in the more devolved, larger federation, Canada, which is responsive to both Anglophone and Francophone identities?

In Canada, less has been made of systemic instrumentalism, allowing pragmatism to play the more prominent role. The emphasis is explicit in commentary about public service culture and public sector reform being pragmatic and evolutionary (Aucoin 2002; Gow 2004; Lindquist 2006). Elements of the Canadian character may also be reflected in the use of specific instruments for public purposes. The attachment to an array of central agencies and officers of the parliament has signified not only a focus on incrementalism and process, but to a top-down stress on oversight and a greater reliance on veto points (e.g. the Public Service Commission being responsible to parliament).

The United Kingdom has been in many respects towards the opposite pole to Canadian incrementalism. Of all the Anglophone systems, it has been the most prone to a change dynamic in the reform era, typified as 'chronic reformism' (Pollitt 2007) in contrast to its historic pragmatism and incrementalism. Pollitt (2007), who argues for UK's exceptionalism (2013b), poses the challenge as to whether other countries have displayed this intensity of reform and organisational upheaval, including Australia and New Zealand. This can be attributed to the 'awfulness of the English' (Castles 1989, p. 267) in first embracing neo-liberal ideas in the 1980s, or to the relative decline of the economy producing a distinctive trajectory for restructuring (Hoggett 1997), although they do not account for what emerged from a longitudinal perspective on reform. Contextual factors allowed serial government interventions that absorbed the tenets of managerialism. The instrumental possibilities of managerialism took hold (Pollitt 2007). Manifestations of managerialism and politicisation have undoubtedly been exceptional as depicted by the UK Blair government's performance regime through the scale of indicators, target complexity and the grip over delivery (Matthews 2016), and the control and direction of central government (Blick and Jones 2010; Diamond 2019a and b).

The United Kingdom has shared with other Anglophone countries the relative lack of constraints on reformist political leaders, although arguably it was more pronounced. There is a propensity for governments to engage in reform as an end in itself without much regard for evaluating the evidence (Pollitt

2013b), although this and the political symbolism of reform occur elsewhere (Salamon 1981; March and Olsen 1989). The UK also became more complex with internal devolution to subnational jurisdictions and its supranational membership in the European Union, remaining unitary for some purposes and quasi-federal for others. The role of the Brussels 'policy-making state' is unique to the UK (Richardson 2018). The notion of the UK as an outlier has continued to receive support (Pollitt and Bouckaert 2011; Wilks 2013; Pollitt 2016), and its new public management credentials have usually been the strongest.

New Zealand can be argued to have displayed exceptionalism in two respects. Of the four it was once the most 'unbridled' in terms of the constraints on the power of governments, which was 'the product of a largely uncodified (in statutory terms) constitution, highly centralised unitary state, a small uni-cameral parliament, and a[n] . . . electoral system that invariably generated single-party majority governments' (Boston and Eichbaum 2014, p. 375). Under traditional constitutional arrangements, New Zealand exemplified an extreme variant of a tradition that facilitated change: 'it was possible to change too much, too quickly, with too little public input' (Boston and Eichbaum 2014, p. 375), and imposition of the radical model was an expression of this. The position was moderated to 'bridled power' following a changed electoral system (mixed-member proportional replacing first-past-the-post), in itself a marked departure from Anglophone practice, coalition government and other constitutional changes (Palmer and Palmer 2004), which, 'on balance, slowed the pace of legislative reform and constrained the available policy options' (Boston and Eichbaum 2014, p. 375). Replacing one-party majority with multi-party government smacked of European models (James 2002). The combination of a small-scale and unitary centralised structure has contributed to a sustained emphasis on societal outcomes. Second, in the heyday of public management reform (from 1988) its radical model was unlike that of any country internationally and went further with new public management (Boston et al. 1996; Scott and Boyd 2017b). A case can be made for arguing that the modified New Zealand model is different from the other Anglophone countries on several counts that will be apparent later.

REINFORCING GROUP DISTINCTIVENESS: INCUBATOR, FACILITATOR AND CONDUIT OF REFORM

Beyond institutional traditions, several factors reinforced the identity of the Anglophone group. Continuing patterns of interaction – historically formed and culturally supported by language and heritage – have been highly important. Endogenous communication patterns influence members of this group through bilateral relations between countries and various types of network. The formal networks derive from relationships developed between Britain and its colonies and deepened following their recognition as autonomous 'Dominions'. Alliances for defence and war have been entrenched features involving all members of the group. The Commonwealth has provided a mechanism for communication between Canada, Britain, Australia and New Zealand based on a common language, cultural legacy and institutions (Patapan et al. 2005).

The formal networks have included agency-level exchanges of staff, importing senior experts to conduct reviews, annual meetings of networks and constant informal contacts and associated epistemic communities. The specialised networks have been an important source for circulating ideas and the documentation of experience. Over time, these functional-based and relatively informal systems within the Anglophone group have facilitated reform transfer within a sector, which often occurred independently of general reform programmes (e.g. Inland Revenue or specialised service delivery agencies). They have existed in several policy fields, for example social security.[6] Politicians from the left and right have had their own looser political networks.[7] The networks are tapped and reflected in reviews of 'best practice' internationally, which typically feature Anglophone systems (e.g. OAG 2001; DFD 2012b; IPPR 2013), and the role of management consultants in policy and practice transfer (Saint-Martin 2004; Accenture 2008; KPMG 2009).

Location and institutions were also apparent in specific linkages and relationships. Apart from the long-standing relationship with the United Kingdom, it has continued to furnish the head of state. Canada's development placed it in an intermediate position for some purposes between its North American neighbour and the others. The combination of federalism and Westminster has linked Canada and Australia, whereas unitary government has produced a bonding between Britain and New Zealand (the latter once depicted as the perfect example of the Westminster model: Lijphart 1984). The antipodean countries of Australia and New Zealand have been close because of physical proximity and specific agreements for trans-Tasman relations (e.g. trade and social security).

Reform Model

The reform era was initiated in Thatcher's Britain, although its origin can be traced back to the 1960s if formative, but largely unimplemented, inquiries in the four countries are included.[8] For OECD countries, the main indicator that things were different was that reform featured managerialism and was more comprehensive and rapid in contrast to past incrementalism. Despite substantial variations between countries in the process, type and impact of reform, there were strong similarities between some programmes, especially among countries, with early parallels drawn between the United Kingdom, the United States and Canada (Pollitt 1990; Savoie 1994), and Australia, New Zealand and the United Kingdom being grouped because they adhered more to precepts of 'new public management' than other OECD countries (Hood 1996). At the peak of the OECD's fixation on NPM, the Anglophone experiments were upheld as the ideal (OECD 1995).

The emergence of this distinctive set of reforms was the product of a pattern of interaction that accorded legitimacy and relevance to initiatives within an administrative tradition facilitating rapid transmission and acceptance of ideas and practice. The early identification of managerialism came from UK writers who discerned the trend under Thatcher (e.g. Pollitt, 1990). In addition to the major reforms (e.g. privatisation and executive agencies), individual country programmes gained international significance with New Zealand's 'public management model'. The reform movement served to reinforce the notion of the Anglophone group's identity as distinctive and contrasting with that of other countries. The four systems often exhibited similar patterns of development (Halligan 2007a). The age of reform was a leveller in that all the countries in the Anglophone group studied and borrowed from each other's reforms, the processes of institutional isomorphism operating within the group.

Diffusion and Policy Transfers

The long history of the transfer of ideas and reforms between the four countries dates from the transplanting of Britain's institutions into its colonies during the eighteenth and nineteenth centuries. The subsequent dominant pattern reflected hierarchical diffusion: the larger or more developed countries adopted new policies at an earlier stage. A country such as Britain traditionally operated as a repository of a distinctive form of government that exported institutions.

A basic principle of communication networks in the diffusion literature concerns the development of relationships between units with similar characteristics, and decisions about whether to adopt a particular innovation are largely dependent on the experience of comparable systems that have already adopted it. For small countries it was standard practice to scan the activities of other systems: UK and US reforms received attention. Australia, Canada and New Zealand were more externally oriented because of colonially induced reactions and an inclination to consider the experience of larger, kindred systems (Halligan 1996b). The propensity of countries to look externally and their preparedness to borrow the innovations of others shaped diffusion patterns.

The historical links were based on networks centred on the British Commonwealth (and earlier the Empire) and countries with similar cultural and linguistic traditions (Halligan 2007a, 2015c). The pattern of transfers for

Australian public policy and legislation (Carroll 2006) changed from coercive transfers from Britain in the nineteenth century to more selective borrowing and increasingly localised innovation. Transfers also became more complex as inter-colony transfers and adaptation increased towards the latter part of the nineteenth century. Following the Australian federation, itself based on a constitution (1901) that borrowed from the UK (responsible government) and the USA (federalism), the twentieth century was first characterised by intra-federation transfers usually from the states to the federal government, but then by 'polydiffusion' as multiple sources were drawn on. The declining influence of the UK was apparent during the twentieth century (Carroll 2006) as country contexts became important and national consciousness stronger.

The role of environmental influences was discerned 70 years ago by an American observer of New Zealand (Lipson 1948, p. 10), who pointed out that while inherited traditions permeated society and government, the system was not just an imitation of the British model. When it took the initiative, the results were 'more analogous to those of other English-speaking democracies than of Britain. The United States, Canada, Australia . . . are the countries in which some parallel features can be observed. In certain cases, New Zealand has deliberately followed an American or an Australian rather than a British precedent. In others, she has independently arrived at results like those of America and Australia'.

Reform Transfers in Public Management as an Endogenous Process

In the early years of reform, the strong influence of the UK and the USA was apparent as indicated by policy transfers. These included financial management and efficiency scrutinies from the UK as well as a raft of other reforms such as privatisation and joined-up government. Central personnel management, pay-for-performance (Peters 1997), the senior executive service (Halligan 1996b, 2012), policy tsars (Levitt and Solesbury 2012) and the prime minister's office (Gow 1994; Savoie 1999) could be linked to the USA. With some exceptions – e.g. accrual accounting and the charter of budget honesty (New Zealand), citizen surveys (Canada) and Centrelink (Australia) – the UK has generally been the leader in reform initiatives. Several cases indicate the complexities of diffusion and transfers, and the difficulties with establishing connections.

The case of financial management shows how countries facing like environmental pressures chose similar solutions, but different contexts meant that this did not necessary lead to the same results or that implementation was straightforward. The UK's Financial Management Initiative (FMI) and the Australian Financial Management Improvement Program (FMIP) can be compared (Zifcak 1994), FMIP (1983) following FMI in time (1982) with a similar purpose and content. Both formed the initial basis for managerialism in the two countries (Halligan and Power 1992; Pollitt 1993; Pollitt and Bouckaert 2011).[9]

Performance became of increasing significance (Bouckaert and Halligan 2008) with the 1980s and 1990s being years of expansion as all countries designed performance management systems, and new generation forms were implemented in the twenty-first century. Despite their strong focus on results and performance, there were variations in commitment to and application of such principles. Australia favoured outcomes, New Zealand outputs, Canada refined its system in the 2000s, and the UK opted for public service agreements and targets, but the different schemes were often transient and the long-term results debatable (Bouckaert and Halligan 2008).

The public–private partnership has been widely diffused within and beyond the Anglophone group. Originating as the UK's Public Finance Initiative (PFI), it was renamed and reconceptualised by the Blair government as the public–private partnership (PPP). PFI was retired in 2012, but schemes continued to have currency in the remodelled form of Private Finance 2 (PF2), only to be critiqued after failures and lack of benefits (NAO 2018b, p. 5; Plimmer and Parker 2018). This is a complex case with debates about ambiguities in applying the concept, the results, and the widespread diffusion effect internationally. What is clear was the UK's leadership in this area in the 1990s (Wettenhall 2010), and the extensive use made of the PPP by other Anglophone countries (although much of this was at the sub-national level).

There were also 'hard transfers' associated with programmes, instruments and implementation (Evans and Davies 1999; Nutley et al. 2013). Direct transfer seems to be associated more with specific techniques or review processes. A case in point was the efficiency scrutiny model that Australia borrowed from Britain in 1986, which was officially acknowledged and included its methodology and the documentation (Halligan 1996b). The UK's use of delivery units influenced Australia (Barber 2007; Gold 2014, 2017), and Canada subsequently adapted a variant of deliverology for results (Shepherd and Stoney 2018). A simple case of diffusion of a tool was the Gateway Review process, which originated in the UK in the early 2000s as an adaptation from the private sector that was branded and franchised, and adopted in Australia and New Zealand. The process involved reviewing procurement projects at six decision points and was deemed successful in terms of savings and as a policy (Marsh and Fawcett 2011).

A set of explicit transfers in the 2010s involved a review process, with the content going to the core of a public management system. Known as capability reviews in the United Kingdom and Australia and a performance improvement framework in New Zealand, they provided systematic assessments of departments' capability. The latter two were modelled on the original British scheme but modified to fit country contexts. That these countries needed to use this instrument reflected similar weaknesses in their management systems, but that they could readily use a similar instrument to address management capabilities indicated how well it translated between the three countries (see Chapter 5).

A mixture of borrowing and mutual learning is apparent from the interaction among policy units in the four countries. The network concepts of 'professional' and 'functional areas' were transferred from the United Kingdom to New Zealand (Davison 2015) and subsequently mutual development and learning about policy projects has occurred among the systems (Washington and Mintrom 2018; Shepherd and Stoney 2018; Policy Profession Board 2019).

Disconnects and the Role of Context

The debate about convergence led to a renewed interest in the influence of contexts on the borrowing of reform ideas (Pollitt 2013c), and the extent of modifications and adaptations to local conditions. The 1990s trend towards 'agencification' centred on separating policy formulation from implementation, the best-known and most influential example being the experiment with executive agencies in the UK, although the impact within this group was variable. The United Kingdom made a major commitment to the executive agency concept under the Next Steps reform programme. New Zealand also offered an 'agency' form of a type that differed from standard cases of agencification (Pollitt et al. 2004, p. 31), which was one element of a larger management framework in which policy advice and service provision were decoupled by using small policy ministries and large delivery departments. The two federal systems, however, resisted this trend, in part because most potential agencies were at the provincial or state level. Australia and Canada pragmatically applied this principle on an 'as needed' basis, whereas the experiments with separating policy formulation from implementation took the form of systemic separation in the UK and NZ.

Another case was the incorporation of the UK concept of the accounting officer in the Canadian Federal Accountability Act 2006. The Canadian variant lacked key features of the British approach and introduced problematic elements (Heintzman 2013, p. 92), in particular, an assumption that the accounting officer would be accountable (rather than answerable) to a parliamentary committee rather than to the treasury department.

The shared services approach was a complex area in terms of the processes of adaptation and was fraught with difficulties. The origins of the concept are unclear, although management consultancy firms were promoting this option in the 2000s, and early starters included two Australian states (Queensland and Western Australia), and Canada. The UK also picked the concept up and

Australian government agencies were required to enter into such arrangements (Elston and MacCarthaigh 2013; Commonwealth of Australia 2017). That the results of shared service schemes have been uneven, even disastrous, did not deter conservative governments in Australia, Canada and the United Kingdom, but not New Zealand, from pursuing them for corporate services in the 2010s.

As the source of more reforms than other countries, the UK continued to be influential during the reform era, but there was asymmetry when it came to solutions to its own problems, such as the unwillingness to adopt Australia's strong prime minister department model despite its being advocated as a solution to weaknesses at the centre of Whitehall (e.g. Lee et al. 1998) or New Zealand's State Services Commission approach to senior civil service appointments. In the latter case, there was a view that successful reforms in a small system like New Zealand could not be translated in Whitehall (IPPR 2013).

CONCLUSION

A significant trend during the reform era has been the reification of the potential of instrumentalism and pragmatism as governments rose to new levels of reformism. The consequences for managerialism and politicisation are explored later. At this point it can be noted that the inner contradictions of the administrative tradition have exposed significant tensions and dilemmas. On the one hand the tradition has enabled unparalleled reform and flexibility often centred on maximising further flexibilities and few constraints, but on the other hand core elements of both the tradition, and Westminster more generally, have been discarded, and fluidity in understandings has fostered ambiguity. The consequences have been disruptive in both senses of the word: preventing progress and effectiveness, and facilitating innovation.

A test of administrative tradition is to examine how well it survives different phases of reform and how the dimensions discussed above have been worked through. The application of an instrumental approach has become much more expansive in the reform era while the norms and conventions that prevailed historically have been regularly challenged. Pragmatism has moved from being a hallmark of incrementalism to facilitating constant reform. The durability and international standing of the administrative tradition and the efficaciousness of the associated reform model are assessed in Chapter 9.

NOTES

1.   For example, the administrative tradition of the Anglo-Saxon group is depicted as 'Administrative law/legalism less developed than' the 'rule-of-law legalism' of Continental European countries (Pollitt and Bouckaert 2017, p. 63).

2. The Westminster model is used even though the term is redolent of a context as much as a system (but see Aucoin 1995; and Rhodes et al. 2009).
3. The 'old instrumental view of administration' was centred on efficiency (Goodin and Wilenski 1984, p. 512).
4. Australia has long relied on government as a developmental agency. The instrumental view is attributed to utilitarianism with government regarded 'as the instrument of the people' (Emy and Hughes 1991, pp. 117–18; see also Encel 1960; Wettenhall 2006).
5. Several of these cases influenced other Anglophone countries (e.g. scientific management), but the influence of the United States on Canada has been more pervasive and direct.
6. There is also the International Organization of Supreme Audit Institutions and the Commonwealth Association of Tax Administrators. See also Legrand (2015).
7. The networks may extend to ministerial advisers, e.g. the head of communications for Australia's Prime Minister Gillard was a former Blair adviser in the UK.
8. Canada was a leader in the early diffusion of management ideas (Glassco Commission on Government Organization (1960–63), although influenced by the US Hoover Commission. The UK's Fulton report (Committee on the Civil Service 1968) was also influential. Australia had the Coombs Royal Commission (1976), New Zealand the Royal Commission into the State Services (1962).
9. Canada's Increased Ministerial Authority and Accountability (IMAA) (1986) bore some resemblances to these programmes as an attempt to change management practices, but never registered much impact (Savoie 1994). New Zealand did not engage public management reform until its original model was introduced under the State Services Act 1988 (Boston et al. 1996).

3.   Politicising the executive branch: changing roles, resources, relationships

This chapter examines the expansion of the political executive's influence within the executive branch focusing on the dynamics of change in ministers' roles and relationships, and their use of instruments and levers for exercising control over the public service and obtaining action on their preferences. There is also recognition that the pattern of change is more complex than a linear representation of increasing politicisation. There have been fluctuations between regimes, the dynamic often being dialectical, and variations in behaviour have emerged both at the level of individual political actors, and between country styles.

While each country has moved significantly from a traditional arrangement, they have exhibited distinctive approaches to handling the relationship. Three dimensions account for most of the change: the ministers' roles vis-à-vis the senior public service; the use of ministerial resources in extending political influence; and the relationship between ministers and senior public servants. A fourth dimension, the handling of appointments to the senior civil service, and the consequences of political change for the public management system are analysed through different models and contending theoretical perspectives in Chapter 4. A core question centres on the implications of discarding the traditional norms that regulate the relationship, and how to obtain a new fit between politicians and public servants (Plowden 1994) when divergent principles and expectations are in play.

POLITICISATION AND ITS INSTRUMENTS AND LEVERS

Politicisation has attracted various definitions. A standard approach is to view politicisation in terms of appointments, usually of partisans (Mulgan 1998), and as substituting political for merit criteria in the recruitment and handling of public servants (Peters and Pierre 2004a, p. 2). In the Anglophone system this has usually entailed individual cases rather than being systemic as in the United States and other countries, although tenure has become more tenuous.

The expanding forms of 'politicisation' have been recognised, including public servants assuming political responsibilities as political bureaucrats (Campbell 1988a; Peters and Pierre 2004a, 2004c), political interference in daily routines and decisions (Oberg and Wockelberg 2016) and the subordination of the public service 'to a partisan political agenda' (Varghese 2016, p. 2). There is also 'procedural politicisation' focused on the interventions of ministerial advisers who constrain officials from playing professional roles (Eichbaum and Shaw 2008).

Politicising tendencies over time (Peters and Pierre 2004a) points to a secular trend in the long term, which may be represented in several ways. One type of progression is illustrated by analysis of the changing policy roles of bureaucrats and politicians (Aberbach et al. 1981). The existence of optional political and bureaucratic roles, and movements between them, is well documented in the literature (Peters 1987) and shifts between bargains have been illuminating (Hood and Lodge 2006). Peters and Pierre (2001) depicted the relationship as best regarded through a continuum that ranges from the classic model (ministers decide, officials deliver) to public service dominance. A more relevant version is to substitute political dominance for the classic model with movement towards either end of the continuum producing an imbalance in the system as either highly politicised or highly bureaucratised. A multi-dimensional approach is favoured here, using models of interaction between officials and ministers (Peters 1987), which reflect two of the theoretical positions outlined in Chapter 1. The trustee conception identified with the administrative state variant of traditional public administration accords a prominent role to officials, who nevertheless operate within Westminster precepts in terms of the minister. The principal–agent formulation preferences the political executive over officials who function as subordinates in the relationship.

Politicisation is defined as the expansion of the influence and control of the political executive within the executive branch. There is a range of potential indicators of change involving either the expansion of roles that extend political influence (e.g. communications), or the displacement of roles performed by the public service. The three dimensions addressed are the growth in ministerial roles, staff resources and influence over appointments. The public service has traditionally performed the roles of advice to and support for ministers, policy development and implementation. The countries are examined for systemic changes in relations between ministers and the senior public service, while noting individual exceptions that represent precedents and the cumulative impact of incremental interventions.

The instruments associated with political roles, policy development and implementation and management appear in Table 3.1. Two models underlie the organisation of roles and instruments, one defined by the prime minis-

Table 3.1   Political and policy roles and instruments

Roles	Prime minister and centre	Minister and department
Priorities and strategies	• Prime minister monitoring • Cabinet and committees	• Ministers and their office
Policy initiation and development	• Prime minister's office • Cross-dept. reviews/task forces*	• Ministerial policy leadership • Ministerial advisers' roles
Policy implementation and department management	• Prime minister's office • Central implementation units* • Performance plans*	• Executive ministers • Departmental boards • Ministerial staff roles

* Addressed in Chapters 6 and 8.

ter and his or her private office that drives the system from the centre, the second focused on the minister and decentralised political instruments for minister-centric roles in policy, implementation and management. Pure variants of these types are uncommon, but they provide a basis for comparing systems according to where the emphasis is placed. The latter depends on prime ministerial style (centralised or decentralised with ministers) and the circumstances confronted by the government (e.g. working majority or not) (Berlinksi et al. 2012).

POLITICAL EXECUTIVE DYNAMICS OVER THE REFORM ERA

The country systems once reflected the traditional model. The permanent senior public service was the conduit through which interaction with the political executive was funnelled. In most fields ministers relied on advice from their permanent secretary who usually had the undisputed role of primary policy adviser. The few ministerial staff were usually provided by the department.

Four forces have largely accounted for the new directions: institutional needs and demands, environmental change (ranging from pressures on the centre to the 24/7 media of the twenty-first century), the reform environment, and the changing policy roles of leaders (prime ministers and ministers). These can be associated with several phases (noting variations between countries in terms of timing and intensity). First is the expanding role of the state and the need to strengthen central capacity (1960s–1970s). Second is the emergence of more assertive political executives who sought policy implementation because of real or imagined opposition from the public service, and to define an asymmetrical relationship under the influence of new right ideas about the role of the state and the political executive (1970s–1980s). The third phase is tightened control over the public service using different instruments ranging from direct political control to performance indicators and results (1990s–2000s). Fourth is the emergence of time-fixated politicians and new variations on politicisation, an influential statement position being 'new political governance' (2000s–2010s) (Aucoin 2012; Bakvis and Jarvis 2012; Diamond 2019a, 2019b).

Strengthening the Centre – Cabinet and Departments

The expanding role of the state and the need for strengthening central capacity were apparent from the 1960s. This entailed taking charge of the central machinery and bolstering it. In Canada, Pierre Trudeau was credited with reducing the policy influence of departments and giving cabinet the ability to make policy based on competing advice. The cabinet process and central capacity were augmented to break the control ministers and deputy ministers had over line departments, major policy decisions and administration (Aucoin 2006; Savoie 2011). The shift from individual to collective responsibility also occurred under Menzies in Australia (Weller 2010). There were several well-documented experiments in the UK with central units for enhancing capacity on policy and strategy (Diamond 2014), and interventions in departmental policy formulation (Campbell and Wilson 1995). Other harbingers of change included permanent secretaries' loss of their domination of departmental advice (Heady 1974).

Responsiveness and New Right Ideas

The political reaction to the traditional arrangement emerged most explicitly in the 1970s and reflected both political frustration with the implementation of government programmes and mounting reservations about the performance of the senior public service. The influence of new right ideas was strongest with leaders of conviction like Thatcher and Mulroney (Savoie 1994),[1] but the revolt against the status quo was a product of several influences including the left's aspirations for political control and reform of vested interests in the public service (Hawker 1981). There were institutional variations between the countries; in particular, the British generalist (and elitist) approach to its administrative class differed from new world approaches, but overall similar critiques emerged. The rise of the career politician and the emergence of ideological politics were apparent across the four countries (Campbell and Wilson 1995).

The reaction in Britain surfaced early, as expressed through Prime Minister Wilson and the Fulton report (Committee on the Civil Service 1968). Thatcher's view was of an 'over-large, under-responsive public service' (Fawcett and Gay 2010, p. 27), but a 'more reasoned critique' emerged of complacent civil servants 'wallowing in their own collective self-esteem', the product of a narrow social class and out of touch (King 2007, p. 218).

The pressure to expand the influence of Australian politicians emerged in the 1970s when a Labor government confronted a public service that had served a Conservative government for over two decades by introducing political advisers and partisan appointments. A formal review saw the bureaucracy as being too elitist, independent, unrepresentative and unresponsive (RCAGA 1976). The public servants' positions were challenged because 'the balance of power and influence ha[d] tipped too far in favour of permanent rather than elected office holders' (Commonwealth 1983), and Labor's priority was political control to implement party policy and redistribute power (Wilenski 1986; Halligan and Power 1992).

Canadian government was dominated by the Liberal Party in the 1960s and 1970s, which had a close association with the public service. Nevertheless, stirrings began under the Liberals in the 1960s (Aucoin 2010).[2] Progressive Conservative Prime Minister Mulroney sought to refocus attention on ministerial departments while buttressing minsters' offices and the prime minister's office (PMO).

New Zealand operated under principles and constitutional conventions established at least 70 years previously when the public service was small and concerned with implementation. This produced 'bureaucratic stasis': Westminster administrative conventions supporting continuity. The system was regarded as inflexible, inefficient and insufficiently accountable (Roberts 1987; Boston et al. 1996). Pressures emerged to break the 'old-boys' network', diversify senior staff and define the minister's role (Boston and Halligan 2012).

Responding to New Public Management and New Environments

A rethink occurred as major complex policy issues required greater attention and the limitations of new public management experiments were exposed by vacuums at the centre. Political and central control was heightened from the mid-1990s across the four countries (see Appendix 3), which included strengthening the role of PMOs (Savoie 1999; Christensen and Lægreid 2006). By the turn of the century, ministers' offices were undertaking more work and staff in PMOs were playing more active and interventionist roles in developing and implementing policies (James 2002; Norman 2003; Savoie 2004; Tiernan 2007a, 2007b; Blick and Jones 2010).

New Political Governance

There were indications of change in media relations before the reform era as greater control of information flows about government policy was sought through some form of coordination (Lee et al. 1998), but the immediacy and intensity of the pressures were far greater from the 2000s. The changing environment led politicians to become fixated on controlling the agenda in the present time and responding rapidly to the media. Aucoin's (2012) new political governance consists of four features: the integration of executive governance and the continuous campaign, partisan-political staffs as a third force, personal politicisation of senior appointments, and a public service that was promiscuously partisan to the government (Aucoin 2012). These characteristics were most strongly expressed at that time in Canada and to varying extents elsewhere (Boston and Halligan 2012). The combination of forces affecting new political governance (NPG) became more influential: in addition to 'masses of media', the components were competition in the political marketplace, political volatility and polarisation, as well as transparency and openness and auditing of government performance.

The dynamics of governing were affected by the permanent election campaign by which 'the techniques for winning power have been transferred increasingly to the processes of government' (Thomas 2013, p. 54; Savoie 2019c, p. 359). This 'fusion of campaigning and governing' was influenced by the circumstances of minority government, the media environment and the prime minister's leadership style (Savoie 2019c, p. 66).

Following heightened control and friction in several jurisdictions (Richards and Smith 2016; Zussman 2016) and the occasional respite or lull (not unlike that reported by Rouban 2004), political and centralising pressures intensified in the UK under Brexit prime ministers and new political leadership in Australia where the permanent campaign as a mode of governing became more evident (Savoie 2019c, pp. 300–301; see also Thomas 2013; civil servant interviews in Whitehall 2018; Evans et al. 2019).

MINISTERIAL POLICY AND MANAGEMENT ROLES

Four policy modes are distinguished (Table 3.2). In each the principal or dominant actor is indicated, unless a role is shared, but this does not preclude contributions by secondary actors: for policy initiation under Mode 1, election policy was relevant, and portfolios might be exempt (notably defence and foreign affairs). The demarcation of roles is clear under the first mode, which has public servants taking a lead on policy roles and being responsible for implementation. Under Mode 2, the ministers exercise policy leadership. Mode 3 envisages that ministers have roles across the spectrum, including

Table 3.2   *Ministers' increasing influence in policy and management roles*

	Mode 1	Mode 2	Mode 3
Values	Ministers	Ministers	Ministers
Strategy	Shared	Shared	Ministers
Policy initiation	Public servants	Shared	Shared
Policy implementation	Public servants	Public servants	Shared
Management	Public servants	Public servants	Shared

Note: Ministers includes their political staff.

implementation and management. Mode 1 represents a traditional type of conception with defined roles. In Mode 3, ministers are engaged in both policy initiation, and implementation and management.

The most interesting categories are forms and levels of sharing in strategy, policy initiation, policy implementation and management, which is where much variability may occur. Despite the stance of some political executives that strategy is their responsibility, there may be provision for strategic advice in specialised areas: e.g. Canadian deputy minister committee on Governance (of democratic institutions) (PCO 2019).

The contrast between traditional operations and those in the reform era is striking as illustrated by the UK. Policy during the 1950s, 1960s and 1970s was 'generated from within the machine at a high level' (Marsh et al. 2001, p. 171). In effect a duopoly existed with the civil servants running the country while ministers provided political direction (King and Crewe 2014). Policy was left to departments, which coordinated through interdepartmental committees where appropriate, and was then worked through a hierarchical committee system of officials, ministers and cabinet (Lee et al. 1998). Starting in the 1980s, ministers took on a range of new roles, and 'a politicisation of the policy process' was the result (Richards and Smith 2016, p. 503). Policy leadership roles (legitimation or rubber stamping, selection from options offered and initiation) and management roles, first delineated by Heady (1974), were both changing in significance with initiation becoming more salient. The 'agenda-setting' role was added for ministers seeking to change the broader departmental policy agenda or stance (Richards and Smith 2002, pp. 211–12).

Ministers' Roles in Policy Initiation and Development

The transformation of roles from the 1980s was dramatic with the rise of the activist minister in conjunction with governments that wanted to accomplish change and prime ministers that favoured and rewarded effective minsters.

Some ministers had previously regarded themselves as policy initiators, but this was largely 'paying lip-service to a constitutional norm' about their role (Heady 1974, p. 71). Ministers rarely took major initiatives except for colonial and defence policy (King 2007).

The role of ministers was recast by Thatcher, 'to be initiators and leaders, the dynamos of change' (King and Crewe 2014, p. 334), and she was prone to early intervention in policy development and involving select ministers on an ad hoc basis. Traditional procedures were short-circuited by ministerial handling of cross-departmental matters. Central public servants had less control of processes (Lee et al. 1998, pp. 5–6). Many ministers believed that they were the initiators of policy and made the decisions while civil servants were responsible for execution (King 2007, p. 225).

Policy initiation from the public service was replaced by greater ministerial direction in Canada, Prime Minister Mulroney arguing that policy formulation belonged to ministers (Zussman 1986; Aucoin 1988). Ministerial roles in New Zealand changed from 'policy legitimators' (according to a former prime minister) to 'policy initiators' by the early 1990s, and policy-making shifted from being inductive to 'largely . . . a deductive process, proceeding from "first principles"' (McLeay 1995, pp. 120–25). Policy active ministers have regularly initiated policy, two cases being Michael Gove, a high-profile Secretary of State in the Cameron and May governments (Diamond 2019a, 2019b), and Andrew Lansley the policy architect of reform to NHS, 'a text book policy failure . . . in the Brexit league' (Edwards 2019, p. 4; see also King and Crewe 2014, pp. 400–402). The different levels of ministerial priorities in the UK have also been recorded (Freeguard 2018). Governments as a whole have required repositioning of major policy (e.g. Mulroney: see Sutherland 1993).

Much of the running was made by political advisers as policy actors. Advisers acquired extensive roles in policy-making working with the department by supervising, orienting and mobilising; and being involved in generating ideas, and both policy development and implementation expanded (Maley 2015). Interdepartmental coordination once performed by interdepartmental committees (IDCs) could occur via advisers' networks or in conjunction with public servants. The tracking of implementation at the departmental level was central where government or minister's priorities were involved.

Canadian advisers have been in a special position. They were direct providers of policy advice to a range of policy actors but also acted as intermediaries who transmitted the advice of other actors within and beyond government. There were unique in at least three respects. First, in the formalisation of a system of partisan/political advice under Harper (2006–15) that operated in parallel to public service processes. The written advice took the form of 'notes on policy issues that percolated up the system in lock step with public service advice', or responses to prime ministerial requests for advice on specific issues. The provision of policy content was bureaucratic, systematised, and strengthened political control of policy-making. Secondly, PMO's advisers shaped the content at the planning and execution stages, and engaged in 'procedural moving (e.g. monitoring, sequencing, coordinating) of policy as it is advanced through government'. Thirdly, PMO staff were able to influence the policy process at 'the front end', 'had access to unique policy and governance levers, and help[ed] craft amendments to the strategic and day-to-day strategy of government' (Craft 2016, pp. 43–4).

Ministers in Policy Implementation

Implementation was once the core function of public officials, and largely an exclusive one. However, this function received direct attention in the reform era through agencification (giving delivery to executive agencies) and outsourcing delivery to third parties in the private and not-for-profit sectors. The most relevant instruments here are the use of monitoring and reporting, and direct engagement and interventions by ministers and their advisers.

The convention used to be that departments should have the responsibility for implementing government decisions without interference from ministers. Political and managerial change had an impact. A core principle of managerialism, best articulated in the New Zealand variant, was the association of one function with one organisation unit (Boston et al. 1996). This type of specialisation was regarded as preferable to the confusing and conflicted arrangements of multipurpose ministerial departments. The severing of departments from implementation established precedents, which came to mean that this responsibility was no longer exclusive but simply one of the structural options in play. Similarly, shifting the specialisation to external agencies underscored this, even though now twice removed. In addition, boundaries that once existed by convention regarding political and administrative interaction meant that assertive political executives were scrutinising departmental activities more intrusively and were more demanding about achieving results. This occurred most explicitly through either the centre (PMO and implementation units) or executive ministers.

Central implementation units were used in Australia, Britain and Canada (see also Chapters 6 and 8). The political component was present where the reporting was directly to the prime minister, even in person, or through cabinet taskforce and ministerial oversight, and where the prime minister's office was responsible. The units were pioneered by the British experiment with the Prime Minister's Delivery Unit (PMDU), which established clear goals, delivery maps and reports, trajectories, league tables, stock-take sessions with the prime minister, and a working relationship with Treasury to align spending with the desired outcomes (Barber 2007, 2015). The central capacity for implementing the prime minister's objectives was unprecedented (Jones 2016). An Australian Cabinet Implementation Unit was established in the Department of the Prime Minister and the Cabinet (DPMC) to seek effectiveness in programme delivery by ensuring government policies and services were delivered on a timely and responsive basis. The 'traffic light' report to the prime minister and cabinet provided an incentive for public servants to be responsive (Wanna 2006). The delivery unit concept was also adapted in Canada under Justin Trudeau and run out of the Privy Council Office (Gold 2017), but the public service's role had already been reduced to implementing policy directions (Shepherd et al. 2017).

Of other experiments, New Zealand did not use a delivery unit, although the Better Public Services (BPS) agenda (discussed in Chapters 6 and 9) arguably performed this function for several government priorities. Another variation was the use of implementation taskforces of ministers in the UK to monitor and resolve implementation issues and drive cross-cutting priorities (Cabinet Office 2015b; Rutter 2015a; see also Chapter 8).

In the UK environment of the 2010s, ministers' roles in policy implementation have regularly been of an executive nature (NAO 2016a, p. 4). Political drivers had assumed greater importance. The emergent executive role of ministers appeared to be less about managing the department and more about dictating requirements, such as implementation details and timing. Examples of their involvement in implementation have included central efficiency measures and payments by result schemes (e.g. welfare and justice), but there were many others (Hallsworth and Rutter 2011; NAO 2016a; interviews with think tank experts, London). An exchange in the proceedings of the Committee of Public Accounts indicated contrary positions. According to the chair, Meg Hillier, ministers were increasingly assuming, 'more of a semi-executive role', instancing ministers with Gantt charts, who developed and designed policy details, and who were more closely involved in project delivery than previously. Jeremy Heywood (Cabinet Secretary) rationalised the greater ministerial involvement in implementation that had occurred since Blair's early years when ministers were closely involved in monitoring performance through Barber's delivery unit by being, 'very engaged in the data, holding people to account and getting really stuck into whether performance was being delivered'. What could now be observed was, 'an extension of that, or another variation on that same theme . . . If ministers are more involved in the practicalities of implementation, it helps us to design policy more effectively' (CPA 2016b, Q108, Q109).

A second instrument that rose to prominence under Blair was the policy tsar, a ministerial appointment, who often had a significant role in implementation in specialised fields (Smith 2011a; Levitt and Solesbury 2012).

Ministerial staff provided a major source of support, particularly where there was a profusion of political advisers, as in Canada, who frequently dealt with programme implementation: 51 per cent, rising to 69 per cent if occasional involvement is included (Wilson 2016a; see also Maley 2000 for Australia, and Eichbaum and Shaw 2011 for New Zealand).

Ministers' Roles in Management

The management role of ministers has intermittently appeared as a matter that needed to be addressed, but rarely systematically (Di Francesco 2012a). A purchasing role for the minister was envisaged as part of the original reform model in New Zealand (Boston et al. 1996; Di Francesco and Eppel 2011), but politicians were neither interested in, nor capable of handling the task (Scott 2001). There continued to be debate about the extent to which ministers engaged with performance management (Di Francesco 2012a; Van Dooren et al. 2015). The question has since re-emerged from three different positions: as a bulwark against core executive domination, to avoid the risk of a separation between policy and management (Di Francesco and Eppel 2011), and to entrench a ministerial role in internal departmental processes. Political agents may of course be the main actors.

The executive minister has been evident in Anglophone countries, but as the exception, and mainly in the United Kingdom. The classic study of UK cabinet ministers identified management as one of five roles, although most ministers did not mention it (Heady 1974). The micro-managing minister could be expected in any cabinet. The executive minister assumes management responsibilities, possibly arguing that policy and implementation cannot readily be separated. The number of executive ministers at this time was small, and they usually had a bent: motivating staff, organisational change and introducing management processes and techniques.[3] A celebrated example was Michael Heseltine, 'a Whitehall "freak" . . . fascinated by the machine, avid to trim it and supercharge it' (Hennessy 1989, p. 607). His advocacy of the Financial Management Initiative and a management information system in 1982 represented the 'minister as manager' (Metcalf and Richards 1987). The concept of their becoming chief executives, in addition to ministers overloaded by existing responsibilities, was widely dismissed (Hennessy 1989; Riddell et al. 2011). A New Zealand minister, Simon Upton, also showed a 'strong interest in organisational management' in the 1990s (Di Francesco and Eppel 2011, p. 130).

Of course, the minister could operate above the management fray if he or she had a special adviser working in an area. The UK code of conduct was progressively extended from 'giving advice' to encompass 'assistance on any aspect of departmental business'. Advisers may 'undertake long term policy thinking and contribute to policy planning within the department'. In their work with civil servants, they can convey Ministers' views, instructions and priorities . . . request officials to prepare and provide information and data, including internal analyses and papers'. They could review civil servants' advice to the minister. Advisers may also direct civil servants regarding their day-to-day work where they provide support to them (Cabinet Office 2019, sections 3, 4 and 6). This was interpreted to mean that a special adviser could exercise management functions in relation to career officials, although the code prevailed. Special advisers were reported to be giving orders to civil servants and engaging in active management roles (Palmer 2015). In effect the surrogate performed a management function.

Canada is often depicted as the most politically centralised administration (Savoie 1999; Aucoin 2006). The propensity of advisers to play a role in departmental management has been recognised for at least three decades, such as working through medium-level staff, attempting to direct staff (particularly in areas such as contracts and grants) and affecting the reporting relationship between senior executives and the minister (Osbaldeston 1989; Craft 2016). Media attention to even a minor matter quickly escalates its significance, and the policy/administration distinction becomes irrelevant (Savoie 2011). Public servants have become less assertive in operational work, while the activities of ministerial staff are more accepted in operations: 'access to information legislation and the media have made government operations and programs more sensitive to politics and political direction' (Savoie 2010, p. 209). Guidelines indicate 'a more pronounced "operational role" in that advisers are actually buffering and bridging and moving and shaping in relation to the work of the department in addition to the political needs of the minister' (Craft 2016, p. 45). Most ministerial advisers are involved in departmental operations – 63 per cent at least occasionally, 39 per cent frequently or very frequently dealing with such matters (Wilson 2016a, p. 347).

More generally, a European survey indicated that politicians in 'Anglo-Saxon countries' (i.e. the United Kingdom and Ireland) were much more likely to 'interfere with routine activities' in organisations than countries from four other European traditions (Oberg and Wockelberg 2016, p. 67).

A different tack was the use of the departmental board introduced into the UK's departments in the 2000s (HM Treasury 2005), but then channelled as vehicles for Secretaries of State to exercise influence in departments. Corporate management boards became mandatory in 2005 because of concern about management at the top level of the civil service (Parker et al. 2010). Aucoin (2008, pp. 21–2) argued for boards where central management agencies dominated governance, as in Canada (see also Di Francesco and Eppel 2011).[4] Secretaries of State subsequently became chairs of UK departmental boards, comprised of the permanent secretary and senior departmental staff, non-executive members and the cabinet minister plus junior ministers (HM Treasury and Cabinet Office 2011; Cabinet Office 2013; PACAC 2018). The argument was made that departmental challenges, in particular budget cuts, 'overrode traditional distinctions between policy making, delivery and management and required a single concerted effort, focussing on priorities.'[5] If there were further developments this would mean a shift to a collective model and accountability by departmental boards (CPA 2011). Meeting agendas focused on management not policy questions (Waller 2014), and the role was advisory and supervisory (CPA 2011, ev3), although one insider's view was that the board did address policy (Civil service interview, Aug. 2018). The reality was that most boards were not regarded as particularly effective, and this was largely because Secretaries of State were poor at chairing meetings (whether because of a lack of skills and preparation or disinterest) and the advisory character was dominant (Hazell et al. 2018; PACAC 2018).

A final extension of this ministerial role is micromanagement. Once associated more with sub-national governments, the practice became more evident in central governments, at least under specific regimes focused on centralised control of processes, branding and day-to-day operations of departments (Delacourt 2016; Zussman 2016). It is particularly salient where decisions of government authorities are reversed (e.g. research grant decisions, the contents of the census or scientists are muzzled).

POLITICAL RESOURCES AND INSTRUMENTS: THE ROLE OF MINISTERS' AGENTS

The expansion of ministerial resources came through their private offices. The early modern stirrings of interest in advisers occurred in the two largest systems. Canadian political staff began to increase in the 1950s from a modest ministerial office where almost all 'exempt staff' were clerical. The modern institutional role began in the 1960s when the Pearson Liberal government sought to implement an ambitious party policy agenda (Aucoin 2010). Labour Prime Minister Wilson was credited with laying the foundation for the British system in 1964 when 'special advisers' were employed in the Cabinet Office, Foreign Office and Treasury (Fawcett and Gay 2010).

Prime Ministers' Offices

Prime ministers' offices (PMOs) have played critical but variable roles. They come in two basic forms offering either core support for the prime minister or as political machines for driving the prime minister's agenda, with variations in between. The former may have a narrow range of functions; the latter an extensive number of responsibilities and greater policy and strategic authority.

Much depends on the level of decentralisation the prime minister permits within the political executive and how the PMO is constituted. A powerful PMO has a propensity to come into conflict with central agencies and the domains of ministers and their departments. Indicators of a PMO's character have been the degree of partisanship of staff, and the relative significance of process and policy content. The prime minister's office was depicted as calling the shots in Canada, and at times in Australia (Aucoin et al. 2013), whereas in the UK, No. 10's roles have been more variable but often pivotal.

Canada set the pace with the PMO in the 1960s. The modern version of the PMO was attributed to Pierre Trudeau but there were already about 40 staff in the office of his predecessor, Lester Pearson, whom he succeeded in 1968 (Radwanski 2016). The PMO functioned mainly as a 'switchboard' for the prime minister (rather than the 'nerve centre of policy making') with most roles (apart from nuts and bolts) supporting the prime minister in terms of public image, party politics and increasingly short-term tactics and firefighting (Campbell and Szablowski 1979). The Canadian PMO became larger after Trudeau with staff ranging from 80 to 120. It was reorganised along the lines of the Executive Office of the President in the United States, and PMO staff members were described as more like those employed there (Savoie 1999, p. 101). Of Aucoin's (2012) components of NPG, prime ministerial power became greater, and the PMO much stronger. The centralisation and concentration of power in the Canadian government was frequently acknowledged (Savoie 1999). The staff were depicted as 'partisan, temporary, and above all loyal to the prime minister', in a structure that was highly centralised (Savoie 1999). One result was that deputy ministers had 'fraught' relations with the PMO (Bourgault 2014, p. 377). Much depended on the prime minister's style as indicated by a 'directive' approach under Harper compared to the 'facilitative' approach under Justin Trudeau (interview, senior official, Ottawa 2016).

Canada's PMO was the model for the Australian office (Tiernan 2007b), which dates from the 1970s and evolved greater responsibilities and complexity over time as the government's reliance on it increased. The office existed not principally to initiate policy, but to focus on process and extend the prime minister's capacity to control the public service (Walter 1986; Campbell and Halligan 1992). Early on the PMO was quasi-partisan, becoming less so as the value of public service expertise was appreciated more (Campbell and Halligan 1992). The transition to a more political PMO occurred in the following two decades (Rhodes and Tiernan 2014a), when central agencies were weakened by decentring, and continued while recentring was under way with the most impact on the Department of the Prime Minister and Cabinet. The chief of staff role was emerging towards the end of the 1980s, influenced by the 'Chef de Cabinet' in Europe and management ideas (Behm 2015). The PMO covered policy advice and coordination and increasingly became a concentration of partisans committed to the prime minister's objectives. Advisers accounted for 75 per cent of PMO staff (40 of 53) in 2012 (Rhodes and Tiernan 2014a; 2014b, p. 69).

A shift from strategic policy to short-term politics and more intervention in coordinating, such as centralising of policy development in selected areas, occurred under Howard (Bennister 2012, pp. 100, 113). Under Rudd, the Australian PMO acquired more comprehensive authority and power (Waterford 2009).[6] Under his successor, Tony Abbott with Peta Credlin, the chief of staff of the PMO, the arrangements were highly centralised, authoritarian and created a climate of fear; yet policy-making was ad hoc, and coordination and strategy were lacking (Patrick 2016). Credlin, 'redefined the role of the prime ministerial chief of staff . . . she turned a backroom position into a proxy for the prime minister himself' (Patrick 2016, p. 19).[7]

The United Kingdom's centre has been weak by comparison with other Anglophone countries (Yong and Hazell 2014). The Cabinet Office and No. 10 have fluctuated in capacity and different organisational arrangements. There is no doubting the authority of No. 10, which could exercise decisive influence in specific areas but less so more comprehensively. However, under Tony Blair, No. 10 staff assumed highly active and interventionist roles in developing and implementing policies and in organising the machinery of government. The prime minister's support was based on commandeering parts of an augmented Cabinet Office and an enlarged prime minister's office (Blick and Jones 2010). Theresa May's two co-chiefs of staff (until their demise in the 2017 election debacle) made decisions without regard to cabinet, including developing Brexit policy (Shipman 2017).

The Minister's Office

The other prominent addition to the executive branches during the early reform era is the ministerial adviser, who has become an integral fixture in that position (Shaw and Eichbaum 2018). The political executive used advisers to increase the influence of the ministerial office, and to enlarge the partisan element within the executive, to extend the minister's authority at the interface with the public service and to redistribute power between administrative and political systems. They often performed tasks that otherwise would be undertaken by public servants; and acted as the main communication link between the minister and other institutions.

Ministerial or political advisers have also been known as special advisers (or spads) in the UK, and 'exempt staff' in Canada. It is unclear how comparable the terminology is for it may apply to several types of ministerial staff ranging from media to technical and policy experts (see Craft 2016). Whether they have been members of a political party has varied between governments (e.g.

Halligan and Power 1992), but partisan appointments have increased over time in Australia, and still vary with governments and ministers. Regardless, staffers operating politically rather than as professionals within core executives has markedly increased in significance.

The Canadian minister's office expanded in tandem with the PMO. An explicit rival to departments was most clearly articulated by Canadian prime ministers, first by Pierre Trudeau, and then Brian Mulroney when he introduced the chief of staff position for ministers' offices in 1984 (Bakvis 2000). Over the past four decades, political staff have added a significant new element to the Canadian government as the agent of the minister to whom they were responsible and accountable (Aucoin 2010). Under Mulroney the number of political staff rose to 460 in the early 1990s (with 99 in the Prime Minister's Office), and subsequently the combined staff exceeded 500, a level maintained despite fluctuations (Aucoin 2010). By the 2010s the PMO figure was as high as 112, and the total exempt staff was 570 (Table 2.2 in Craft 2016).

In Australia, the Gough Whitlam Labor government introduced an advisory system in 1972; although partisan advisers existed before, they now became the norm and the size of the ministerial office increased (Halligan and Power 1992). The Bob Hawke Labor government sought to strengthen political direction (Campbell and Halligan 1992) by proposing a political tier within the senior public service, but compromised with a new position, the ministerial consultant, and the minister's office was accordingly expanded as an alternative to overt politicisation. Ministerial advisers were increasingly interposed between the bureaucracy and politicians, and became an institutionalised part of government with numbers as high as 470 (2007) (Halligan and Power 1992; Maley 2010). The Member of Parliament (Staff) Act 1984 provided for ministers to employ and be responsible for staff, and interventions by parties supported the professionalisation of staff and careers (Tiernan 2007b). Working in a minister's parliamentary or electoral office has been one pathway to a career in parliament (Behm 2015).

In contrast with other Anglophone countries, New Zealand was more reluctant to develop ministerial offices. Ministerial suspicions of senior departmental advice in the 1980s led them to rely less on the public service and more on political appointees in their offices, but the position was not institutionalised. The number of ministerial advisers has increased during the last two decades: there were about 30 political advisers (excluding press secretaries) in 2006 (Eichbaum and Shaw 2007b, p. 465), but numbers have remained small until a jump in the 2010s (Table 3.3). In addition, ministers usually agreed to the placement of departmental staff in ministerial offices to provide policy advice and liaison (Shaw and Eichbaum 2018; Boston and Halligan 2012).

The UK numbers fluctuated (Richards 2008, p. 180), but jumped under Blair, and have increased overall until recently. Despite constant reviews of

Table 3.3   *Ministerial staff in Australia, Canada, New Zealand, and the*
                   United Kingdom

	Minister's Offices	Prime Minister's Office	Total
Australia	402	50	452 (2019)
Canada	490	91	581 (2018)
New Zealand	126	23	149 (2015)
United Kingdom	62	37	99 (2018)

Source: Table 5.1 in Craft and Halligan 2020.

the role, the overall numbers have remained comparatively small. A distinction is drawn between the minister's private office staffed by public servants (who perform roles such as correspondence, departmental liaison and the ministerial diary, elsewhere undertaken by staff in a partisan office) and special advisers appointed by ministers. The latter were fixed at two per minister with the notable exceptions of the prime minister and deputy prime minister. In addition, there might be an expert policy adviser employed on a temporary contract (Paun 2013; Yong and Hazell 2014).

While all countries developed systems of ministerial staff in the reform era there were significant variations between them: the smallest and largest systems have fewer advisers, while the two medium-sized federal systems have 450–580.[8] Getting a comparative fix on the composition of the staff can be problematic as it varies over time (e.g. in the extent of their partisanship and the use of public servants), and covers various types of assistant in addition to advisers (Craft 2016). Australian ministerial staff covered a range of occupations from administrative and support staff, political, departmental liaison, and the major growth areas, media and ministerial advisers (Tiernan 2007b). Ministerial advisers accounted for 71 per cent of staff in Australia (Maley 2011). The average number per minister in 2015 was highest in Canada (19) followed by Australia (12), New Zealand (6) and the UK (4) (Ng 2018, p. 51). Numbers alone do not of course indicate the influence of advisers, for many have been young and inexperienced (Aucoin 2010; Yong and Hazell 2014; Behm 2015).

British special advisers were, 'the lightning-rod for debate . . . about the politicization of the public service' (Fawcett and Gay 2010, p. 25). The roles of individual advisers have attracted public debate, such as the two senior advisers given authority by Prime Minister Blair to issue instructions to civil servants (an authority subsequently rescinded by Prime Minister Brown). Advisers have been the subjects of several investigations over the years, and again by parliamentary committee inquiries in 2012. The UK appeared to be edging towards the arrangements of other jurisdictions as the ceiling continued to rise but it remained well short of the federal systems and the trend was halted. This ambivalence was epitomised by the 'extended minister's office' (covering civil servants, special advisers and external appointees) introduced under the coalition government; but ministerial demand for more staff was low, and the practice was terminated under May.

The frayed nexus between the political executive and senior officials in Australia often centred on the impact of ministerial advisers on public servants and their lack of accountability when involved in major public policy issues (Tiernan 2007b). However, the mechanisms for holding advisers accountable remained problematic, one implication being that they have not been contained (Moran 2011). There is considerable evidence of advisers acting beyond the limits established by official guidelines and codes of conduct (Wilson 2016a; Craft 2018b). The position can be subject to high turnover because of the rigours of the job.

The sheer numbers often matter less than the standing and influence of specific advisers and the level of direct support marshalled by prime ministers. Thus, the UK has maintained a modest complement compared to Australia and Canada, but there have been a few celebrated advisers of great influence. Ed Balls advised HM Treasury in 1998 that their new performance management framework for the civil service was being replaced. Alistair Campbell and Jonathan Powell (chief of staff, Downing Street) were given the authority to direct civil servants (Blick and Jones 2010). Fast forward to the mid-2010s and concern was being expressed at the appointment of 'increasingly influential' advisers able to act on behalf of the government (NAO 2016a, p. 4). On the question of direct support, the aggregation of resources by Blair across his quasi-fusion of the PMO and the Cabinet Office was unprecedented with almost 800 staff supporting him in leading the government in 2005–06, and multiple policy units reporting to him (Blick and Jones 2010; Jones 2016).

The roles of advisers have long been institutionalised. They have supported ministers in four ways: helping ministers perform their jobs, steering policy, coordinating work within the ministry and supporting cabinet work (Maley 2010). One valued role of political advisers has been to reduce the pressure on heads of department to provide partisan political advice (Osbaldeston 1989; Yong and Hazell 2014). However, issues have persisted. The calibre, expertise and experience of advisers has been a chronic problem, more so in specific contexts. One example of an issue has been the propensity of Australian ministers to appoint 'miniature versions of themselves: political thrusters who place a premium on playing the political game at the expense of building the national community and its resilience' (Behm 2015, p. 43). An extended critique came from a former head of the Australian public service who derided the limited experience of the 'teenagers' (see Chapter 3, fn 13).

Ministerial staff have assumed the job once held by the senior public service of protecting the minister. This may entail working against the public service except that they may be more zealous and less restrained in how they operate. Familiar machinations of key advisers have been observed in the United Kingdom (McBride 2013; Palmer 2015; Shipman 2017) and in Australia (Behm 2015; Patrick 2016). A small number of New Zealand advisers attempted 'to limit the scope of requests for official information or change an agency's proposed decision for unwarranted reasons' (Wakem 2015, p. 4; see also Legault 2016 for Canada). Codes of conduct exist but can be readily ignored in practice (Palmer 2015).

Policy Tsars as Political Appointees

An alternative to expanding the use of political advisers in the PMO or ministers' offices in the UK is the appointment of policy tsars (Smith 2011a; Levitt and Solesbury 2012).[9] A definition of a tsar is 'an individual from outside government who is publicly appointed by a government minister to advise on policy development or delivery on the basis of their expertise' (Levitt and Solesbury 2012, p. 4). They are ministerial appointments and have mainly been external experts, although some have been serving MPs or ex-ministers. There were 267 appointments between 1997 and 2012, the annual rate of appointment increasing across the four governments (Annex 1.1 in Levitt and Solesbury 2012).[10] Tsars have been ad hoc and temporary appointments, the majority of whom (70%) completed their task in less than 12 months – one-fifth took less than six months. Their advice has been made directly to ministers thereby providing another source of policy advice, although there were other reasons for making appointments (including delivery coordination and patronage: Levitt and Solesbury 2012).

Australia, Canada and New Zealand have regularly used independent review processes for a range of issues, but their institutionalised basis may be less identified with ministers and policy advice, and without documentation their role is indeterminate.

OVERALL SHIFTS AND SWINGS BETWEEN ROLES

Roles and Advice

The pattern of change was fairly consistent across countries once the new leadership role of ministers emerged most explicitly in the 1980s. Australian ministers were now in charge, but the public servants' role was acknowledged (Campbell and Halligan 1992). Thatcher was best known for an active (even strident) role in political assertion and policy initiation. Howard harboured medium-term suspicion of the Australian public service, and political control was intensified through a significantly stronger PMO. Blair established a new top-down model through a central machine of civil servants and special advisers in units for pursuing performance and implementation. There was a flurry of activity under Cameron's government with debates about roles and highly interventionist ministers under his decentralised approach.

The central machine in Canada seemed to squeeze out the identity of ministers after Mulroney's mixed success with placing more emphasis on them. Canada was renowned for centralised control featuring the PMO (Savoie 1999), which increased further under Chrétien and Martin (Savoie 2008), reaching a new level after Harper was re-elected with a majority. The level of direction from the PMO was emphatic and elaborate in the later Harper years when command and control affected ministers and their advisers and departments alike.[11] The Harper case was a more complete takeover of a public management and governance system by a prime minister. Australian centralisation peaked under Abbott's brief term as prime minister.

Policy advice was once the primary role of senior public servants, but ministers then styled themselves more as policy initiators and perceived the public servant in terms of department management but became engaged with implementation to an increasing extent. Policy development work shrank as ministers became more forthright in policy pronouncements and less interested in the analytical work of departments, or even in policy options, and drew on external policy sources. The bottom line is that all systems have demanding ministers, prioritisation of ministerial and government business, and diminished internal policy capability. The general movement was from Mode 1, a traditional type of conception, towards Mode 3, although variations were evident, particularly at the individual minister level (Table 3.3). A Mode 4 can also be articulated where the public service focuses on delivery and the sharing of the policy initiation role is replaced by ministers and advisers with the officials as a support team.

Of the roles in governing, the public service is less likely to be involved in articulating values and mediating interests (cf. Aberbach et al. 1981). Management options involved contracting, marginalising, use of executive agencies, devolution, external oversight through boards, special reviews, central monitoring and policy development, and consultants and political advisers. The public service has been consolidated, redefined and curtailed. The progressive reduction of public service roles from advice and support, to policy initiation and formulation to policy implementation has been apparent across the systems over time. However, there are qualifications: the direction is not solely one of expansion and contraction for this would have meant the demise of the public service, and the 2010s provided reflections on how to position roles and resources. For example, despite the rhetoric in Francis

Maude's push for a new relationship, most UK ministers chose not to expand their private office. The three modes therefore provide a sense of the direction of change over time, but do not reflect finer variations. With ministers' roles more generally, the move between different relationships has continued, with the ministerial leadership using either a mixture of partisans and public servants or directing political control through partisan staff.

Unbounded and Ambiguous Spheres of Operation

The internal contradictions embodied in management and political reform are grounded in conflicting conceptions of the roles of top public servants and ministers that have entailed more authority and discretion for both. The former, especially in the case of NZ's chief executives, expected to exercise greater freedom to manage their departments. However, reforms were also designed to ensure that department heads worked more explicitly under ministerial control (Aucoin 1988, 1990; Gregory 2001).

Political actors acquired greater flexibility, more discretion and worked under fewer constraints. In almost all the main departments, UK ministers, 'pursued their own large and risky policy agendas at pace' (Page et al. 2014, p. 17). Ministers, unless formally circumscribed, could move across a range of roles, including implementation and management, once the preserve of the public service. In the UK the Armstrong Memorandum (1985) defined civil servants' duties and roles in terms of ministers who were willing to take advantage of what was provided for constitutionally. It was observed that the, 'demarcation between ministerial responsibility for policy and Accounting Officer responsibility for implementation has blurred as Ministers in successive administrations have taken a closer interest in how their policies are delivered' (CPA 2011, p. 4). Ministers' close involvement in implementing policy has been referred to earlier (NAO 2016a). According to a former cabinet secretary, understandings about outcomes, responsibilities and constraints on delivery were opaque: 'we are living in a '50 shades of grey' world where none of the above is clear. As result public servants and ministers can blame each other – the former privately, the latter publicly. This is a recipe for mutual distrust' (O'Donnell 2013, p. 384).

Policy tsars added to the ambiguity as both creations of ministers and the media, often with uncertain responsibilities and operating under informal arrangements (although there was some dependence on formal institutions like the civil service if they wished to be effective (Smith 2011a).

Analysis of agency bargains between ministers and civil servants indicated that several types (directed or delegated) existed and that movement within and between these categories occurred (Hood and Lodge 2006). The working arrangements could vary so much between ministers, between different types of issue and over time, that they were unpredictable and unclear to the participants, and often depended on individual cases (e.g. precipitous actions by ministers – see Chapter 4). Where there was a high turnover of ministers and departments (e.g. a UK permanent secretary could experience three Secretaries of State in as many years) the 'bargain' could be constantly renegotiated.

In Australia political advisers were often unrestrained where there were either large numbers or few formal constraints, or where they were specifically empowered and could be unleashed regardless of competence (although there were many exceptions: see Behm 2015). The lack of public accountability remained an issue, even where guidelines or codes existed for how they related to public servants.

Tension in Reformulated Relationships

Different formulations of the roles of ministers and public servants have long been apparent (Peters 1987), according to whether there was an understood demarcation of responsibilities and the character and tone of the relationship. On the one hand, there is the conception of a department head with some measure of independence on operational matters, or as a parliamentary 'accounting officer' where that role is defined or linked to stewardship roles. On the other there is the conception of the strong minister operating as a political master, running both political and non-political agents and with a pervasive reach (including possibly a departmental board and dictats from the prime minister's office). In the UK it was argued that there was an artificial distinction between policy and delivery which should be characterised as a continuum because officials were engaged in developing policy (Francis Maude, CPA 2011, ev1). This argument could be used to rationalise ministers' involvement in delivery. Yet a contra argument about separating policy advising from implementing, which arose most explicitly in practice in New Zealand (Boston et al. 1996), allowed for implementation to occur independently of the public service.

Another dimension of the relationship is the extent to which it is adversarial or complementary. The latter is identified as cosy relationships between political and bureaucratic elites (e.g. 'village life' in Whitehall: Heclo and Wildavsky 1974) or others supporting integration and the indivisibility that once characterised the Whitehall relationship (Peters 1987; Richards and Smith 2016). The former was once more likely with new governments confronting a public service thought to be close to its predecessor. But now short-term reconciliations of new governments with the public service are replaced by ongoing tensions as might befit a principal–agent relationship.

Ministerial Performance

These tensions in the relationship between ministers and officials have a long history, but the focus in the reform era has been to address them by making the public service more responsive (PACAC 2018). This one-sided approach has neglected ministerial responsibility in the relationship even though ministers' roles and authority have expanded. The relationship has been depicted as the 'fulcrum' of the UK system, which must be based on 'strong mutual trust' to be effective. Without trust, the 'fulcrum can become a fracture point. Under the circumstances, honest conversations do not take place as this affects the atmosphere throughout the whole department. In the end, policy and delivery suffer' (PACAC 2018, p. 3).

One long-term issue has been the qualifications of ministers, many of whom have lacked competence and/or relevant experience. Heady (1974) argued that ministers were not qualified to be policy initiators because of their short time in office and the length of time required for policy to be enacted. The training of many ministers was unsuitable for decision-making and cabinet ministers were not qualified to initiate policy (Heady 1974; Heclo and Wildavsky 1974). Four out of ten were capable of 'administration' (Hasluck 1995, an experienced Australian minister). The Blair government decided that there were insufficient members of parliament appropriate for ministerial rank, so appointments to the House of Lords were made and policy tsars created.

Contradictions in Empowering Ministers

Ministers do not necessarily take advantage of the options provided to them. This was most clearly demonstrated by New Zealand ministers who were given explicit responsibilities under the 1988 public management model. They turned out to be either uninterested or lacked the ability to address their role as purchasers (Scott 2001). UK ministers have also not availed themselves of a prime option for enhancing their resources through the extended ministerial office (although the process may have deterred some). A few have not bothered with their full quota of special advisers. Secretaries of State have also not made effective use of their role of chairing departmental boards, in some cases through poor chairing skills or a lack of interest beyond the political agenda (PACAC 2018). Some prime ministers have given attention to evaluating ministerial performance.

The limits of ministerial responsibility, which have historically been subject to evasion, has new manifestations when the blame game is employed (see Chapter 7). It is more difficult to pinpoint where public servants succumb to political pressure. Under austerity and deficits as an ideological mainspring, percentage cuts in the public service are made, but departmental heads take responsibility for specific actions (Mulgan 2016).

CONSEQUENCES OF POLITICISING THE POLICY PROCESS

There have been consequences for policy advice and tensions about understandings and operations within the executive branch where pressures were intense. Unintended consequences have included weaknesses in internal policy capability, the disregarding of evidence and official advice, and the nature of decision-making about policy.

Policy Advice and Analysis

Externalising and pluralising of advice have been long-term features in Anglophone countries (Craft and Halligan 2017, 2020). There was a four-pronged attack on the policy function of the public service which included downgrading the policy role at senior levels, separating policy from implementation, reducing departmental capabilities and the cultivation of the generalist. The upshot of this manipulation of different options was the deterioration of policy capacity in their countries (see Chapter 5). As part of the general erosion of public service policy capacity (Edwards 2009; Gleeson et al. 2011; Craft and Halligan 2017) there was a decline in officials' content experience in favour of the generalist and process forms of policy work (Page and Jenkins 2005; Tiernan 2011; Howlett et al. 2014). This was attributed to the externalisation of policy roles, policy competition, and politicisation through more directive ministers and their offices (Craft and Halligan 2017, 2020). The official advice about how to improve the public management system exhorts change from within the public service (e.g. Scott et al. 2010; Shergold 2015) but underplays the significance of an often volatile but inviolable political executive and its policy dominance.

Externalising Advice

The use of external consultants has been a prominent feature of public management in Anglophone countries (Saint-Martin 2004), although distinguishing policy work in public data can be problematic (Howlett and Migone 2017) and much may be process-related (Howlett and Migone 2013). The UK is best known for its heavy reliance on third parties for implementation, but there was once a Francis Maude initiative to facilitate the acquisition of external advice, the Ministerial Contestability Policy Fund (2012–15). It was designed to provide and financially support ministerial access to alternative sources of policy advice. In the end, 18 projects were funded (Rutter 2015b).

There have been broader issues with the extent of reliance on consultants, prompting public inquiries in Australia and the United Kingdom (e.g. CPA 2016d; ANAO 2017a; Craft and Halligan 2020). The issue with the use of consultants was made most explicit by the then head of the Australian public service, Martin Parkinson, who castigated departments for being excessively dependent on consultants, thereby repudiating their core role (Easton 2018).

Scotching the Policy Process: Ministers, Evidence and Policy Style

There is a substantial body of cases of ministers making policy declarations without first acquiring evidence. Senior policy officials surveyed in Australia, New Zealand and the United Kingdom (2012–14) have provided concrete indications based on their experiences. The majority agreed in the three countries that ministers were indifferent to facts; three-quarters (over 80 per cent in New Zealand) agreed that retrofitting of evidence occurred after decisions were made. More experienced public servants believed that there was a dramatic decline in using evidence in policy-making (Stoker and Evans 2016). Policy-based evidence-making (or PBE: policy-based evidence) had entered the lexicon of Whitehall and was reportedly endemic (interview Whitehall Aug. 2018; see also Diamond 2019b).

A second exclusion process involves the role of interest groups, which used to be a component of traditional governance policy style that incorporated collaborative and deliberative elements in the policy process. An 'imposition policy style' of pre-determined decisions – with some resemblance to 'pop-up' policy-making – has meant that affected groups lack opportunities to contribute (Richardson 2018), and this has a deleterious effect on policy outcomes.

A substantial number of the 'blunders of government' investigated by King and Crewe (2014, p. 339) were the product of hasty processes. Speedy policy-making by activist ministers and the reticence of civil servants were responsible. A comparative contribution to the blunders of government literature argues that a combination of explanations account for policy failure. In addition to the rushed policy choices emerging from 'hyper-excited politics' there are two related factors, instrument choice (wrong tools) and administrative capacity (assumptions about the availability of skill and capabilities, inadequate resourcing and inattention to oversight) (Jennings et al. 2018). High turnover of ministers and senior leaders were significant in some cases (Page 2015; Jennings et al. 2018). Analysis of eight high-profile Australian policy decisions against ten criteria produced only two cases that approximated 'best practice' (Per Capita 2019).[12] Other Australian cases were a product of precipitative decisions, design issues and mishandled implementation (Shergold 2015).

Impact on Public Policy

It has been established that ministers under pressure have been prone to acting with haste in the short term, and this has become a stereotype of how governments operate in the 2010s, feeding a lack of faith and trust. The policy process no longer matters much as it has become more political and less deliberative (Richardson 2018). Moreover, a perverse effect of the delivery culture that Thatcher and Blair instilled at the centre was that ministers and officials produced results, but 'the wrong commodities' (King and Crewe 2014, p. 343). The mounting range of policy failures has huge costs for society.

Political Advisers: Accountability and Capability

Policy advisers increase the policy capacity of ministers and exact responsiveness from public servants (Wilson 2016a). The latitude either offered to or taken by ministerial staff has continued to provide a potentially unpredictable dynamic within the management system. Apart from those empowered at the centre to exercise power (usually chiefs of staff of PMOs) there is substantial evidence of staff being more interventionist in departmental operations than allowed by guidelines or codes of conduct (Craft 2016) and of interference in the disclosure of information (Legault 2016; for further cases, see Ng 2018). Insider indictments of political staff include the depiction of 'the closed world of callow political advisers and their disastrous impact on the performance of many Ministers'.[13] The judgement that Australian ministerial offices functioned 'like the primordial soup, and in an organic and somewhat chaotic fashion' (Ng 2016) was applied to some offices across all countries but not the well-managed ones or a PMO machine at its most effective. Central oversight of recruitment and practice was also a moderating factor under some prime ministers (e.g. Helen Clark's requirements for matching advisers and minister's competence in New Zealand). Scrutiny of appointments has occurred in the UK but not consistently (King 2007; Yong and Hazell 2014).

CONCLUSION

Politicisation has moved the goal posts within the executive branch. The expansion of ministers' roles represents a firming up of an undeveloped position that was sanctioned constitutionally. Ministers have become stronger and more directive. Their ministerial offices have expanded, and their advisers have become integral to and institutionalised within the system of government. The fundamentals of the relationship between the political executive and the public service have changed substantially. The policy active minister wants to direct portfolio action and to mobilise the public service to achieve his/her objectives. The senior civil service has to accommodate this greater assertiveness.

Three observations can be made. First, while all four countries have developed systems of ministerial advisers in the reform era there is significant variation between three with two tracks being apparent: the smallest and largest systems have smaller ministerial offices and make more use of public servants, while the two medium-sized federal systems have large political offices. The numbers of ministerial staff were not the only indicator of the magnitude and impact of change; the role of pivotal advisers, particularly in the PMOs, could be decisive. Secondly, distinctive pathways are apparent. Australia and Canada moved further down this politicisation track than New Zealand and the United Kingdom and relied more heavily on partisan staff. The United Kingdom experienced heightened political interventions under specific prime ministers, extended ministerial roles in the 2010s and made extensive but variable use of several types of political actor. New Zealand was an all-rounder, showing features of politicisation, but usually at a lower level of intensity (see Chapter 9). Thirdly, cycles of political intensity are apparent because of the changing governance style of prime ministers and fluctuations in the agitation for change.

Once system imbalance came from the dominance of mandarins and the compliance of ministers, now this imbalance was reversed. The traditional formulation of relationships envisaged the minister providing the dynamic element, while the public service offered a stable dimension. With the senior public service no longer permanent, and political intervention pervasive, the governmental system has become vulnerable and susceptible to politicians seeking a level of political control that can only be acquired through expanding partisanship in the executive branch. In the new world of policy ministers, they have either done policy themselves or played the policy leader who sources and selects policy advice from preferred providers and advisers. The consequences of this (often amorphous) reconstruction of policy management are twofold: demand is missing so supply declines leading to slumps in policy capability and skills; and the development and selection of many policy options do not benefit sufficiently from the collective understandings and expertise of the public service. Nor is it clear that expanding the range and intensity of partisan instruments necessarily produces what is desired by the political executive in terms of implementation and results.

NOTES

1. Richards and Smith (2016) note that Thatcher was 'partly informed by public-choice accounts of bureaucracy'. More generally, see Pollitt (1990).
2. Canada had also been distinguished by some movement between the public service and political spheres with deputy ministers crossing over.
3. One ran the department through a management team involving seven junior ministers in decision-making (Heady 1974).
4. 'Boardization' was used by Wilks (2007, p. 456), whose purpose was, 'to capture a significant institutional dynamic generated by the confluence of political strategies of depoliticization and administrative reform strategies of managerialism'.
5. According to Francis Maude, 'having roughly an equal number of ministers, civil servants and non-execs on the board gives the chance to create a genuine collective leadership for the Department, bringing together the political and official leaders with the support and challenge from the non-execs' (CPA 2011, ev1).
6. 'Never, even in John Howard's day has so much power been concentrated in the prime minister's private office . . . among the tight core of minders, advisers and managers focused exclusively on the political survival of the Government and the Prime Minister' (Waterford 2009, p. 8).
7. Apart from dictating policy agendas, Credlin's role extended to controlling the appointment of the heads of ministers' offices, ministerial consultation and the overseas movements of senior cabinet ministers (Patrick 2016). This was not dissimilar to May's chiefs of staff (Shipman 2017).
8. Canada has operated with 35 or more ministers, compared to Australia's 29 (plus 12 parliamentary secretaries).
9. The practice was associated with the United States where it refers to high-level officials (czars) who have oversight of a particular policy or problem area.
10. Levitt and Solesbury (2012, p. 13) excluded about 110 national clinical directors who are expert practitioners appointed in the Department of Health; business ambassadors; and non-executive directors appointed to boards of departments and public bodies.
11. Discussions with current and former senior public servants, 2016.
12. The Jennings et al. (2018) analysis covered cases from seven countries including Australia, Canada and the United Kingdom. The most frequent process omissions in the Australian study were: did not establish need, identify options, brainstorm alternatives, design pathways, consult further or publish proposals. Two of these federal cases scored 2/10 (Per Capita 2019, pp. 8–9).
13. T. Moran, former head of the Australian public service, quoted in Behm 2015, cover jacket.

4. Ministers and mandarins under political management

Heads of departments traditionally provided a linchpin in the Anglophone system of government. As one-time permanent secretaries,[1] they were both professional public servants and bastions of public service independence who presided over their departments of state in Australia, Canada, New Zealand and the United Kingdom. Their status has since been transformed in an era of responsiveness, with activist ministers and management change, which has also produced departures from internal recruitment and volatility in some arrangements. Governments have exercised their authority to appoint (and dispense with) department heads and not necessarily in transparent and consistent ways.

The political executive's most important means for exerting influence over the public service is through its senior appointments. However, political executives vary as to the extent to which they can control such appointments, sometimes having an open hand, in other cases being constrained by convention and law. The operation of senior recruitment systems also needs to be set against a backdrop of major changes in the overall relationship between the political executive and the public service in Anglophone systems (Aucoin 2012; Halligan 2012). Political executives now have a range of instruments for mobilising bureaucrats, including the resources of ministers' private offices and increased influence over appointments. The breakdown in traditional norms regulating the relationship has produced problems with achieving a stable fit between ministers and department heads.

Early studies of politicisation in the reform era were inclined to focus on appointments, and the application of partisan over merit principles in filling senior positions (Mulgan 1998, 2007; Peters and Pierre 2004a). Here a distinction is made between appointment *systems* and individual and ad hoc ministerial actions. Appointment systems can be distinguished according to whether they operate through processes largely dominated or strongly influenced by the senior public service and those where the process is largely or wholly controlled by the political executive. Different outcomes arise from the two approaches.

The revisionist view of politicisation is centred on public servants' behaviour, a difficult dimension to investigate beyond individual cases. One conception addresses the distance that professionals keep from ministers, politicisation denoting excessive zeal in crossing the line while pandering to responsiveness (Mulgan 2007). This does not capture a further dimension, which is how senior public servants defer to ministers against their professional judgement. Mutations of the professional public servant defaulting to a ministerial preference are touched on later, but the focus here is on the minister as the actor who seeks in one form or another to be more directly engaged in a range of departmental decisions.

Three theoretical perspectives on relationships are addressed before analysing their relevance and assessing their relative importance in terms of the impact on officials. More specifically, the chapter examines the recruitment and review of department heads in systems operating under revised rules. Explanations for the different patterns are then outlined, including contextual factors, the role of appointment mechanisms and rules in influencing outcomes, long-term trends towards politicisation, and whether these explanations apply across the four systems under examination. Finally, there is discussion of a set of issues about tensions between approaches (the results of dominant principals versus the stewardship movement for supporting public purposes), and the continuing tension between path-dependent aspects that favour neutral competence and pressures for responsive competence. The interplay of these issues can be seen in the dialectics of change as conflicts continue to be re-run.

TRUSTEES, AGENTS AND STEWARDS

The trustee, agency and stewardship conceptions can be used to examine changes in the relationship between ministers and senior public servants. The trustee form is associated with traditional mandarins. One formulation argues that in a trustee relationship, 'public servants are expected to act as independent judges of the public good . . . to some significant extent, and not merely to take their orders from some political master' (Hood and Lodge 2006, p. 25). Authority is delegated to either a professional bureaucracy or an agency that is insulated from politicians. Trustees sometimes can best serve principals by not being responsive to the principal's interests, especially when the principal's pursuit of self-interest threatens the public interest in the long run (Knott and Miller 2008).

The second formulation is agency theory, which focuses on the divergence between the interests of the principal and the agent. It has been heavily critiqued for the assumptions made about footloose agents (but not about principals: cf. Miller and Whitford 2016). Agency theory resonates with an instrumentalist conception of the Anglophone tradition, which regards the public service as a tool of government with heads of departments a central expression of this, and a focus on the means for assuring their compliance with political preferences. The political executive actively engages in managing the top leadership through determining the assignment of responsibilities, where the appointees come from, and the conditions of their appointment and their assessment. Some reform initiatives were designed to produce a relationship that was 'agency-like' (Hood and Lodge 2006, p. 45).

The third position, stewardship, serves as a counterpoint to agency theory. It is based on a different conception of the individual, focusing on the responsibilities of the manager for the system, specifically its capacity and sustainability. It emphasises the centrality of the manager and of service. In contrast with the economic theory of principal/agent, stewardship theory is grounded in sociology (Davis et al. 1997). Core elements are collaboration across the service (or whole-of-government) and responsibility for public policy over time.[2]

Reign of the Trustees: Mandarins

Modes of demarcating politics and administration range from a model that firmly separates political and public service careers and roles to that in which the careers intermingle and boundaries are weak (Pierre 1995). The traditional British system approximated the former: an explicit separation combined with distinctive boundaries. The relationship was based on well-understood norms: a neutral public service based on permanent officials served the political executive regardless of party, and the political executive in turn respected the integrity of the civil service by supporting its apolitical and professional character (Aucoin 1995; Campbell and Wilson 1995; Halligan 2001).

A common element of the four Anglophone systems was the mandarin who stood astride the department of state and was typified as a strong and influential personality. The Canadian public service was overshadowed by such a group during the Liberals' domination of government for two decades (1935–57) described as 'the presumed glory days of the public service, led by a handful of legendary mandarins' (Aucoin 2010, p. 67). The role of guardian was associated with mandarins and encompassed the public interest, public purse and administrative order (such as protection from irregular partisan interventions and illegalities) (Bourgault and Dunn 2014a, pp. 430–32). In the United Kingdom, the years after the Second World War were depicted as 'a mandarin's paradise' where senior civil servants mainly ran the affairs of government (King 2007, p. 217). Australia had the so-called 'Seven Dwarfs' (Furphy 2015), a group of permanent secretaries who ruled the Australian public service for decades and tended to dominate policy advice. The continuity of New Zealand's permanent heads was also recognised (Martin 2015).

Creating Agents

The position of agent was foreshadowed by a political leader's priorities and planning style in Canada (Campbell 1988b), requiring a chief executive to preside at the apex (Aucoin 2012). The modern version is formulated as that of the agent, the departmental secretary and other senior officials, who are subject to the preferences and expectations of ministers. This type of relationship has been a running theme of the reform era since Thatcher demanded certain types of appointment, prompting claims about 'personalisation' of the civil service, through to Blair's extensions of the type of appointments, to the 2010s (Campbell and Wilson 1995; Aucoin 2012; Diamond 2019b). The position was also defined as the right of ministers to appoint the executives they wanted and needed, and linked to the argument that ministerial accountability for departments required control of the key management tool (IPPR 2013). Overt displays under the Cameron government were the advocacy of ministers' roles in appointing permanent secretaries in the 2012 Civil Service Reform Plan, minister Maude's championing of secretaries of states' rights to appoint permanent secretaries, and minister Gove's implementation of this by determining who the secretaries were in two departments, having dispensed with the incumbents (HM Government 2012; Diamond 2019b). In Australia, Abbott made 'captain-calls' in appointing quasi-outsiders as heads of three central agencies, all of whom left prematurely before the next election, which implied that they would be unacceptable to a new government. Assorted other cases at different times provide further examples. These are of a different order to the informal processes that have long operated (and pre-date the discovery of agency theory: Kellner and Crowther-Hunt 1980) by which ministers have been consulted about candidates.

The alterations in status are illustrated by the Australian process of changing the standing of the department head that went through several stages. The first formal change (1984) was to tenure, redesignating the permanent head as the departmental secretary on a fixed term. In 1994, the fixed-term statutory appointment of secretaries was introduced. In a further stage (from 1996), performance review was introduced for secretaries along with a bonus system. This device might have been unexceptional in another context, except one government employed the review as a means of scrutiny and to reinforce vulnerability (Podger 2007). In the meantime, the stripping of the policy function had occurred, the role of heads of department as chief policy adviser became more tenuous, and their tenure subject to principals.[3]

There were important extensions to the use of agents beyond treating public servants as such; other types of agent were heavily used, all of whom were subject to complete political control because they were short- or medium-term contractees directly employed by ministers. The most notable was the political adviser in the minister's office, but there were also policy tsars reporting to ministers, and ministerial reviews. These agents can be regarded as either substitutes for or playing additional roles to another type of agent, public servants, where control was less complete.

APPOINTMENT SYSTEMS: POLITICAL AND PROFESSIONAL

By the 2010s, the traditional features mentioned earlier had long been changed by public management systems adjusted to accommodate more influential partisan actors. Advice was no longer derived mainly from the public service. The principle that the public service could readily serve a new government had long been challenged, and department heads could be readily displaced where they were no longer permanent. The apolitical service could still be detected but was impacted by political infractions over time and continual political pressures (Aucoin 2010; Boston and Halligan 2012). Two issues continued to be relevant – the institutional standing of the public service and how demands for responsiveness were accommodated – both of which arose in the appointment process for department heads.

Reconstituting the Relationship

In analysing the Anglophone systems, it is helpful to focus on two elements: the process and the source of the appointments. For the source, appointment systems can either rely on internal, public service appointments or draw on external candidates. The second element addresses the nature of the process of recruitment and the main players. To focus the analysis, two categories are used to examine the formal systems: political appointments where decisions are dominated and controlled by the political executive, and professional appointments where non-political actors influence decisions. In both cases the prime minister signs off on appointments. Where political leaders exclusively undertake the task, the expected result is the freedom to recruit executives from inside and outside the public service, including partisan appointments (for examples, see Rouban 2014). In contrast, where the permanent civil service is in control, they can be expected to appoint insiders. The concern here is with approaches that fall between the two, which evince features of each but are inclined to one rather than the other.

While all four systems have changed in the last 30 years, the question of how they have evolved needs to be explained. Several types of factor assist in accounting for different patterns, including politicisation trends internationally (Rouban 2012, 2014), contextual factors, and culturally embedded norms concerning the role of appointment mechanisms. Of interest is the extent to which appointment systems are shaped and constrained by institutional factors or by the drive to achieve results. The two logics of appropriateness and consequences are relevant here (March and Olsen 2006; Christensen et al. 2007). What factors influence whether appointments are made according to processes and rules that are understood and adhered to, or with regard to the consequences for the government in terms of delivering its policy? Similarly, to what extent are the processes legitimised by including explicit roles for public servants and transparency regarding choices as opposed to that derived from the authority of the political leadership? It is well established that various combinations of factors are often important (Christensen et al. 2007).

Australia and Canada provide mixtures of the two types of appointment process, the political and professional, but have tended to move towards more political elements. The UK has also recorded non-professional exceptions, but the political role (i.e. the prime minister's) is more formalised and professional dimensions continue to be influential.

Professional Appointment Systems in New Zealand and the United Kingdom

This category is defined by the process followed, which constrains the actors, but otherwise there have been important differences. New Zealand has had specific institutional arrangements that have made the politicisation of senior appointments difficult. In contrast to the other Anglophone countries where the responsibility for appointing (and dismissing) departmental heads lay with the prime minister, the New Zealand process has differed. Prior to the State Sector Act in 1988, the State Services Commission appointed permanent heads and ministers were usually consulted informally. While the appointment procedures worked reasonably well and provided protection to the public service from improper political interference, it was criticised for being cliquey. As a result, changes were made to the recruitment process under which the State Services Commissioner acquired the formal responsibility for making recommendations to the government on the appointment of chief executives on contracts for departments. Once an appointment was made, the Commissioner became the employer and was responsible for overseeing and reviewing each chief executive's performance (although ministers contributed to the performance management regime) (Boston and Halligan 2012). Ministers participated in the appointment process by advising the Commissioner on relevant matters (e.g. skills) to be considered and suggesting both suitable and unacceptable candidates. Ministers could reject the Commissioner's recommendation but were then required to either obtain another recommendation or make their own selection, providing the decision was published in the *New Zealand Gazette* so that it was clear that a 'political' appointment was being made and the ministerial intervention was transparent. Since 1988 there has been no such appointment by a government and only one recommendation had been rejected (Boston and Halligan 2012). NZ chief executives in the state services have individual employment contracts for terms of three to five years with the possibility of reappointment.

In the United Kingdom, the independent Civil Service Commission (CSC) has a long-standing legal responsibility for merit, fairness and openness; has oversight of the process; and is responsible for approving the appointment. The selection panel is chaired by the First Civil Service Commissioner and includes external members. The prime minister's approval of appointments was formalised in 1920, and ministerial consultation in the 1960s (Halligan 1997). There has been debate since Thatcher's time as to whether the senior civil service was being politicised because promotions to permanent secretary were influenced by being 'one of us' (Richards 1997; Fawcett and Gay 2010). Thatcher's influence over appointments has been documented, but her successor (Major) backed off such involvement (Campbell and Wilson 1995; Richards 1997).

The intricacies of the UK appointment procedures have been regularly modified over time including the last decade or so, with tinkering under the Cameron government (for earlier details, see Halligan 1997; Richards 1997, 2008). The CSC revised its guidelines in response to the government's Civil Service Reform Plan (HM Government 2012) to formalise, clarify and increase the role for the minister in providing feedback on candidates and to allow for objections to candidates. The Commission argued that according ministers a choice would be incompatible with the Constitutional Reform and Governance Act 2010 but acceded to allowing the prime minister that role. The guidelines also provided for the Secretary of State to be involved at all stages. The prime minister may ask the panel to reconsider and re-rank the candidates, but the approval of the full board of Civil Service Commissioners was required (CSC 2014, section 36; Maer and Ryan-White 2018). The matter was debated in the Committee of Public Accounts (CPA 2016b, Q78). When asked whether the prime minister's role was new, the cabinet secretary (Jeremy Heywood) responded that the prime minister chooses from several candidates judged by a panel of the Commission and Cabinet Office permanent secretaries 'to be above the appointable line' and that the process codified long-standing best practice. The UK has opened many civil service positions to external competition, including the permanent secretary level, but the process must reflect the CSC's principles. Few recent appointments have come from outside the civil service.

These two appointment systems are differentiated by the attention to a formal process that incorporates an independent element while providing opportunities for the political executive to contribute. There has also been provision for the resolution of differences and some degree of transparency. The

New Zealand arrangements have a more significant degree of independence, and provide an international benchmark, whereas the British formalities belie the role of informal influences and processes (Kellner and Crowther-Hunt 1980; Richards 1997; Diamond 2019b). There is a continuing role for the UK Civil Service Commission in auditing compliance and maintaining safeguards in the process (Maer and Ryan-White 2018). There is also some continuity across governments in the tenure of the top appointment.[4]

'Political' Appointment Systems in Australia and Canada

This categorisation can be qualified because there is something of a process in Canada and appointees are normally internal professionals; and partisan appointments are not the norm in Australia. Nevertheless, political elements are more apparent. Regime change in the mid-2010s in both countries meant the resumption of less politicised executive branches. However, in both countries there were enough precedents to argue that they were either disposed to or susceptible to political appointments (and terminations).

The Australian guidelines for the appointment process for departmental secretaries moved from official input, akin to comparable countries, to political domination. Prior to 1976 the chair of the Public Service Board advised the minister of possible candidates, consulting with the prime minister as appropriate before the nomination went to cabinet. Under the revised process, the Board chair recommended candidates to the prime minister based on advice from a committee of mainly departmental heads, but this committee stage was subsequently omitted. After the abolition of the Board in 1987, the Secretary to the Department of the Prime Minister and Cabinet, was the sole person to provide formal advice to the prime minister about the appointment of secretaries (Keating 2003). The other aspect of continuity was the association of turnover with loss of tenure. The changes to the head of department's tenure and standing were mentioned earlier. Increases in secretary turnover in the 1990s became significant because loss of position now meant termination of employment. Several departmental secretaries were replaced during Keating's prime ministership, and one other secretary was summarily sacked. The Rudd government (2007–10) promised to preserve traditional continuity and retained the existing departmental secretaries at least initially.

The first political appointments occurred under the Whitlam Labor government in the 1970s. The Keating Labor government dispensed with three departmental secretaries because ministers wanted their own 'doers' (two had past associations with the party) (Halligan 1997). More significant were turnovers associated with further changes of government because they institutionalised the practice and set precedents. The coalition government disposed of six secretaries in 1996 for reasons that remain unexplained. A new coalition government in 2013 dispensed with two secretaries because their department was associated with policies it opposed when in opposition. A further precedent was set with the announcement that the Secretary of the Treasury was displaced, and that the heads of the three central agencies were to be external appointments (albeit with past Australian Public Service (APS) experience). A procession of secretaries departed prematurely in 2016 and 2017, several because of differences with ministers. For a professional public servant, the most antithetical action was the sacking of department heads because it was 'highly corrosive of the culture of impartial service' (Varghese 2016). There was also the readiness of successive new governments to appoint a new chief adviser (the Secretary of the Department of Prime Minister and Cabinet).

In Canada, the prime minister has long appointed the numerous deputy ministers (not all of whom were heads of departments) as well as the second-tier associate deputy ministers, and they can be dismissed 'at pleasure'. Deputy ministers have traditionally regarded the prime minister, not the minister, as the person to whom they are accountable. Deputy ministers' appointments have come mostly from the public service (although there was an increase in external appointments in the 2000s) and there have been instances of partisan political appointments (initially under Mulroney). In contrast to other Anglophone systems, the public service and political spheres have been slightly less separate because of cases of deputy ministers moving to the lower house of parliament (Aucoin 2010). The prime minister's power of appointment of top public servants has been enhanced in the reform era with the increase in the number of positions: approximately six dozen serve at the 'prime minister's pleasure' (Aucoin et al. 2011; Aucoin 2012).

Recruitment in Canada has used an advisory process involving recommendations to the clerk of the Privy Council from the Committee of Senior Officials (composed of deputy ministers), which has reviewed and appraised candidates.[5] The clerk then makes 'suggestions' to the prime minister (Bourgault 2014, p. 367). It is unclear how much the process matters when a prime minister wants deputy ministers supportive of the government's agenda. The appointments and tenures of deputy ministers are at the prime minister's discretion for open-ended terms with no guarantee of their retaining the position. The prime minister can also 'demote or transfer senior officials, since the power to appoint includes the power to dismiss'. Consequently, deputy minister appointments are 'essentially political' and the 'professional' public service is depicted as falling 'between the "career system" and the "spoils system"' (Bourgault 2014, p. 366). Both countries have developed systems involving a high level of political control and a reliance on the prime minister's office. Canada has given more attention to a formal process in appointments, but the concentration of power in the prime minister overrides its significance.

Variations on a Theme: Politicising Central Agency Positions

There are now indications that the position of secretaries of central agencies are subject to new forms of politicisation. In contrast to the unitary systems, Australia and Canada have turnover of the heads of the public service with new governments, the precedent having been set by Trudeau's appointment of his favourite as clerk of the Privy Council in 1975 and 1980 (Campbell 1983; Savoie 2004). Moreover, the position of Public Service Commissioner in Australia has been subject to constant debate, most recently because the incumbent (until resigning in August 2018) was subject to allegations about inappropriate conduct. The head of the Department of the Prime Minister and Cabinet (DPMC), a professional public servant, was previously displaced as head of the Treasury by an incoming prime minister. The 2018 appointment to the Treasury attracted opposition allegations that his career (including his immediate previous position) had been dominated by working in the private offices of the Treasurer (although such experience was not uncommon). In other words, appointments that were once free of debate have become part of partisan conflict (Bagshaw 2018; Koziol 2018), and the rules of the game have again changed in Australia.

Managing Appointments

The managing of appointments has been a concomitant of the growth of the centre of government (Dahlström et al. 2011a) and of ministers' expanding perceptions of their roles. As the position of head shifted from being internal to a department to a system-wide arrangement, rotation became normal, and experience in a central agency essential for many positions. This is important for appointments in two respects.

First, the reappointment or transfer of department heads is another dimension of the appointment system and one that is often opaque in terms of process. The 'managed move' as it is known in the UK for the sideways shift to another permanent head position, accounts for a number of appointments without requiring a 'competition' (Paun et al. 2013; Haddon 2016). The UK's Senior Leadership Committee does consider options on a systematic basis. In Australia five new departmental secretaries were appointed 20 months after the 2007 election in a process that involved the movement of 11 senior executives as the government sought to place appropriate officials in significant positions. In contrast, recommendations by the NZ State Services Commissioner for the re-appointment of departmental chief executives have been rejected, although such cases have been relatively rare (Boston and Halligan 2012).

Secondly, the departure of secretaries is quite often a consequence of ministerial intervention. Australian cases have already been mentioned. The high turnover under Cameron in the UK is attributed to Secretaries of State forcing the issue of suitability, which also occurred under Blair. The high turnover of UK permanent secretaries in the two and a half years following the Cameron government's election (May 2010) was extensive with 18 of 20 departments experiencing one or more changes. These changes inevitably had an impact on the length of secretaries' tenure. The departmental average of two for this period was the same as that for the years 1997–2010 (Dash 2012). This latter figure compares to a drop in the departmental tenure of Canadian deputy ministers: 2.3 years in the ten years up to 2005, and 19.4 months in 2010 (Savoie 2008; Mitchell and Conway 2011).

Finally, the formal processes of recruitment do not cover the full story. Informal processes of consultation operate in all systems and can be highly influential in appointments (Podger 2007). Ministers' informal roles in the UK have been stronger than the specifications in the guidelines (Halligan 1997; IPPR 2013; Richards 1997).

POLITICISING EFFECTS ON BEHAVIOUR

What effects do these changes and pressures have? Three issues are addressed here: the consequences of job insecurity and turnover, the different types of political influence on appointments that have emerged, and the fate of stewardship.

Ministers and Secretaries' Careers

The clear message from dismissals, high turnover and contractualisation are illustrated as follows. The lower use of contractual appointments in Canada and the UK did not preclude dispensing with top public servants; nor was it a pre-requisite to attracting the full attention of heads of department. A common pattern was exemplified by UK civil servants depicted as, 'self-censoring in the face of political determination' (Taylor 2015).[6] More significantly, the accountability officer (usually the permanent head) lacked the confidence to challenge the minister where concerns existed about 'the feasibility or value for money of new policies or decisions'. Standing up to ministers was regarded as damaging to the careers of civil servants (NAO 2016a). Moreover, despite reports of more public roles for the senior public service (Grube 2014), overt policy leadership by public servants could also be career-limiting.

The incentives for Australian secretaries were shaped by strong political control and the contract system leading them to: 'hedge their bets on occasions, limit the number of issues on which to take a strong stand, be less strident, constrain public comments, limit or craft more carefully public documents and accept a muddying of their role and that of political advisers' (Podger

2007, p. 144). Departmental secretaries had long been devoted to supporting ministers, but political messages had become 'more explicit, and secretaries . . . more cautious in avoiding disputes with ministers and in ensuring any public image of themselves is aligned with the government's position (Podger 2007, p. 144). The ultimate 'test is when a less powerful secretary knows that telling a minister what he or she does not want to hear will certainly result in being sacked – or not having the appointment renewed' (Burgess 2017).

The limits of ministerial discretion remained unclear. Many ministers valued independent advice but were intolerant of challenges. A common pathology in NZ was the minister's preference for 'a weak and compliant department rather than one that questions and tests ministerial initiatives that it thinks are flawed: "this compliance can go as far as ministers telling officials . . . not to question and test proposed initiatives". Weak officials too frequently acquiesced' (Scott 2001, p. 95). Senior civil servants in the UK and elsewhere too often lacked the resources and institutional support to raise significant issues with ministers because of the need to maintain good working relationships. The default position was to defer to the minister. An alternative but potentially haphazard strategy was 'picking the battles' by determining which policies to challenge. There was extensive feedback about cases of incomplete candidness in the relationship (Hallsworth et al. 2011), and a reluctance 'to speak truth to power' because objections were regarded as obstructive and had career consequences (as instanced for the UK by King and Crewe 2014).

Politicisation and Public Service Behaviour

Politicisation covers covert and overt forms of pressure on public servants. It has been recognised that the line has moved, meaning that what was once regarded as acceptable behaviour has changed. Nevertheless, overt political and partisan appointments were the exception. From the minister's point of view, this may not matter if the public service is responsive and compliant.

Underneath the carapace of political management, the senior public servant has remained committed to professional values, especially impartiality, and provision of written advice to ministers, making clear where the line is drawn and understanding how to handle advice. Although department heads' roles have moved from guardian to policy adviser to manager (Bourgault and Dunn 2014a), and there has been more of a marketplace for policy advising, there has been a continuing role for policy advice. However, twenty-first-century ministers want their priorities to prevail, and they tend to be highly risk averse with a focus on the short term. The institutional guidelines for public servants can be ambiguous, inconsistent or insufficient to cover all options. The agent therefore must exercise discretion (Grube 2014), and may exhibit contra-

Table 4.1   Politicisation impacts on senior public servants

	Form of appointment	Functioning in office
1. Reactive	Professional	• Compliant because of incentives to be responsive.
2. Proactive	Professional	• Highly responsive, can do enthusiasts.
	Line crossers	• Overly promiscuous, nominally partisan?
	Political bureaucrat	• Professional seconded to political arena.
3. External	Political manager	• Attentive to patron needs and partisan requirements.

dictory tendencies, either underperforming (yielding to demands that raise professional issues) or overperforming (crossing the line).

Following Campbell (1988a), three categories of top public servant are distinguished: the reactive civil servant, the proactive civil servant, and the political appointment (adapted in Table 4.1). In the first case professionals come under pressure to respond in ways that exceed a conventional understanding of their professional role. The incentive system requires responsiveness and compliance that may reinforce political risk aversion, avoidance of policy leadership and even professional subservience. In the second case, the civil servant is more actively engaged in ministerial (and possibly political agendas), with issues arising where professional enthusiasm becomes more promiscuous, while the more direct involvement of bureaucrats in policy and political processes leads to the identification of 'political bureaucrats'. In the third case the minister appoints senior staff who are either partisans or lack insider professional standing and are expected to preference political priorities. The external, senior appointment may have past public service experience, and have been a serial political adviser, but will be unacceptable to an alternative government.

Mulgan (1998) traverses the complexities of specific Australian appointments (at a level of detail that is inappropriate here), which indicate the need for caution with simplistic judgements. He makes three telling points: the need to differentiate between different types of appointment (partisan, policy and managerial), the distinction between the appointment (not necessarily politicisation) and the process (that can be politicising); and a test of politicisation – would the appointee survive a change of government? The purpose of specific appointments may be to show to the outside world (e.g. the business sector) and internally the public service that there is a different government. A further test is whether an appointee is introduced to shake up the public service. Politicisation has been used in this book to register extensions to the political executive's control and influence. Therefore, the act of making unconventional appointments serves this purpose.

The demarcations in Table 4.1 are not necessarily explicit in practice, and individuals can alter their behaviours to fit different contexts (even the serial political adviser who alternates with being a senior executive in the public service). The ambiguities would seem to be greater in the Australian system where public servants are regularly seconded to ministers' offices. Australia is unique because of the number of public servants taking leave from the public service to join ministers' offices as so-called 'temporary partisans' (Maley 2019).

Once the primary role of senior public servants is lost and the political executive no longer accepts that the public servants' skills are sufficient – serious problems arise as to how to reconcile the two. The proactive category contains three types of hybrid. There were early 'hybrids' when public servants were used in PMOs and ministers' offices, a practice that still occurs (and has obvious benefits including their civilising presence and their learning about political processes). They were recruited for their expertise, but it was difficult for them not to operate politically to some extent (Campbell and Halligan 1992). Experience in a minister's office was regarded as expanding the experience and understandings of high-fliers who later became secretaries. The proactive professional ('one of us') took responsiveness to a new level but was also vulnerable to being displaced because of a change of government. The 'hybrid' public servant was said to have increased – one Australian advertisement for staff sought people who would be 'apolitical and "like-minded", impartial and "passionate"' (MacDermott 2008, p. 40).

The inclusion of politicos in senior public service positions (but not as a departmental head) has represented a distinctive type of political bureaucrat. In Australia, John Howard appointed a partisan to be head of the cabinet secretariat within the DPMC. An intriguing variation was Justin Trudeau's Canadian government parachuting the person who produced the party's manifesto into a senior position in the PCO. Yet Tony Blair's semi-fusion of the Cabinet Office and the PMO had earlier provided UK precedents (Jones 2016). It was observed that Canadian public servants had skills that were 'much more akin to the political world than those found in Weber's bureaucratic model' (Savoie 2011, p. 158). A further type was willing to behave unprofessionally out of misplaced loyalty to a minister (Mulgan 2008).

There has been much debate in the past about whether senior public servants were willing to provide professional challenges in the face of a determined minister ('speaking truth to power'), but this has now been restated to fit contexts. The professional advice of the department should be provided (where possible in writing: Craft and Halligan 2020), but apart from declarations on legal, ethical or value for money grounds secretaries are inclined to step aside (see also Chapter 3, and the cases of ministerial directions traversed by the UK's National Audit Office and the Public Accounts Committee below).

The self-limiting behaviour of departmental heads can mean being reduced to advice on procedures or implementing policy (the new Australian prescription) with stark implications for the nature of professionalism. Departments of course continue to generate advice but the instances of either being ignored or by-passed are legion (routinely under Harper in Canada: see Zussman 2016; also, cases under Howard and Morrison in Australia).[7]

Shifting Boundaries in a Promiscuous Partisanship

This concept has two meanings. The first is a characterisation of the way things have worked within government with an emphasis on the impartial professional. The expectation of the civil service, 'is not to be neutral, but partisan for whatever government the electorate has returned . . . The professional skill . . . lies in being able to perform these functions for any duly constituted government; . . . in being sufficiently promiscuous to accommodate to changes in the party in power . . . The implicit deal at the heart of British government is that in return for such political promiscuity, the senior civil service will enjoy a monopoly on advising ministers' (Wilson 1991, p. 328). However, one side of the arrangement has been withdrawn, and there has been greater political influence on appointments and ministerial roles in policy and appointments are less influenced by members of the civil service. As a result, there have been continuing pressures and issues with boundaries, and maintaining and avoiding semblances of partiality.

The second formulation, a central tenet of Aucoin's (2012) 'new political governance', uses the term with a normative connotation that focuses on crossing the line. Officials act as enthusiastic supporters of government policy. This behaviour is not consistent with what might be expected from agents. Public servants are expected to be promiscuously or serially partisan; that is, to be the agents of the government of the day in relation to stakeholders, organized interests, citizens, media, and parliamentarians as they engage in consultations, service delivery, media communications, reporting to parliament, and appearing before parliamentary committees (Aucoin 2012). There are numerous cases of breaches of impartiality (Aucoin 2012; Diamond 2019b).

These notions have been subsequently picked up by others (Grube 2014; Grube and Howard 2016b; Diamond 2019a, 2019b). Aucoin's identification of the 'promiscuous partnership' owed much to the conditions of the Canadian public service under Harper, and to political excesses elsewhere. The unease with how that was handled was significant where the Harper appointments of deputy ministers favoured public servants regarded as sympathetic to the government's agenda (Aucoin et al. 2011, p. 40). There is said to be a fine line between professional commitment and promiscuous partisanship: 'many would argue that the line has been crossed more frequently than in the past'

(Aucoin et al. 2011, p. 44). A series of cases, usually of an exceptional character are now available (Aucoin et al. 2011; Aucoin 2012; Heintzman 2013, 2016; Grube and Howard 2016b; Diamond 2019a). The multiple roles of the most senior Canadian public servant, the clerk of the Privy Council Office was a factor in the incumbent crossing the line between being partisan and non-partisan, which eventually lead to his resignation (Savoie 2019a, 2019b). The judgement that Canadian public servants had become more politicised has applied more generally, but they had not become more partisan (Savoie 2011). In the case of Australia, there have been more exceptions to this rule.

Countervailing through Stewardship?

Most of the running in this area has been unidirectional, but one countervailing concept has surfaced to varying degrees across the four countries. The Anglophone countries have approached stewardship in different ways. Australia addresses capability and buttressing departmental secretaries' whole-of-government role. The one-time most contractualised of the four systems (Boston 1995a), New Zealand, has swung to stewardship with support from the professional centre (and the government). Despite actively reviewing deputy ministers and fostering the 'deputy minister community', Canada has espoused a narrow management conception. The United Kingdom also has a formulation of financial stewardship through the accountability officer with formalised responsibilities and reporting to parliament (HM Treasury 2013, 2015).

The New Zealand position has more centrality because of support from the key central agencies and the political executive. The promotion of a stewardship culture was incorporated in legislation (State Sector Amendment Act 2013). There was an endorsed agenda that embraced stewardship and recognition that stewardship must be brought to the fore. It was designed to ameliorate acute problems arising from a fragmented structure and the emphasis on outputs that undermined collaboration and whole of system attention. The State Services Commission (SSC) has priority interventions to lift system stewardship: setting expectations, aligning executive management to system performance, leadership and capability development and deployment, and an integrity roadmap (SSC 2014, 2016). Accountability was one issue identified as requiring reframing. The traditional distinction between accountability and responsibility was regarded as still important because they involve distinctive managerial tasks, both of which are required (Schick 1996, pp. 84–5). Reform of the NZ system needed to achieve a balance between them: 'chief executives are accountable for the stewardship of the people, assets and resources entrusted to their agency's care, but they also have a responsibility for stewardship of the whole public services system' (Morrison 2014, p. 45).

The Australian relationship between secretaries and ministers has at times been fraught with issues about boundaries. Under Westminster tenets there was a tendency for successive governments to claim ownership of the public service. This had significant implications for transitions between governments when tensions arose with a public service perceived by the new political leadership to have been too close to its predecessors. Politicians' lack of strategic focus and 'short-termism' during the fourth term of the Howard government indicated that an alternative to a heavy reliance on political direction was needed. A significant clarification of the secretary's role was provided by the introduction of the stewardship function, which had previously been recognised (e.g. ANAO 2003; Egan 2009), but not accorded official significance. Leaders had, 'a stewardship role . . . beyond the immediate term and beyond their own organisational unit to build the long-term capability of the APS as an institution' (APSC 2012b, p. 18). The stewardship role was designed for the public service to have 'the capacity to serve successive governments. A stewardship capability must exist regardless of the style of any one Minister or government'. Stewardship covered 'financial sustainability' and efficient resource management, and 'less tangible factors such as maintaining the trust placed in the APS and building a culture of innovation and integrity in policy advice' (AGRAGA 2010, p. 5). The roles were given a statutory basis in 2013 that distinguished three roles of secretaries including two dimensions of stewardship, one within their department, the other public service-wide in partnership with the secretaries board (Public Service Amendment Act 2013). The secretaries' board has responsibility for the stewardship of the public service. Evidence of how these roles are enacted is difficult to come by and interviews with departmental secretaries point to continuing difficulties with a long-term focus.

The 'public interest' aspect had become stunted because of the day-to-day emphasis on departmental operations, but now potentially received a new expression through stewardship. There was the prospect that the stewardship role might allow the leaders of the public service collectively and individually to engage more explicitly in matters deemed to be in the public interest (Halligan 2013a). This, however, depended on ministers and governments allowing diversions from their priorities.

In the United Kingdom, the question of stewardship has centred on the role of the accountability officer,[8] usually the permanent secretary of departments, but questions have been raised about whether the role has been thwarted by their genuflecting to ministers. There is provision for the ministerial direction, which is a formal instruction from a minister to an accounting officer (AO) to proceed with the implementation of a policy, where the AO has expressed concerns that the spending involved does not meet the tests of regularity, propriety, value for money and/or visibility. Once a direction is issued the minister becomes responsible for spending. Directions have allowed permanent secretaries to discharge the responsibilities for stewardship of public funds, while not undermining the duty to carry out the instructions of ministers. Treasury guidance requires the publication of ministerial directions before the next annual report (NAO 2016a, 1.17). However, there have been 'major reforms or projects which raised serious value for money or feasibility concerns, but where no directions were requested'. In several cases warnings were issued by oversight bodies (NAO 2016a, p. 25).

The Treasury did not record 'near misses', where 'AOs raised concerns but stopped short of seeking a direction'. Margaret Hodge, chair of the Committee of Public Accounts (CPA), which has responsibility for holding 'the government to account for stewardship of all public funds and assets' (CPA 2011, p. 4), observed that these 'cases indicated that the ministerial direction mechanism was not working effectively. She cited the case of the decision to enter a contract for aircraft carrier procurement when the committee had expressed concerns over the affordability of the defence budget: "Someone should have stopped it at that point, but the permanent secretary did not request a letter of direction. We went ahead and, because that money was not there, we delayed the building of those aircraft carriers and property including £2 billion of extra cost"' (quoted in NAO 2016a, p. 25; see also CPA 2016a, 2016b). The NAO argued that the 'crucial relationship between ministers and civil servants was under strain from a combination of factors, which affects the balance of incentives on AOs'. The CPA had earlier noted that ministers' greater interest in policy delivery had led to blurring in the 'demarcation between ministerial responsibility for policy and Accounting Officer responsibility for implementation' (CPA 2011, p. 4).

Canada's Privy Council Office refers to its values as including stewardship: 'Federal public servants are entrusted to use and care for public resources responsibly, for both the short term and long term',[9] without articulating or developing a stronger position. The mishandled transfer of the 'accountability officer' concept from the UK (Heintzman 2013) precluded stewardship being pursued through that route. It was therefore left to the Treasury Board Secretariat to run with a management conception of stewardship, but not for its core areas, only for information management, information technology, asset management and service stewardship (TBS 2017b), and to refer in general terms to the stewardship of financial management systems.

Stewardship, then, has been part of the discourse in some contexts but has not been institutionalised even where enshrined in legislation. The agent and stakeholder conceptions may have an uneasy co-existence in some form creating potentially unresolved consequences for public policy and management.

VARIATIONS BETWEEN SYSTEMS

Matters raised from this and the previous chapter indicate variation in the use of levers. Political advisers and the PMO were suffused within the systems. Otherwise there was a degree of specialisation in terms of what instruments were favoured. There was also a waxing and waning in the use of levers depending on the governing style of prime ministers and how different levers were perceived. The reliance on the prime minister's office was apparent everywhere, but its centrality and influence has been strongest in Canada and Australia, which specialised in using the PMO and the partisan staff of ministers' offices. The UK utilised a range of instruments to some extent, including ministers' roles in implementation and management. The least politicised country, New Zealand, had a lower reliance on these instruments, but made effective use of ministers for cross-departmental priorities. More generally, political actors were involved in implementation.

In all four countries there was a shift from using public servants, to a mixture of public servants and partisans, to the dominance of political appointments. Three distinctive pathways have operated: the centralised political management model that emphasises top-down political control using the prime minister's office as the enforcer; the political implementation model that entails the direct engagement of ministers at the centre and portfolio levels in a wider range of policy roles focused on direct monitoring; and finally the across-the-board or corporate model that involves using a range of levers to some extent (see Chapter 3).

Explanations

Several types of explanation emerge from the analysis. The changing international environment in which senior executives operate, and the long-term international trend towards politicisation, have been raised in the previous chapter. The four countries experienced an increase in the size and significance of the minister's office, essentially staff appointed by the minister. The former reliance on the senior public service to replenish its own ranks has faded. As the independence of the institution was eroded the significance of its trustee role declined, but to different extents across the four countries. The instrumentalist conception of the minister's role came to the fore thereby relegating the senior public servant to the role of agent.

Another explanation is 'change continuity', which arises when politicisation becomes 'endemic in a Westminster-type public management system because one or more political regimes *permit* their application rather than *actively pursue* them'.[10] In examining the extent to which NPG was apparent in the

New South Wales public service, Di Francesco (2012b) reports that a range of indicators revealed 'institutional and practice changes in recruitment and termination conditions for chief executives (and senior executives, because such politicization "cascades")'.

The variations between the four systems centre on two factors and the interplay between them: institutional factors that constrain change, and political factors that shape specific contexts and give impetus to ministerial agendas. Institutional constraints are greater in the contexts of New Zealand and the United Kingdom where values are sufficiently embedded and non-political actors entrenched, possibly with veto powers (e.g. the Commissioner for Public Appointments). These are also the countries that have not made extensive use of political staff.

The balance obtained in New Zealand between professional, political and managerial principles is unmatched elsewhere, although not without its limitations. While regarded as providing a benchmark in several significant respects, it is not pristine. Despite arguments that NZ stands outside the politicised pack (Boston and Halligan 2012), it still exhibits basic politicising elements; ministers assert their priorities, and advisers intervene in departmental processes and seek to control (and manipulate) Official Information Act processes.[11] The provision of free and frank advice has variously been depicted as absent in the 2010s (Palmer 2017) or declining (53% of mainly public sector respondents surveyed agreed that such advice was less likely in 2017) (Eichbaum 2017).

The UK has experienced volatility in the relationship between the civil service and the political executive commencing with Thatcher's disruption to institutional continuity and personalisation of appointments. The Blair government used several instruments to control and influence the civil service but did not seek to rely on partisan appointments to the top positions (Richards 2008). Under the Cameron government the civil service was subject to intense pressures, and challenges to the appointment and performance review processes of permanent secretaries (HM Government 2012, 2014). In the face of opposition, the government modified its more radical proposal for ministers to make their own appointments of permanent secretaries. As well, the Civil Service Commission rejected the proposal for the PM to have a choice because the House of Commons Select Committee on Public Administration was conducting an inquiry and it should 'proceed on the basis of political consensus' (CSC 2014).

Several political factors have driven modifications to appointment processes. In terms of managing the senior public service as an instrument of government policy, Australia's and Canada's appointment arrangements have distinctive features. Appointments (and terminations) are less trammelled by process or public disclosure allowing political executives greater latitude and encouraging departures from conventions. For example, some political executives have not cared about the arbitrariness or consequences of their actions: 'the Howard and Abbott nights of the long knives were simple acts of political bastardry' (Burgess 2017). It is also apparent that systems where appointments have been most readily subject to prime ministerial determinations were those that cultivated large ministerial staffs of political operators and maintained strong PMOs that have been pivotal within the executive branch for both ministers and the senior public service. In other words, the political elements are more systematically embedded in the Australian and Canadian systems.

Australia has been prepared almost willy-nilly at times to selectively make unconventional appointments (and terminations) for over 40 years. These include terminations of professional public servants, and appointments from outside the fold. Ignoring occasional appointments of secretaries from state governments, there have been appointments from the business sector, and several others with backgrounds deemed to be political (Mulgan 1998). These occurred without the processes evident elsewhere.

Canada has emphasised political executive domination of the public service, the prime minister aided by powers of appointment and a US-influenced machine for supporting the leader. The explicit influence of the United States (Gow 1994) explains the early inclination to expand ministerial staff, and the development and operation of the PMO. The power of appointment of the prime minister dates from the nineteenth century, but what is important is how he or she chooses to use the position. Prime Minister Chretien, for example, argued that appointments were needed as a form of political control and to demonstrate that the government was in charge (Aucoin 2012).

The new political governance (Aucoin 2012) is relevant here as is the argument that Canada displayed distinctive features that have continued to evolve and be extended by successive governments. Some elements of high intensity politicisation have been pronounced, including the strong centralising prime minister's office (the largest of the four systems), and the largest cadre of ministerial advisers of the four countries (Savoie 1999; Zussman 2008, 2016; Aucoin 2010). Moreover, there were issues about the degree of subjugation and demeaning of the stature of the public service (Heintzman 2013; Zussman 2013; Campbell 2014) with an implication that behaviour went beyond boundaries regarded elsewhere as acceptable for a Westminster system.

While UK prime ministers have varied between passive (Harold Wilson), and active roles (e.g. Thatcher) in the appointment process (Richards 1997), the tendency there and in other systems is for activism to become a normal operating procedure. The nature of Thatcher's interventions had two elements: appointing candidates who had the appropriate 'can do' style, who could relate more effectively to the emerging managerialist environment (in this respect, Britain was no different from Australia at that time: see Halligan and Power 1992); and opting for 'one of us', which could either mean demonstrating a willingness to implement government policy (already an assumed responsibility of a permanent secretary in a Westminster system) and/or a belief in elements of that policy.

In this environment, two traditional precepts have, however, prevailed in the four systems: each maintains the concept of an apolitical public service and relies on internal recruitment of heads of department. They have remained committed to appointing experienced professionals from the civil or public service, with occasional exceptions. This consistency can be interpreted as reflecting the relative strength of the Anglophone administrative tradition (Halligan 2010b), which has continued to provide an evolving and pluralist vehicle that can accommodate the complexities of country systems. It has been fairly resilient in general respects and adaptive in specifics. The administrative tradition is modified in content, but is durable in terms of some fundamental elements that are explicit in debates about political incursions into the realm of the public service.

Dynamics and Dialectics of Politicisation

Politicisation has not evolved unabated, and the dynamics of change have been subject to fluctuations in intensity, which owe something to the shared understandings of the Anglophone administrative tradition and its role as a constraint on deviations affecting core values. It is apparent elsewhere that phases of 'politicisation' and 'neutralisation' may alternate (Rouban 2004, p. 82), and that political tensions are heightened around elections that produce changes of governments (Aucoin 2010). It is important therefore to be able to demonstrate whether a secular trend has existed over the long term and whether movement is unidirectional or involves shifts between different levels of intensity.

The politicisation process takes something of a dialectical form: a radical departure is followed by public debate eventually producing modified principles and/or behaviour. Several cases have exemplified this process: the appointment of externals and partisans to department head positions (Australia and Canada), the peremptory dismissal of professional public servants (Australia), public questioning and discourse about loss of traditional values (e.g. New Zealand: see James 2002), the enthusiasm for critique and reform of the UK civil service (especially the revision of the process for appointing permanent secretaries: detailed in Maer and Ryan-White 2018), and adjustments that occurred following public critique by the NAO: in the first half of 2018, five permanent secretaries received ministerial directions (Johnstone 2018b).

Similarly, the succession of reports on the condition of 'frank and fearless' public servants in New Zealand (Eichbaum 2017; Kibblewhite and Boshier 2018) may be reflected in a new State Service Act (Hughes 2019). Is this an irrevocable trend or a position that will fluctuate with regimes? This cycle also applied to dramatic changes in the use of political advisers (e.g. practice under Mulroney and Blair) and the subsequent reversal of these initiatives under ensuing prime ministers (Diamond 2019a). The weakened role of the administrative tradition in constraining deviant behaviour is addressed in Chapter 9.

A change of government is commonly the cause of departures and also of short-term resolutions to politicising behaviour. It needs to be noted that the outcomes of a dialectical process may modify departures from practice but do not prevent incremental change so that cumulatively over time the position is markedly different.

CONCLUSION

The recruitment of department heads in the public service changed in all four Anglophone countries as ministers became more policy active and determined to be in the cockpit directing their portfolio. The departmental head had to complement and adapt to this greater assertiveness and to the rise of the ministerial office and the political adviser at the interface between them. Overriding the relational basis was the government's perceived need to mobilise the public service to achieve its objectives. There have been significant differences between the four countries in terms of how they have responded, which depended both on the pressures for change and the ease with which it could be accomplished, and the strength of the institutional brakes on the pace and degree of change.

The four countries remained attentive to an administrative tradition that has dictated that at a minimum department heads should usually come from the public service and be impartial professionals. The enactment of this latter principle came under challenge with political pressure raising issues about professionalism in the age of responsiveness to ministerial preferences. Similarly, while prime ministers in all systems had a significant role, the level of intervention was less contained in specific cases. Where the political executive favours a strong instrumental position the attitude to the public service has had several components. First, the political executive cannot automatically be expected to rely on all senior public servants to transfer professional behaviour from one government to another. There is a strong expectation that the public service will work in terms of ministers' agendas, and heads are deployed accordingly. There may also be rejection of those who have supported the agendas of another government, and doubts about whether public servants have the expertise to handle certain fields, the solution being to import executives with private sector experience.

Elements of the traditional Anglophone model of the relationship between ministers and department heads can still be discerned despite the role reversals and the reduction of the public service position. However, the element common to all four systems – the retention of the impartial public service – has continued to be under pressure, both in the appointment process and through the institutionalised political advisory system. Having moved from the traditional model of an independent public service, the Anglophone systems like Australia and Canada now share features with non-Anglophone systems (cf. Rouban 2014).

A continuing point of contention is the co-existence of the agent and stakeholder conceptions and the tension between the two has had significant implications for public policy and management. The swing towards the agent appears to be in a holding pattern in some systems. The climate is not conducive to the re-emergence of the trustee even though there is the odd expression of it (e.g. the popularity of the parliamentary budget office) and stewardship approaches have a foothold but hardly a firm base for revolutionising public policy and governance. There is therefore movement in the cycle, but otherwise tensions between the different positions continue. The broader implications of the new normality in relationships between ministers and senior public servants are explored in Chapter 9.

NOTES

1. The countries use different terms for department heads: see the Glossary.
2. Stewardship is also used in the sense of system steering (e.g. Hallsworth 2011 in relation to the UK's devolved arrangements involving local government); strategy, monitoring and human capital (Barber 2015); and the government role of 'stewardship of the collective interest' that entails 'monitoring, anticipating and course correcting' (Bourgon 2009).
3. Augmentation of the position occurred 15 years later when their salary packages were greatly increased, and roles were given a statutory basis (Halligan 2013a).
4. Gus O'Donnell was cabinet secretary and head of the civil service for three prime ministers; Jeremy Heywood has been cabinet secretary for two. Recent chief executives of the New Zealand Department of Prime Minister and Cabinet have served two prime ministers.
5. PMO advisers also provide advice for selected positions (Aucoin et al. 2011).
6. The observation continues: 'As the minister . . . described the policy . . . you could see the officials wrestling with the need to provide a reality check – but all too often deciding it was better to nod sagely than look career-threateningly unhelpful.'
7. For example, 618 applications for community sports infrastructure recommended by Sports Australia were rejected by the then minister: see Karp 2019).
8. System stewardship of the policy process has been advocated for civil servants (Hallsworth 2011).
9. http://www.pco-bcp.gc.ca/index.asp?lang=eng&page=about-apropos&doc=mission-eng.htm.
10. Personal communication from Michael Di Francesco, 27 June 2019.
11. A few ministerial staff sought to affect the scope of requests or to alter the proposed decision of an agency (Wakem 2015).

5. Management dilemmas

A central argument about managerialism was that it empowered agencies and managers. New management processes were the key to invigorating an ossified bureaucratic system, and an inclination for management improvement maintained the momentum. This chapter addresses what happened to several principles of managerialism in reformed systems, with the advantage of hindsight and experience provided by a twenty-first century lens.

Five dimensions are addressed across three chapters. The application of management controls; devolution of functions and authority; and supporting capability and management processes and the drumbeat of reform and change are covered in this chapter. Relevant management themes are further developed in discussing performance management in Chapter 6. The effects of rules and regulations, an interrelated dimension, are featured in Chapter 7. The five dimensions can be linked to periods of reform according to when issues became prominent. The first surfaced as neo-Taylorism early in the reform era when old controls were not relinquished, and new central controls were instigated, and subsequently with contract management, and then performance targets for results from the late 1990s. Devolution of functions and authority date from the 1980s and issues have mounted over time. The need to enable management processes and support for capabilities was present for most of the reform era, becoming most salient in the twenty-first century. The fourth was the built-in commitment to management improvement, change and reform that was enabled by greater flexibility. Finally, factors shaping these management choices are addressed to provide explanations for the results of reform, focusing on institutional and contextual factors, and to what extent they entail managerialisation and politicisation.

Management dilemmas arise at the interface between hierarchical levels and relationships: central and line departments, departmental and portfolio agencies and political executives and bureaucracies. The dilemmas examined here entail central questions for public management and governance regarding control and discretion, and central authority and managerial flexibility. The scope for enabling management flexibilities and greater autonomy in an Anglophone system depended on several institutional factors, such as the roles of ministers and responsible central agencies.

A signal that public management was ailing was the poor performance reviews that commenced before the global financial crisis of 2008.[1] It was officially recognised that reform-era gains could be dissipated either by unintended dysfunctions or by insufficient internal adaptation and support for maturing management and externally by environmental change. The role of 'reverse effects' has been recognised for interventions that lead to the opposite result from that intended, which have been common in public management (Hood 1998; Gregory 2001). The several potential constraints on a management approach reflect different but often interrelated processes: contradictory requirements of managerialism (Pollitt 1993), political impera- tives requiring responsiveness, externalisation of activity, institutional factors including bureaucratisation, incentive structures, procedural demands, and environmental pressures, such as those producing an austerity agenda (Pollitt and Bouckaert 2017).

MANAGEMENT CONTROL AS COMPLIANCE AND PROCESS: INTERNAL CONTRADICTIONS OF PERFORMANCE

Questions about management control emerged early in the reform era as part of managing for results, appearing starkly in New Zealand which was first to advance the injunction about not simply letting the managers manage but making them manage. The early generations of reform exposed issues and unintended effects (Gregory 2001), and the position of NPM, based mainly on the 1990s and earlier, was represented as middle aged and suggesting a para- doxical future (Hood and Peters 2004). Three issues can be identified: the role of management control, compliance as a routine, and the necessity for process. The difficulties were self-inflicted and can be attributed to interrelated internal factors: design issues and the conflict between letting and making managers manage, the propensity of central agencies to impose controls of a particular type, and the accretion of requirements (which may have been partly influ- enced by external factors).

A central imperative of management is control, but what form of control and for what purposes? In the New Zealand case, it was about 'extracting the value of the concept of controllable outputs for tightening management process' (Scott 2001, p. 176). Using control and contracts through purchase and performance agreements and other documents, compliance reporting to exact performance, and relying on tight specification of requirements had consequences, producing examples of goal displacement. A regime focused on outputs was devoted to a plethora of processes, unnecessary compliance reporting, and rules and compliance procedures. The over-emphasis on speci- fications and the increasing elaboration of requirements meant compliance was rewarded instead of 'responsibility and responsiveness'. As well there were doubts as to whether organisational performance was necessarily improved by control routines that promoted low-level compliance rather than efficiency or effectiveness (SSC 1999; Norman 2003). The demands on management engaged in formal transactions were even argued to compare to, or exceed, those for the traditional bureaucracy (Gregory 2001). The Treasury both pulled back and pushed harder on specifications, but a decade later departments were pushing against excessive specifications. The claim was made that managers may have had greater discretion before the shift from controls over inputs to outputs (Hitchiner and Gill 2011).

There were extensive reporting requirements in public management. Even where principles or value-based management were being applied there were still formal expectations. Departments demonstrated high levels of compliance, and conformance in performance management systems and practices to the formal system. Central agencies used departments' performance information mainly for checking compliance and conformance (Ryan 2011b).

Process controls were expected to be replaced under public management that emphasised results. Departmental devolution of corporate services and other responsibilities were at different stages (Aucoin 1990; Hoggett 1997). The New Zealand case revealed the complications that arose when making the managers manage dominated the concomitant objective of letting managers manage, with negative consequences (Gregory 2001). Across the public service much time and substantial resources were devoted to monitoring processes and outputs, usually for reporting and accountability rather than outcomes. This occurred because 'the system' required it (Ryan 2011b, p. 450; see also Brady 2009). The traditional Australian public service focused on procedures rather than outcomes, and experienced early difficulties in shifting across the board. Despite the formal shift from process to programmes, about 40 per cent of senior officials thought the process emphasis was excessive. There continued to be discrepancies in letting and/or making managers manage and promoting a results focus, and then being prescriptive about inputs and models (TFMI 1993, pp. 94, 469, 471). Fast forward twenty-five years and there were still reports that 'the culture and habits of process, caution and direct control run deep' (de Brouwer 2017, p. 8). The performance movement produced a reliance on top-down performance indicators and targets, which as in the case of the UK could produce a highly intrusive centralised performance measurement system (Pollitt 2012).

MODES OF DECENTRALISATION

Departments and managers acquired new responsibilities and freedoms for managing resources (with variations in timing between countries). Early managerialism was 'riven with contradictions' on decentralisation (Pollitt 1993, p. 118). Four forms of decentralisation principles and practice are examined for the level of discretion that was enabled: devolution to departments, deregulation to allow line departments authority over resources and managers freedom to manage, delegation within departments, and disaggregation of departments using different agency forms (really a variation on standard non-departmental organisation). Early debates and tensions between central agencies and departments are not reprised here (but see Zifcak 1994 for Australia and the United Kingdom), although they are symptomatic of later difficulties. Of interest are the reliance on 'first order' controls (micro-managing and rules and regulations) (Perrow 1977), the potential contradictions inherent in centralisation and centralisation, and the recurrence of issues.

'Devolution' to Departments

The term 'devolution' was favoured in Australia and New Zealand to underscore the contrast with traditional practice and the emphasis on management freedom over resources. It referred to transferring functions and decision-making authority within the public management system, either from the centre to departments or within departments (TFMI 1993). A range of financial and human resource transactions and other delegations were given to departments. Typically, this allowed departments scope for moving resources around within their allocation. Managers acquired greater responsibilities and greater accountability (TFMI 1993; Scott 2001). The piecemeal delegation of responsibilities was replaced by management initiatives, but every so often there were major flourishes supported by reform principles: the most significant involved assigning transactions to line departments and emphasising principles and values at the centre.

Devolution presented several types of issue when contextual and contingent factors came into play. First, there was a familiar short-changing (which applied also to agencies (discussed later in this chapter)); levels of delegation varied and could be withdrawn; and re-regulation had the effect of countermanding potential delegations.

OECD surveys indicated that in a formal sense Australia and New Zealand ranked high on human resource delegation; the United Kingdom was also high and Canada low (Table 6.5 in OECD 2005). More generally, the UK was also somewhat more complex because of expansions and contractions of delegations in the reform era (Haddon 2016). Canada conveyed ambivalence towards delegations with a disjunction between rhetoric and practice (Juillet and Rasmussen 2008), and the retention of central controls and monitoring.

The demise of New Zealand's central personnel function represented 'a bureaucratic "roll-back"'. Agency heads acquired greater authority over 'hiring and firing' of staff and were no longer subject to a 'cumbersome system of centralised classification, grading and appeals', but there was little evidence that agencies otherwise had more autonomy (Gregory 2001, p. 239). The problems experienced with the accretion of requirements and associated issues were sufficient to justify being singled out by the State Services Commission (SSC 1999; Norman 2003). Political controversy was generated by certain types of issue, including inputs for 'property management, redundancy payments, information technology developments, bonus payments and the use of consultants', which led central agencies to increasingly require greater detail (Norman 2003, p. 209). A turning point in New Zealand was the 1995 Cave Creek crisis (Gregory 2002); management freedom to explore different management options internally and externally was supplanted by greater risk aversion (Norman 2003). Similarly, the Canadian 'trend to increased flexibility was abruptly reversed as the result of several major mismanagement scandals . . . there has been an increase in requirements for public disclosure of expenditures for hospitality and international travel for senior executives and contracts. And the Office of the Comptroller General has been re-established to strengthen financial management and internal audit' (OECD 2005, p. 98).

Perceptions of the success of Australian devolution varied widely – many staff still believed it had a long way to go (TFMI 1993, p. 111). There was also a disjunction within the Australian centre as to how they dealt with department managers leading to issues about discretion and the commitment to letting managers manage. The 'forked-tongue' problem arose because on the one hand the leadership of Finance pursued the macro agenda of FMIP (discussed later on), while resource control seemed to continue as before with its supply division still focusing on inputs and 'burrowing' (Campbell and Halligan 1992, ch. 5).

The Australian 'principles-based approach' was applied from the late 1990s as part of its devolution to line departments of transaction management, with particular reference to human resource management where Australia was listed as one of the most devolved systems in the OECD (OECD 2017b, 2017c). It meant that responsibility for regulating a substantial amount of activity dropped to department level, but without accompanying guidelines. A significant process was the filling of the large gaps created when the centre vacated a space. By moving to principles and values as a basis for central frameworks, a vacuum was created that was filled by departments making their own rules. This process also occurred in Canada's less devolved system, where responsibilities delegated from the Public Service Commission and the Treasury Board Secretariat were not used effectively (as discussed in Chapter 7). These experiences echoed the UK paradox that greater managerial discretion in the UK was accompanied by increases in the process rules of regulators (Hood et al. 1999).

Delegation and Centralisation within Departments

Devolution was a significant plank of early reform. The initial experiences were mixed, with lack of delegated authority a key issue; devolution was the most neglected reform agenda (Halligan and Power 1992). Central agencies expressed concerns that the transfer of responsibilities to departments did not extend within them to programme and operational levels (TFMI 1993, p. 489).

Countervailing pressures to centralise intensified as external demands and scrutiny and results-fixated governments lifted levels of risk aversion, producing greater centralisation and hierarchy within departments (see Chapter 7). The 'vertical solitude' was well-established in both Australian and Canadian public services early in the reform era (Jabes et al. 1992), differentiating the most senior from feeder groups and others in departments. A cognitive divide existed between NZ's senior management and front-line managers in their thinking about performance. Fewer than 50 per cent of New Zealand public servants experienced much discretion for organising and prioritising work. Only 17 per cent had substantial freedom with budget and staff allocations (Laking 2011, pp. 425–6).

Canadian human resource advisers tended 'to avoid performing higher risk staffing actions and using alternative sourcing methods, except in cases where there was support from senior management'. The Public Service Employment Act stipulated that staffing authority was to be delegated to the lowest appropriate level. However, many departments introduced further internal controls, including committees of associate deputy ministers for certain types of appointment (TBS 2016a). A priority area of the 2010s reform agenda was empowerment of staff because there were 'few occasions to work directly with senior leaders, apart from annual meeting and greeting events'. Employees' work was 'often filtered through many layers of approval' (Government of Canada 2014, p. 14).

The nature of decision-making at very senior levels in the Australia public service meant limited responsibility was delegated to middle management (or lower levels). Thirteen of the 18 capability reviews (undertaken between 2012 and 2014), reported 'centralised decision-making at senior (often very senior) levels' (Belcher 2015a). The most common reason for raising clearance levels was that the impact of media and parliamentary scrutiny increased the caution and risk aversion of politicians and consequently senior public servants. Work shifted from the middle level to the senior executive service, which became more concerned with administrative detail. Middle-level staff were unwilling to take responsibility for minor matters (e.g. approving internal emails about process) (Belcher 2015a, pp. 19–20). Increased risk was linked not only to greater external scrutiny, but to ministers demanding a rapid response rate on advice and programme delivery. Senior and experienced staff had to be employed to handle risk mitigation (Beale 2011).

Disaggregation to Agencies through Agencification

A keynote reform, reflecting the identification of disaggregation of multi-purpose departments, was the executive agency model. 'Agencification' centred on separating policy formulation from implementation and providing greater scope for resource use. Four different responses were apparent within the Anglophone group with the principle applied on a cross-system basis, ad hoc, pragmatically and according to different forms of agency (see Appendix 3).

The United Kingdom's major reform commitment to the executive agency concept shifted the focus to the extensive use of the executive agency. Executive functions were transferred to executive agencies, which operated within departments, each with a chief executive directly accountable to ministers and a policy and resources framework designed to provide a focus and targets. The other significant feature was systemic application: during the first ten years of the scheme it was extended to most potential candidates for agency status, meaning that around 75 per cent of staff in the home civil service were employed in executive agencies. The UK experience provided the most influential case of agencification, although debate continued about how effective the system was in practice (Pollitt et al. 2004).

New Zealand also offered an 'agency' form of a type that differed from standard cases of agencification (Pollitt et al. 2004). This was one element of a larger model for public management. The core was restructured according to two principles: the separation of responsibilities for policy and delivery, and the identification of specific functions with specialised organisations. In addition to the three central agencies, the result was 17 policy ministries, 11 delivery departments, and three that combined both responsibilities.

Australia's and Canada's responses differed. Australia had several well-established delivery agencies but did not proclaim them as part of a system-wide reform programme. It also remained attached to combining policy and implementation roles within a department in order to maintain effective feedback on implementation, with one major exception. Centrelink was created as a new agency model that was multi-functional, delivered services to several departments, provided an integrated cross-portfolio service, and accounted for about 30 per cent of the Commonwealth's budget (Halligan 2008a). Canada experimented with special operating agencies (SOAs), modelled on the UK's executive agencies, but there was a lack of drive to create an SOA system and it did not proceed very far with these arrangements (Savoie 1994). That neither Canada nor Australia needed an agency system may be partly attributed to their federal structures and the smaller scope for creating agencies at the national level.

How much autonomy were executive agencies accorded? In the United Kingdom, the Cabinet Office and Treasury allowed delegated authority for recruitment, but this could be revoked. There were constraints on developing individual recruitment systems (James 2003, p. 82). The original model accorded agencies substantial freedom with employment and staffing, but despite general satisfaction with delegations (given constraints on departments), 40 per cent of chief executives surveyed agreed that 'more flexibility over the use of financial and human resources' would enable more effective service delivery. The results for delegated freedom and controls were 'confusing and sometime perverse'. Departmental headquarters tended, 'to enforce controls over inputs in place of systems to ensure that outputs are delivering desired outcomes'. The ability to deliver was negatively affected by reductions in management freedoms (HMT and OPSR 2002, pp. 14, 40), and the Next Steps agencification programme was over-bureaucratised (Talbot and Talbot 2019).

Departments were reluctant to give up controls in some cases. The lack of success of the Canadian SOAs was largely a result of how central agencies and line departments handled the delegations. The Treasury Board Secretariat enabled SOAs to operate more flexibly through delegating management authority, but departments retained much of it in head office (Savoie 1999). Some UK departments did not pass a range of freedoms to their agencies (James et al. 2012).

Over the longer term the United Kingdom reduced the number of executive agencies by mergers with ministries (and other fates) (Elston 2012); there was some rationalisation of New Zealand's fragmented system, and Australia's Centrelink was not durable because controls increased, and it was eventually merged with other agencies to create a mega-ministerial department (Halligan 2015a; see also Chapter 8). This was not dissimilar to the experience of the UK's 1980s executive agencies under the 2010s reform agenda under which agencification was 'advocated as centralized, politically proximate and departmentalized governance' (Elston 2014, p. 11), and agency staff were reduced to 25 per cent of the civil service (Talbot and Talbot 2019).

CORE MANAGEMENT CAPABILITIES: CONSTRAINED BY CONTEXTS

The condition of core management is indicated by the state of management capabilities and processes central to the functioning of the public management system, and how capability is lost and retained. Several basic departmental capabilities are considered: human resources, financial, performance and risk.[2] Each represents a key management process that dates from the outset of reform. In addition, policy capability logically fits here because of its centrality to the public management systems. Other capabilities could have been chosen (e.g. leadership, delivery, strategy and digital), a list that has expanded since corporate weaknesses were identified in the 2000s (e.g. Cabinet Office 2009, 2013). The key questions are why were capabilities in a state of neglect in the twenty-first century, and how is capability lost and retained? The inattention could commence early: within a decade of the introduction of the NZ's public management model, an official judgement was that capability was 'largely ignored' (SSC 1999, p. 21). The focus here is on the middle and longer term.

Central intervention through capability reviews forms part of the analysis. While departments have lost capability through government cutback programmes and outsourcing, they still have had choices to make about how they deploy their resources.

Financial Management: A Linchpin of Managerialism

Management inertia, even slippage, has been apparent in the field of financial management for two of the four countries, Canada and New Zealand being apparent exceptions.[3] Consanguinity existed between Australia and the United Kingdom with the UK's 1982 Financial Management Initiative (FMI) and the Australian 1983 Financial Management Improvement Program (FMIP) providing a basis for examining their condition after three decades (Halligan 2013b). Both formed cornerstones of managerialism in the two countries (Pollitt 1990; Halligan and Power 1992; Pollitt and Bouckaert 2011).

The Australian FMIP was designed to achieve clarity about and linkages between the elements of a resource management cycle. It signified the shift from inputs and processes to programmes and outcomes and was based on a simple cycle of planning (objectives and strategies), budgeting and operational planning, implementing, monitoring, reporting and evaluation (DFD 2012b, p. 14; see also Halligan and Power 1992). This focus was at the core of the new managerialism and was regarded as relatively successful in changing culture and practice (Zifcak 1994). Fast forward 30 years and the achievements of the 1980s were dissipated through neglect of the basics across the Australian public service (senior executive, Finance Department, Canberra 2012). The condition of departmental financial management was woeful. The position was described euphemistically in a review of financial accountability as follows: 'some of the clarity provided by this simple conception has been lost over time. Moreover, the financial framework does not currently draw links to planning, budgeting or evaluation activities' (DFD 2012b, p. 14).

In the UK, the critique from oversight bodies (House of Commons and National Audit Office) extended over more than a decade. The Public

Accounts Committee reported that obstacles to improving financial management included the lack of financial skills among non-finance staff, the need
to improve the quality of financial information, and the ineffective use of
information. Most departments did not have accurate, timely and integrated
financial and operational performance information to enable their boards to
make informed decisions on resource use and to evaluate its utilisation. Policy
and operational decisions, for example, were rarely based on a full assessment
of their financial implications. Financial management was yet to be properly
embedded within the cultures of departments (CPA 2008). The National Audit
Office's review of progress in improving financial management provided
insights into the state of play (NAO 2011b). Top Whitehall leaders were
castigated for not demonstrating commitment to good financial management.
The centre – Cabinet Office and Treasury – had not strategically employed its
expertise to produce fundamental improvements in the maturity of financial
management (NAO 2011b). The NAO argued that 'transformational change'
was required across the civil service to achieve appropriate financial management, including senior civil servants with relevant expertise, incentivising staff
through assessments and rewards, and a culture of making decisions based
on good financial information and with regard to the financial implications
(NAO 2011b). Following trenchant critiques (Bouchal and McCrae 2013;
NAO 2013c), and an analysis of the condition of management information in
government (Read 2013), the Treasury produced its response (HM Treasury
2013), and the oversight for registering its new attention. This agenda continued to be pursued and was upheld as a successful functional reform that
produced progress (McCrae et al. 2016).

Meanwhile, financial management featured as one of the main areas of
the Canadian Management Accountability Framework, which meant regular
monitoring on an annual basis, and a specialist group in the Treasury Board
Secretariat devoted to promoting the profession in government (Lindquist
2009).

Human Resource Management

Human resource management has long been a poor cousin to other forms of
management and a loser under cutbacks. In Australia, there were continuing
gaps between staff expectations of leaders and their current competencies. In
making judgements about leaders and their competencies, considerable reliance is placed on the results of employee surveys. One of the most significant
capability and performance gaps for the senior executive service (SES) and
the SES feeder group was people management (AGRAGA 2010). As well,
surveys of employees indicated low satisfaction with senior leaders as a continuing trend (Taylor 2010; JCPAA 2012). From the capability review pro-

gramme of departments, the results extended across dimensions of leadership, strategy and delivery, and provided insights into strengths and weaknesses. For leadership, 76 per cent of agencies were 'well placed' (or better) in terms of motivating people, but 71 per cent were ranked as a 'development area' (or worse) for developing people. These and other results indicated considerable variations in departmental assessments. The category, 'staff performance management', ranked poorly in the assessments with three-quarters of reviews rating agencies below the required level (APSC 2013, p. 215). More generally, recruitment was identified as one of two areas that involved 'significant time and resources . . . much of the administrative burden associated with these activities is due to the imposition of agency requirements' (MAC 2007, p. 23). The capability gap in strategic human resource management was still evident in 2019 (Whyte 2019).

In the first decade of reform, NZ departments were unable to invest in staff because of constant 'downward pressure on the operational budget' (SSC 1999, p. 26). For New Zealand's performance improvement framework, 'management of people performance' results were poor with 71 per cent of agencies needing development – the second lowest ranking. Both 'engagement with staff' and 'leadership and workplace development' received low rankings with 62 per cent (or worse) of agencies in both cases needing development (Te Kawa and Guerin 2012, p. 32).

The UK capability reviews included a category, 'Build capability', which assessed how staff were managed and developed by their department. This was the weakest of the reviews' ten elements with 95 per cent of departments classified as a 'development area', many of which were described as urgent, even serious. Those departments reviewed again were still rated as 'development areas' or worse (Cabinet Office 2009, pp. 10, 12).

Canadian human resource management has been beset by cumbersome operating procedures and divided, largely centralised responsibilities, and a sense that it was a 'neglected dimension' of deputy ministers' managerial responsibilities: 'Decades of an approach emphasising delegation of authority had . . . deputy heads as primarily responsible for administering a centrally prescribed framework but had failed to make them HR leaders by making human resources management an integral part of their management responsibility' (Juillet and Rasmussen 2008, pp. 201, 206). A mid-2010s reform review identified people management, specifically recruitment and staffing processes, as one of five priority areas (Government of Canada 2014). Nevertheless, the investment in talent development has remained limited and subject to bureaucratic approaches that affect productivity and ignore diminished capacity (Public Policy Forum 2016, p. vi).

Performance Management

Anglophone systems have been highly committed to performance management for around three decades during which time they have refined their
measurement and performance frameworks and increased their capacity to
monitor performance (see Chapter 6). The countries followed different pathways with their performance management frameworks, while corresponding
on the basic planning and reporting requirements. However, practice fell
short of aspirations with persistent issues with the quality and use of performance information, internal decision-making and external reporting, and the
variable engagement of departments. The limitations of country approaches
included questions about how well the framework was working, the fixation
on compliance, and top-down complexities in a unitary system (Halligan
2007c; Bouckaert and Halligan 2008; Talbot 2010; Gill 2011a). The level
of performance measurement capability was often judged to be indifferent.
For example, capability in the United Kingdom was still at a 'low level' in
the mid-2010s, with departments struggling 'to develop outcome-based and
longer-term indicators'. This was attributed in part to limited resources resulting from cutbacks to the civil service (NAO 2016b, pp. x, 35).

Risk Management

Risk management had been an element since the early days of reform but
acquired significance in the 1990s as greater attention was paid to systematising and formalising it (e.g. Barrett 1996). Some hesitation occurred following
9/11 as border controls were tightened, but a new momentum for addressing
weaknesses emerged during the 2000s, particularly where risk was perceived
to be increasing (e.g. most UK departments reported facing more risk than
three years previously: NAO 2004), and as a focus on innovation became
fashionable.

All departments must confront risk issues that impact on basic roles,
which take several forms: external (e.g. political, technological, legal and
environmental), operational (e.g. delivery, capacity and capability, reputation,
governance, resilience and security) and change (e.g. new projects and policies) (HM Treasury 2004). Despite sustained attempts to improve financial,
performance and risk management, pervasive weaknesses persisted. Risk management was 'found wanting in a number of recent policy failures and crises'
(Cabinet Office 2002, p. 3). Most departments in the United Kingdom had
well-developed risk management processes, but they were unintegrated with
financial and performance information. How then did management connect
risk management and efficient and effective service delivery? (NAO 2011a).

Canada has had an elaborate integrated guideline for risk management (TBS 2016a). However, there had earlier been a problem in a risk aversion environment with incorporating risk management in the administration of grants and contributions (TBS 2006). A modern risk management system was advocated to replace the reliance on central regulation for preventing mistakes and misconduct (Canada Treasury Board 2005, 2007). However, departmental transactions continued to follow cumbersome processes regardless of the level of risk, and without using existing flexibilities (TBS 2016a). A core area of the Management Accountability Framework (see Chapter 6), 'integrated risk, planning and performance' was not scrutinised for integration beyond establishing that most departments did not use performance information to identify risks (TBS 2017a).

In New Zealand, insufficient attention was given to managing risk (BPSAG 2011, p. 20), and risk management was rated below the level regarded as acceptable in the Performance Improvement Framework system for 38 per cent of agencies (Te Kawa and Guerin 2012, p. 32).

Implementing risk management has been hard work in Australia (see DFD 2012a, 2012b). The APS grappled with making risk management work effectively, and some progress occurred but it remained variable across the system, and a culture of risk management remained elusive (DFD 2012a, p. 57). In organisational capability assessments, risk management ranked poorly; two-thirds of Australian agencies ranked below the required level (APSC 2013). According to 'external and self-assessments of APS practice . . . too often risk management is a compliance exercise rather than a way of working' (APSC 2014, pp. 11–12). There are indications that entities have pursued risk management more seriously under the Public Governance, Performance and Accountability Act 2013 (PGPA), although progress for the majority was uneven. Given the rather tortuous engagement with risk management (in a risk averse environment), this could either be interpreted in the short term as a continuing problem or alternatively progress from a low base. Risk practice has remained relatively immature. A more effective risk culture is unlikely without support from political leaders (Alexander and Thodey 2018).

POLICY CAPABILITY

Policy capability is an integral component of the public management system but has been identified in the twenty-first century as an ailing field not readily amenable to resuscitation. Managerialism had earlier pushed management to the forefront as both an activity and a primary responsibility of senior public servants (the relegation of policy is also attributable to externalisation and politicisation (Craft and Halligan 2017, 2020). Several assessments of departments' capability were undertaken, which had elements in common for three countries, and a comparable framework in the fourth.[4] The position across countries was similar.

First there was the pre-eminence accorded to management in sustained reform agendas for upwards of two decades or more. The Australian public service's policy role changed with the rise of managerialism as senior executives and department heads were pushed to manage and the near monopoly role within the advisory system was disbanded as political executives became more assertive (Halligan and Power 1992). Studies have since reported that the policy capability of departments has been eroded (Edwards 2009; Tiernan 2011; Tingle 2015, quoting former heads of Treasury; Vromen and Hurley 2015), and their policy expertise valued less (Head 2015). An official view was that the policy capability of the public service required strengthening, particularly in relation to innovative and strategic advice (AGRAGA 2010). The ambiguous status of the policy role of departmental secretaries was such that it required legislation to revive it as a formal responsibility of departmental secretaries (Halligan 2013a). The contestability of policy advice was one plank, the argument being that 'competition for the ministerial ear' increased the range of inputs and improved decision-making. However, this was only likely if ministers wanted it to happen, and it was not apparent that government was open to a range of options (MacDermott 2008). The new fashion for policy first and development of evidence later became more prevalent outside the 'headline policy' of new governments (Varghese 2016).

The bias in the United Kingdom's reform programme was officially acknowledged by registering the emphasis on management reforms for 20 years, and the lack of attention to the policy process (Cabinet Office 1999; Hallsworth et al. 2011). There were more policy process generalists below senior levels (Page and Jenkins 2005), and weaknesses in policy-making have been tied to deficiencies in advisory practices (Institute for Government 2011a, p. 7). The government pushed for the outsourcing of delivery to encompass policy analysis (Diamond 2014). Policy implementation without evidence was pursued by policy active ministers, such as Michael Gove while Minister of Education. Policy was described as being initiated by hunch (or ideology) rather than by evidence (Bousted 2017; Wilby 2017; Rutter 2018).

In the Canadian case, the managerial function of senior executives increased from the late 1960s, policy planning units declined in importance, and a shift towards generalist managers occurred (Carroll 1990). The policy advisory group within the federal bureaucracy flourished in the 1970s, but its fortunes declined from the 1980s with successive purposeful expenditure reduction and public management reforms (Savoie 2014). In the 1980s the management emphasis affected policy work. The managerialist reforms of the late 1980s and early 1990s produced a decline in policy capability. The emphasis on management was linked to a de-emphasis on policy work and discouragement from engaging in active inter-departmental policy dialogues (Fellegi 1996; Lindquist 2014). The federal public service's policy capacity declined with widespread shortages, particularly of policy analytical capacity (Peters 1996; Dobuzinskis et al. 2007; Howlett and Wellstead 2011).

New Zealand resources were being put into advisory work and capacity within the public service departments, but often capacity was unavailable in key areas or was unaligned with government priorities (Scott 2010). The long-standing policy problem was diagnosed to have multiple dimensions, including variations in quality, skill shortages, evidential shortfalls, cross-agency weaknesses, and a series of contradictions and divergent goals resulting from the changing environment (DPMC 2014; NZPC 2018).

Specific details about the loss of departmental policy capability offer insights about the extent of the problem in Australia and New Zealand. Capability reviews were used by the Australian government to provide systematic assessments of departments' capabilities from 2011 to 2015.[5] Departments varied widely in terms of the quality and extent of their policy capability, ranging from well-developed to laissez-faire, but were generally weak in six dimensions: policy development, strategy, research and analysis, policy implementation, stakeholder engagement and evaluation (Halligan 2016).

There were substantial variations in departments' ability to offer choices, ground advice in evidence (particularly where departments had a large data base), draw on effective consultation internally and externally, and be forward-looking; other qualitative factors also varied. Most departments either lacked a strategic focus or made inadequate provision for it or simply neglected it in practice. Strategic policy was often ad hoc and siloed. Departments were reactive and disinclined to be forward-looking, which was attributed to day-to-day pressures and issues, a culture of problem-solving, and a prevalence of tactical and transactional considerations. There was a need to recognise strategic policy development as a capability, organisationally and within a policy framework aligned with departmental objectives. The policy and implementation relationship was a perennial issue. For departments, there was often a lack of systematic feedback loops from the service delivery coalface to those who developed policy and designed national programmes. Departments generated rich intelligence from the interactions of networks with clients and service providers, but the evidence was largely untapped or unstructured in being relayed back to the national office. Stakeholder engagement on policy was a pervasive theme, but consultation was usually inadequate for various reasons (e.g. too late or lacking proper engagement). Evaluation was not formally embedded in contrast to other countries (e.g. Canada), and was patchy or under-developed, except for a few departments. The most telling result was the passive approach to policy overall, which was reflected in the relative lack of policy advocacy and leadership (Halligan 2016).

In New Zealand, policy resources were 'under-managed', departments were making an insufficient contribution to the policy agenda, the big policy issues were not being responded to, there were gaps in 'policy advice leadership capability' at the chief executive level, an imbalance existed between the emphasis on process at the expense of analysis and advice, the quality of data was poor, and consultation was mishandled (Scott 2010). The key issue was that policy analysis (i.e. the content of policy) was 'weakened in favour of a systemic focus on policy processes and advice – the process and presentation aspects of policy. Capability in basic policy analysis disciplines . . . [were] degraded across the public service in favour of increased expertise in risk and process management' (Scott 2010, p. 37).[6]

New Zealand and the United Kingdom have given the most serious attention to resurrecting the policy function through mounting programmes for developing the policy profession. New Zealand's Department of the Prime Minister and Cabinet's 'policy project' was established because of complex policy problems (DPMC 2014).

REFORM AND CHANGE

The final dimension is the propensity to reform the public management system. The early emergence of Anglophone countries as active reformers was traversed in Chapter 2, and this was attributed to fewer obstacles than elsewhere and the nature of the administrative tradition. The shift to management was in part because it was depicted as being proactive, flexible and responsive. Once management replaced administration as the central concept and the private sector experience became reference points, the identification with stability, permanence and process was succeeded by management improvement which became a routine objective of departments and central reformers (Zifcak 1994). Other conceptions of change were also incorporated including change management as a means of obtaining acceptance of new ideas and processes. Each generation has its own formulations, a typical injunction being 'A high performing public service is relentless in its commitment to continuous improvement' (MAC 2010).

Reform may address relations with either the external relationships – private sector, ministers and society – or internal to the public service itself (see Chapter 1). Most analysis focuses on one of these. The questions to be addressed are what the reform pattern has been and why it continues to be intense in the 2010s.

Reform or planned and designed change comes in different sizes and scales: general programmes and system design, often identifiable by an official document; specialised reforms issuing from the centre; and department-led reform. Simultaneously, other types of change occur, both intended and unintended. Structural or organisational change are the most obvious: mergers and demergers of departments (surveyed for the UK: White and Dunleavy 2010), agencification and reintegration (e.g. Elston 2014). Change may occur by stealth, be emergent or display institutionalist characteristics. There have also been 35 years of the disruptive effects of a change of department heads and/or ministers (Dunleavy and Carrera 2013; Freeguard et al. 2019; Riddell 2019). The efficacy of reform is often difficult to determine, in part because of a relative lack of official evaluations (Pollitt 2013b). Of importance is unintended change: incremental adjustments and processes that occur without seemingly being planned or designed. The important lesson to be drawn is that there are multiple currents running, which may only be arrested when blanket austerity measures are imposed.

Here the focus is mainly on general reform programmes of government, and a few specialised reforms of systemic significance. An overview of types of reform initiatives can be obtained from Table 5.1 (with country details in Appendices 1 and 2). Australia and the UK are higher reformers and more prone to swings in emphasis than Canada and New Zealand, judged by the regularity of and directional change in reports (Appendices 1 and 2). Of the four the UK has been judged to be a hyper-reformer characterised as displaying serial re-structuring and accelerating re-disorganisation (Pollitt 2007), which reflects early and continuing NPM elements that create greater rifts and swings (cycling or alternating) in public management reform (Pollitt 2011) and the alacrity with which initiatives are profiled and then disbanded or replaced.[7]

The currency of constant change is indicated by the regularity of agendas initiated by the centre of government. The incidence of reform programmes in the 2010s in all four countries is significant (Appendices 1 and 2). The Anglophone countries have placed a premium on reform programmes, which are usually attached to the political executive (or its main agent, e.g. the UK Cabinet Office), and exhortative reports associated with central agencies driving change.

The ease of reform can be overstated. The urge to reform the NZ model has been the longest running narrative (Morrison 2014). Reform in some respects had become harder. Reform plans lacked coherence or a narrative ('t Hart 2010; Pollitt 2013b); and in the Canadian bottom-up approach ideas float up from the mass of public servants (Government of Canada 2013). Knee-jerk approaches could be seen in Cameron's early reform flourishes (which were designed by ideological gurus), or in cutbacks (and not really reform). The response of the most reformist countries in the OECD after two decades of reform was, predictably, more reform initiatives. These replays are not simply about responding to environmental change but are about fundamentals. At the end of the 2010s, New Zealand was seeking the most significant changes to its public management model in 30 years (SSC 2018a, 2018b). Australia has

Table 5.1   *Management results and status of dilemmas*

Dimension	Results	Status of dilemmas in 2010s
• Management control relaxation	Efficiency dominated compliance and process. Often chronic	Internal contradictions. Ongoing
• Decentralising management	Mixed results at systemic level	Non-issue
• devolution		Centralisation
• delegation	Agencies often under-empowered	Intra-dept. centralisation
• agencification	(delegations withheld)	Agencies used as required (as they were historically)
• Management capabilities	Struggled for attention with outputs and results prioritised	Intermittent attention often prompted by central reviews.
	Inadequately managed	Ongoing
• Policy capability	Demand declined with management focus and contestability	Uneven revival attempts. Ongoing
• Steering flexibility	Outsourcing in specific systems	Continuing focus
• Reform and change	Constant change, punctuated by major reforms at intervals	Implementation failures. Continuing focus

mounted (but not published at the time this book went into production) what has been represented as the most significant inquiry in 40 years.

MANAGEMENT ATTRITION, MARKING TIME, AND REVERSALS

Five areas examined have been summarised in terms of management results and status in the 2010s and are summarised in Table 5.1. In each case there have been discontinuities and fluctuations, and attenuation of purpose and results. All but one dimension is ongoing.

In accounting for the management trends in which the reformers' original intentions were not sustained, several factors emerge as important. The naivety of the early and more radical reformers need not be recapped, except to note that original reforms were not 'a simple shift from "bureaucratic to post-bureaucratic forms of control"' but a combination of 'strong elements of innovation with the reassertion of a number of fundamentally bureaucratic mechanisms' (Hoggett 1997, pp. 11–12). The literature may refer to a reform paradigm change, but a management approach had to fit into the institutional context vacated by public administration. The contextual obstacles to sustaining reform existed from the beginning and mounted (and were magnified) because of the influence of external factors and ministerial stances. The 2010s have been identified as a time of greater uncertainty and risk internationally (BPSAG 2011), and there were similar reactions in the 2000s with international terrorist threats, a global economic crisis, and boundary issues that impacted directly on how risk management was applied.

The focus on factors internal to the executive branch is either because of the apparent loss of the reform achievements and momentum of the 1980s and 1990s or the re-enactment of conditions that confronted early reforms in the 1980s. What is clear is that the constraints on discretion and capability persisted into the 2010s, and in some cases increased. More generally, managerialism (including externalisation) and politicisation affected all dimensions of reform in Table 5.1.

Management Control and Discretion

The lack of thought given to design issues meant that empowering the centre while promoting managerial discretion could not be reconciled simply. The problems with reconciling rules and flexibility were exposed in Australia's devolved budgeting and financial management through FMIP and budget reforms with a rules-based explanation accounting for the domination of central control over devolved financial authority (Di Francesco 2016; Di Francesco and Alford 2016, ch. 5). Take also the case of NZ, famous for making managers manage while simultaneously hampering them while they tried to do so. The output drive negated the principle of managerial freedom. The UK pattern of managerial freedoms was often 'strangled at birth or subject to a process of attrition through proliferating rules and regulatory oversight' (Hood 2000, p. 7). Was this a case of management begetting management (Gregory 2001)? Managerialism, while paradigm-changing in many respects, was introduced into established governance and accountability regimes. It added to the multiplicity of accountabilities as well as being subject to their increasing complexity (Mulgan 2003). Politicisation came into play where external exposure or public embarrassment produced greater central rules or intra-departmental centralisation (see Chapter 7).

Management Processes and Capabilities

The neglect of financial and human resource management at different times in several countries is not entirely explicable, particularly in the case of financial management. Human resource management is commonly susceptible to fiscal constraints pertaining to levels of investment in staff development. Public service personnel were 'simply "resources" . . . to be managed in the most efficient manner possible, including being substituted for by other resources' (Aucoin 2006). The two were given insufficient attention in the flux of modernising public services. For example, financial management was in practice detached from incentive systems with the inadequate incentives for officials in the UK civil service being attributed to the lack of the cultural embeddedness of core principles (NAO 2011b). In human resource management, contrasts were regularly made with the private sector (e.g. Korac-Kakabadse and Korac-Kakabadse 1998) an implication being that it is more readily able to handle this form of management. Australian departmental and agency investment in learning and development was considerably lower than within the private sector (APSC 2010).

The attrition of management processes and capabilities over time can be attributed to several factors. For performance, there were questions about the design of management systems that were unattractive operationally to both departments and politicians. Departments would revert to 'local rules' because they were simpler and more readily comprehended and applied. For senior management, several considerations affected the enhancement of capabilities: they were displaced by other priorities, there were implementation challenges and conflicting demands, and unfavourable incentive systems and structures. The swings in support for programmes were of particular importance, whether because of fashions, reform fatigue, or a change of government (as discussed next). New capabilities (or old ones reprioritised) came to the fore (take the UK case of Manzoni's 2018 agenda that emphasises skills in commercial, technical and project execution).

Propensity to Change

Overall there has been a high incidence of reform initiatives. The propensity to change can be attributed first to the ease with which it can be accomplished in Anglophone countries. Moreover, there is the access to and ability to use a wide range of instruments that may address the fundamentals of public governance and management. A consistent feature has been the 'thinness' in the evidence provided in support of reforms which is often reliant on anecdotes or mini-cases (Pollitt 2013b). This is in an age when 'policy-based evidence' (i.e. evidence in support of policy is found after it is decided) has become standard practice.

The role of radicalising managerialism in the reform agenda needs specific consideration. The move from contained and relatively closed public administration systems to less constrained and open public management systems had a major impact with a range of results that were not necessarily as expected. As discussed, the demands of managerialism were not just about greater freedom but also about tighter control in the pursuit of management results. The addition of the more radical NPM-type reforms both subverted further the identity of the public service and extended its exposure. New instruments and techniques were added to leaders' toolkits. NPM was often associated with different conceptions of the role and size of the state. Austerity became a reinforcing factor for NPM approaches: maintaining management capability while reducing staff and resources was problematic, cutbacks contributed both to running down capability and holding back the revival of programmes, and the spike because of attention given to NPM led to neglect of other management features that needed attention.

One manifestation of this neglect is 'disruptive steering' (see Appendix 3). Major swings and counter-swings in approaches to the state, the public service, governance and public management became routine, more so in some systems than others. However, radicalisation was not sufficient in itself to explain the issues with controls and capabilities. Issues with capability had arisen prior to the GFC (the UK capability reviews were launched in 2005). Unintended consequences (e.g. turnover of staff as a by-product of career incentives and the actions of government) were a product of the managerialist environment more generally. Austerity was regarded as 'driving out evidence-based policy-making' particularly in the unitary systems. 'Large-scale retrenchment . . . had short-term impacts on strategic policy capability, such as the loss of specialist expertise and institutional memory (Stoker and Evans 2016, p. 17; Pollitt and Bouckaert 2017).

Important political factors were the demands made on departments to attend to ministerial priorities, the 'minister as leader' syndrome and, more generally, risk aversion. Much of the decline related to the lack of priority given to maintaining and enhancing management capabilities and other agenda. Self-assessments of Australian agencies and the results of numerous capability reviews indicated that generally, 'little progress has been made in rectifying . . . capability deficiencies in recent years. Perhaps the urgent has crowded out the important' (APSC 2014, p. 9). There have continued to be major capability issues and a need for rebuilding (Burgess 2019). The lack of sustained interest and support by ministers affected the long term impact of Next Step agencies in the UK (Talbot and Talbot 2019).

New Zealand ministers pressured public servants 'to juggle priorities' (Norman 2003, p. 88). Chief executives under pressure both from ministers' requirements for greater 'output for the same budgets', and from Treasury expectations for financial performance resorted to cutbacks in discretionary areas (e.g. 'research and development, staff training, computer upgrades') while focusing on mandatory outputs (Norman 2003, p. 198). A decade later, survey results indicated that ministerial engagement was very strong while improving efficiency and effectiveness was very weak. Departments were 'better at managing issues and keeping their Ministers happy than . . . building core institutional capability that adds substantial and enduring value' (Francis and Horn 2013, pp. 10–11). Inconsistent demands on UK civil servants created problems for business planning that involved matching single department plan (SDP) deliveries and capacity because it was difficult to resist new ministerial priorities (NAO 2018c, p. 11). New governments wished to overturn practices associated with their predecessors (e.g. the Cameron Coalition rejection of targets and a central delivery unit, only to restore them when the need became apparent). More generally, ministers focus on the short term, the political dynamic becoming influenced by polarisation, continuous electioneering, and the influence of media in general and social media in particular.

The use of external consultants for management and policy has been well established in Anglophone countries (Saint-Martin 2004; Craft and Halligan 2020) compared to those in different administrative traditions. Its importance varies between systems, over time, and whether policy advice is central. High levels of outsourcing have impacted on the role and performance of public services. The head of the Australian public service critiqued the excessive reliance on consultants for core APS policy work (Parkinson 2018a).

CONCLUSION

This chapter has been concerned with understanding why core management elements are often poorly realised and sustained in practice. It has considered the dysfunctions of dimensions of public management: the dips in and problems with improving capability and the entanglement of process features, all within contexts that display (to varying extents) exaggerated risk aversion. Moreover, this apparent insouciance to capacity issues is pervasive.

There are numerous cases of departments responding to problems, such as compliance and hierarchy, although often after they have been exposed by a central review. Examples of good practice (e.g. Belcher 2015a) have not necessarily addressed the factors that created the problems in the first place, consequences being attenuated management capabilities and issues in sustaining management improvements in Anglophone countries. The early years of reform were notable for centrally driven internal deregulation. The immediate impact of agendas was to produce something of a reformation in which public management became the dominant approach. However, internal contradictions in managerialism meant that the intended effects were not achieved.

A number of explanations have been canvassed. A core managerialist problem is that the built-in focus on results – whether defined as outputs or political priorities – has been pursued at the expense of processes and capabilities that support and enable a well-functioning public management system. The political interpretation is that ministers have focused on their priorities and the achievement of results, which led to the exclusion or neglect of institutional factors. The management paradox is that internal contradictions in the managerialist paradigm in fact undermine its performance. It is possible for a programme to be bureaucratised by centralised requirements on the one hand while experiencing neglect because of political disinterest and lack of institutionalisation on the other (Talbot and Talbot 2019). Management dilemmas and the complexities of the interaction between management, political and bureaucratic factors are further explored in the analysis of regulatory practices in Chapter 7.

NOTES

1. The country system most heavily affected by the crisis introduced capability reviews in 2006 because of weaknesses in capability, management and skills (see the comments by the Cabinet Secretary, Gus O'Donnell in Cabinet Office 2006).
2. Four have been used by Canada for its Management Accountability Framework: TBS 2017b.
3. New Zealand benefited from a low threshold in performance improvement framework (PIF) ratings (Francis and Horn 2013).
4. These were known as capability reviews in the United Kingdom and Australia and performance improvement frameworks (PIFs) in New Zealand, the latter two being modelled on the original British scheme but modified to fit country contexts. Canada's Management Accountability Framework (MAF) has covered some of the same ground (i.e. capabilities) without posing the interesting questions of the others, but the model differed in providing annual oversight.
5. Main sources are http://www.apsc.gov.au/priorities/capability-reviews, and APSC 2013, 2014.
6. The disciplines included cost benefit/effectiveness/utility analysis, rigorous programme evaluation, micro-simulation modelling, and quantitative and performance analysis (Scott et al. 2010).
7. For example, the Financial Management Initiative, Next Steps agencies, Citizen's Charter, and in late 2018, the Public Finance Initiative (PFI).

6. Contradictions in implementing performance management

Performance has been a leitmotif of the reform era and the centrepiece of managerialism. Its pervasive influence has dictated the operations of government departments, subsidiary agencies and third parties (Radin 2006; Bouckaert and Halligan 2008). It is impossible to envisage public management without regard to results, targets and performance measurement. However, a paradox of performance has been that the information generated for management frameworks has been largely unused. Tension between the managerial and the political purposes of performance management has been a continuing dynamic of the reform era, which is one reason why the architecture of performance systems remained unresolved.

The performance movement shifted the focus from inputs and process to outputs and outcomes, or more generally results. The underlying proposition was deceptively attractive: to establish a process for advancing objectives with the promise of measurement and accountability, and then reporting results against indicators. There were, however, complications, for purposes were not always clear and often competing, their relevance varied with stakeholders (Behn 2003) and different logics were in play (Gill 2011b; Pollitt 2013a). The practice was also demanding as it entailed both the intricacies of performance measurement and reporting, and complex interactions with politicians focused on results. Given the pitfalls it was not unexpected that the efficacy of performance management was mixed.

The performance management framework was largely the domain of officials as a whole-of-government arrangement that provided for continuity and accountability to parliament. In this sense there was a guardianship role for a foundational component of the governmental system. However, once the framework was converted into outputs and outcomes, performance indicators, targets and other accoutrements of an expansive managerialism, ownership was more problematic. The motives of managers and politicians differed in terms of the purposes and uses of performance management. Public managers wanted a consistent and stable whole-of-government framework within which to operate which would allow them to fulfil the compliance requirements for parliamentary reporting. Political executives signed off on the formal documents, but how the process served their purposes was questionable, a core question being whether it was a managerial or political exercise.

The Anglophone countries were more committed at an early stage in the reform era to performance management and measurement than most OECD countries (OECD 1995; Bouckaert and Halligan 2008). This high level of commitment has lasted for over three decades during which countries have reworked their measurement and performance frameworks and expanded the range of performance instruments. The four countries have emphasised instruments that were both similar to and different from each other. The variations in approaches to performance ranged from a common type of arrangement for all departments – the whole-of-government performance framework – to specific performance instruments for measuring efficiency or for tracking priorities and progress against targeted results. Different levels were encompassed by a performance system: the macro level (public service/sector) organisations (departments and agencies), programmes or projects, and the individual official.

The high and sustained support for performance management raised questions about the results over four decades of reform, and also how the performance management framework evolved as countries wrestled with design issues and the utility of a central outputs and outcomes framework. The countries' distinctive pathways allow comparisons of approaches to managing performance systems, the clusters of instruments used, and whether the performance system was actively managed. However, performance arrangements keep changing, which raises questions about whether there has been progressive development either in the core performance management framework or in the performance system. This chapter therefore examines what became of performance management and to what extent the limitations of a performance approach were addressed.

THE PURPOSES AND INSTRUMENTS OF PERFORMANCE

Several purposes have been differentiated for performance information (Van Dooren et al. 2015), but essentially there are between three and five: public accountability, central control, management improvement and learning, business planning and strategy, and results or priorities. The last three have assumed greater centrality for several countries. It can be argued that the standard purpose has always been about performance and therefore results, but they have been subject to different interpretations and practice.

Performance measures can be used for multiple purposes (Behn 2003; Micheli and Neely 2010; Gill and Schmidt 2011; Van Dooren et al. 2015), but the extent to which more than one (or two) can be appropriately achieved simultaneously through measuring information can be problematic. Much depends on the degree of clarity and understanding of the accountabilities, the handling of multiple stakeholders, and the complexities of attending to several purposes. The primary purpose of a performance instrument has been first and foremost about reporting, of putting on the record what has been done, in other words accounting against intentions. Or is it about attaining progress on an activity, which is then documented through measurable results? If the first it leans towards accountability, and at worst becomes a matter of compliance and retrospectivity. If the latter, it may be primarily focused on achieving a government agenda. Of course, it may purport to be about both, and have other purposes.

The solution under the standard logic model has been that outcomes will provide the effects or results. Outcomes are, however, subject to two primary difficulties that often seem insurmountable: first, articulation and application (credible measurement), a constant problem being consistency in applying an outcomes approach; the second is about accounting for achievements where there are factors that cannot be controlled for. This has led to a focus on intermediate outcomes or the language of results. These are well-established understandings about the weaknesses of performance management (Radin 2006), and major issues have also arisen with the unintended consequences of performance assessment at the delivery level, which are particularly salient in unitary systems of government (van Thiel and Leeuw 2002).

Performance Instruments and Systems

Performance is multi-faceted and extensive. The focus here on the organisational and systemic performance of the central government raises two considerations. First, in demarcating the performance system, much performance activity is excluded: the macro or whole-of-government level is central as is the meso level (performance of joint activity) and to some extent the micro level (the department). An understanding of cases (Gill 2011) and factors affecting performance at this level form one basis for generalisations.[1] In this study, the performance of individuals, inter-government programmes (sub and supra) and substantive policy areas at the sub-system of delivery within specific sectors (e.g. education and health) are not addressed.[2] Secondly, different instruments have been used for judging performance, ranging from the general framework for departments to specific and highly focused tools.

The generic performance management framework is conceived in different ways depending on what is expected of it (e.g. a strategic framework: NAO 2016b), but the core element is the parliamentary estimates (or plan) and annual reporting. A compliance accountability focus is narrow and limiting. While the focus is on the overarching performance framework, other specialised instruments of performance have been recognised, and six are identified here: implementation in furtherance of government priorities, chief executive assessment, capabilities, efficiency, corporate, and programme evaluations. These may be either ad hoc or ongoing, published or unpublished (the latter not being of demonstrable public significance), or hybrids (either largely unpublished or opaque to the public and of questionable value). Departmental head reviews are private, although the integrity of the system depends on the clarity of the assessment criteria and the process. The results category needs to be singled out because it can be either integrated with the performance management framework or form an 'overlay' of government objectives.

Different players (politicians, treasury, PMD and departments) focus on their own brand of performance. The targets used may be for specific activities (delivery, back office, leadership, management skills and corporate governance), chief executives' performance or specific types of organisation (ministerial department, other agencies).

In order to consider the focus and role of the country frameworks, five dimensions are derived from the literature and official documents (Table 6.1). The first is the degree of focus or spread of the purposes (ranging from the basics to a comprehensive 'road map'). The significance of planning and whether it has been used internally by departments is relevant here. Also important is the political executive's role and the centrality of its priorities (which are also related to ownership of the framework, either by one or two central agencies). A corollary of the last two is the question of the range and relative importance of stakeholders (Talbot 2008). Third is the question of whether the framework has been stable and durable across governments (NAO 2016b). The cross-cutting component is the fourth element. The fifth is the question of whether evaluation is built into performance management (Talbot 2010).

PERFORMANCE MANAGEMENT FRAMEWORKS: HOW HAVE COUNTRIES HANDLED THEM?

The core of the performance system has been the performance management framework for departments and agencies. The four countries have had a fully fledged model that fitted within the 'performance management' ideal type differentiated by Bouckaert and Halligan (2008). The official model has usually been based on an outputs and outcomes framework that covered organisational dimensions and their management interrelationships. Their frameworks have been pursued in some form since the 1980s and have provided the longest records of most countries – an exception being the United States – in wrestling with how to make performance management work.

Australia: Path Dependence

The Australian agenda since the mid-1980s has involved three phases, each initiated by a new performance framework, the first dating from the inauguration of a new system (1986); the second from its reformulation (1997–9); and the third implemented in 2014–16. The first two frameworks reflected two reform phases: managerialism and the new public management variant (Halligan 2007b). In the first, the elements of performance management were developed through the Financial Management Improvement Program (FMIP). The focus on results, outcomes and performance-oriented management dates from this time (Wanna et al. 2000). The core was programme budgeting and management, which was to assist managers' assessments of programme development and implementation relative to objectives. All programmes had to be reviewed every five years and departmental evaluation plans produced annually for the Department of Finance (Keating and Holmes 1990; Campbell and Halligan 1992; TFMI 1993). In this phase, the elements of performance management were developed within a centralised approach. The strengths were institutionalised performance management, and the experience of formal evaluations by the centre. The weaknesses were the quality of objectives for, and performance information on, programmes.

The second formulation was based on an outcomes/outputs framework, devolution, principles instead of formal requirements, and an emphasis on performance information. Departments and agencies were required to identify explicit outcomes, outputs and performance measures, and their heads were assigned responsibility and accountability for performance. However, problems with the design and implementation soon became apparent, and a succession of piecemeal interventions occurred during the 2000s, which failed to prevent a continuing critique. Departmental *programmes* were reincorporated because ministers argued that they lacked the information required for making decisions.[3] Even where a principle-based approach was used controls were re-imposed in the form of inputs and 'front-end processes'. The framework became more compliance focused and less about performance and achieving results (DFD 2012b, p. 34).

A succession of studies by the audit office and a ministerial review, Operation Sunlight, raised serious questions about the efficacy of aspects of the framework and the need for renewal (e.g. Tanner 2008; ANAO 2011; Hawke 2012). There were strengths, such as strong ownership for departments and reliance on managing through. Weaknesses included insufficient information for parliamentary needs and sound management (Mackay 2004), weak support for evaluation, and problems arising from combining a centralised budgetary process with devolved departments.

After 30 years, Australia still lacked an effective system according to political and oversight sources (Halligan 2007c; Tanner 2008; Hawke and Wanna 2010; Mackay 2011; ANAO 2012a, 2013a). The framework was the subject of a multi-year review by the Department of Finance (DFD 2012a, 2012b; DoF 2014). Under the Public Governance, Performance and Accountability Act 2013, a new framework was implemented with outcomes and programmes retained. It was intended to resolve limitations, to report more effectively and to integrate departmental planning and performance management, using corporate plans, plus other aspirations (e.g. improved risk management). An initial survey reported that notable challenges remained including overcoming risk aversion and improving performance (DoF 2015; Podger 2015). The third framework is a progressive development (Hawke 2016), but the quality of reporting on performance information still required improvement. In key areas (e.g. management of risk and cross-government cooperation) little had changed (Alexander and Thodey 2018).

Canada: Confronting Conundrums

Canada's pathway is notable for an early succession of trials and acknowledged failures, followed by a gestation period before a fully fledged and durable performance management framework was installed in the 2000s. This has now been somewhat overtaken by the 'results and delivery' agenda in the late 2010s.

The shift from structuring the main estimates as a traditional programme budget occurred after 1995 with the introduction of the Planning, Reporting and Accountability Structure (PRAS). Departments and agencies reported on their plans and priorities in the main estimates to inform parliament about the outputs and outcomes they wanted to achieve. There were issues with the quality and coverage of financial and performance data and the lack of outcomes focus (Talbot et al. 2001). For each strategic outcome and programme, resource allocations and performance indicators had to be defined, but reporting on outcomes was difficult. Assessments of departmental performance reports showed a limited focus on outcomes (TBS 2002, 2003; Bouckaert and Halligan 2008).

By the mid-2000s, these issues had been responded to, if not convincingly addressed in practice. The Management and Accountability Framework (MAF), was introduced in 2003, and the Management, Resources and Results Structure (MRRS) replaced PRAS as the basis for departmental reporting. A standardised approach was used to incorporate performance information in management and policy cycles. The MRRS established the link between results and the results of programmes that connected with departmental management and structure. The requirements for departments were codified and integrated through reports on plans and priorities and departmental performance that were designed to indicate the links between plans, performance and achievements. The whole-of-government planning and reporting framework provided a comprehensive overview of resources and results. There was a shortage of independent analysis, and scepticism existed about performance management and the mandatory federal agenda (Thomas 2004; Clark and Swain 2005). The approach was heavily top-down featuring central agencies, particularly the government's 'management board', the Treasury Board Secretariat. Nevertheless, by the mid-2000s, Canada had a developed performance management framework, which continued to evolve and be refined, one that readily fitted within the 'performance management model' (Bouckaert and Halligan 2008). The Management Accountability Framework created a broader framework to anchor the performance focus by providing deputy ministers with tools to assess and improve management practices, and the framework was revised in 2017.

The Policy on Results supplanted MRRS in 2016 with the purpose of improving the attainment of results. Departments were expected to be clear about objectives and the measurement of success, and to measure and evaluate performance and use the information for managing and improving programmes (Lindquist 2017).

New Zealand: Escaping the Constraints of the Original Model

A range of financial management reforms were introduced in New Zealand in the late 1980s with the emphasis on outputs.[4] A key feature of the original model was the distinction between outputs and outcomes, and their assignment respectively to chief executives and ministers. Under the Public Finance Act, departments acquired responsibility for financial management from the Treasury. Chief executive officers (CEOs) managed inputs to produce outputs that ministers purchased. The focus was on CEOs and their responsibilities for managing departments under contract as specified through performance and purchase agreements, and the annual assessment of their performance by the employer, the State Services Commission (Boston et al. 1996; Scott 2001).

New Zealand was slow to tackle weaknesses to the model in the areas of accountability, performance measurement and strategic management. Two limitations were the emphasis of the output orientation on managerial accountability at the expense of public and parliamentary accountability, and gaps in the system's capacity to learn from experience (e.g. routine policy evaluations). Performance judgements ultimately involved ministers and there was considerable investment in seeking improvements to performance information. The link between outputs and desired outcomes was variable because of how the political executive engaged: ministers were expected to utilise the connection and performance targets (Boston et al. 1996; Schick 1996; Scott 1997; Kibblewhite and Ussher 2002). The requirement under the Fiscal Responsibility Act 1994 for government to specify 'broad strategic priorities' only produced 'statements of broad direction' (Kibblewhite and Ussher 2002, p. 86). Managing for Outcomes was implemented to address long-term strategic thinking through the statement of intent (SOI). Incremental improvements occurred in the quality of departmental planning, but most SOIs did not show much improvement (NAO 2006), and there was a need to refine output and outcome indicators and improve the links between them. Performance also stood for a broad agenda for better overall performance of the state services, and development goals were introduced with indicators for monitoring progress (Prebble 2005; Whitehead 2006).

The focus on outputs and CEO responsibility for delivering goods and services produced distortions, while ministers let their purchaser role override their responsibility for outcomes (Schick 2001). The system addressed outcomes conceptually but had problems integrating them into public management because of specifying and measuring difficulties (Kibblewhite and Ussher 2002; Cook 2004). In a system 'hard-wired for single agency production' (Wintringham 2003), outcomes represented more 'an overlay to the outputs system' (Norman 2006, p. 11; see also Ryan 2011b). Performance information was not used much in the budget process, and the effectiveness of annual budgeting for assessing public performance was questioned (Shand and Norman 2005). Changes were difficult because removing the output focus 'would strip the system of its magnificent conceptual architecture' (Schick 2001, p. 2).

The Public Finance Act 1989 was amended in 2013 to improve reporting on intentions and achievements, and address results and outcomes more explicitly. Agencies must still describe and evaluate performance, but Treasury prescriptions are more flexible and allow agencies to specify how performance is to be assessed.

A turning point was the report of the Better Public Services Advisory Group which stipulated improved performance by the state services by 'securing the outcomes that matter most to New Zealanders' wellbeing'. The system's strength, service delivery (outputs), was insufficient because, performance was not 'gaining traction on the big outcomes that matter' (BPSAG 2011, pp. 14, 15). The report led to extensive activity centred on ten result areas, and government prioritising ensured progress on targets (Morrison 2014; Scott and Boyd 2017b). The 2019 budget has been produced on a well-being basis (James 2019; Malpess 2019), and the 2019 reform process is intended to support higher performance.

United Kingdom: System Churn – Governing without a Framework?

The Financial Management Initiative (FMI) in the UK was designed to focus on objectives and measure outputs and performance but was only partly successful although it laid a foundation for the next stage. The sequence of change was the domination of the three 'Es' in the 1980s (efficiency, economy and effectiveness), particularly the first two; outputs and service delivery from the late 1980s to the early 1990s; while outcomes became significant in the late 1990s (Talbot 2001; Bouckaert and Halligan 2008). The last decade has been notable for a succession of frameworks.

The political executive's drive for performance, delivery and results was relentless and reflected in instruments for aligning government priorities with progress in implementation. A turning point was when ministerial adviser, Ed Balls, informed the Treasury that its new performance framework, Output and Performance Analysis (OPAs), was being replaced by Public Service Agreements (PSAs). The OPAs provided continuity with previous systems (i.e. FMI) but, 'were not aligned to the key election pledges . . . and did not include targets, which would make it difficult to demonstrate measurable improvements in public services' (Panchamia and Thomas 2014, p. 47). The substitution of a complex set of reporting documents based on different institutional linkages and requirements in the planning, control and reporting cycle was a new direction for a performance framework.[5]

The PSAs were linked to spending reviews, the first being the 1998 Comprehensive Spending Review which examined resources for each field of expenditure and the related service delivery in order to integrate a multi-year policy perspective with a budgetary process. Linking resources to objectives and performance standards and creating the opportunity to transfer unused budgets to the next year, increased incentives to focus on efficiency and effectiveness. Further spending reviews occurred mainly at two- or three-year intervals.

The PSA system underwent several iterations between 1998 and 2007. Departments had a PSA, a two-yearly agreement with the Treasury consisting of an aim, objectives, performance targets, value-for-money targets, and a responsibility statement. They were operationalised through plans for reaching targets and reported to the Cabinet Office and the Treasury on implementation. They were presented to a cabinet committee, but not to parliament or the public. The PSA was 'a novel and ambitious tool' for bringing central government under a performance framework (James 2004, pp. 398, 400). Limitations were frequent changes to targets, use of presentation strategies for blame avoidance, unclear objectives and weak incentive effects on priorities (James 2004). The Treasury made limited use of departments' performance reports (Talbot 2010). The PSA evolved, and was simplified (fewer PSAs and targets), enhanced (joint targets), and linked to spending reviews, which resulted in 'strengthening coordination processes between resource input, policy making and delivery' (James and Nakamura 2013, p. 1).

Departmental business plans (DBPs) were introduced by the Cameron Coalition to provide democratic accountability and to hold departments centrally accountable for implementing the reform programme. Each plan addressed the Coalition's priorities and programme for the department, focusing on areas that the government could control in contrast to 'aspirational outcomes' (Stephen et al. 2011, pp. 8–9). Issues about usability were apparent, including ambiguity with the data, format inconsistencies, and difficulties with accuracy, analysis and comparability (Institute for Government 2011a, 2011b). No evidence plans were being used by the Cabinet Office, and the prime minister was not systematically tracking reform progress, indicating that the political link was lost (Institute for Government 2012). The business plans were not serviceable for measuring performance for many departments (Bull et al. 2013).

The DBPs were replaced in 2015 by a new business planning and performance management system, single departmental plans (SDPs) that were designed for reporting on key priorities, crosscutting goals spanning departments and departmental day-to-day business. Oversight bodies observed the lack of a 'cross-government approach to business planning, no clear set of objectives, no coherent set of performance measures and serious concerns about the quality of data that was available . . . quite apart from the gap in public transparency' (NAO 2016b, 12; see also CPA 2016b). The government argued that these processes added up to a management system. The contrary position was that the 'collection of processes does not amount to the coherent strategic framework for planning and managing public sector activity . . . and that without such a framework the way government plans and manages its business will not be able to tackle the pervasive problems it faces' (NAO 2016b, p. 7). The SDPs were judged to be potentially a step forward, but their effectiveness remained untested, and the need for significant further development was officially recognised (CPA 2016c). Priorities of departments were 'vague statements of intent or platitudinous aspirations', the link between priorities and resources was tenuous and there remained 'weak incentives to prioritise, make realistic plans and consider long-term value' (NAO 2018c, p. 12; PACAC 2018, p. 16).

OTHER PERFORMANCE INSTRUMENTS

In addition to the generic performance management framework, each country had developed specialised ongoing and ad hoc whole-of-government instruments for pursuing performance by the 2000s. Many efficiency reviews are not subject to public reporting and do not qualify here. Where they are economy exercises, they also fall outside this consideration.[6] The Canadian case is unusual in relying on the Management Accountability Framework as more of an omnibus approach (without precluding other more specialised instruments).

Implementation/delivery and results. Results and government priorities agenda are reflected in implementation/delivery units: (e.g. the UK's PMDU), minister-led cross-departmental priorities, such as those resulting from the New Zealand's Better Public Services report (BPSAG 2011), and the UK's cabinet taskforces.

Executive performance. The development of secretary performance assessment has been an element, often important, in the panoply of performance instruments. All Anglophone systems have some form of performance assessment for department heads. Of the four, the Australian arrangement appears to have been less developed, and scepticism has been expressed about the significance of the exercise even where a formalised process exists as in Canada (Aucoin 2008 on Canada). There is also ambiguity about its purpose where a remuneration component is central. Is the system about rewards for good performance or judgements about the extent to which public service leaders have achieved predetermined objectives? There is also a possible underlying sanction entailing career prospects other than short-term rewards (Podger 2007).

Canada has formalised guidelines for deputy ministers, which have existed in some form since at least the early 2000s (Fleury 2002; Privy Council Office 2015). The Privy Council Office's (2015) performance guidelines for deputy ministers, reads prima facie as a compensation plan that includes performance pay (presumably reflecting its origins in reports from 1998 of the Advisory Committee on Senior Level Retention and Compensation). Performance Agreements are made between the clerk of the Privy Council Office (PCO) and the deputy minister, comprised of commitments in the results areas of policy and programme management (as specified by the Management Accountability Framework), leadership and corporate, and associated measurements.

New Zealand redefined the relationship between ministers and departmental chief executives appointed on performance agreements, and associated outcomes with the former and outputs with the latter. The relationship was contractually based: the government purchased outputs from departments, while the government was defined as the owner with an interest in the return on its investment. The renamed CEOs, whose predecessors were permanent officials, held contract appointments based on performance agreements and their performance was evaluated. The State Services Commission has been responsible for performance agreements of chief executives which constitute a cornerstone of performance management. The Commissioner has appointed, employed and reviewed the performance of chief executives, including the achievement of results and the investment in organisational capability. The

SSC refocused this performance management responsibility from a retrospective compliance emphasis to a 'proactive approach focused on management that achieves results' (SSC 2006; Scott 2016).

Permanent secretary objectives have been used in the United Kingdom for the performance management of the most senior civil servants. The objectives of each permanent secretary are agreed with ministers and the prime minister, and have been publicly available since 2012. They are reviewed annually by the cabinet secretary (or the head of the civil service, where that position has existed). The 2015–16 objectives covered four priorities: strategic, business, diversity, and personal leadership (previous objectives had included cross-government working, civil service reform and capability). There were also generic responsibilities: contributing to the corporate leadership of the civil service and supporting civil service reform (but for issues about permanent secretary objectives, see Freeguard et al. 2017).

Organisational capabilities. A focus on management capability addresses the performance of particular skills. Capability reviews have been used in Australia and the United Kingdom, and Performance Improvement Frameworks (PIFs) in New Zealand. The Canadian MAF (see below) has an integral capability element. Capability reviews have been discontinued in Australia and the United Kingdom; self-assessments have been used in both countries and critiqued in the UK as a poor variant. New Zealand continued to make use of its adapted version, PIFs, which have also had a more explicit performance aspect (School of Government 2017).

Management Accountability Framework (MAF). Canada's MAF is in many respects in a class of its own. It has existed for over 20 years and is subject to regular reviews and revisions. Unlike the other countries, the MAF has entailed a top-down system of monitoring and compliance by the Treasury Board Secretariat. There has been a strong performance element to the framework. MAF 'is more audit and process-based' (Dean 2009, p. 31). It has been used to comprehensively assess departmental performance for ten areas: governance and strategic direction, values and ethics, people, policy and programme, citizen-focused service, risk management, stewardship, accountability, results and performance, and learning, innovation and change management. The Treasury Board of Canada Secretariat (TBS) has compiled annually a wide range of indicators to evaluate MAF reports and to overview and assess the quality of management and key systems of departments. It is guided by a framework, 'a high-level model of the attributes of a "well-performing" public sector organisation, but MAF increasingly has the look and feel of a quality assurance and risk management assessment system' (Lindquist 2009, pp. 49, 56). The value of MAF has continued to be hazy (and debated) given the transaction costs. It has provided an instrument for monitoring departmental performance and MAF results do feed into deputy ministers' assessments

(Lindquist 2017), but the data is not as freely available as alternative instruments, the regulatory compliance aspect lingers despite modifications over time, and the level of learning and application of that knowledge at the central and departmental levels has not been clearly established. MAF is part of an extensive oversight system of instruments (including plans and priority reports, performance reports, internal audit groups, programme evaluations, and Office of the Auditor General (OAG) reports) which according to the auditor general existed to prevent the Phoenix fiasco but did not (SSCNF 2018).

Corporate performance assessment. New Zealand has used the annual Administrative and Support Services Benchmarking (BASS) exercise since 2010 for systematising information about corporate services. It has provided agencies with performance information on expenditure on back office services, consistent performance data across agencies and an 'evidence base' for performance assessment.[7] It was pitched as a benchmarking analysis to assist agencies with achieving efficiencies by using targets. Initial improvements were not sustained for a small sample of agencies suggesting that the instrument was not driving performance improvement (Bonner 2014). System-level impacts were modest, and the degree of comparability was unclear (Bonner 2014; Henderson 2014). The published document provides transparency for performance information.

Programme evaluation. The use of evaluation has been highly variable in the Anglophone systems, which have not been responsive to renewed international interest in a central role, with one exception. An outcomes approach requires measurement based on evaluation (Hughes and Smart 2012). For Australia, evaluation was a component in the management cycle and a crucial element in 1980s managing for results because it linked policy development and programme implementation (Keating and Holmes 1990, p. 174; Halligan and Power 1992, pp. 103–104; Di Francesco 1998). Following an experiment with mandatory programme evaluation there have been over two decades of indifference to evaluation except for a few departments. Some form of evaluation advocacy and capacity at the centre has been argued for by experts who took a system viewpoint, but the lack of departmental agreement meant nothing emerged, although an independent review (Alexander and Thodey 2018) has supported greater use. In New Zealand evaluation has also been essentially a departmental responsibility, and several have had evaluation capacities (Scott 2016, p. 5). The use of evaluation for policy advice processes has been limited compared to other countries (Scott et al. 2010). UK evaluation was at a low ebb prior to 1997 (Talbot 2010, p. 12). Since then 'some progress' has occurred, although doubts exist about whether it produced meaningful learning, and the obstacles to quality evaluation were substantial (NAO 2010; Hallsworth et al. 2011).

The exception has been the central government of Canada, which has had a long history of mandatory evaluation with formalised arrangements through the Treasury Board Secretariat (Shepherd 2016). Under the TBS's policy, all programmes were to be reviewed every five years. Departments were expected to maintain 'a robust, neutral evaluation function' (TBS 2016b). The impact of this formal process remains unclear, although 'the track record . . . in assessing management performance or evaluating the impact of government's policies and programs has not lived up to expectations' (Savoie 2011, p. 163). The growth of the evaluation industry is problematic and programme evaluation is about 'turning a crank that's not attached to anything' (Savoie 2014, p. 149).

Cross-cutting programme performance. New Zealand's Better Public Services is arguably the best documented exercise at the sub-system level (see Chapter 8). The concept of a leadership superstructure overlaying several departments in pursuit of defined objectives is not new (although it, like other international experiments, has not been durable: Peters 2015).

PERFORMANCE FRAMEWORKS IN FLUX?

There was an ever-growing catalogue of weaknesses in performance management by the third decade of the reform era that were not resolved by framework development (Radin 2006; Bouckaert and Halligan 2008; Van Dooren and Hoffmann 2017), which need not be reproduced here beyond noting the most salient and intractable issues. Practice generally fell short of aspirations, and significant questions remained about the quality and use of performance information in the budget process, internal decision-making, relevance of external reporting, political relevance and the variable engagement of departments and agencies. The limitations of country approaches included questions about the effectiveness of their frameworks, particularly a compliance emphasis focused on external reporting rather than other objectives. Performance management systems were regularly modified to improve operability, but their effectiveness was undermined by tardiness in and reluctance to modify the framework, and churn (in the case of the United Kingdom). Common features were disconnects between outputs and outcomes, internal planning and reporting, and reconciling demand and supply of performance information (i.e. what politicians want) (Flynn 2007; Bouckaert and Halligan 2008; Talbot 2010; Gill 2011a; Edwards et al. 2012; Burnham and Horton 2013; NAO 2016b).

Outcomes and outputs. All management frameworks have featured outputs and outcomes in some form. Both Australia and New Zealand were talking outcomes in the 1980s, but their paths diverged. New Zealand identified outcomes with ministers and outputs with chief executives, with a performance agreement between them. This was perceived in Australia as institutionalising the separation of policy and delivery, a perennial issue in public administration. In contrast, Australia wished to bring them together as part of FMIP, but ambiguity, even blurring, remained as to responsibilities (Holmes 1989). In the long term neither approach was sustained. The outcomes side remained underdeveloped or unresolved, eventually being either assigned to politicians or overshadowed by an output focus. New Zealand's 'managing for outcomes' approach was discontinued because performance measures lacked the rigour of those for outputs (Hughes and Smart 2012, p. 6). The inclination in New Zealand was to reject outcomes in favour of some form of results. Australia eventually opted for 'programmes' instead of outputs. As mentioned in Chapter 5, performance management capability in the United Kingdom has been poor with respect to performance measurement for developing 'outcome-based and longer-term indicators' (NAO 2016b, p. 35). The UK Treasury has acknowledged the challenge of moving from inputs to outputs to outcomes, and inputs have continued to be a focus reflecting the central agency's role in public spending and because manifestos have focused on levels of expenditure (CPA 2018, Q23).

Quality of performance information. UK oversight agencies, like counterparts elsewhere, have long had issues with the quality of performance information. Insufficient information was provided 'to hold departments to account for all costs, outcomes and value for money on both the coalition agreement and across all of a department's work' (CPA 2011, p. 4; NAO 2016b, p. 24). The Committee of Public Accounts found no improvements, concluding that AOs lacked the cost and performance data required for undertaking effective oversight. This was regarded as a long-standing problem as the National Audit Office had previously reported that 'variation in the scope and completeness of information currently available limited its ability to inform public choice and accountability' (NAO 2016b, p. 24). The Canada Revenue Agency misrepresented its performance in dealing with taxpayers: 'Too often . . . performance measures do not reflect the actual performance' (OAG 2017; SSCNF 2018).

Decoupling of functions. The decoupling of functions – outcomes and outputs – from operational practice (Dormer and Gill 2010) was a commonplace response to central performance management systems. The frontline may be either disengaged from the senior management's preoccupation with outputs and outcomes that was expected at the whole-of-government level, or reflective of departmental operating principles.

Australian departments went through the routine of producing the material for reporting purposes but were inclined to rely on their own internal planning for operational matters under the second model, while the third framework sought to integrate performance and internal corporate reports. One dimension was organisational incentives. The performance framework did not require departments to integrate their own internal planning processes with the performance process, which was an external imposition. Consequently, the two processes were run in parallel. Priority was given to external reporting, while performance information was not generally made use of for internal purposes. Since the incentives didn't exist for departments to apply the framework for their own purposes, there was insufficient attention given to organisational culture, and the embedding of performance. The inclination of departments to deviate from performance management frameworks has been long argued for by the Australian National Audit Office (McPhee 2005; Bouckaert and Halligan 2008).

Targetism. The use of targets has been commonplace but pursued with particular zeal in the UK. The fixation on targetism under Blair extended from the composition of Public Service Agreements with departments, mainly defined in terms of outputs and outcomes, to delivery organisations operating under tough sanctions for missing targets, such as threats of job loss, agency termination and publicity of results (Flynn 2007). In New Zealand, achieving results through targets became simply another control function (Gill 2011a).

Performance in Canada became 'the product of many hands, from the political level down to the most junior front-line worker. There was no incentive for public servants to draw attention to problems, to explain what has gone wrong, or to suggest why performance targets may not be realistic'. Savoie quotes Michael Warnick (then deputy minister and later a clerk of the PCO) who reported that departments dealt with central agency demands by producing 'fake stuff', which is 'the stuff you pretend to do that you feed to the central agencies to get them off your back' (Savoie 2011, p. 160).

Use of information. Who uses performance information and why is it not used (Van Dooren et al. 2015)? A range of factors have contributed to the mixed use of performance information (e.g. the standard problems with devising indicators for outcomes), the organisational level performance gaps derived in the first instance from the design and implementation of the framework, and the inability of political and public service leadership to respond to the weaknesses. This situation can be argued to be a consequence of a combination of an NPM-type solution and the political nexus that is diffident about the role of central leadership in performance management.

Pollitt (2006) pointed out that research has rarely focused on the 'end users' of performance information in the traditional model of representative democracy (i.e. ministers, parliamentarians and citizens), and that if they used performance information it would, 'constitute the definitive justification for the practices of evaluation, performance management and performance audit as components of a *democratic* polity, rather than as merely an artefact of technocratic administration' (p. 38).

More generally, the use of performance information to underpin budgeting has long been an unfulfilled objective, although it may inform certain aspects (Cangiano et al. 2013). Politicians have four types of response in which they can either opt out or in on their own terms.[8] The first is for politicians to regard departmental performance as a responsibility that is delegated to public service leaders. Performance information is used for compliance purposes and accountability, learning and management improvement. Politicians may play an indirect role through involvement in formal evaluation of public service leaders. The second is for politicians to engage with performance information, but this either occurs at a general policy level (ministers signing off on legislation) or through a parliamentary committee charged with performance oversight. Politicians may also operate as either an executive minister (see Chapter 3) or a concerned parliamentarian with strong performance interests, but these roles do not necessarily cover regular attention to performance information. Several studies have indicated a limited use of performance information in Anglophone parliaments. Australian parliamentarians used performance information infrequently, but reportedly more than Canadian counterparts (Thomas 2009). It has been argued that senate review processes serve the purposes of financial accountability, but performance information is not generally apparent in estimate and standing committee hearings, and reference to performance information is scant in both houses of parliament (Bowrey et al. 2015; Smith 2015).

Under a third alternative, politicians redefine formal performance management systems for their own purposes, such as government results and priorities. The numerous attempts to improve the supply-side involving the quality and relevance of information have either been inadequate or insufficient to make a difference with politicians' use of performance information. Instead, a demand-led process is employed to engage politicians directly (perhaps incorporating supply-side adjustments). The UK focus on political objectives is the clearest case (see discussion of SDPs above). The fourth response is to substitute alternative instruments for performance monitoring and evaluation. This can take the form of cabinet committees driving the implementation of performance in a priority or cross-ministry area and/or the use of cross-ministry structures to address significant societal issues. High profile cases entail performance information about progress towards targets agreed to by politicians.

RENEWAL THROUGH PLANNING AND PRIORITIES?

The four systems have followed different pathways within a performance management framework. Their early implementation styles differed in terms of conceptions of the relationship between outputs and outcomes, the responsibilities given to chief executives, and the roles of the central personnel agency in handling performance oversight. There continue to be differences in approach and with the treatment of outcomes and outputs. Several generations of performance management provided extensive experience of potential limitations.

The management discipline, efficiencies and accountabilities achieved under these frameworks sustain commitment and the quest for system improvements in managing performance.

Three of the frameworks have undergone recent transformations: Australia's third framework formally incorporates business planning, Canada's two-level results focus combines the revised performance management framework of the TBS with a political overlay for driving the focus through the Privy Council Office. The UK approach has had the most discontinuity and poor public articulation although ambitious and multi-purpose. In the case of New Zealand, the inability to move from an entrenched focus on output accountability, which served the system well for efficiency purposes, left the framework otherwise unserviceable (Morrison 2014; NAO 2016b; Gold 2017). For some time 'the language of outcomes was replaced by results. Results in this context were effectively bite-sized pieces of an outcome (similar to what was previously called intermediate outcomes)'. The government wanted 'tangible progress towards its larger objectives, which in effect was a renaming of outcome indicators' (Morrison 2014, p. 47). A switch back to outcomes has occurred under the Jacinda Ardern government.

The dissatisfaction with obtaining results through outputs and outcomes has not led to a focus on results instead of outcomes. The knitting together of performance with planning and/or priorities caters for different purposes. The expansion of purposes means that distinctions could be made between keeping to the basics and more comprehensive schemes.

The later part of the 2010s has been a time of evolution and experiments with frameworks in all four countries, with the level of change and other details not necessarily yet publicly available. With that caveat in mind, several dimensions are distinguished in Table 6.1. In terms of purposes, all systems provide for formal accountability, and usually some measure of internal department planning, with the level of central control variable. Results are more formally recognised in two countries for the whole-of-government framework.

Framework stability and continuity across governments have been apparent in three cases, the exception being the United Kingdom. Attention to fundamentals for planning, managing and changing priorities has been lacking in the UK's SDP framework: 'Government needs a proper framework for planning to the medium term and beyond, that will allow it to make achievable plans, and to understand what it needs to know to stay on track. This framework should be stable and enduring, existing independent of political priorities' (NAO 2016b, p. 6).

The stakeholder approach was generally focused, but the UK's aspirations were more broadly conceived. The SDP framework was designed by the Cabinet Office and HM Treasury 'to cover a large number of different stakeholders' needs, by capturing for the first time the whole range of departments'

Table 6.1   *Dimensions of frameworks*

	Australia	Canada	New Zealand	United Kingdom
1. Purposes	Focused	Multiple	Focused	Comprehensive
Planning	Yes	Yes	Yes	Yes
Priorities	In development	Still evolving	In selected areas	Still evolving
2. Stakeholders	Focused Formally broader	Focused	Focused	Broad in concept
3. Stability	Yes, but evolved	Yes, overlay	Yes, but evolving	Changeable in
Continuity across	Yes	effects unclear	Yes	2010s
governments		Yes, but augmented		No
4. Cross-government	Limited provision	Unclear	Recent experience	Unfulfilled so far
5. Evaluation	Left to depts	Central role	Left to depts	Left to depts

aims and objectives including departmental commitments, cross-department goals, day-to-day service delivery, business transformation programmes and efficiency improvements' (NAO 2016b, p. 14). It was subsequently judged to require a range of changes without which, 'government will continue to be trapped in a cycle of short-termism, over-optimism and silo decision-making, which creates real risks to value for money' (NAO 2018c, p. 13).

The greater interest of political executives in results and priorities has varied between countries. It has also been underpinned by the stronger role of the prime minister's department in performance management (e.g. the Privy Council Office in Canada and the Cabinet Office in the UK). Of the others, there is relatively limited cross-government activity. Evaluation was mainly a matter for departments.

PERFORMANCE SYSTEM?

The performance system consists of the core framework, and other possibly complementary, instruments with a public identity working towards common objectives or a specific dimension of performance. This approach goes beyond the conventional focus on the performance management framework that provides the centrepiece for measuring and reporting on performance. The specialised instruments may be ongoing or ad hoc, and public or private, although lack of information about the latter reduces their import here. To operate as a system two features are required: there needs to be a conscious focus on system performance, which raises questions about who has formal rights for steering (Talbot 2008); and attention to the interaction between the different instruments as dimensions of the system. These two criteria are not necessarily

Table 6.2   Performance 'system' by country and performance instrument ownership

	Prime minister's dept. (CO, DPMC, PCO)	Finance, TBS, Treasury	State Services Com.
Australia	• Secretary performance • Priorities and implementation	• Performance framework	
Canada	• Performance framework* • Deputy minister performance • Results and delivery	• Performance framework* • Capability (MAF) • Program evaluation	
New Zealand	• Implementation (BPS)*	• Performance framework• Implementation (BPS)* • BASS	• Results (BPS)* • Chief exec. performance • Performance improvement framework^
United Kingdom	• Secretary performance • Implementation	• Performance framework • Efficiency review	

* Joint PCO/TBS OR SSC/Treasury/SSC. BPS until discontinued in 2018.
^ DPMC/Treasury/SSC.

realised. Performance instruments are usually owned by individual central agencies (although less so now in the case of the performance framework), and much depends on how corporate the systems are (see Appendix 3) (Table 6.2). System performance has been writ large in Canada and New Zealand. Canada has long maintained a national performance structure at least on paper and in rhetoric. New Zealand has had performance at the forefront of its goals (as articulated by the SSC and Treasury).

New Zealand has maintained its core performance management framework but worked around and beyond its limitation to address performance more systematically at several levels. Two types of selective performance have been developed, the performance improvement framework (PIF) focused on the organisational level, and the Better Public Service (BPS) approach on cross-departmental priorities. The chief executive assessments have evolved as a central performance instrument. There was also the annual BASS exercise for systematising information about corporate services. Unlike the other systems, an implementation/delivery unit has not been used in New Zealand (although arguably similar results may be accomplished through the other instruments). A conscious focus on system performance has been apparent. The PIF program, 'a key artefact in the performance management toolkit' for monitoring organisational performance in the public sector (Allen and Eppel 2017), has been maintained for seven years, and is regarded as successful, although the decline in reviews suggests that it may be tapering off (School of Government 2017). The BPS yielded results for ten priorities and was renewed and then discontinued by a new government.

New Zealand has had a more conscious approach to using a range of performance instruments, although the elements in its system of performance were not linked effectively (Allen and Eppel 2017). The centrality and strength of the State Services Commissioner's role is such that the performance agreement has been depicted as the 'main vehicle of performance management, rather than performance budgeting' (Shand and Norman 2005, p. 22). The performance improvement framework was designed to assist leadership of performance improvement in departments by identifying gaps and opportunities in current and future capability and performance (School of Government 2017).

Australia has focused on enhancing its core framework. The capability review programme ran for four years but was not followed through. Efficiency reviews have since been conducted as part of a contestability programme, but these were designed as covert operations, with their veracity not subject to public scrutiny. An implementation unit was used from the early 2000s but discontinued in 2016. Departmental secretaries have been subject to an annual 'discussion', but the methodology now includes assessments against leadership capabilities and stakeholder feedback (APSC 2018, p. 113). There was awareness of other ad hoc options for performance measurement, but they were inclined to be 'soft' instruments, such as benchmarking, evaluation and surveys, advocated because key performance indicators (KPIs) were incomplete (Halton 2015). The United Kingdom's system was depicted in terms of 'the performance management machinery of PSAs and PMDU' when they co-existed (Panchamia and Thomas 2014, p. 58). The capability review programme was innovative in the second half of the 2000s but didn't survive a change of government. Political intervention produced targetism, but also established a precedent whereby the framework changes almost with governments. The scope of the SDP is broad and can be envisaged as an expanding centre point, but a strategic framework and performance system was still missing (NAO 2016b). Canada's Management Accountability Framework is more of an omnibus approach, which provides a stronger monitoring and guidance role than elsewhere. The new results process promises to add a new dimension, and the Canada Performance focus is also original.

These performance instruments can be represented as being part of a system. It makes sense to go beyond the core framework because much lies outside it. Performance instruments can be designed for distinctive purposes (e.g. accountability to parliament or implementing government priorities). However, there is a question as to what extent the centre operates corporately in using levers for modulating and strengthening systemic performance (and there are issues in seeking to steer performance systems: Talbot 2008).

CONCLUSION

Bearing in mind the introductory questions, how has this uneven record been worked through? Performance management frameworks have neither gelled nor become durable as multi-purpose fixtures. The 2010s have been a decade of experimentation with instruments for improving performance. What form of performance is appropriate is not amenable to a consistent answer beyond the basic requirement of satisfying a public accounting for results against objectives. In responding to multiple objectives and stakeholder expectations, two polar options are to rely either on an omnibus document (more like the UK) or several instruments (the New Zealand way). The purposes of performance remain unresolved, particularly where they are subject to turnover with governments. This is where managerialism meets politicisation as politicians take control where solutions falter and implement priorities.

The place of 'results' in the overall scheme of things remains a conundrum. Performance has become more focused on achieving political agendas. The framework is likely these days to be skewed in that direction rather than serving the needs of departments or the public, although the former is catered for if the renewed emphasis on business planning works. However, inflexibilities are still present, and the cross-departmental aspect problematic.

The 'performance system' has been used to denote the clusters of instruments used and represent mixtures of ongoing components plus short-term exercises. To what extent they operate as a system is dependent on design questions and the attention given by a corporate centre to systemic questions and impacts of performance.

To what extent have the four countries devised stable performance instruments to provide the information expected by stakeholders? One has persisted with progressive iterations of a core framework (Australia). Two have worked round limitations with the framework overlaying a results reporting facility (Canada and the United Kingdom); or retained a narrowly focused framework and parallel arrangements, which has prompted use of instruments for specific purposes (New Zealand). The UK has opted for regularly replacing the framework, and while its ambitious 'road map' remains unrealised, if successful it will provide a new model.

There have been long-term difficulties with engaging effectively with a performance approach. Frameworks take time to develop and implement, and perennial issues continue to resurface. All systems are working through new arrangements, the results of which remain unclear. What is apparent is the performance story is still in progress after over three decades and, without resolution of chronic issues, will remain a contested area.

NOTES

1. See Talbot (2008) for the problems with levels of analysis in performance regimes. The matter of delivery under differently structured governments was raised in Chapter 1.
2. Recent examples are Taylor 2009, 2011.
3. There was also a renewed emphasis on cash accounting; and improvements to cash management, budgeting and programme reporting and financial information systems.
4. For the rationale for outputs, see Scott 2001.
5. The Output and Performance Analysis eventually played a submerged role.
6. Such reviews had performance implications. Australian functional reviews were concerned inter alia with the identification of barriers to performance (Cormann 2015).
7. See http://www.treasury.govt.nz/statesector/performance/bass.
8. These categories were clarified in discussions with colleagues at the University of Caligari: Patrizio Monfardini and Alessandro Spano.

7. Management and bureaucracy in a political milieu

Management reform was meant to produce 'debureaucratisation' under which public servants acquired the freedom to manage without being overly constrained by inflexible procedures and the red tape of traditional public administration (Aucoin 1990; Hoggett 1997; Gregory 2001). As discussed in Chapter 5, there was difficulty realising this ideal because a single-minded focus on results had costs and unintended consequences. This chapter takes up the story from a bureaucratic perspective: given the association of government organisation with bureaucracy, how could some reliance on rules and regulation be evaded (Wilson 1994)? But the central question here is about *excessive* dependence on rules and regulation, and how bureaucratisation becomes salient.

The analysis examines questions about the conditions under which reforms are enacted. Several parallel and interrelated conditions that were seemingly anti-managerialist in nature became most publicly apparent in the twenty-first century. They included regulation of the 'red tape' variety, a risk-averse culture, mounting political control, and heightened internal and external scrutiny. Factors that influence risk culture include political control, levels of formalisation and red tape, and incentive structures (Bozeman and Kingsley 1998).

The central argument is that unintended consequences were engendered by managerialism and politicisation, and that over time bureaucratisation became entrenched with the accumulation of rules and layers of regulation. The chapter examines the incidence of rules and regulations in the four countries with attention to cases of over-reliance, typified as red tape. Secondly, it reviews the factors that accounted for the excessive use of rules and regulation, both ad hoc and systemic: intensification of risk-averse behaviour, political control, and the multiplication of accountability, oversight and public scrutiny. The third consideration is the consequences of bureaucratisation for core aspirations of managerialism, incentives and innovation (Pollitt 2016), and its impact on the public management system.

CONTROL, RISK AND CULTURE

The nature of rules and regulations in public management systems is affected by a range of internal and external factors. The external factors cover environmental changes that result in a mismatch of skills and needs that produces red tape (Walker and Brewer 2009) and includes both complex policy questions (e.g. the UK's Brexit) and cataclysmic events; fiscal austerity that leads to budgetary cutbacks; technological change; and the intensification of the public scrutiny of government. The institutional contexts within which public servants operate are based on the configuration of roles and operating routines for ministers, central agencies, oversight agencies, departmental cultures and the embedded logics of management systems.

'Over-control' is the main reason for 'rule-inception red tape' (in contrast to 'rule-evolution red tape: Bozeman and Feeney 2011) and assumes managerial and political forms that are discussed separately because they differ in terms of cause and effect. Four factors have been identified as highly significant.

On the management side, the reliance on formal rules (formalisation) is a frequent response to ambiguity and uncertainty, and highly rule-bound organisations are more likely to produce red tape (Bozeman and Feeney 2011). The evolving nature of managerialism produces a greater use of contracting and performance, the first inserting another layer of accountability and oversight for departments; the second imposing new reporting requirements on managers (Hoggett 1997; Bozeman and Feeney 2011). Important were the inconsistencies between managerialist conceptions and real-life applications.

Political 'over-control' affects most public organisations to some extent and is a second factor influencing risk culture and the level of risk engagement (Bozeman and Kingsley 1998; Walker and Brewer 2009; Bozeman and Feeney 2011). Systems characterised by increasing politicisation (Peters and Pierre 2004b, 2004c) and new political governance (Aucoin 2012) display strong political control, which affects the incentives of officials and therefore the level of risk aversion. Individuals and organisations adopt 'defensive routines' as buffers from environmental threats (Argyris 1990).

Oversight and scrutiny make up the third factor. The reformed systems inherited existing accountability systems, which have since been augmented in response to public management reform and as new issues lead to extensions to oversight. The multiplicity of accountabilities has been a characteristic of the reform era (Mulgan 2003; Halligan 2007d; Doern et al. 2014).

Fourthly are the rules arising from implementation and evolution, which have been termed 'rule-evolution' red tape (Bozeman and Feeney 2011). One contributory factor is the unintended consequences of organisational processes of change that have a cumulative impact. Incremental change emerges 'in the "gaps" or "soft spots" between the rule and its interpretation or the rule and its enforcement' (Mahoney and Thelen 2010, p. 14). One type of gradual change is 'layering' (Mahoney and Thelen 2010). Rule drift may result from inadvertent changes to the meaning or intent of rules created in the past by 'organisational phantoms' (Bozeman and Feeney 2011, p. 63). When these individual actions become standard operating routines, they affect the culture of a field and, if pervasive, the public management system.

INTERNAL REGULATION AND RED TAPE

Regulation involves the use of rules for influencing or requiring specific behaviours within government that entails some measure of compliance. Such use of rules is not in itself problematic, but the excessive use of and reliance on regulation is, and is commonly termed red tape. There are methodological questions about how red tape is handled in official documents, in part because the term can be loosely employed to cover a range of defects. The analysis may lack sophistication and necessary compliance may not be clearly differentiated from negative red tape (cf. Bozeman and Feeney 2011). What is important is that there is a strong and consistent official diagnosis, and that red tape is creating problems not readily resolved.

The regulatory patterns over time are represented here as consisting of two generations that exhibit some differences. The first covers the impact of managerialist and regulatory reforms in the late twentieth century, particularly financial, performance and contract management, and the early awakening to the contradictions in reform agendas. An increase in regulation was observed in the United Kingdom (Hoggett 1997; Hood et al. 1999) and as a result of performance requirements in New Zealand (see Chapter 5). Oversight regulation within government increased during the first two decades of reform although much of this activity involved sub-national functions and local government (Hood et al. 1999, although fields covered are less relevant at the national level in federal systems). Risk aversion was identified as resulting from fear of failure in the civil service culture and was regarded as excessive (Cabinet Office 1999).

In the second-generation, long-running red tape cases were extensively identified and documented in Australia and Canada which indicated an entrenched problem. Red tape became an issue in all countries, but the focus was the regulation of external actors (including earlier initiatives: Harries and Sawyer 2014; Savoie 2015a). In the twenty-first century, governments became fixated on relieving the regulatory burden on business.

Prime Minister Cameron in the UK proclaimed that there were over 21,000 statutory rules and regulations in 2011 (without differentiating the good from the bad). The UK Civil Service Reform Plan (HM Government 2012) provided a superficial diagnosis (sclerotic, slow, process-focused, unnecessary activity) and announced that the regulatory burden in the public sector and its impact on the policy-making process in Whitehall would be addressed. However, the Red Tape Challenge concentrated on regulations affecting business and society.[1] The UK efforts appeared to be focused on the impact of regulation beyond the centre, such as Blair's concern with reducing red tape for general practitioners (Travers 2007). Such cases also apply in federal systems: take the Australian case of micromanaging delivery by third parties, in this case not-for-profits. The focus on reducing business regulation is relevant in that it is symptomatic of a mode of operating with internal implications. In the latter case, public servants' motivation was 'to avoid political risk on behalf of the ministers' by imposing 'red-tape standardisation' to reduce the agency's risk (Shergold 2013, p. 10; NZPC 2018). The Canadian federal government may have the record for micromanagement, accepting 60,000 reports annually from Aboriginal communities (Savoie 2011, p. 160).

The focus here is on documented cases of *systemic* internal red tape, and this is particularly evident in the two federal systems. This is not to say that red tape is not extensive in the unitary systems, only that it has not been as frequently and systemically documented, at least in the centre of government. For New Zealand, 35 per cent of public servants perceived a great deal of red tape, 46 per cent some red tape, and less than one-fifth no red tape (School of Government 2017, p. 19). There is also an indication that red tape is more commonly perceived by the private sector in federal than unitary systems (Kaufmann et al. 2018).

Debureaucratisation was central to early managerialist reform agendas in Australia, yet within two decades internal 'red tape' was diagnosed as an expression of a generalised condition (Shergold 2003). Five public inquiries have since addressed the issue in less than a decade, two mapping its growing incidence and three focusing solely on red tape. The first defined red tape as 'regulatory or administrative requirements that are unwarranted, ineffective or not the most efficient option for delivering the required outcome' (MAC 2007, p. 1), with procurement and recruitment identified as problem areas. A reform review derided red tape because it reduced agency agility and the capacity to achieve objectives and was regularly cited as an issue by public servants who specified the volume of regulatory and compliance requirements (AGRAGA 2010). In addition, finance departments mapped the level of red tape within the public service, identifying more than 2,000 legislative and administrative compliance requirements that applied to agencies.[2] A major challenge was identifying and paring red tape and regulations, according to a review of financial accountability (DFD 2012b, p. 3), which sought to understand the 'causes of regulatory creep and red tape', declaring that the compliance burden would increase if inaction persisted.

The position was deemed to be a whole-of-government matter by the most recent and definitive review with issues applying across the public service: regulation was excessive, inefficient, unclear, inaccessible, and embedded in a risk-averse culture. The level and volume of internal regulation was growing (covering more than 600 documents entailing 8,000 requirements) and had increased since the previous count five years earlier. The main regulators were the central agencies and agencies with cross-government jurisdictions. The inefficiencies derived from the scale of data collected and compliance reporting that involved duplication and wasted resources. A common issue was the level of ad hoc reporting on a specific task without a clear purpose. Confusing regulatory requirements created further problems because it was unclear whether compliance was mandatory, and meaningful guidance was lacking. Many practices existed that were not required for internal control purposes and added to the burden of process (Belcher 2015a, pp. 5, 9–15).

Canada had reviews ten years apart with the Web of Rules Action Plan (TBS 2009a, 2009c) and Blueprint 2020 being pursued in the interim. A reform agenda for Canada identified 'unnecessary levels of scrutiny and cumbersome processes' as an issue to address if Blueprint 2020 were to be realised: 'many rules and processes are overly complex, top-down, siloed, and lack coherence and consistency . . . [which] become internal red tape when they are perceived as unjustified, overly burdensome, and a hindrance to action or decisions' (Government of Canada 2014, p. 14).

Canada was earlier reported to have 'over 12,000 pages of personnel policies, with over 70,000 rules in the area of pay alone' (Desautels 1997). The management culture was depicted a decade later as one of over-control: 'the sheer complexity of the current "web of rules"' produced confusion with accountability and frustrated managers (TBS 2006, p. 44). Another decade later, a major review argued that red tape encompassed unclear rules and direction, policies and guidelines, poor client service by the central agency, process overload (too many steps and processes for simple tasks), burdensome policy and cumbersome technology. Transactions usually followed similar processes, regardless of the risk level, and available flexibilities were ignored. In this environment, services were secondary to process, and staff felt powerless. The problem areas were 'procurement, staffing, internal processes and approvals' and grants and contributions (TBS 2016a, pp. 3, 10–16).

RISK AVERSION

Risk aversion refers to the behaviour of ministers and public servants who seek to reduce uncertainty by choosing lower risk options and adopting measures or regulations that cover activities with compliance requirements. The perception of risk was similar across jurisdictions, for example damage to an organisation's reputation, political embarrassment, and failing to achieve objectives (NAO 2009). It was often closely related to red tape, the negative side of regulation. All countries had a problem with risk aversion: it had been deep-seated and systemic in Australia and Canada during the twenty-first century (Belcher 2015a, 2015b; TBS 2016a), and prevalent in the other countries (Hallsworth et al. 2011; Hood 2011; Morrison 2014; Brecknell 2016).

The striking feature in Australia was the pinpointing of the problem in major reviews by central agencies during the 2010s: the Blueprint for reform advocated reducing red tape because of excessive risk aversion (AGRAGA 2010); risk aversion was reported to be growing and dominating departmental culture (DFD 2012b); of 18 departmental capability reviews (2012–14), 72 per cent had 'significant levels of risk aversion' (Belcher 2015a, p. 19); and most recently, risk aversion was seen to be, 'deeply embedded in the psyche of Commonwealth officials, and . . . business practices' (Alexander and Thodey 2018, p. 19).

A culture of risk aversion was also reported by a Canadian review of red tape. This was most pronounced within staffing and more generally in human resources, with advisers tending to avoid high-risk staffing matters (TBS 2016a). An earlier report commented how frequent references were made to a 'risk-averse' management culture, which was expressed in regulations and written policies and in managers' expectations of staff (TBS 2006, pp. 15–16). In none of the other three systems was there the same preoccupation with risk aversion and this has continued until the late 2010s (Clarke 2019).

There were of course wide variations among departments in terms of their exposure to risk. All countries had cases of vulnerable agencies. The Australian Department of Immigration and Citizenship was 'heavily risk adverse' (APSC 2012a) because of the department's preoccupation with crisis (associated with highly political and contentious issues about how to handle illegal entry by boat people). (Compare the case of NZ's Department of Corrections discussed in Chapter 5 in Laking 2011; see also Ryan et al. 2011.)

Four sources of risk aversion have been identified: ministers concerned with media demands and a focus on the 'gotcha' behaviour (Doern et al. 2014), public scrutiny and electoral factors; central and oversight agencies' reporting and accountability demands on departments; fear of failure and external scrutiny; and senior management afflicted by politicians' angst and the public accountability framework and other staff afflicted by all the above (see Chapter 2 in Hood 2011 on the blame game).

Public Scrutiny, Failure and the Blame Game

Scrutiny of the public sector, especially by the media and parliament was generally greater than that for the private sector, which meant that decision-making processes in a 'politically charged environment' were affected by criticism about performance, regardless of the risk level. In the UK a succession of very public implementation failures with large projects raised questions about the government's ability to handle implementation and administration (PAC 2009, p. 18). One of two causes of Australian risk aversion was 'overreaction or a detrimental reaction to minor mistakes or embarrassment'; small and large failures, and strategic and operational failures, were not necessarily distinguished (Belcher 2015a, p. 19; see also DFD 2012a).

Different factors produced similar responses: public disapproval led the NZ Department of Corrections to adopt defensive practices (e.g. focusing on process) and to retreat into rules (Laking 2011). Perceived risks and failures in an Australian environment of increased risk aversion resulted in more rules, tighter controls and increased reporting (DFD 2012b); and mistakes induced staff to add checks and clearances, and to elevate decision-making (Belcher 2015a). Canadian central agencies responded to public scandals involving bureaucrats and politicians with new controls and reporting obligations (Savoie 2008).

Risk aversion in New Zealand was significant at the top among the ministers and their chief executives (BPSAG 2011). The continuing problems in Australian government were attributed either directly to politicians (Head of oversight agency, March 2013) or to perceptions of and anticipated reactions by senior public servants. Hyper-sensitive Australian ministers overreacted to media reports and exaggerated the impact of embarrassment and 'rage' against staff, including criticism and mockery over minor mistakes (Belcher 2015a, pp. 19, 22). The UK government's manoeuvres over the Windrush generation of Commonwealth citizens were symptomatic of the blame game (Johnstone 2018a; Moreton 2018).

Similarly, Canadian ministers indulged in public blaming of public servants for embarrassing new stories (Zussman 2016). The effectiveness of Canadian management was undermined by the deep permeation of 'fear of criticism or blame' (TBS 2006, pp. 15–16) and the 'error-free government' ethos of politicians (Clarke 2019). Canada's 'web of rules' was usually the result of knee-jerk reactions to crises requiring the government to have a remedy (Lépine 2007).

Fear of Audit

A major source of risk aversion was the fear of an audit by central or oversight agencies, with different types of agency nominated. Departmental processes and procedures were more elaborate and restrictive than required by the central agency policies of the Canadian Treasury Board or the Public Service Commission (PSC). Instead of using the flexibilities provided for in whole-of-government policies, departments interpreted and applied policy requirements in the strictest sense. Transactions often followed the same internal process, resulting in little activity, and outweighing the risk. This was most acute in human resources and focused on one central agency, the Public Service Commission. The fear of being discovered by PSC audits to be engaged in wrongdoing affected advice on staffing options and flexibilities. Fear of audit was repeatedly cited as the driver for increased procedures, demands for documentation and encouraging a risk-averse culture where functional groups had a policing function rather than a client service role (TBS 2016a).

In the United Kingdom, the activities of parliamentary oversight agencies, the Public Accounts Committee and the National Audit Office were perceived to be a significant deterrent to risk-taking because of the high profile given to failure in reports (Cabinet Office 2002). The impact of negative external coverage, even about isolated incidents, could intensify risk aversion. Frontline staff were concerned about innovation because it involved risk, and failure would impact on service users (NAO 2009).

ALL THEIR OWN WORK? REGULATORS IN ACTION

Regulators and managers have relied heavily on rules at central and departmental levels, sometimes for inexplicable reasons save that the culture or lackadaisical behaviour dictated such an approach. Regulation construction was commonly central agency-inspired and routinely by default: 'a first option response . . . without adequately examining the relative costs and benefits of alternative approaches' (DFD 2012b, p. 3; see also Savoie 2008); red tape for managing actual and perceived risk lacked 'a proportional approach to regulation' (Belcher 2015a, p. 9). Even where a principle-based approach was used, as in Australia's second performance management framework (see Chapter 6), controls were re-imposed in the form of inputs and 'front-end processes'. The framework became more compliance-focused and less applicable to performance and achieving results (DFD 2012b, p. 34).

The implementation of a deregulation agenda to reduce external red tape increased internal regulation within government that was inflexible and a compliance burden. Ironically, the Australian Red Tape Reduction Framework, focused on external regulation, required internal reporting annually and quarterly on deregulation compliance cost savings, and was deemed to be 'onerous, fragmented and duplicative'. Portfolios duplicated reporting information for both the centre and their own reports on deregulation (Belcher 2015b, pp. 101–102).

Departments were also complicit. Canada's Treasury Board policies made provision for flexibility in establishing reporting requirements for transfer payments and other aspects of policy affecting recipients. However, the intention was buried in the numerous requirements of a dense and inconsistent policy framework. As a result, the rules were poorly understood by departmental programme managers and even by Treasury Board officials. Although basic policy requirements remained stable, there was a perception that they were constantly changing because of perpetual adjustments to rule-related procedures and paperwork (TBS 2016a).

Departments were also inclined to self-inflict regulatory burdens. There were many cases of agencies engaging in unnecessary regulation. An example was the tendency of agencies to view policy guidance material from regulatory bodies, or Better Practice Guides from the ANAO, as setting the minimum standard for compliance, rather than as a source of useful information to inform the setting of internal procedures according to business needs and risk appetite. Some agencies imposed additional internal processes well in excess of the minimum requirements set by regulators, particularly in human resources and procurement (Belcher 2015a).

Another syndrome was dysfunction arising from managerial design that was not implemented. The Australian 'principles-based approach' was introduced as part of devolution to line departments of financial transaction management. This also applied to human resource management where Australia was listed as one of the most devolved systems (OECD 2017c). It meant that responsibility for regulating a substantial amount of activity dropped to the level of the department, but without accompanying guidelines. A significant process was the filling of the large gaps created when the centre vacated a space. By moving to principles and values as a basis for central frameworks, a vacuum was created. Internal deregulation had the effect of diffusing the handling of rules across the public service to a multitude of different agencies, which developed their own regulations in addition to the reimposed central rules. In Canada's less devolved system, responsibilities delegated from the Treasury Board Secretariat were not utilised, and also produced reregulation at the department level. The Public Service Commission, which continued to play direct and indirect roles in staffing well into the reform era (Juillet and Rasmussen 2008), moved towards a values-based approach to the staffing system. However, despite the Public Service Employment Act 2003, departmental managers were unable to consistently operationalise and apply the values (PSC 2011, p. 10).[3]

Organisational culture has not been adapted to accommodate the advent of risk approaches of modern public management (see Chapter 6); rather, an antipathy towards risk has been manifest. The culture of risk aversion was one of two causes of excessive internal regulation in Australia (Belcher 2015a). Similarly, Canadian departments were 'heavily rule-bound', and disinclined to use existing flexibilities because they were risk adverse (TBS 2016a, p. 32;

see also TBS 2006). Canada's management culture of over-control and the widespread acceptance of the complex 'Web of Rules', officially defined as 'the accumulation of unclear and overlapping rules, reporting requirements and inefficient business processes' (TBS 2009a), indicated the problems were systemic. The rule accumulation diminished programme efficiency and effectiveness, undermined accountability and management (TBS 2006, 2009c) and was so entrenched that staff became inured to their operating context.

In the United Kingdom, risk was affected in some cases by departmental procedures developed over a long time, which had in some cases become 'gold plated' to handle 'every conceivable circumstance and need however small or remote' (NAO 2004, p. 8). Similarly, the Australian financial framework developed by multiple processes over a long period became overly complex, and contained principles, rules and guidelines that were introduced to address specific issues at specific times. Organisations employed 'a wide range of inconsistent practices and processes' (DFD 2012b, p. 34).

MULTIPLE DEMANDS AND ACCOUNTABILITIES

The concern is with the 'totality of controls that defines the lived experience of the bureaucracy' (Garvey 1993, p. 200). Canada's provision for flexibility in establishing reporting requirements for transfer payments and other aspects of policy were 'lost in a mass of other admonitions and requirements and a policy framework so dense and inconsistent that the rules [were] poorly understood by departmental program managers and even by Treasury Board officials' (TBS 2006, p. 30). A difficulty in Canada was that 'a single action, in its various dimensions, can trigger a series of simultaneous accountability requirements to different parties with sometimes diverging points of view' (Bourgault 2014, p. 379; see also Clarke 2019). Similarly, New Zealand's chief executives were subject to multiple accountabilities as well as more complex roles and limited agenda control (James 2002).

A further dimension was overlapping requirements from different sources. The intersection of different demands on public servants was widely experienced as different professions and oversight agencies prescribed standards and requirements. The problem was that a combination of factors was often present. Thus, requirements for accounting, audit, legal and management overlapped significantly, thereby adding to complexity (for Australia, see DFD 2012b; cf. Hood et al. 2004). It was not just a matter of many deeply embedded requirements of agencies, but 'unproductive tensions between the conditions required for sound management, the political process and accounting for public resources' (DFD 2012b, p. 3). A New Zealand case study showed a 'department's "retreat into rules", of bureaucratisation from the top in response to conflict and ambiguity' (Ryan et al. 2011, p. 287).

Table 7.1   Changing environments and types of accountability for Australia

	Environment	Accountability type	Character of accountability
1970s	Traditional public administration	Hierarchical Ministerial responsibility Regulatory	Transaction control of inputs Political New administrative law, FOI
1980s	Management Political responsiveness	Accountability management Political control	Devolution and control Political intensifying over time
1990s	External/client focus Market/Competition Performance	Customer/client Contract management Performance	Customer choice; assurance Markets, contestability, Output/Outcome framework
2000s	Reclaiming central state	Centralised control, delivery Horizontal	Top-down direction Joined up; networks
2000s	New political governance	External	Media focus on short term

Source: Adapted from Halligan 2007d.

Accountability Layering

Accountability has been an evolving dimension across several decades of public sector reform as the environment of the public management system changed in distinctive ways. Associated with each major change has been an enlargement of accountability responsibilities from the traditional ministerial responsibility and bureaucratic hierarchy to cover inter alia successive new management, market and governance environments. Each experiment, however, had limitations and challenges that in turn engendered new responses. A paradox of accountability was that attempts to satisfy needs for control, reporting and scrutiny invoked new forms and variations on existing arrangements (Halligan 2007d). They led to the multiplication of mechanisms – of plurality in accountability (Mulgan 2003) – over time because each new element did not necessarily replace another, but instead added complexity, layers, ambiguity and conflict (Table 7.1).

The environment continued to change in quite distinctive ways across the reform era with major implications for accountability. The traditional focus on inputs and process was converted to a management environment emphasising outputs and results, and then to a market environment emphasising competitive elements (e.g. contestability), choice, outsourcing and contracts, and hybrid forms. Associated with each change in the environment was an extension of accountability responsibilities from the traditional core (i.e. minister and departmental hierarchy) that featured ministerial responsibility, to cover successively the 'new administrative law', accountability management, political responsiveness, markets and sharing accountability (Table 7.1). Accountability requirements were commonly entrenched in specific areas, often a specialised central agency making compliance demands (financial, human resources, procurement; central regulation unit). Some accountabilities were constantly significant in the landscape. Political control has been a dominant feature of the reform era as the range of measures was extended. The media's role featured more prominently with the advent of the 24-hour news cycle.

Countries had their own variations in forms and timing. The UK system was subject to supra-national EU requirements. New Zealand's accountability system was already highly complex in 1999 because of incremental additions over time and the growing detail and control (SSC 1999, p. 21). Canada's system had similar forms of accountability (plus the additional oversight following the Sponsorship scandal[4]), but a total of nine parliamentary watchdogs, also termed 'gotcha' agencies (Doern et al. 2014, p. 22; see also Pastré and Cain 2012; Savoie 2014). It also has a unique feature of internal oversight, the Management Accountability Framework, the most comprehensive and systemic form of internal accountability of the four countries. What began as a quality initiative in the early 1990s was transformed into a top-down performance system for monitoring and compliance. At one time, departments had to respond annually to as many as 134 lines of evidence for 41 areas of management (Lindquist 2009, p. 56).

Demands and Responses

The main components of the demands on, and the evasive and defensive responses of, the bureaucracy, are summarised in Table 7.2. The demands focus on those actions that provoke responses. The minister may engage in a range of blame avoidance behaviours (Hood 2011), most of which are not directly relevant here unless they impact on the functioning of departments for which they were responsible or on public servants. The burgeoning requirements from central agencies and oversight bodies has taken two forms: those which scrutinised performance and made public judgements that implied inadequacies, shortcomings or 'failure' (more usually oversight and parliamentary bodies); and those that represented a propensity of central agencies to default to rules as a policy lever.

At the department level push and pull are prevalent. Staff down the line are pleased to relinquish responsibility for routine decisions with a risk element to senior leaders, while the latter are prone to pulling up anything that hints of risk vulnerability. The result is that the tendency to centralise basic decisions is strong (and possibly to very senior levels). Otherwise the defensive routines are to adhere to rules and risk minimisation.

Table 7.2   *Effect of demands inside government*

Political/oversight demands	Ministerial/political	Central and oversight agencies/committees
	• Ministers' angst regarding external scrutiny and critique	• Central agencies prone to default to rules • Exposé and ambiguous oversight guidance • Parliamentary reviews focused on failure
Systemic effects	• Government/ministers' fears and priorities dominate	• Multiplicity of requirements • Layering of accountability
Agency response	Departmental top officials • Echo ministers' angst re risk and need to minimise failure • Centralised decision-making	Department operations • Push routine decisions up the hierarchy • Rules as defensive routines • Incremental accumulation from defaulting
Agency effects	• Sanctioning procedural layering and red tape	• Layering of procedures ('gold plating') • Risk aversion embedded in culture

Many of the processes discerned by institutionalists have been evident in the four countries: incremental accumulation from defaulting, automatic application of rules of uncertain value that originated in the past, and layering that was multifarious and built on rules from different generations of organisational development. The condition was so institutionalised in one jurisdiction that the 'web of rules' entered the official lexicon as something that was accepted because it could not readily be eradicated.

The pattern is therefore complex with the different components being mutually reinforcing. Governments and ministers in contending with intense scrutiny from the media and parliament were cautious and risk adverse, thereby afflicting senior public servants. It is not simply a matter of contending with how intense 'media and parliamentary scrutiny has made governments, individual ministers and therefore senior public servants more cautious or risk adverse' (Belcher 2015a, p. 20). The rigours of multiple demands have been challenged (Doern et al. 2014), and the influence of accountability and transparency requirements declared to be problematic, and not necessarily essential (AGRAGA 2010). The inability of the accountability system to adapt to the developing maturity of departments was another rigidity (SSC 1999).

All countries have a large number of rules, but it is unclear whether this is reflected in red tape levels and the extent to which it is systemic. Red tape may be associated more with types of agency (e.g. one subject to close public scrutiny) or a field (e.g. human resources, procurement), but how does this become systemic? The political climate established by a government – asserting strong political control, questioning the standing of the public service or hyper risk avoidance – provides the conditions for a collective response. It is argued that the 'more blame heat is perceived, the more blame-avoidance strategies are likely to be joined up' (Hood 2011, p. 138). Where blame pressure is intense and sustained, greater integration can be expected, producing a system-wide culture.

IMPLICATIONS FOR THE PUBLIC MANAGEMENT SYSTEM

Three types of implication are addressed: the impact on innovation (long a clarion call for reformers), management flexibility, and distortions and confusions associated with incentives.

Innovation and Risk

The incentives to innovate are likely to be undermined by the penalties for failure outweighing the rewards for being successful (Ritchie 2014). In many public organisations there is a focus on 'downside risk', the handling of potential or actual failure (Alexander and Thodey 2018).

A central aspiration of all four countries, innovation, was repeatedly thwarted. A stronger fixation on risk emerged with the interest in innovation, but the conditions of the four countries indicate similar patterns. Innovation was often directly and negatively linked to either the inability to manage risk or managers' unwillingness to undertake risky endeavours.

The trend towards a compliance culture had adverse effects on innovation (Bourgon 2011). In Australia and New Zealand, innovation was constrained by an unnecessary level of risk aversion by NZ ministers and chief executives (BPSAG 2011) and restricted by systemic risk aversion and decision making centralised at senior departmental levels (Belcher 2015a). The imposition of 'red-tape standardisation' on delivery agencies stifled creativity and weakened innovation (Shergold 2013, p. 10; see also APSC 2009). Many departments had 'an almost exclusive focus on downside risk, identifying and managing what could go wrong (or has gone wrong)'. The public sector would lag behind other sectors in handling citizens' expectations and technological change if risk aversion was not attended to (Alexander and Thodey 2018, p. 20).

UK departments had addressed the culture of 'risk passivity', but there was still widespread 'lower-scale risk aversion inhibiting creativity and innovation' (NAO 2006, sec. 3.3). Public servants' risk-averse attitudes inhibited innovation processes (NAO 2009). The incentives to innovate were unevenly distributed: only 50 per cent of civil servants surveyed believed their organisation provided incentives for staff to produce innovative ideas. A comparison of innovation in the private and public sectors indicated that risk in the latter was conceived as negative effects on organisational reputation, embarrassing politicians, and failure of policy implementation. The consequences of failure might mean service quality and careers being adversely affected. Innovation was not necessarily regarded as essential to achieving objectives. External pressures also affected innovative processes (NAO 2009, pp. 12, 38).

The Canadian 'web of rules' discouraged innovation and impaired the capacity to deliver services (Lépine 2007; TBS 2009a). The highly risk-adverse public service meant that innovation was 'an uphill struggle' which often required extensive and time-consuming documentation, analysis and discussions, including with ministers (Charko 2013, p. 113). Innovation was not prioritised and had to occur in department silos (Clarke 2019, p. 145).

Implications for Management

The consequences for public management have been dysfunctional across a range of processes because managing is hampered. The reliance on rules was part of a trend towards a compliance culture, a product of increasing controls and reporting demands that undermined good management (Bourgon 2011). In those countries where regulation and risk aversion were strongest the departures from the managerialist ideal were stark, and the kinship with bureaucracy strongest. The dilemma was that managers were exhorted to reflect the management mantra, 'to engage with risk, be innovative, flexible, agile', while simultaneously having to contend with extensive specifications detailing how they were to function (Belcher 2015a, p. 10). A second dilemma was that deregulation in a devolved system produced more regulation (see earlier discussion), and other requirements placed constraints on obtaining benefits (DFD 2012b).

Implications for Incentive Structures

Incentive structures are argued to shape public servant behaviour in specific directions (Heinrich and Marschke 2010). In all four countries there is extensive evidence of public servants responding to the signals given by those who influence them and by reacting to calculated attempts to shape incentives. Specific structures and processes have been adopted as part of the calculations required to achieve results (commonly minister's priorities), notably reporting and targets. However, there are limitations on the efficacy of such incentives. They may be simplistically conceived (e.g. 'rational man'), particularly where competing incentives exist or are ambiguous and obfuscating. The owners of the structures may not act in conformity with them. They may ignore the contexts in which people operate and the range of other expectations that exist. The costs may outweigh the benefits. The traditional ambiguity of incentives (e.g. size matters, inputs prevail over results) has not been fully reversed (Barber 2017). There are several explicit approaches, one focused on the minister, the other on scrutiny and accountability; in combination, they can have significant effects.

An imbalance in incentive structures was widespread (e.g. Boston 2017). Issues about incentive structures usually involved the political executive. Several cases illustrate the point. UK accounting officers had weak incentives to give priority to 'value for money' instead of routinely satisfying ministers (NAO 2016a, sec. 8). A significant issue for department heads was the range of incentive structures, but the primary focus was delivering the government's agenda (APSC 2014). The tension was expressed through being task-focused rather than strategic or capacity oriented (Interview, former Australian agency head 2017). Ministers were the arbiters of incentivising behavioural change and the engendering of a positive risk culture (Alexander and Thodey 2018).

When a prime minister was engaged, the incentive pathway was clear. This was illustrated by Blair's leadership in the United Kingdom on the priority PSAs, which was essential for formalising accountability arrangements and incentivising people to focus on the delivery (Panchamia and Thomas 2014). Compare also Howard's monitoring of policy implementation in Australia, and Deputy Prime Minister English's role in state services reform in New Zealand. The tenor of specific governments had system effects on the reactions of staff, such as in Canada under Prime Minister Harper's directive and controlling government (Zussman 2016), and the Mulroney government's antipathy towards the public service led to political control and risk aversion.

Lack of delegation by senior management and overreaction to errors were primary behaviours influencing the creation and maintenance of regulations. The reason for external scrutiny led to a chain reaction down the hierarchy of caution with risk aversion affecting governments and ministers first, then senior public servants who reacted by centralising, and finally the reliance of other staff on rules. The frequent response to mistakes and misjudgements was to increase checks in place and centralise responsibilities for clearances and decision-making (Belcher 2015a).

The incentives for public servants may be either lacking or difficult to sustain in terms of their handling of risk. The expectations of superiors in the United Kingdom mostly seemed to emphasise 'avoiding mistakes far more than accomplishing change' because senior managers were unwilling to take risks and to accept some measure of failure. Many staff believed that a single 'black mark' would affect their careers, which encouraged 'very risk-averse attitudes'. Consequently, common attitudes were avoiding embarrassment to ministers and maintaining a stable job brief, which inhibited innovation (NAO 2006, p. 28). There were no career incentives for officials to express reservations about the policy adventurism of ministers (King and Crewe 2014). In muted public service terms, the question was posed whether more durable modifications to the accountability framework would 'better balance the incentives that agency heads face to both deliver for the government of the day and be effective stewards of an enduring organisation' (APSC 2014, p. 17).

POLITICISATION AND BUREAUCRATISATION

Political Control

Politicians want political control and high levels of responsiveness to their priorities, but this tends to lead to risk-averse cultures and to constrain innovation. Despite the changes to relationships between politicians and senior public servants, one element of continuity has been the primary purpose of the ministerial department. Under the traditional system, the public servant's first duty was protecting the minister, and according loyalty to the government (Stone 2011). Departments of state give centrality to this function despite the addition of political advisers in the minister's office, and the attendant ambiguities and potential fracturing of loyalties. Nevertheless, ministerial engagement and priorities remained at the forefront (Te Kawa and Guerin 2012).[5] A managerialist approach may suffuse the operations of the public service, but it remains subject to the conditions that define the public realm.

The effect of political dynamics was highly significant for management development, particularly with the handling of risk. Politicisation in its various manifestations placed the political leaders more starkly in the public frame at a time when public policy, media engagement and public expectations became more demanding. No longer was political contact routed through the head of department, but ministers and their staff routinely dealt directly with public servants. Thus, the political executive was often the major source of risk aversion in all countries. When politicians were overly dominant, obsessively controlling and intervening there were consequences. Not only was there the likelihood of 'a dampening effect on risk' (Bozeman and Kingsley 1998, p. 117), but risk aversion could be magnified. Ministers strongly influence departments' risk appetites, which need ministerial support to instil an effective risk culture, but 'there is no evidence the risk appetite of ministers . . . has shifted in recent years' (Alexander and Thodey 2018, p. 19). Paradoxically, the politicians' advocacy of a highly responsive public management system was the main reason for the expansion of protective barriers through regulations (along with increased accountability and oversight requirements that flourished under their watch). Combine this with Canadian conditions and the result is:

> Dense, elaborate, top-down approval processes, risk aversion, information control, and strictly defined and siloed responsibilities for particular tasks all respond to a context of hyperaccountability, but accountability of a particular brand, one

that emphasises 'naming and blaming' and seeks to mitigate failures at all costs. Ministers demand 'error-free government' that in turn inspires a 'cover your ass culture'. (Clarke 2019, p. 186)

Bureaucratisation under Public Management

Bureaucracy can be viewed as the organisation of traditional public administration or as a product of managerialism and enhanced politicisation. They are similar in some respects, particularly where process and compliance apply, and may of course co-exist. A country like Canada appears to be subject more to old bureaucratic principles, while more managerialised systems like Australia's reflects more the new 'iron cage' (Gill 2011a). The range of pressures on public servants was shared between old and new – accountability and public scrutiny of those in the goldfish bowl occurred in the past – except they were magnified in the twenty-first century.

It is apparent from this chapter that red tape has been extensive and intractable. Canada's 'web of rules', 'the irrational layering of superfluous regulation, controls and processes' was widespread (Lépine 2007), and Australian red tape extensive, and the syndrome of risk aversion and excessive regulations occurred in all countries. The sedimentation of regulations was commonplace. According to Savoie (2011), Canadian decision-making processes can be reduced to two, one directly controlled by the prime minister, political advisers and agencies at the centre; the second exists to maintain control by avoiding or managing political or bureaucratic blunders. The process is depicted as 'slow, cumbersome . . . laden with elaborate reporting requirements. Its purpose is in part to assess the management performance . . . but also to enable those at the centre to steer departments away from political or bureaucratic gaffes and to establish an early warning signal to manage politically difficult situations' (p. 163).

Managerialism led to the transition from a relatively closed to a substantially open public management system. This meant greater exposure to external influences and an expectation that public management would be more responsive to environmental change. However, greater exposure for public organisations placed higher demands on public servants. The first refuge of an insecure public servant remained the protection offered by rule dependency.

There was also the intractability of embedded rules and regulations in Australia and Canada. The TBS (2009a, 2009c) claimed that measures had been implemented for dealing with the problem but went back to the drawing board in 2016. Australia finally reviewed the position in 2016 after desultory responses to 'creeping' bureaucratisation over a decade, but the conditions for its perpetuation remained.

The over-reliance on rules and procedures indicates bureaucratisation had become a standard feature of the public management system in the twenty-first century. The initial decades of the reform era provided a grounding through different types of performance specifications and new regulatory roles. The unabated accumulation of rules and procedures over time registered as a critical condition by and following the turn of the century, particularly in Australia and Canada, where bureaucratisation became more explicitly a systemic matter.

CONCLUSION

In significant areas of the public management system, bureaucratisation has stifled creativity, precluded innovation and smothered good public management. The processes discussed in this chapter highlight the multiple factors that contribute to the imbroglios confronting reformers: risk aversion, oversight demands and creeping red tape have produced a fixation on compliance and over-regulation in otherwise managerialised public services. There are strong and complex pressures involved in rule-making and it remains unclear whether they are surmountable on a sustainable basis. Red tape reviews regularly appear but the record of responses has tended to be insufficient to withstand the pressures to regulate. Single loop solutions on an ad hoc basis only provide short-term Band-Aids. Attempts to reconcile aspirations for a smart, agile, flexible service and the bureaucratic requirements of a formal public service produced tensions and dilemmas that were not readily resolved.

The nexus of political intervention and embedded risk aversion has continued to permeate all systems. The bureaucratisation of Anglophone public management systems arose with the onset of full-on performance regimes and was elaborated with the maturation of the systems as they contended with complex demands. Over the long term, bureaucratisation has become a fully fledged component of the public management system.

NOTES

1. UK's Red Tape Challenge (2011–14) was based in the Department for Business, Innovation and Skills. See http://webarchive.nationalarchives.gov.uk/20150423095857 and http://www.redtapechallenge.cabinetoffice.gov.uk/home/index/.
2. The listing of compliance requirements for different fields did not, however, differentiate beneficial from negative red tape: cf. Bozeman and Feeney 2011.
3. See also the discussion of centralisation and hierarchy within departments in Chapter 6.

4. Canada's federal government ran a sponsorship programme in the province of Quebec until corrupt practices were revealed and publicised by an auditor general's report, leading to a public inquiry by the Gomery Commission.
5. Two of the three strongest ranked elements in New Zealand's performance improvement survey were 'engagement with ministers' 81%, and 'government priorities' 72% (Te Kawa and Guerin 2012, p. 32).

8.   Coordination and collaboration

The twenty-first century has been marked by divergent, even contradictory tendencies, with pronounced centralisation as political executives, in response to new policy and governance movements, reasserted their authority over fragmented systems (Halligan 2010a). Politicisation has favoured top-down coordination which has impacted on operational and non-hierarchical activities, but reform trends have also supported strengthening the ministerial department. This chapter looks at the choices made with coordination, and the consequences for public management.

The Westminster tradition incorporates a political executive organised in terms of specialised ministers with defined portfolios and the ministerial department as the primary organisational form. Departments based on the functional principle provide an explicit conduit for funding as well as a hierarchy of authority and accountability that leads from the department to the responsible minister, who is in turn accountable to parliament. These features have dictated a vertical focus within bounded organisations producing the so-called silos that have dominated the public sector landscape. Managerialism in the late twentieth century produced more specialisation, and a multiplicity of agencies and fragmentation that reinforced vertical accountability through performance reporting based on outputs and targets.

The limitations of functional silos underscored the need for coordination, which was reinforced both by burgeoning policy issues that could not be contained within one department, and the shift to cross-boundary approaches in response to complex problems (O'Flynn et al. 2014). A further factor was that the joined-up movement stimulated conceptions of and experiments with coordination, such as collaboration with new roles for networks and partners interacting horizontally. Another complicating factor is the expansion of ministerial staff with roles that often included significant coordinating activities. These trends promoted a cross-department focus that required less formally bounded organisations, although departmental self-interest remained central. Finally, the concern with coherence and coordination at the macro level led to an emphasis on whole-of-government agendas.

The first dynamic addressed is the central axis of the public management system, the vertical relationship, and how this impacted on the declared need for greater cross-departmental arrangements; in other words, how vertical pressures could be reconciled with horizontal needs. A second dynamic is the role of political executives in directly utilising coordination instruments to achieve their priorities. How the contending approaches play out is examined through three questions: how to reconcile the need for specialisation in the machinery of government with that for coordination of function-based organisations and programmes; what types of coordination have been used, including the relative importance of vertical and horizontal instruments, including the burgeoning use of digital tools; and why the continuing struggle to achieve viable horizontal coordination and collaboration is not being addressed.

MODES OF COORDINATION

Coordination addresses the instruments designed to produce an alignment of tasks and activities and greater coherence, while minimising contradictions (a simplified version of Bouckaert et al. 2010, p. 16). There are several ways of viewing coordination: levels (Metcalfe 1994), administrative, political and policy domains (Davis 1995), governing principle – hierarchy, markets and networks (Bouckaert et al. 2010), instruments employed (Bouckaert et al. 2010; Lægreid et al. 2014; Peters 2015), partisan-political and administrative-technical (Craft 2015) and variations on horizontal and vertical dimensions (Lægreid et al. 2014; Halligan 2015b). Modes of coordination can also be analysed with a functional approach that considers the role of different actors, for example components of political advisers' coordinating roles: 'buffering' (Craft 2015, 2016); and brokering policy agreements (Eichbaum and Shaw 2011; Maley 2015). Mutual adjustment and cultural change are non-structural alternatives for horizontal governance (Lindquist 2014).

Two basic forms of coordination are distinguished as both vertical and horizontal. Vertical coordination is the relationship between levels within a public management system, which means between the political executive or central agencies (including the prime minister's office) and line departments (and/or ministerial advisers). Horizontal refers to coordination between departments within one level of the system (or 'the same hierarchical tier within government': Bouckaert et al. 2010, p. 24). A rider may be added about peers being precluded from exercising authority over each other in a 'predominately voluntary' association (Bouckaert et al. 2010, p. 24), but agencies are often induced to coordinate by a higher authority (e.g. the horizontal and vertical mix in the UK's joined-up programmes) (Peters 2015). Where a relationship is fundamentally about departments (and/or political advisers) working together – providing central controls do not dominate – it is deemed to be horizontal.

Coordination instruments have been identified as either primarily vertical or horizontal (although hybrid cases have been common) (Peters 2015), and the relationship between vertical and horizontal initiatives can be complicated (Whitehead 2003; Howard and Phillips 2012). Instruments may be institutional, such as cabinet, treasury, the PMD and PMO (Bouckaert et al. 2010), or specialised instruments employed by them (e.g. implementation units, task-forces and specialised networks). Key factors are the type of control used vertically, and the level of engagement for horizontal coordination. Instruments of control vary from mandatory to permissive, while forms of engagement range from loose to tight couplings. At the centre, there is a strong meta-governance inheritance from years of reform which could entail choices between markets, networks and hierarchies, but within government the range of options for these modes of governance is more limited (but see Peters 2015), and there are numerous other instruments to choose from for controlling, prioritising and other purposes.

Coordination is an area where ambiguities (Christensen and Lægreid 2007) and grey areas exist. Apart from the intricacies of vertical and horizontal relationships, there is the question of distinguishing between political and administrative coordination. The difference is often clear-cut, but political offices often include seconded public servants, and partisans (or political bureaucrats) may operate in departments. There are also difficulties with evaluating the effectiveness of instruments (Sarapuu et al. 2014), often because public information is unavailable or is too superficial. This is also a field where conceptual clarity is often missing or subject to variations in usage. A case is 'collaboration', which has been in vogue for some time, but has been used for a grab bag of activities, ranging from voluntary interaction to formal shared commitments. The term has continued to be loosely employed (O'Flynn 2009; O'Leary 2014). Where greater precision is sought, collaboration can be positioned in relation to other forms of interaction, one approach being to locate it within a continuum, such as 'cooperation-coordination-collaboration-service integration', in which the level of intensity in the relationship varies (Selden et al. 2006, pp. 413–14; Eppel 2013; Keast and Mandell 2014; Halligan and Smith 2019). Compare also a structural spectrum ranging from loosely coupled to full integration (Hughes and Smart 2012, p. 6). Analysis of the scale of coordination is another option, a well-known hierarchy providing a policy spectrum that ascends from independent ministers to government strategy (Metcalfe 1994) but focuses on resolving differences between ministers. For the purposes here, a broad distinction is made between steering and driving change from the centre (often of a macro and whole-of-government character) and settling departmental divergences (meso in nature).

Types of coordination that extend outside the core public sector are omitted, an example being the substantial field of collaborative governance focused on public, private and civil society interaction (Williams 2002), and portfolio coordination involving non-departmental organisations. At any point in time, a variety of types of coordination are in operation, ranging from the informal

Table 8.1   *Vertical coordination: political and administrative instruments*

Purpose	Political	Administrative
Government policy and priorities	Cabinet committees Prime minister's office Lead minister	Central agencies Public service delivery units
Management (ongoing)		Central agency prescriptions and guidelines Governing and leadership bodies Performance management Management programmes and reviews (ad hoc and whole-of-government) Digital

and barely visible to highly formalised top-down control, but their extent and layers remain indeterminate (Peters 1998b).

In terms of explaining preferences for specific instruments there are macro-type interpretations about changing environments (e.g. fiscal austerity) and distinctive reform programmes, such as neo-liberal or reintegration. At this macro level, a 'whole-of-government' literature locates cases within broader patterns of change, and greater coordination as a product of fragmentation, but context matters as indicated by the choices of instruments in an austerity environment. Where there is a multiplicity of different types of agenda (Christensen and Lægreid 2007) tensions exist between those that strengthen hierarchical structures and instruments (e.g. efficiency) and those favouring horizontal arrangements.

VERTICAL COORDINATION

Vertical coordination occurs between levels involving central agencies (including political offices) and line departments (Table 8.1). It generally entails the alignment of departments and ministerial offices with government and central priorities. Whether hierarchical relationships entail mandatory prescriptions, or an admixture of sanctions and incentives depends on the instrument.

The instruments of vertical coordination are grouped according to whether they are either *political* (directly involving the political executive and their partisan agents) or *administrative* (undertaken through a department or programme) in character. For vertical, *whole-of-government* refers to arrangements that issue from a central source and cover all or most organisations in a public management system. The term seems to be associated more with particular countries,[1] although the meaning resonates more generally where central agencies are steering a public management system to overcome fragmentation and lack of coherence or implementing a modernisation agenda.

Central coordination was primarily about control, and therefore prescriptions, according to Kernaghan and Siegel (1991, writing on Canada). It would be an overstatement now to regard central coordination as simply a matter of control because more nuanced approaches are also used. Yet the instruments in Table 8.1 reflect strong control elements. Vertical coordination takes explicit forms ranging from strongly hierarchical with mandatory prescriptions to mildly interventionist and permissive. The middle ground is one of interaction, negotiation and exhortation (compare Christensen and Lægreid's discussion of two versions of an instrumental perspective, 2007, p. 1061). The integration of back office management and transactions may involve a strong element of choice at one level (who to join and whether to lead), but it has been mandatory in Australia, Canada and the United Kingdom.

POLITICAL COORDINATION

The political executive (prime minister and cabinet) is not the focus of this study, although its instruments are central to the coordination of the core executive. As discussed earlier, political executives have extended their influence by enlarging the partisan element within the executive branch and ministers' authority at the interface with the public service, and this has included coordination and implementation. Politicisation can be regarded as a coordinating strategy (Dahlström and Pierre 2011). In addition to the 'shadow of hierarchy' (Scharpf 1997), the 'shadow of politicisation' is highly significant.

Political coordination is dominated and controlled directly by the political executive, and entails organisational processes run by ministers and their agents. It typically involves political control at the centre through the prime minister's office and special units designed to control prime ministerial agendas, and may include appointments to strategic central agency positions. Primary central instruments have been cabinet and its committees and the prime minister's office.

Cabinet and its Committees

Cabinet and its committees are the ultimate coordinating units of government (Weller 2007, 2018), although reliance on them varies. 'Court government' was rife under specific prime ministers in Australia, Canada and the United Kingdom (Savoie 2008; Rhodes et al. 2009; Rhodes and Tiernan 2014b) but a greater use of cabinets re-emerged by the late 2010s. This has implications for levels of centralisation and decentralisation and for the roles of ministers.

UK cabinet committees were employed in conjunction with cross-cutting PSAs (Panchamia and Thomas 2014). They were then used to focus on horizontal coordination of mainly intractable issues following the Blair precedent (Beuselinck 2010). Cabinet Implementation Taskforces composed of ministers, with Cabinet Office support, were established to monitor and resolve implementation issues with service delivery and drive the main cross-cutting priorities, often 'wicked' issues (Cabinet Office 2015b, 2016; Rutter 2015a). The taskforces reported to the prime minister and cabinet, but not publicly. The original ten (or eleven) taskforces under Cameron shrank to five, and then seven, under May. Despite a commitment to working across organisational boundaries by monitoring and driving the delivery of priorities, the approach failed to support joined up activity and the taskforces did not affect planning and performance management and had no visible impact (CPA 2016c; NAO 2018c, p. 11).

The more ambitious committees are used to drive government priorities. The New Zealand cabinet's Social Wellbeing Committee addresses strategic and policy matters, but is also meant to ensure coordination and delivery of government priorities, plus monitor achievement of outcomes.[2] A core cabinet committee in Canada – Agenda, Results and Communications – has had responsibility for driving the 'results' programme of the Trudeau government (Results and Delivery Unit 2016), and establishes 'the government's forward agenda, tracks progress on priorities, and considers strategic communications', with the prime minister as chair (Canada Government 2018).

Lead Ministers

Ministers have important roles to play coordinating the management of sectors and the implementation of cross-departmental priorities. One option is the appointment of ministers of state for coordinating a government's approach across departments in either a specialised field or broadly conceived sector. A second is to have focused priorities and reporting at a high level.

Special ministries were created in Canada for broad priority issues (e.g. urban affairs and social development). However, ministries were small in size and budget, had limited programme responsibilities, and were unable to contend with powerful line departments (Adie and Thomas 1987).

New Zealand illustrates three approaches. Early experiments involved sector groupings in fields such as justice, natural resources and social policy, each with a sector leader. However, this approach was depicted as: 'a Procrustean bed, a forced fit to an existing standard, using a work-around to combine a horizontal role with a vertical accountability framework' (Boston and Gill 2011, p. 229). The Better Public Services review (BPSAG 2011) elevated the approach to a new level by addressing the poor coordination under the New Zealand model, a defining characteristic being the concentration of 'decision-rights and accountabilities with the chief executives' (BPSAG 2011, p. 21; Eppel 2013). The mode of coordination changed from inter-agency consultation to a more tightly coordinated arrangement under which ministers had to agree and be aligned around a small number of measurable sector-wide results. Chief executives were appointed to lead sectors in delivering results that reflected government priorities, and to organise the means to deliver results, including working with central agencies on system-wide changes. Legislation provided for strengthened collaboration in the state sector, including a new type of multi-category appropriation that allowed grouping of different types of expenditure for a purpose. The ten BPS results were to be achieved within a time frame. The results approach was deemed to have been successful (Jensen et al. 2014; Scott and Boyd 2016b) and was renewed with a new set of targets (Key 2017). It was terminated by the Ardern government, which opted for new structures – boards or joint ventures – composed of relevant chief executives, each board being accountable to one minister and being resourced by a budget appropriation and staff (Ardern 2019).

Prime Minister's Office and the Political Advisory System

The prime minister's office role ranges from offering basic support for the prime minister to providing a political machine for driving the prime minister's agenda, with variations in between. The former may have a narrow range of functions, the latter an extensive number of significant responsibilities and authority underscored by partisans unequivocally committed to the prime minister's objectives. The powerful PMO is inclined to dictate to central agencies and ministers and their departments, depending on how centralising and controlling the prime minister is. Prime ministers' offices have played significant roles in Australia, Canada and the United Kingdom. Of Aucoin's (2012) components of 'new political governance', prime ministerial power had become greater, and the PMO's position has generally been strengthened over time in the two federal systems (Savoie 1999; Rhodes and Tiernan 2014a).

The ultimate expression of a dominant office was the 'directive' role of the Canadian PMO under Prime Minister Harper (Zussman 2016). The transition to a much more politically active and controlling PMO has also occurred in Australia during the last two decades (Rhodes and Tiernan 2014b) and when central agencies were weakened by decentring. Australia's Howard coalition government (1996–2007) was distinguished by strong central control and coordination of ministerial offices, including the employment of senior ministerial staff, under a dominant prime minister who placed a premium on political control of the apparatus. The PMO staff was large and turnover was contained (Maley 2010, p. 98; see also Tiernan 2007b).

The high level of activity of some PMO's and ministerial offices has meant that they have taken on more of the coordination roles. These include support for the operation of the cabinet system and formal contributions to cabinet and committee meetings (Maley 2011, 2015; Craft 2018a). Its location and relationship with the prime minister ensure that the PMO has significant authority both in relation to other ministers and their offices, and to central agencies and line departments. The effective PMO pursues government strategies and priorities, often cross-cutting, through working with other actors. The Canadian case shows how the command and control type of PMO can stultify the apparatus (Johnson 2017; Shepherd and Stoney 2018).

The UK's No. 10 has greatly expanded its role through various instruments, but ambivalence about its capacity to exercise consistent and effective influence has been a general judgement (Parker et al. 2010; Diamond 2014; NAO 2015).

The overall political advisory system also needs to be incorporated as part of vertical and horizontal control if ministerial staffers are used as part of a general strategy. The network of ministerial staffers is an important element of vertical control where the ministerial advisory system has an identity of its own and is organised under the prime minister's office. The advisory system can be used for political coordination across the public management system, including meetings of advisers chaired by the head of the PMO.

Policy Tsars

A coordination mechanism for confronting a policy problem (Peters 2018) has been the tsar, a term mainly employed in the UK presumably for the large number operating there over the last two decades. They are appointed either by the prime minister or ministers and may have an implicit or explicit coordination role. Tsars have been a response to fragmentation for dealing with delivery issues within policy fields such as health (Smith 2011a; see also Chapter 3).

ADMINISTRATIVE COORDINATION AT THE CENTRE

This category covers central coordination that occurs through central departments and programmes as opposed to political mechanisms, although the instruments will normally represent government initiatives. Under the hybrid arrangements apparent in the reform era, political appointments may play key roles, an important consideration being the problems with the traditional machinery in coordination (Smith 2011a).

The centre of government provides the strategic focus and direction and coordination across the governance system. A set of central agencies exist with common core functions in the four systems, although how these are configured varies, and one of the three or four agencies is essentially political. Much depends on how the functions are constituted, the engagement with the political executive and relationships with other parts, central capacity to respond to complex demands on government, and finally the overall performance of public management and governance. The basis of specialisation at the centre is well established for core functions and is generally durable. Individual central agencies specialise in coordinating policy advice for the prime minister, financial management and personnel, and use different types of instruments (see e.g. Table 6.2 for performance).

The centre may adopt inter alia a command and control approach (hierarchical), a corporate approach (whole-of-government and system coherence), a networked approach (light coordination of operational agencies), or differentiation can be based on management principles with the centre establishing either strategies or principles and values within which departments function.

Prime Minister's Department

The prime minister's department (PMD or its equivalent in Canada and the United Kingdom) is responsible for policy coordination across sectors or whole-of-government. While categorised as 'administrative' the PMDs primary focus is supporting the prime minister in a political environment that is often directed by the partisans of the PMO. The PMD has responsibility for the interface with the political executive, in particular the prime minister and cabinet support and is therefore closely linked with the political agenda. It works closely with the prime minister's office, and together they provide for the centralising tendencies in the federal systems, particularly Canada (Savoie 1999). There is a symbiotic relationship between the PMO and the PMD, its character depending on how prime ministers use it, which affects the level of centralisation within the public management system. The partial fusion of the Cabinet Office and the PMO under Blair is one example (Jones 2016), presenting an exception to the view that the Cabinet Office normally has a more collective ambit than simply the prime minister.

Divisions or units are created to suit prime ministers and their agendas. The level of coordination has depended on centralising pressures. One response to complex policy needs was to build coordinating units within current structures, particularly the PMD. Australia developed a capacity in the 1970s to advise across a range of policy fields (Weller 2018).

A strategy unit was significant under Blair while Rudd's strategic focus for the PMD overshadowed departments. In contrast New Zealand's PMD was small and sought to avoid being overly policy interventionist. The task force has been used to pull together departments the level of central control depending on how it was led.

Implementation had been the neglected end of the policy spectrum (Gold 2014), although it was an original reform goal in Anglophone countries. Governments reviewed internal constraints on implementation in response to public perceptions of the performance of delivery agencies. The solution was to extend central control to remove implementation obstacles and delays. Implementation and delivery units have provided a distinct type of vertical coordination role that supports active political engagement in 'oversight' at the centre for monitoring and negotiating with delivery departments over issues (e.g. blockages), and formal reporting on progress with delivery and political priorities (see Chapter 6).

This approach, pioneered by the UK's prime minister's delivery unit (PMDU) under Prime Minister Blair, established clear goals, delivery maps and reports, trajectories, league tables, stock-take sessions with the prime minister, and a working relationship with the Treasury to align spending with desired outcomes (Barber 2007). It was regarded as successful when it had the PM's attention, but declined once political backing was lost. Misjudgment led to its termination by the Cameron Coalition (2010) only for it to be revived as indispensable (Panchamia and Thomas 2014). An Australian variant, the Cabinet Implementation Unit was an effective instrument when used by one prime minister but fell into desuetude and was absorbed into the cabinet division of the department. Implementation units have produced results in the short term, particularly when political leaders were engaged, but were inclined to falter over time (Gold 2014, 2017).

Of a different ilk is the unit that addresses priorities and their achievement, Blair's Strategy Unit being a forerunner. The Results and Delivery Unit established in the Canadian Privy Council Office in 2016 under an external appointee has been an ambitious exercise because of its systemic aspirations and was in some respects inspired by the Barber formula (Results and Delivery Unit 2016; Gold 2017). It has focused on core government priorities, operating with political actors and reporting on departmental progress. Australia established a Priorities and Delivery Unit in 2019 under a deputy secretary (see Chapter 6).

Whole-of-Government: Management Coordination and Coherence

This category covers central agency frameworks, programmes and instruments for coordination and coherence across the public service, ad hoc interventions by governments for engineering efficiency and schemes for reforming public management. They generally have had a whole-of-government basis, which meant that they have applied to public service departments (and agencies) in general, and entail giving effect to policy and management decisions, whether mandatory or advisory. Whole-of-government requirements can be sourced directly from the government, but routinely derive from either central agencies or collective groupings of senior public service leaders. Whole-of-government may be a hybrid instrument of both vertical and horizontal coordination.

The former is best represented by centralisation of departmental responsibilities because of issues with distributed management. Management capacity at the centre fluctuates over time, but a most concerted initiative to augment infrastructure in the 2010s was in the United Kingdom with inter alia centralisation of procurement, consultancy oversight and digital websites. Of the second approach, typical reform agendas have addressed cross-government efficiency, capability reviews and reviews of the performance management framework.

Performance management has been significant for coordination with respect to relationships between the centre and operational departments, whole-of-government, and among political actors at the centre. The core was the performance management framework based on an explicit template that featured reporting requirements that shaped budget documents (see Chapter 6).

An efficiency agenda refers to the employment of a distinctive family of instruments as an overriding objective, more usually in austerity contexts. These instruments address either modifications and reductions in organisational operations, or measures to extract greater productivity. The UK's Efficiency and Reform Group developed plans in conjunction with departments. This work was led by the centre, and implementation by departments was obligatory (NAO 2015). The Australian Efficiency through Contestability Programme examined government activities and services with reference to contestability (Department of Finance 2015; Halton 2015). The Canadian strategic and operational reviews were not released as public documents (Lindquist 2014), which was also the case with comparable Australian exercises (but see ANAO 2018).

The shared services fashion represented both a return to some form of centralisation of departmental corporate services, another form of savings where austerity agendas reigned, and a potential stepping-stone to privatisation. Shared services can be regarded as horizontal coordination in some cases, but the heavy hand of the centre and government agendas have been responsible for this type of organisational change and its prominence in three countries in the 2010s. They combine partial integration of departments' functions and meso or macro level centralisation, which generally has been centrally driven usually for efficiency reasons – the savings to be acquired from pooling departments' corporate functions – and the rational logic appears persuasive (despite the reality checks from the history of shared services in Anglophone countries: Elston and MacCarthaigh 2016). However, the credibility of shared services as a mode of coordination has floundered at times with issues in different contexts. For the UK, benefits occurred but were less than expected. Both customers (ministries) and suppliers experienced increased costs because of implementation delays. There were weaknesses in the design and the Cabinet Office's management role. Shared Services Canada provided email, a data centre, and network services to 43 departments and agencies, plus purchasing IT equipment for all of government and being responsible for transforming IT infrastructure, but the agency was unclear about what service levels partners might expect, reporting was poor, and savings from the transformation could not be demonstrated. The administration of Australia's shared services had been effective, but the client base was small, and departments had not determined whether it was efficient and resulted in savings; it was terminated (OAG 2015; NAO 2016d; ANAO 2017a; Savoie 2019c). The structures and systems have been reworked and the roles of central agencies (such as the UK's Cabinet Office and Australia's Department of Finance) have become significant and the savings claim substantial from Australia's six hubs providing corporate services to 30 agencies and the UK's new strategy (Commonwealth of Australia 2019, p. 9; see also Cabinet Office, Government Shared Services 2019).

Capability reviews employ an external panel of experts to examine departmental management improvement using a template that incorporates potential areas of strength and weakness. This focus arose as governments and oversight agencies confronted the downside of the aftermath of NPM and as major weaknesses in overall capacity became increasingly stark. This led to programmes of capacity development through formal reviews, first in the UK, then Australia and New Zealand (see Chapter 5). The reviews were designed to provide systematic assessments of departments' capability and the specific skill weaknesses and apparent failures of core management.[3] Here the purpose is to consider how this approach might contribute to coordination. Initially this was arguably the case, but the attrition of coordination followed decentralisation. The two systems that withdrew from a central role faded; whereas the two with institutional support at the centre accorded more attention to capability. The British reviews went through two rounds that showed improvements before becoming voluntary exercises that were disparaged (Panchamia and Thomas 2014). The Australian reviews registered impacts, but the follow-up process was discontinued. The New Zealand PIF was maintained in a modified form, although not as a mandatory requirement across the system. The potential benefit of continuing some measure of central coordination was not properly tested.

In contrast, the Canadian Management Accountability Framework has operated differently as the most elaborate central mechanism for monitoring capabilities covering ten management dimensions. This has an explicit coordinating dimension in seeking standardisation across departments through templates, public reporting and central guidance in the relationship with the Treasury Boards Secretariat. It has also been part of an overall management system with information from annual departmental reports being used in assessing deputy ministers. This ultimate oversight mechanism has been heavy handed in the past but exemplifies continuous top-down compliance-based coordination (Lindquist 2017).

Governing and Leadership Bodies

Collective leadership instruments exist in each country, the most important being those convened by the head of the public service. These groups and committees can play a number of roles ranging from briefings and information exchange through to collective strategies and addressing government priorities. How they operate depends on the emphasis of coordination: steering from the centre or pulling together organisations, and whether coordination is primarily vertical or horizontal. There are elements of both and given the governing dimension they are listed here.

The main governing body of the UK civil service, the Permanent Secretaries Management Group, considers strategic issues for the whole civil service and provides corporate leadership where a collective position is necessary. Canada's Coordinating Committee of Deputy Ministers functions as a forum for discussing government policy and priorities and ensuring coordination across the numerous deputy minister committees. The Australian Secretaries Board sets the overall direction for the public service, drives collaboration and cross-boundary solutions and promotes a shared culture. New Zealand's State Services Leadership Team focuses on collective interests, promoting the unified public service and working across boundaries.

Below the top group there is either a single or multiple committee(s) that either undertake tasks assigned to them by the governing body or have responsibility for an area. The UK's Civil Service Steering Board role is to enhance the performance and reputation of the Civil Service by focusing on specific areas delegated to it. The NZ Public Service Leaders Group is a cohort comprised of senior public servants in the largest and most complex leadership roles across 36 agencies. Members hold a special role leading across the Public Service and their chief executives support their development and career progression. Canada has an extensive record of using senior leadership committees with an accessible list of 21 deputy minister committees covering a wide range of functions: integrated policy development in support of government priorities and medium-term planning, government-wide policy coherence, and departmental engagement in a whole-of-government approach to management and policy planning (PCO 2019). In contrast, the Australian arrangement largely operates under the radar with several committees of the Secretaries Board pursuing issues and modernisation.

Digital Coordination

The burgeoning impact of the 'digital era' (Dunleavy et al. 2006) has been penetrating public sectors in similar ways across countries. Usually, a central agency has been assigned a role in coordinating and supporting departments with digital 'transformation'. A central agenda for coordinating departmental websites into a single dot.gov applies to varying extents across the four and is seemingly of uncertain standing. The most ambitious attempt at imposing a top-down approach was Gov.UK, which registered an impact with standardisation of departmental presentations through a template focused on delivery to citizens, but less so with recognising alternative customers, and the needs and requirements of departments (Brown et al. 2017; NAO 2018a). Some form of central digital agency operates with varying degrees of success as relationships evolve, but generally with responsibility for an information and communications technology (ICT) strategy. The priorities of the Australian digital transformation strategy include whole-of-government strategies and policies; government-wide platforms and services for enabling transformation; and collaboration and partnerships to support digital transformation of government services (DTA 2019). However, the aspirations for strong central control have waned across the systems, and the level of coordination is highly uneven (for the complexities of the Canadian case, see Clarke 2019).

Technology-enabled joint provision of service has been a hallmark of the twenty-first century, enabled through either outcome or priority focused arrangements or within conglomerate departments. There has been movement towards significant collaborating arrangements and priority-driven agendas. The extent to which holistic approaches to individuals and their needs have been embedded varies widely. IT debacles in several countries have also complicated acceptance of and disrupted digital and IT agenda (Bagnall 2016; SFPAC 2018). In Canada, GCTools (a suite of digital collaboration applications) with the potential to enable horizontal activities in government are still not widely used (Clarke 2019, p. 222).

HORIZONTAL COORDINATION

Horizontal government approaches have been developed to promote inter-agency coordination because of complex policy problems and the need for joint implementation. A range of instruments reflecting horizontal and whole-of-government principles have been used to address 'wicked' and other issues that cannot be handled within a functional department (Christensen and Lægreid 2007). An important layer has been the new roles and behaviours of ministers and their retinues.

Table 8.2   Instruments of horizontal coordination*

	Political	Administrative
At the centre	Inter-ministerial organisations Chief of staff and political advisers: PMO and other ministers' offices	Corporate central agencies (Governing and leadership committees)*
Networks	Political advisers	Inter-departmental committees Functional and professional
Programme delivery and inter-agency	Lead ministers and advisers	Horizontal management Collaboration
Horizontal organisation		Integration/mergers Interdepartmental executive boards; joint ventures**

* Horizontal dominated by vertical. ** Prospective organisations in New Zealand (SSC 2018b).

Horizontal coordination entails interaction among agencies at the same level within a public management system. As with vertical coordination, classification is not free of problems in characterising inter-departmental (or equivalent) arrangements, but several are clear cut: centre of government coordination is readily delimited for most purposes, although less so where the prime minister's office is ubiquitous. Others are grounded in one level but shadowed by hierarchy and/or political processes. Ministers' staff have long 'mediated' minister–departmental coordination in Australia and Canada (Hamburger 2007, p. 220; see also Craft 2016). The discussion here focuses on the administrative column (Table 8.2).

The instruments of horizontal coordination are grouped according to whether they are either 'at the centre' or department/minister-level forms: networks, horizontal management, collaboration or integration. Most of these modes of coordination relate to segments or slices of coordination: a 'wicked' issue, capability development, and inter-agency cooperation. Coordination is commonly used as the generic term, but the concepts that appear in the Anglophone literature are clarified by levels of intensity or complexity on the horizontal dimension. *Horizontal management* is 'the coordination and management of a set of activities between two or more organizational units, [which] do not have hierarchical control over each other and where the aim is to generate outcomes that cannot be achieved by units working in isolation' (Bakvis and Juillet 2004, p. 8). This definition can be restricting where there is a hierarchical element, but is fairly inclusive, the relevant instruments ranging from 'informal networks to jointly managed secretariats' (Bakvis and Juillet 2004, p. 8). *Networks* entail both informal and formal mechanisms of interaction with some degree of longevity. *Collaboration* involves the sharing of resources and authority and is used here in this narrow sense of shared objectives, results and accountabilities (cf. Dutil et al. 2010). Similarly, organisational *integration* covers strong structural coordination over variously policy, programmes and delivery, including linking policy and implementation.

Horizontality has been a core value in Canada since the 1990s (Lindquist 2014), flowering in the UK with the 'joined up' phase (Bogdanor 2005) and Australia's 'culture of collaboration' in the 2000s (ANAO 2010b, p. 13), and flourishing in New Zealand at the same time (Boston and Gill 2011). The commitment to horizontal government remains constant, at least at the level of rhetoric.

Programme Delivery and Inter-Agency Cooperation

Horizontal management covers various forms of arrangements between agencies. Canada was arguably the earliest country to engage with horizontal public management commencing with the Task Force on Managing Horizontal Policy Issues (TFMHPI 1996). The horizontal initiatives programme dates from this surge of interest in the late 1990s (Lindquist 2014). The TBS undertook oversight, and horizontal initiatives have been listed on the TBS website. Bakvis and Juillet (2004) reported mixed results. There was no systematic monitoring or evaluation of the horizontal initiatives. Performance reports did not record the shared outcome contributions of partners (Auditor General of Canada 2003). It took the Auditor General (Auditor General of Canada 2005, 2016) 11 years to review another initiative. A sense of inertia exists with regards to horizontality. The agenda nosedived in the 2000s because of lack of political interest but may be revived under Trudeau.

Australia recorded over 1,800 inter-agency agreements for 21 departments (including two large agencies), 'signifying a breadth of cross agency activity and interdependencies' (ANAO 2010b, p. 30). Of these agreements, three types of service were provided by one agency for another: delivery of services to the public; provision of advice or data to another department (e.g. data collection and provision); and shared services between two agencies (e.g. the provision of corporate services by one department to another) (adapted from table 1.1 in ANAO 2010b). Then there were relationships based on joint programme implementation (e.g. shared oversight for delivering international climate change adaptation); and border security support (e.g. national security coordination). A recent case is the Data Integration Partnership for Australia, which is designed to make more effective use of government data assets and involves 20 Commonwealth agencies and includes networks and units (DPMC 2020).

Integration and Mergers

An integrated form of coordination is at one end of the spectrum of options for handling the provision of services. Complete integration means that inter-departmental relationships have been largely internalised. Seen as a means of obviating problems with cross-boundary relationships, integration does not necessarily preclude problems with horizontal and vertical coordination within large and complex organisations.

Integrated organisations can result from consolidation of non-departmental organisations in reaction to NPM disaggregation together and/or with departments (e.g. New Zealand and the United Kingdom). Economies are commonly the purpose for austerity-fixated governments, although the rationalisation is usually expressed in terms of improving the efficiency and effectiveness of policy and delivery. The social services field has produced integrations across all four countries, which indicated a preference for the ministerial department as illustrated by the conversion of Australia's multi-purpose delivery *agency* (Centrelink) into the core of a multi-functional delivery *department* (Human Services) (Halligan 2015a).[4] Other cases of super departments have aimed at creating greater government coherence (Halligan 1987). There are also one-offs such as the Australian Department of Home Affairs in 2017 that seemingly absorbed everything to do with borders and security.[5] Mega-departments struggle with the clash of cultures and may not be long-lasting, often dependent on government preferences. Structural solutions to coordination issues can be problematic in part because of complexity, as indicated by the mixed UK experience. The question arises as to whether the trading of hard for soft internal silos is necessarily achieved in practice (Talbot and Talbot 2014).

The overall trend in OECD countries is from single-focus siloed departments with specialised skills and approaches (e.g. defence, foreign affairs and justice) 'towards non-siloed approaches, combining connected functions (as with agriculture, environment and business) – again an area where UK patterns seem broadly consistent with the overall OECD trend' (White and Dunleavy 2010, p. 25). A further variation is to seek some degree of integration within a super-portfolio such as the Australia Jobs and Innovation Portfolio within which departments are nested (Smith 2018).

Meanwhile, experiments are planned in New Zealand under the reconstituted public service legislation in 2020 which will allow interdepartmental executive boards and joint ventures as structural means of furthering collaborative arrangements. The use of a board composed of chief executives would represent a shift from voluntary to formal arrangements and from single executive to collective decision-making about funding and staffing (SSC 2018b).

NETWORKS

Internal networks have become a fashionable area of inquiry (Maley 2011), although they were also prevalent under traditional public administration. Three forms of network are: political; functional and professional; and interdepartmental committees and task forces.

Political Networks

Political advisers use networks to interact with counterparts and their ministers in the development and advancement of agendas. Various roles may be employed – negotiating, brokering, buffering and bridging (Craft 2016). They may be informal and ad hoc or more formalised. Political staffers' political affiliation and ties with ministers mean they can be influential 'within multiple networks that criss-cross government and politics' (Wilson 2016b, p. 191). Advisers are often short- to medium-term appointments, which affects the character of networks. The full impact of political advisers on coordination remains unclear because of the lack of studies that also incorporate public servants, but it can be extensive.

Ministerial advisers have played several coordinating roles. The first was the resolution of policy conflicts, particularly where there were internecine differences between departments and other logjams. The second related to new policy that involved several portfolios and entailed brokering agreement and a whole-of-government result. The detailed work was undertaken by departments but to maintain political control groups of advisers often worked on policy development, negotiating and refining policy packages that mirrored public servants' IDCs (Maley 2015, p. 52).

The location of advisers as a 'primary node' in multiple networks was well established at an early stage (Bakvis 1997; Maley 2000; Eichbaum and Shaw 2010; Craft 2016; Wilson 2016b). The examination of 'the horizontal dimension . . . illuminates the mechanisms of coordination and information transmission on the political side and provides insight into how decisions are shaped within the black box of ministerial offices' (Wilson 2016b, p. 191). UK spads work with officials and external networks, but it appears that coordination between portfolios and ministers' offices did not have the same centrality as in the Australian and Canadian political advisory systems (Yong and Hazell 2014).

Australian PMO advisers have played 'a key role in coordinating and steering the development of these policy packages, to ensure they deliver both policy coherence and political advantage' (Maley 2015, p. 52). Canadian PMO staff have played a unique role 'at the front of policy making and also on a more day-to-day basis, in working horizontally to give coherence to the shape, and help coordinate the pace, of governing' (Craft 2018b, p. 44).

IDCs, Forums, Task Forces and Working Parties

Interdepartmental committees (also called working parties or study groups) have long been common, covering administrative matters, programmes or policy negotiation. There were, for example, as many as 180 permanent and ad hoc committees under the traditional Australian system (Spann 1979). IDCs were variously regarded as inconsequential and process-oriented fiefdoms that lacked productivity (see MAC 2004). Public service arrangements were affected by the growth of ministerial advisers with their associated networks, interventions from the centre and the greater preference for short-term, task-oriented processes. Nevertheless, IDCs, informal interaction and networks continued to be significant and commonplace (Boston and Gill 2011).

Officials routinely worked across departmental boundaries to deliver services and collaborate in formulating national policies through IDCs, task forces, joint working parties and other cross-agency mechanisms (ANAO 2010b). Task forces rose to prominence in Australia as a means of avoiding the defects of IDCs and as short-term vehicles for giving focus to government agendas. The task force becomes 'semi-formalised as a device to develop new policy or to deal with significant, urgent issues' (MAC 2004, p. 29). Whereas once task forces were distinguished informally from other cross-agency structures, the understanding was now entrenched of the task force as 'a discrete, time-and-purpose limited unit responsible for producing a result in its own right'. Their capacity for operating independently from policy departments is strengthened by the Department of the Prime Minister and Cabinet being assigned administrative responsibility for them in many cases (Hamburger 2007, p. 218). Task forces have been used by the Australian DPMC for several decades to address questions by combining central coordination, generalist and whole of government skills with line department (or external) policy expertise. At times there were around ten a year (Hamburger et al. 2011, pp. 384–6).

The IDC has remained a core component of interdepartmental interaction, but without the rigidities and permanency that characterised its predecessors when they dominated many internal advisory processes. Following the termination of the UK's public service agreements, in lieu of formal arrangements informal working groups were established for specific problems, but lack of formalisation and the high turnover of members meant that influence was limited (Paun and Blatchford 2014). The more open internal processes with ministerial staff constantly interacting with public servants and being able to range quite freely across the policy spectrum (as depicted by Craft 2016, 2018a) provide checks and counterpoints.

Functional and Professional Networks

Networks for learning and capability development operate horizontally to link specialists across departments. These might be a bottom-up product, a semi-official guided entity or a more formal centralised mechanism for enhancing capacity and communication among professionals. Networks used to be more informal, short on resources and multi-purpose, while others have been more developmental, geared to tasks, and led by senior public servants. There are also variations between the two.

Two approaches, functional areas and heads of profession, have taken off in New Zealand and the United Kingdom as a means of capability development (Jensen et al. 2014).[6] The UK push towards specialisms and cross-department activity derived from the 2012 civil service reform agenda and led to the differentiation of functional areas and professions of which policy is one.[7] The UK's functional model covers 11 corporate functions: commercial, communications, corporate finance, digital, finance, human resources, internal audit, legal, project delivery, property and a more recent addition: fraud, error, debt and grants. A core purpose is the leadership of corporate functions on a cross-departmental basis. In contrast to the professions which focus on skills, the functions approach emphasises central coordination and may address duplication, efficiency and shared systems. The benefits sought have therefore ranged beyond cross-departmental strategies and aspire to modernise government operations (Cabinet Office 2015a; McCrae and Gold 2017; PACAC 2018). The New Zealand approach, conceived as cross-agency leadership, relies on functional leadership from designated chief executives of line departments, and covers three functional areas (ICT, procurement and property). The focus is cutting total costs for common activities through efficiencies, capability development and improving service delivery (SSC 2017).

The heads of profession approach was confined to five areas in New Zealand (finance, human resources, ICT, law and policy), but has risen to 28 in the United Kingdom, the 'policy profession' being common to both and considered further here. Previous attempts at enhancing policy advice across the New Zealand government, including central prescriptions and guidelines, failed at the implementation phase. The 'policy project' has been based on collaboration and co-design involving a community of policy leaders with the overall purpose of embedding collective responsibility and improving the quality of advice across the state services. The objective of collective ownership has yet to be achieved (Davison 2015, 2016). There has been significant sponsorship: the head of the policy profession has been the chief executive of the Department of the Prime Minister and Cabinet, who is supported by a policy profession board comprising chief executives and deputies (Washington 2016). There has also been political support from senior political leaders. One-third of policy agencies were reported as having taken up the policy quality framework; another third used the policy skills framework; and several agencies applied the policy capability framework. There has been funding and institutional commitment and plans to measure improvements in the quality of policy advice and the usage of the frameworks (Washington and Mintrom 2018, pp. 40–41). The Board has since taken on the role of a policy career board with responsibility for cross-agency support for developing a cohort of about 90 policy leaders (Kibblewhite 2018b). A new stage occurred in 2019 when all chief executives agreed to the development of a revised policy quality framework, which has been accepted by the profession and used by all agencies.

The UK policy role has been a core generic activity of civil servants (and over half the permanent secretaries have backgrounds in policy and economics) (McCrae and Gold 2017). There is a standard depiction for a profession, in the policy case 'an informal network for civil servants who work in, or are involved with, the formation of policy for government'. The functions are to raise standards, provide career development opportunities, and to promote collaboration, all within a governance structure. There is a cross-government head of the policy profession, a departmental permanent secretary who convenes the leadership group, and the policy profession board, which is responsible for improvement agendas such as professional standards. The policy profession is not well institutionalised as in New Zealand, funding being dependent on amounts negotiated with departments annually. Although one of the largest specialist areas, the support unit is small. The policy profession head is a very part-time permanent secretary. However, membership of the policy profession board covers the main policy departments and has expanded to become more inclusive of Whitehall agencies.

Civil servants are appointed to one of the specialisms. In the new 'transformation' of the workforce commercial, technical and project execution skills have been favoured by the chief executive of the civil service (Manzoni 2018).[8] Policy with 18,400 members is one of the largest of the 28 professions. However, a cognate area, operational delivery, is a separate profession for staff delivering and supporting frontline services with 230,000 members (70 per cent of the civil service).[9] An evaluation of the policy profession assessed the original actions, reinforced the directions being taken, such as collective ownership and the collaborative approach (rather than the centralised and interventionist roles of functional areas) and building links with other centres of expertise (e.g. with Policy Lab) (Policy Profession Board 2019).

Canadian networks have varied between standard forms for exchange and results-oriented developmental activities. The financial management group has been institutionalised and engaged inter alia in recruitment with support from the Treasury Board Secretariat. The Canadian policy community, established in 2017, is funded by departments and has a small team of staff managing it under a board and activities focused on hosting annual conferences, developing training materials and a competency framework, and operating policy mobility through placements (Percival 2018; Shepherd and Stoney 2018).

Australia has had a profusion of networks that operate as communities of practice and information sharing forums, occasionally facilitated by a steering committee or central agency. It final adopted the 'profession-based model' in 2019, as a 'much-needed public service-wide initiative', which took the initial form of an HR Professional Stream Strategy (Woolcott 2019). Australia's policy capability agenda was also formalised under the leadership of a secretaries' group with a dedicated staff in a policy hub and an associated website and roadmap (DPMC 2019). The objectives include policy career pathways, cross-agency policy improvement, developing system leadership for capability, annual assessment of policy capability, increasing 'the demand for long-term policy thinking', and clarifying political advisers' role in policy development (DPMC 2019, p. 5).

SEARCHING FOR COLLABORATION

The trajectory of public sector reform has continued to be state-centric but disposed towards greater collaboration as the broader environment of ideas and practice moved in that direction.

Joined-up government was introduced in the United Kingdom in 1997 with a key aim being to ensure policy-making was more connected and strategic (Bogdanor 2005). Public service agreements (PSAs) were created as a coordination tool and evolved over time to include joint targets, an 'ambitious attempt . . . to re-engineer government along more collaborative lines' (Paun and Blatchford 2014, p. 131). There were problems with joint targets because of difficulties with coordinating 'cross-departmental policy and resource allocation' owing to the siloed departmental structures in Whitehall (James and Nakamura 2014), but they provided a potential foundation until terminated by a new government.

Only two joint bids were submitted to the Treasury for the UK's 2015 spending review (NAO 2016a). The Committee of Public Accounts reported cases of departments working together but 'these working practices rarely lead to formal funding or accountability arrangements' (CPA 2016c, p. 5). Departments had sought to work together but the obstacles were insurmountable, inter alia, 'disagreements between ministers; disagreements about who should fund policy areas; and insufficient flexibility within single departmental plans to enable departments to work together' (NAO 2016c, p. 37). The Spending Review process was unsuited to handling issues that spanned departmental boundaries because it was based on bilateral negotiations between the Treasury and departments. The Treasury's approach controlled departmental spending but prevented the tackling of difficult issues, including 'policy issues such as obesity and structural issues such as interdependencies between departments and the services they provide' (CPA 2016c, p. 12; NAO 2016c, p. 18). However, queried about departmental joint bids in the Committee of Public Accounts, J. Bowler (Director of General Public Spending, HM Treasury) responded that Whitehall is siloed and that there are different mechanisms for joining: 'There are three buckets . . . joint funding, joint targeting and joint delivery and implementation', and an increase in the first. According to Manzoni, Health SDP has some joint objectives with the Department for Work and Pensions but it was unclear whether they were systematically shared (CPA 2018, Q23, 82, 83, 89).

The Australian system displayed the tensions between the strength of vertical accountability on the one hand, and the increasing scale of existing horizontal relationships on the other. Nevertheless, official views supported horizontal approaches, collaboration and collective action (AGRAGA 2010). Only one of the governance agreements in the ANAO's classification, previously mentioned, was close to serious 'collaboration', defined as 'high-level principles and obligations for a collaborative relationship between two or more agencies': see Table 2.1 in ANAO 2010b). An analysis of joint working in audit reports found that only 20 per cent involved more committed arrangements like collaboration (but also argued that for many purposes such a level of agreement was unnecessary) (Halligan and Smith 2019).[10] There was therefore some evidence of movement towards collaboration, and some institutionalisation (Halligan 2015b), as illustrated by two different cases. Project Wickenby was a cross-agency exercise for preventing tax evasion through illegal offshore schemes with eight agencies working together under the leadership of the Australian Taxation Office (ANAO 2012b; DFD 2012a). Working Age Payments covered income support through a partnership between two departments that was underpinned by a formal agreement based on service delivery strategies that met intended outcomes while acknowledging each's operational priorities (ANAO 2013b; Halligan 2015a).

New Zealand emphasised 'horizontally-integrated, whole-of-government capacity and capability' and cross-agency coordination (Boston and Eichbaum 2007, p. 134). System rebalancing and renewing public management outcomes became central. Specific issues were the products of fragmentation under an agency system and the need to integrate service delivery and cross-agency coordination. Some degree of shared accountability was reported as common but included informal as well as formal arrangements. Inter-agency agreements were being increasingly formalised, with a focus on sharing accountability and outcomes (e.g. chief executives working in sector groupings), but there was a shortage of evidence about the incidence and types of collaboration (Boston and Gill 2011, pp. 213–14, 236). This mood was not converted into durable collaborative governance because of many challenges and obstacles (Boston and Gill 2011; Eppel 2013; O'Leary 2014).[11] A joined-up approach, such as the Integrated Service Response, was constrained by a lack of ownership and sharing (Hughes and Smart 2012). Under the sectoral approach, agencies received acclamation for process success (e.g. a joint strategy), the high performing sectors having the most activity (e.g. governance groups, and joint statements) but no obvious public value (Scott and Boyd 2017b, p. 12). Another reality check was that while agencies understood the potential that collaboration offered, the New Zealand system was some distance from routinely operating on that basis (Morrison 2014).

New Zealand continued to ripple with experimentation in this area from 2011. The ten goals of Better Public Service required special coordinating arrangements (see 'Lead Ministers' section above). A feature of the social investment approach was a 'new mode of governance' because it involved 'improved cross-agency working – or better horizontal governance' (Boston and Gill 2017, p. 12).[12] The 2019 well-being budget has involved ministers and departments developing funding bids together. Resource sharing within a policy system remains dependent on amendments to legislation and is still 'more form than substance' but the potential is considerable (James 2019).

PATTERNS OF COORDINATION AND COLLABORATION

The traditional public administration system (pre-1980) was replete with coordination, the IDC being a standard mechanism. How IDCs worked was the subject of conflicting views (see e.g. Kernaghan and Siegel 1991). There were also the claims that 'informal collaboration' among the elite was the most important dimension (according to S. E. Finer in Hood 2005, p. 32). A central dynamic was the perceived failure of the machinery of government to adapt to new circumstances, specifically the weaknesses in policy coordination by central agencies, the permanent character of IDC communities and chronic siloisation at the department level.

Developments with coordination have since taken several directions. The dominant place of interdepartmental committees in the traditional system was eroded. Temporary task forces came into favour, political offices and networks acquired a major role and the central drive by political executives for results increased. Horizontal management became somewhat more extensive, collaboration was popularised (although less so where it entailed sharing objectives and accountabilities), and coordination overall expanded using a greater variety of instruments, a number of which can be linked to governance types.

Vertical coordination was reinforced, although not by a return to the traditional hierarchy and transaction control of departments by dominant central agencies. The character of vertical coordination changed in some respects becoming more important with an expanded range of management forms. A growth area was political instruments directed at priorities and implementation. Prime ministers' offices played influential roles in the web of coordination.

The instruments of coordination varied between countries and over time. The United Kingdom has relied on a string of units variously located in No. 10 and the Cabinet Office for driving implementation of government priorities. Canada and Australia have emphasised the role of the PMO in political coordination. New Zealand has invested in minister-led, CEO-driven results and outcome-focused exercises. The use of some coordination instruments was transient, including those inspired and influenced by specific prime ministers, and ad hoc interventions (e.g. an efficiency agenda) or revisited based on experience and changing contexts.

At the operational level there was extensive activity. British civil servants surveyed indicated that they sought 'to avoid duplication, overlap, or letting issues fall between the cracks', and favoured being joined-up (Page and Jenkins 2005, p. 151). This was nevertheless a passive conception, which reflected behaviour involving low levels of intensity. The Australian survey of inter-agency agreements showed widespread 'cross-agency activity and interdependencies' but concentrated at the lower to middle end of the spectrum (ANAO 2010b). Common-sense dictated that particular tasks required specific forms (Halligan and Smith 2019). However, the issue was whether big ticket questions, intractable problems and siloed matters were being systematically addressed.

The widespread inter-agency activity was more variegated and integral to the operations of departments, but most did not entail high commitment of resources or integrated operations. There was no obvious trend to horizontal coordination at the expense of the vertical as might befit an era proclaimed as one of networks and governance. Rather, the combination of austerity conditions, and/or neo-liberal programmes, and controlling political executives and central agencies reinforced both vertical coordination and the influence of hierarchy on horizontal coordination. Could it be otherwise given the institutional contexts of the Anglophone systems and the reaffirmations of the functional axis and the ministerial department?

Management coordination expanded in specific jurisdictions because of top-down austerity programmes, greater oversight and strategic roles for central agencies, and capability weaknesses at the line departmental level (see Chapter 5) or new or expanding fields. The coordination system nevertheless continued to have multiple dimensions and layers. Central oversight of capability was institutionalised in some cases. Other mandated programmes provided an impetus to central agencies, including efficiency programmes.

Whole-of-government directions were of course steadfast, some with deference to departmental discretion.

Horizontal coordination was inclined to reflect the influence of hierarchy (Peters 2015), or simply the intersection of horizontal and vertical coordination, but this was both predictable (and often appropriate) where central agencies practised different shades of hierarchy. Horizontal coordination remained uneven and problematic (cf. Europe: Lægreid et al. 2016). The complexities displayed in the early wave of horizontalism were still evident, as were the weaknesses at the centre and in interdepartmental workings (Bakvis and Juillet 2004). Cross-agency work was still dogged by silos (e.g. Robertson 2018).

Despite the celebration of 'collaboration' during the last 15 years, the more committed and demanding shared forms remained under-incentivised and under-utilised. The declared passion for collaboration was not necessarily reproduced in inter-agency agreements or sharing results. There was a shift from routine consultation (or less self-conscious forms of coordinative interaction) among departments to results-focused agendas driven by ministerial leadership which used either a set of accountability-based sectors and issues or cabinet committees and task forces.

Explanations for the Rise, Decline and Plateauing of Coordination and Collaboration

Several types of explanation are relevant to the choices of instruments and the fluctuating support for horizontal governance, taking the latter first. Successive reform paradigms have registered a significant impact on what instruments are used and the relative emphasis on specialisation and coordination (Bouckaert et al. 2010), featuring the standard categories like managerialism, reintegrated government and network governance. Starting in the noughties, the lack of a distinctive and coherent paradigm was apparent; eclecticism became dominant with diverse elements being variously drawn on. Consequently, competing organisational principles were more pronounced in reform (Christensen and Lægreid 2012). With the renaissance of central agencies, the centre was empowered with new instruments.

The second set of factors was institutional, in particular, path dependency. Factors favouring vertical silos included specialisation of the functional department; and efficiency reviews that drove top-down departmental savings. Favoured forms of specialisation, the central agency and ministerial department, became more institutionalised, strengthening vertical lines. In the architecture of public organisations, an important trend was the swing back to a stronger ministerial department (Halligan 2006; see also Appendix 3).

The biases in the structure were duplicated across all the countries as departments retained explicit organisational boundaries and hierarchical accountability. Under the Australian framework the 'strong-willed focus on the operations of individual entities' meant that department heads' responsibilities did not 'directly consider concepts such as joint operations' (DFD 2012a, p. 36). The chief executive of the UK's civil service warned against an accountability system with multiple axes: accountability had to be maintained down one axis, the departmental one (John Manzoni in CPA 2016c, Q53). New Zealand's model dictated single-purpose agencies with clearly specified outputs to produce efficient service delivery. Similarly, the UK Treasury focused on inputs and outputs, not outcomes, which were a concern of the Cabinet Office.

Vertically centred financial arrangements were a barrier to greater collaboration. Australia's Finance Department recognised the need for dual and multiple accountabilities (DFD 2012b), but legislation (the PGPA Act discussed in Chapter 6) dealt with collective responsibility and accountabilities in a limited manner, and inter-agency cooperation did not increase (Alexander and Thodey 2018). Shared accountability for system-wide results required a recasting of aspects of governance and institutionalising principles and practices based on outcomes (Edwards et al. 2012). 'Spending reviews have previously been characterised by a bilateral deal-making approach between departments and HM Treasury, and a lack of collaboration between departments – this is consistent with an emphasis on controlling individual budgets but does not encourage a joined-up approach to value for money. SDPs are not formally shared between departments' (NAO 2018c, p. 12). Funding roles and mechanisms have presented barriers to coordination (NAO 2013b).

A third factor was the cycle of reform. The life of a reform agenda is dependent on the levels of commitment and the strength of the obstacles. Once attention deficit sets in, a reform agenda tapers off. The Australian agenda received impetus through the report, *Connecting Government* (MAC 2004), which examined how to work across boundaries through processes and structures, cultures, managing information, and budgetary frameworks. Despite specific successes, overall implementation was 'disappointing', and the report did not have a major impact in the medium term (APSC 2007, p. 247; Halligan 2008b). The early Canadian focus on horizontal management came in the aftermath of the top-down cuts of the Program Review and restructuring (Aucoin and Savoie 1998). Horizontal management was high on the reform agenda in the late 1990s, with consideration of the need for an 'enabling culture' for horizontal matters. Following the peak of interest and discussion on horizontal governance (early to mid-2000s), reports and commentaries on horizontal initiatives tapered, and became piecemeal (Lindquist 2014). Under the Harper government there were no incentives to address such questions. The joined-up agenda in the United Kingdom was prominent under early Blair but faltered as other agendas came to the fore, such as governance beyond the centre. Joining up government was unlikely to be durable because it required a magnitude of change unpalatable to 'high political culture' (Burnham and Pyper 2008, pp. 86–7).

The fourth factor was politicisation as the inclinations, preferences and priorities of the political executive become pivotal and more interventionist. The drive of political executives for performance, implementation, delivery and results has been relentless, and reflected in coordination instruments that pursue alignment between government priorities and progress in implementation. Some instruments are not directly attributable to managerialism, but to the political paradigm (Aucoin 2012) that operated in parallel. Most problematic were government interventions resulting from the electoral cycle that undermined potentially effective coordination and required long set-ups to be credible. Political agendas focused on results ran counter to cross-cutting exercises (e.g. the UK's cross-boundary PSAs were replaced by department-centred plans: Paun and Blatchford 2014).

Fiscal austerity encouraged the use of top-down instruments to secure compliance with efficiency and economy objectives, and stove-piping of organisational functioning (see Lindquist 2014 on the Canadian programme review). Central agency roles were strengthened, particularly those responsible for efficiency oversight (financial and performance management), which were driven through the functional department. Political capacity was augmented through control of vertical instruments of coordination. The greater emphasis on political capacity had limitations as the use of relevant instruments could be volatile, and public policy outside government priorities neglected. The governance climate, specifically the directive style of Canadian governments, produced a decline in corporate discourse (Lindquist 2014).

The proliferation of horizontal instruments registered an impact on capacity development. However, what was systemic could be unimportant, while what was important were specific arrangements for societal issues that emphasised shared results and accountabilities. The latter, however, appeared to remain the exceptions because of obstacles presented by the vertical imperative. A test case was the extent of the flow of New Zealand's experiments with key results to the rest of the state sector.

CONCLUSION

This chapter has examined several forms of coordination, different types of horizontal and vertical instruments, and trends. Over recent decades, the level of coordination has increased substantially, it is more diverse, and the range of forms has expanded. The spectrum ranges from hard-edged mandatory forms (particularly prompted by austerity, neo-liberalism and implementation issues) through to softer network guidance and exhortation. Much of this can be attributed to managerialist requirements that reinforce vertical controls and transformation of roles and processes through politicisation and top-down austerity measures (including centralisation, rationalisation and standardisation). The use of instruments is susceptible to environmental conditions because governments attending to budget deficits emphasise mandatory vertical and political instruments. The political drive for results has influenced the primary modes of coordination in use. There has nevertheless been ongoing experimentation with various instruments that have sustained horizontal innovation. When fiscal pressures are relaxed questions about when to apply sanctions, how best to incentivise, and the right circumstance for intervention receive different attention and are reflected in the choice of coordination instruments.

Collaboration has seemingly faltered or plateaued in several respects. Many initiatives seem to be concentrated towards the light end of the spectrum, which may not be far removed from traditional mutual adjustment, and tends to be short term, ad hoc and either less formal or low intensity. Others, such as the rise of professional and functional networks, reflect capability deficits at the individual and organisational level. The preconditions for greater collaboration are often absent, including incentives for partners to engage. There is a shortage of evidence to sustain the argument that collaboration has become integral to public management and grounded in well-developed relationships. European surveys report that commitment to collaboration is too vague about meanings and practice to be of much assistance, and that paradoxically, 'while coordination and collaboration generally are seen as important contemporary reform trends, few executives see significant improvements in the quality of policy coherence and coordination' (Lægreid et al. 2016, p. 251). The paradox of collaboration for Anglophone systems is that despite being one of the strongest mantras of public leaders in the twenty-first century, it has attracted little sustained action.[13] Despite an increase in coordination activity there has continued to be inadequate evidence of its impact.

NOTES

1. An Australian document referred to 'whole-of-government' in the sense used here (macro-level) and more loosely for other inter-departmental arrangements (meso-level). For the Public Service Commission, whole-of-government covered 'working across portfolio boundaries to achieve a shared goal and an integrated government response to particular issues' (MAC 2004, p. 4), while the Finance Department saw it covering most or all agencies, and giving 'effect to government policy decisions, to improve consistency and control'. See https://www.finance.gov.au/procurement/wog-procurement/wog.html.
2. See   https://dpmc.govt.nz/cabinet-committees/swc-cabinet-social-wellbeing-committee.
3. Sources are the Australian Public Service Commission at http://www.apsc.gov.au/aps-reform/current-projects/capability-reviews and APSC 2013; for New Zealand

Te Kawa and Guerin 2012 and the State Services Commission at http://www.ssc .govt.nz/pif; and for the UK, Cabinet Office 2009.

4. Canada's former Department of Human Resources Development moved through several iterations. New Zealand's Ministry of Social Development was the product of a merger. The UK's Department of Work and Pensions also derived from the mergers of agencies (White and Dunleavy 2010).

5. This contested development (e.g. Gourley 2017), was credited to the clout of an influential minister and bureaucratic politics rather than rational design.

6. Australia adopted a formalised professions model in late 2019.

7. The 'functional model' covers 'priority areas of common, cross-departmental activity for which central leadership is required' and includes many professions. The distinction is not entirely clear, except that professions cover a range of expertise, including niche and broad areas (e.g. policy). See https://assets.publishing .service.gov.uk/government/%20uploads/system/%20uploads/attachment_data/ file/418869/The_Functional_Model.pdf.

8. Manzoni 2018 advocated a civil service composed of specialists (as opposed to traditional generalists). See https://www.instituteforgovernment.org.uk/events/ civil-service-fit-future.

9. See https://quarterly.blog.gov.uk/2018/07/05/top-things-to-know-about-the -operational-delivery-profession/.

10. Only 38 audit reports out of 304 involved working together (Halligan and Smith 2019).

11. Note that O'Leary's canvass included delivery arrangements.

12. In addition to horizontal governance, other drivers were austerity in order to sustain social benefit programmes and using evidence over the long term. These drivers have also been contested: see Head and Di Francesco 2019.

13. See e.g. Hughes and Smart 2012; Scott 2017.

9. Long-term reform and public management systems

Public management and governance have become harder. There is consensus that external demands have become greater in a more turbulent environment – higher expectations, stronger political pressures, protean governments – as have issues internal to the government system including no respite from accountability requirements (Varghese 2016). Diagnoses have continued to report failures to attain results and the desired management levels (e.g. Shergold 2013; King and Crewe 2014) within institutional contexts that were complex and difficult. Anglophone countries – once admired for their ability to initiate reform – struggled to sustain implementation over time. Even so, the drumbeat of change and management improvement has been constant.

Scholars have argued that 'what it said on the tin' – meaning official reform claims about 'containing costs and improving administration' – did not materialise for the United Kingdom, meaning official reform claims about 'containing costs and improving administration' (Hood and Dixon 2015, p. 178). But there were other reform aspirations in Anglophone countries, several of which have been addressed in this book.

Reform in the 1980s was thought to be solving the age-old problem of reform failure. There were accomplishments in the short-to-medium term in the sense of implementing a range of distinctive public management reforms and learning from and building on reform experiments (Halligan 1996a). The settlement of reform types occurred, and they became internalised and institutionalised as routine instruments to be called on. These included management improvement, managerial flexibility, privatisation, outsourcing, performance focus and so on, which were available as menu items should they be required. However, once the ideological zeal had faded and the verdict on key reforms was in, the position changed. Making reforms work and sustaining their positive features long term often proved to be elusive. The second half of the reform era was replete with dysfunctional trends as the consequences of poorly conceived reforms were registered. Implementation was often problematic over time in terms of sustainability (APS Review 2019a, p. 28). Recycling became a theme as governments reworked and repackaged reform agendas (Pollitt 2008), and the results of earlier agendas were dissipated through neglect because improving capabilities was low priority and public management was unable to lift its game. Unintended consequences appeared because of gaps in implementation and through the contradictions in reform agendas.

This suggests another explanation: that public sector reform has not been a serious priority for political executives in the twenty-first century, who have been preoccupied (1) under Hammond (UK) or Cormann (Australia) with efficiency gains, or more explicitly cuts to the public service and outsourcing, masquerading as reform; (2) or with results and government priorities above all else (most governments), or a disinterest in managing reform (Gillard in Australia and Cameron in the UK).

The book has focused on the impacts of specific reforms and change on the public and governance management system, specifically the impact of politicisation over the long term and the effects on managerialism given the institutional contexts in which it has been applied. This chapter explores the condition of public management systems in Anglophone countries after four decades and answers the question of what has changed because of reform with respect to politicisation and managerialisation.

The chapter compares the four countries in terms of components of their public management systems indicating variations between them and raising questions about how sustainable a public management reform agenda is over the longer term. It returns to the initial questions about what has changed because of managerial and political reform; the long-term results of this period of intensive change; and what might account for the shortfalls in performance and the continuing need for reform. There are questions to be addressed about the role and significance of the Anglophone tradition and the public management approach. This chapter addresses ongoing issues, particularly the challenges of finding appropriate mixes in the design of public management and governance, and alternatives for reconstituting the system. But first the impact of politicisation and managerialism is examined.

IMPACT OF POLITICISATION

Politicisation is defined as the expansion of the political sphere within the executive branch. This may be at the expense of other interests, but not necessarily. Underlying politicisation is the drive for implementation and results and the assertion of political authority. Five distinct components have been examined across several chapters: redefining the political–bureaucratic relationships and roles; the appointment process; reasserting the centre and executive authority; driving political control under 'new political governance'; and results and performance.

The extent of politicisation is evident in many respects, although much is private, informal and opaque. Political actors have permeated much of the public management system, their influence becoming pervasive in all four

Table 9.1   Major functions affected by politicisation

Area	Result
Policy initiation	Shared responsibility
Policy implementation	Political involvement
Departmental management	Commonplace
Management processes and capabilities	Typically, political involvement
Appointments	Greater political engagement
Performance	Swing to emphasis on results
Coordination	Significance of central political control and delivery

countries. The contextual nature of the character of politicisation must be emphasised as the level of politicisation varies between countries, regimes, ministers, and over time; inter-country differences are discussed later in this chapter. Few boundaries remain because politicisation has increased greatly everywhere during the last four decades. There are generally legislative limits to political influence over appointments, although they may be malleable and exceptions occur. The reserve powers of departmental heads, where they exist, can set limits, providing of course that they are prepared to draw on them. The over-bearing and peremptory minister, who initiates policy (possibly by PBE) and disregards advice, is difficult to contain. The willingness to 'give the flick' to the department head or other senior staff is one more extreme manifestation of arrogant political actors (noting that there have also been many effective partnerships between ministers and senior public servants).

The types of impact are explicit in the summary and reflected in many dimensions of the public management system: coordination is more political, and performance more results-driven (Table 9.1). With the political executive given its head in the environment of the 2010s there is government on demand. Under the traditional system, more extreme and nonviable policy schemes were often modified by bureaucrats. Under twenty-first-century governments, policy advice may not be sought (or ignored). Professional preferences may be discouraged by ministers and senior public servants may withhold advice with public interest implications. Insistent advisers can be penalised.

The country focus can be distinguished by the breadth of instruments and the intensity of their use (Table 9.2). Within the Anglophone group there have been different emphases regarding the instruments relied on and how intensively they were used. These could be either highly centralised with a prime minister operating through the PMO and central agencies, and/or ministerial initiatives that were undertaken without due collective responsibility (e.g. ministers running major policy preferences under Cameron's decentralised approach).

Table 9.2   *Use of political instruments in Anglophone systems*

	Australia	Canada	New Zealand	United Kingdom
Ministerial roles	Strong	Strong	Strong	Strong
PMO	High	High	Medium	High & variable
Ministerial advisers	High	High	Medium	Medium
Appointments (& terminations)	High	High	Low	Medium
Other instruments*	Medium	Medium	Low	High

* For example, policy tsars.

In the reform era, Canada focused on the centralised system associated with the prime minister and the prime minister's office and more generally an extensive cadre of political advisers (Savoie 2011). The Australian combination was similar, noting that levels of centralisation were not as consistently high as Canada's, but the prime minister and the PMO were the centre-point and there was scope for activist ministers, and political advisers. The UK drive was through the prime minister, but the PMO's organisational capacity was variable and often ineffective. The addition of policy tsars and central units and the role of key partisan actors were significant. Ministers had stronger roles, but the ministerial advisory system was less developed and interventionist. New Zealand rated lower overall on these indicators, but similar elements were present and ministerial agendas registered strongly with similar effects to elsewhere. Overall, Australia and Canada were high for dimensions of politicisation, whereas New Zealand and the United Kingdom varied and were usually lower in the rankings (Table 9.2).

Types of Relationship

Four types are used to distinguish different forms of relationship between ministers and public servants according to several elements including origins (relative importance of trustee-stewardship–agent positions), degree of balance and the approach to appointments. They have been differentiated according to the role of politicisation, the principles underlying the relationship and the extent to which a durable relationship has been forged within the managerialist environment of the reform era. Three of these types are based on varying requirements for responsiveness in which the minister more explicitly stands astride the portfolio reflecting different approaches to developing an effective operating system and the relative importance of countervailing forces (Table 9.3).

A traditional conception (Type 1) is based on acceptance of the complementary roles of ministers and senior public servants with associated features that

Table 9.3   *Types of relationship between ministers and public servants*

Types	Character	Main principles	Stability	Balance
1. Traditional conception	Evolved over time	Public service trustee Westminster	Stable	Conditionally balanced
2. Modernised	New settings for reform era	Principal–agent, Westminster, stewardship	Stable	Rebalanced
3. Oscillating	Swings between positions	Principal–agent versus Westminster	Unstable	Imbalanced
4. Skewed	Asymmetrical	Principal–agent, partisanship	Destabilising	Imbalanced

ensure common understandings and responsibilities. This enables a reconciliation of a prominent policy role for permanent secretaries and the minister's constitutional role, which provides operating conditions that are stable and durable. It is dependent on certain conditions and assumptions, the foremost being that top public servants would not overly exploit their positions as trustees or guardians of the public good, while ministers would accept a reactive leadership role. The potential imbalance in their positions could be activated if the premises no longer apply.

The other types range from less politicised and stable through to highly partisan and unstable. Type 2 is based on a new accommodation (or bargain in the terms of Hood and Lodge 2006) between the actors in which adjustments have been made, and the politicians' desire for control has been acknowledged. Under this type there is a squaring of the contending principles (principal–agent and stewardship) with due regard for Westminster. In the context of management reform modernisation has occurred, and the traditional relationship has been converted into contemporary terms involving redistribution of power in favour of the political executive. This could be regarded as a muted form of principal–agent – ministers are assertive and demanding – but limits exist on the influence of the political executive. There is understanding and articulation of the need to attend to the relationship and the underlying principles.

The two paradigms distinguished by Aucoin (1990) mark the radical shift in understandings about the role of 'politics' and how management functions are exercised. In one, politics is about 'the determination of the basic values or missions, and thus the policies, of an organisation', whereas with the other politics pervades management, and is therefore integral to both policy formulation and implementation (p. 127). A significant line is crossed in moving to Types 3 and 4.

With Type 3, principal–agent principles shape politicians' actions. Notable swings are apparent between high-level political intervention and containment. Typically, this is instigated through incursions by politicians that conflict with accepted principles, and which become subject to public debate (for example, capricious sacking of department heads, political and partisan appointments to top positions). This usually includes some form of dislocation in the short term – an apparent inability to reconcile the respective claims about the relationship which tests the strength of traditional norms. By a form of dialectical process there is movement towards some solution. The inherent lack of consensus and instability means that this process is likely to be replayed at other times. The model, therefore, is characterised by swings between different positions and implicit ownership of the public service, which makes for an imbalanced system.

Under Type 4, partisan self-interest and ministerial capriciousness dominate and conventions matter less. The type represents a pronounced shift in favour of the politicians because of unbridled exercises of executive power producing unstable and imbalanced, unbounded, potential for the full gamut of politicisation activity. If irrevocable and not corrected it is both destabilising for governance and a potentially dangerous departure from the Anglophone tradition.

These possibilities underlay Aucoin's (2008, 2012) argument about the changing conditions under which governments were operating in the twenty-first century, including greater open government and transparency, external audit and review, political volatility and polarisation, media demands and the growth of think tanks, lobbyists and interest groups.

Type 1: Traditional configuration
The four countries approximated this type prior to the changes of the reform era. The relationships in this type began to unravel once the premises of the traditional bargain no longer held. The consciousness of an imbalance became starker and less tolerated by political executives, and the challenges to it more strident. This was particularly associated with politicians awakening to the potential inherent in their positions, and as the role and types of ministers changed.

Type 2: Modernised and rebalanced
An approximation of this type has been New Zealand, which knitted together the old (relative independence) and new (CEOs on contract, appointed by an open and explicit process that went beyond the control, but not the influence, of the political executive). A significant result of New Zealand's distinctive brand of reform was the redefinition of roles including those of ministers and senior public servants. It can claim to have modernised the traditional system through using explicitly managerialist concepts to more clearly delineate an appropriate fit between the two.

Illustrative of the New Zealand position was the weaker evidence in support of Aucoin's (2012) four dimensions of new public governance. An increased concentration of power in the office of the prime minister was not apparent. With regard to appointments to the senior public service, the State Services Commissioner had responsibility for recommending appointments of departmental chief executives. Ministers participated in the appointment process, but no government has made its own appointments, one argument being that it was unnecessary to appoint partisans because of the responsive public service (Boston and Halligan 2012). The removal of a chief executive of a department is the responsibility of the State Services Commissioner with the agreement of the governor-general in council.

Nevertheless, there has been evidence to support marginalisation of the public service, ministerial advisers have consistently been a source of concern (Eichbaum and Shaw 2010; Boston and Halligan 2012), and ministerial pressure has intensified (Eichbaum 2017). The minister's office has a mix of political and public service staff (but not the 'temporary partisans' of Australia: Maley 2019). Considering Aucoin's final dimension, a public service that was 'promiscuously partisan' for the government of the day, the openness of the New Zealand system provided some protection for the public service. New public governance was only weakly applied in New Zealand, in part because of the attachment to traditional Westminster values. Nevertheless, there are tensions (ministers and their political advisers do cross the line) and debates have occurred about the stewardship role of chief executives. New Zealand is not therefore without its limitations, and there have been Type 3 debates (James 2002), and questions about the level of commitment to stewardship. Legislative changes planned for 2020 are intended to fine-tune balance in the system.

Type 3: Oscillating

With Type 3 there are alternating phases of stability and instability pointing to imbalance. The periods of stability are punctuated by outbreaks of divergence and discordance reflecting political dissatisfaction. This oscillation is a product of the divergent views of the principles and contention for influence over the system. The 'new government syndrome' is a factor here.

The Australian handling of responsiveness and public service neutrality has been subject to swings of focus and attention during the last 50 years. The general trend has been towards politicisation, but declarations for, and occasionally measures to reinforce, neutrality have also occurred. The relationship between secretaries and ministers has at times been fraught with issues about boundaries. Under Westminster tenets there has been a tendency for successive governments to exude ownership of the public service. This had significant implications for transitions between governments when tensions arose with a public service perceived by the new political leadership as being too close to its predecessors.

Prime ministerial power is a component of Aucoin's components of new public governance (NPG). Political advisers were accepted as necessary (at times seemingly rampant) and personalisation in appointments occurred. The question of the public service's being 'promiscuously partisan for the government' (Aucoin 2008) is evident. Some instances supported this contention, but it was not an ongoing condition. It was understood that a strong political executive can drive a professional public service using the range of instruments available for securing public service attentiveness. There was mounting evidence of NPG, although unevenly across the countries, and the trajectory was towards a greater NPG that reflected a different synthesis of traditional values and performance-based responsiveness.

The UK civil service experienced volatility in its relationships with the political executive as successive political leaders sought transformation, but there were calmer periods under less fixated prime ministers. It has been subject to intense pressures to outsource policy, and to challenges to the appointment and performance review processes of permanent secretaries (HM Government 2012). The character of the rhetoric would point towards an NPG result, but it shows up as an imbalanced case (Type 3). While the Blair government used several instruments to control and influence the civil service it did not actually seek to politicise it with partisan appointments, adopting 'an essentially conservative attitude in its attempts to reform the SCS' (Fawcett and Gay 2010, p. 27). Nevertheless, the eruption of debates since the 1970s indicated a system vulnerable to new governments and personalities. The rhetoric under the Cameron government was convincingly Type 4 (e.g. the right of ministers to appoint permanent secretaries), but the practice was more muted. Uncertainty remained about the dynamic between ministers and senior civil servants, and the effectiveness of spads (Brecknell 2017).

Type 4: Politically skewed
The final type of relationship recognises a high level of intensity of political interventions by ministers and their staff, which moves the relationship along the continuum towards the highly politicised end. In the process, 'displacement' occurs in which core elements of the relationship – invariably public service roles and positions are either diminished or taken over. Typically, there is a propensity for a prime minister or minister to act as if boundaries and established relationships lack meaning.

Australia and Canada have at times displayed tendencies that fit this category. The 'new political governance' that Aucoin (2008, 2012) observed is most relevant here, Canada serving as the exemplar of this position. Simply put, some of the excesses of politicisation were more pronounced: the strongly centralising prime minister's office (the largest of the four systems), the prime minister's influence over the appointment of deputy ministers (although it was unclear how far 'personalisation' was taken), and the largest cadre of ministerial advisers of the four countries (Savoie 1999, 2003; Zussman 2008, 2012; Aucoin 2010, 2012; Craft 2016; Heintzman 2016; Bourgault 2018). Canadian politicisation is dominated by the control and influence exercised by the political centre over the branches of government, and consequently checks and balances within the system are diminished (Shepherd et al. 2017).

Australia has had arguably the unruliest record of the Anglophone countries with the appointment and displacement of department heads. Heads of department could seemingly be dismissed at the whim of ministers, behaviour that has been unprecedented because of its frequency and public character. A high level of political control has occurred under specific regimes with heavy use of partisan instruments (Halligan 2019; Wanna 2019). During the last three decades, according to Podger (2019, p. 5) the problems 'have worsened . . . raising questions about how well the APS today is able to meet its constitutional responsibilities . . . the thickening of the interaction between the APS and ministers, coupled with professionalisation of politics, has changed the relationship from a partnership to one often more akin to "master-servant"'.

A sure indicator of Type 4 in both countries is when the public service is explicitly consigned to implementing policy directions (Shepherd et al. 2017; Morrison 2019).

Consequences of Politicisation

Three immediate consequences affect the functioning of the public service under politicisation. For the public management system, risk aversion is high in some management fields, which can be largely sheeted home to the role and stance of ministers. Together with other external demands public servants tend to be risk adverse and hesitant to innovate. In the face of political and other pressures, they seek insulation through regulation. The consequence of risk-reducing reliance on rules is the bureaucratisation of the public management system.

A second consequence has been the emergence of porous boundaries and a lack of distinctiveness of the public service. The increased focus on short termism has been startling and the subject of universal critiques. There are also major issues about the quality of public policy and how big issues are being managed (Boston 2016; Diamond 2019b). The institution has been undermined by the movement from a traditional position of relative clarity to one that is ambiguous, and vulnerable and subject to arbitrary infractions by ministers that are often informal and private. For each public service, there was the question of its identity, now more ambiguous following disintegrating boundaries and the attenuation of public servants' policy roles. The prioritisation of government's and ministers' goals is paramount across the countries.

When short-term priorities trump everything, there can be significant implications for good government.

The third consequence has been the neglect of both public management capability and more generally the maintenance and development of the institution.

MANAGERIALISM

The hallmark of public management reform has been the strong commitment to the managerialist approach that supplanted the traditional bureaucratic model. The components of managerialism identified and addressed in several chapters are now brought together to see what has emerged. The dimensions in Table 9.4 address several commonly understood principles of managerialism, and the intended and unintended consequences. Several paradoxes have been raised in earlier chapters. The first was the erosion of management capability over time (although this was less the case where a compliance and control approach was used: e.g. Canada's Management Accountability Framework). The second was that the removal of obstacles to change produced new constraints (internal barriers, centralisation, multi-layered control and over-regulation). Managerialism's combination of devolution and principles-based approach at the centre generated re-regulation. The magnitude of regulation was expanded rather than reduced by relying on a principle- or values-based approach at the centre, leaving departments to control their transactions. The third is centred on how risk-averse politicians generate excessive regulation (i.e. red tape) and more generally bureaucratisation: heightened politicisation begets bureaucratisation. The propitious conditions for bureaucratisation existed under the high political control of Australia and Canada.

Management Improvement: Processes and Capabilities

The question addressed here concerns capability development and retention as might be expected under managerialism, focusing on original core management processes: financial, human resources, performance and risk (see Chapter 5). This emphasis was prompted by the disinclination of departments to pursue capability sufficiently, the actual loss of capability, and pressures that forced departments to be inattentive (e.g. political priorities and the complex demands of modern government). Serial fluctuations, even a decline in capabilities eventuated, which can be attributed in large part to their neglect at the departmental level, which derived in large part from pressures to respond to political priorities (and in specific cases to externalisation). Once attention was given to specific capabilities, ones like financial management could be more readily attended to than others like risk management.

Table 9.4   *Managerialism: long-term results for components*

Dimension	Condition	Comment/ Result
1. Management processes – improved capabilities	Centrality, but condition of capabilities variable	Level of operability variable; continuity questionable Fluctuates, cyclical
2. Decentralisation to departments and managers	Devolution a core principle but compromised in practice Delegation to managers affected by other factors Disaggregation	Departmental roles strengthened Devolution subject to silos limits, agendas and regulation Top-down control and under risk-averse conditions Systemic agencification gone
3. Deregulation	Over-regulation and red tape	Bureaucratisation
4. Performance and results are central	Still being pursued, but in different ways usually focusing on priorities and delivery	Constant striving: holy grail Central compliance Renewed push on results Formalisation and results
5. Policy capability	Uneven; often neglected and rundown; redefined	Countermeasures in place but condition indifferent or unclear
6. System design and reform	Grand reform still applies	Why is major reform still necessary?
Change management: continuous change	Constant feature	Facility for change often disruptive, and not by design
7. Steering flexibility in management choices	Structures, delivery modes, instruments, techniques	Facilitates use of third parties and short-term solutions

That central agencies have had to intervene to promote capability raises questions about the role of the centre versus the ministerial department. Departments were accorded greater measures of autonomy but were then unable to make enough use of managerial freedoms – excessive regulation posed constraints on them.

The case of policy capability was both similar and different. Politicians sought to play more pivotal roles in policy, and this included controlling decisions on policy development. This was also where new understandings about the flexible choice of instruments coincided for the politician and the managerialist: policy advice could be purchased from a range of sources. Policy competition became the vogue in a situation in which the public service might be a handicapped player, or even marginalised. Other policy actors or suppliers were increasingly used from both inside (ministerial staff and political advisers) and outside (consultants) government. The well-documented consequences for all four systems were that public service capacity and specific capabilities declined and, worse, could not necessarily be relied on when government wished to use its services. Moreover, departments were inclined to become entangled in short-term contingencies, demand and supply issues and quality questions. The development of high-profile programmes for retrieving and developing basic policy capabilities attested to their ailing condition, but they are still a work in progress and cannot alone address shortfalls.

Decentralisation

Several forms of decentralisation have been employed across the four systems. These initiatives have also been rescinded, overridden, and constrained by external and internal oversight. Startling deviations have been apparent under risk-averse conditions (see Chapter 7).

Devolution of transactional responsibilities to line departments was a cornerstone of managerialism and made a significant contribution to public management by strengthening the roles and autonomy of departments. Nevertheless, to varying extents line authority over resources did not necessarily flow quite as expected, although departments have had significantly more authority over transactions. The constraints in the form of compliance and performance-reporting appeared early and mounted through to the twenty-first century. A contradiction existed between being assigned authority to manage resources but being subject to highly prescriptive reporting upwards, and its different foci on inputs, outputs or outcomes. The greater emphasis on principles and values at the centre invoked an expansion of regulation both with the freedom fighters and at the centre. The exposure of an issue publicly prompted the imposition of central controls or spurred senior management to centralise tasks within departments.

All systems have made significant use of agencies, although not necessarily 'executive agencies' in the British sense. The two countries (New Zealand and the UK) that led systemic agencification internationally wound back many agencies in the twenty-first century to provide a greater balance between departments and agencies. The rationalisation of agencies, mergers with departments and a stronger attention to corporate governance were prevalent. Departmentalism was reaffirmed in the twenty-first century.

Deregulation and Debureaucratisation

Debureaucratisation was the early expectation of managerialism. The 'bureaucracy problem' emerged because the bureaucratic ideal produced excessive controls over time on public servants. The problem was not bureaucratic power but top-heavy bureaucracies with formal systems of controls (Aucoin 1990).

Central controls were reduced in Anglophone countries, particularly over routine transactions. However, by the time the advanced public management system of the twenty-first century was in place, the conditions for free-spirited managerialism had receded. Politicians had ratcheted up political intervention and controls, and the totality of demands was greater. The problems were also that the recipients of principle- or value-based management coped poorly with the reduction in central regulation, and central agencies resorted to an ever-increasing number and range of controls. Too little attention was given to mitigating the risk-averse conditions discussed in Chapter 7 that contributed to red tape production, which was unlikely to be resolved by implementing formal risk management. Consequently, bureaucratisation became apparent: controls expanded, and rigid and inappropriate procedures were maintained. Bureaucratisation may be concentrated in specific areas (e.g. procurement, recruitment) or systemic. The advantages of managerialism – such as greater flexibilities for managers and agencies and innovation – are lost.

Performance and Results

Early managerialist documents referred to results, but their achievement over the last 30 years has been uneven, despite large investments in different experiments (see Chapter 6). The 2010s has seen a renewal of efforts at not just securing results (as outcomes or whatever), but results that mattered, and made defining contributions. For many successful initiatives this has entailed cross-departmental working. New Zealand stood out with its Better Public Services programme, although this was confined to just ten cross-departmental objectives. The United Kingdom had a form of results buried in its various departmental planning processes, although these are confusing to outsiders because of opaqueness, and it is unclear precisely what was being achieved. Canada also came up with an elaborately ambitious program of 364 results driven by the Results and Delivery Unit in the Privy Council Office. Australia, by maintaining continuity with its framework, has been the odd one out with no comparable interest in a results approach until the Priorities and Delivery Unit headed by a deputy secretary was established in DPMC in 2019.

The struggle for achieving performance has been a central concern for several decades. There are three narratives. The first is of disillusionment with lack of framework sustainability. The second resorts to variations on performance. The third continues to seek effective outcomes through a spectrum of instruments. The lack of agreement on the purpose of frameworks, and the limitations of a reporting focus, has led to other, often complementary approaches. Australia, Canada and the United Kingdom were revisiting their frameworks in the mid-to-late 2010s.

System Design, Reform and Change

Managerialism recognises the need for change and reform at multiple levels: continuous improvement in departments, adoption of new techniques, and fundamental systemic reform. There is extensive evidence in the four countries of the ability to change regularly.

Reformism has been apparent across the four countries with 'chronic reform' diagnosed for Britain (Pollitt 2007; see also Jenkin in Brecknell 2017). Each had major reform documents at beginning of the 2010s, but implementation has been slow, interrupted, erratic and unstable rather than a process of dynamic change. Reformism may be a source of dislocation as well as change (cf. the lack of a management framework: NAO 2016c). It is all very well running with multiple processes, but in a system as complex as the UK's it is necessary to operate within an 'effective management framework'.

Reform is exceedingly complex: apart from the incremental adjustments to environment change that occur regardless of broader agendas, different fields of management and policy often operate within specific cycles (Pollitt 2008). Politicisation does not adhere to any rules about being dovetailed with management reform. An important question that bears on the Anglophone reputation as a reformer is how public management reform has been conducted over time. What is the propensity for reform? It can be argued that the case for reform in the end rests on producing a durable form of public management, but instead there has been constant and divergent reform.

Change became constant, even chronic, in the 1980s and continued in the twenty-first century. Important precepts of managerialism have been continuous improvement and responsiveness to the environment with open systems. The reason can be related to the administrative tradition: a British type of system that 'maximises temptation to re-organize and minimizes the penalties for so doing' (Pollitt 2007, p. 534), has echoes in the others.

Change operates at several levels as a result of various factors: change in leadership (prime ministers, ministers, department heads and other senior staff), in governments, reform agendas and machinery of government, and swings between reform paradigms. Change in itself is desirable under the public management model, but chronic change has manifold consequences. Leadership turnover is pervasive. The change dynamic affects the career movements of senior staff and content experts. Unintended consequences included the turnover of permanent secretaries and other senior staff (Sasse and Norris 2019; Orton n.d.). Otherwise staff were diverted into short-term endeavours, including firefighting.

System Failures?

There are a number of indicators of system failures across the four countries. A UK conclusion – that applies to all systems – is of governments, 'trapped in a cycle of short-termism, over-optimism and silo decision-making' (NAO 2018c, p. 13; cf. Boston 2017 on New Zealand). The documented blunders of the UK government were largely the product of hyper-active ministers (King and Crewe 2014). The 'Whitehall paradigm' was irreversibly changed in the 2010s (Diamond 2019a, p. 10).

The catalogue of deficiencies in Canada is extensive: politicisation, risk aversion, inefficiency, silos, hierarchical structures, and bureaucratic approaches (Public Policy Forum 2016, p. vi; see also Savoie 2014, 2019c; Shepherd and Stoney 2018; Clarke 2019). The Canadian Auditor General's unprecedented critique of the public service following the Phoenix pay fiasco was scathing about the dysfunctional culture of the federal bureaucracy, which, left unchanged, would lead to more colossal failures, mismanagement and further erode trust in government. The Auditor General listed the requirements that were meant to prevent the occurrence of the Phoenix failure in the Anglophone country with the most developed regulations and controls: a management accountability framework, plans and priority reports, performance reports, internal audit groups, programme evaluations, departmental audit committees and Auditor General reports (M. Ferguson, Auditor General of Canada to SSCNF 2018; OAG 2017, 2018).

Australia has also had cases of speedy and mishandled implementation (the Building Education Revolution policy and the Home Insulation Program fiasco: Hanger 2014; Shergold 2015) and shares dysfunctional features with Canada. Finally, the New Zealand public service, once the exemplar of modern managerial reform, 'is neither as strong or resilient as once it was' (Palmer and Butler 2018, p. 79), and must operate collectively in response to NZ's complex societal needs (Hughes and Smart 2012).

COMPARING PUBLIC MANAGEMENT SYSTEMS

The public management systems addressed in this book have all been subject to managerialism, politicisation and bureaucratisation. The four countries can be differentiated according to how they conceived and implemented managerialism. The early research in the 1990s focused on three countries. A comparative basis was established (see Table 1 in Hood 1990), which distinguished New Zealand (for its new institutional economics) from Australia and the United Kingdom (depicted as modern Taylorism). Canada was not included in the group at that time. Subsequent comparisons observed the continuing significance of these distinctions (Dunleavy et al. 2006).

Table 9.5   *Twenty-first-century components of public management*
               systems

	Managerialism	Politicisation	Bureaucratisation
Australia	Strong	Pronounced	Systemic
Canada	Medium	Pronounced	Systemic
New Zealand	Strong	Prevalent	Prevalent
United Kingdom	Strong	Pervasive	Prevalent

All four have had managerialist phases (Table 9.5). Use was made of consultants for twentieth-century privatisation and restructuring, but not the compulsory contracting-out or its extensive use as in Australia and the United Kingdom (Scott 2001, pp. 188–89; Scott and McKenzie 2001; Craft and Halligan 2020).

In the twenty-first century, Australia and the United Kingdom have been the most inclined to NPM-type approaches The United Kingdom has had the strongest propensity to outsourcing of delivery. Australia was managerialised with NPM episodes that involved inter alia extensive outsourcing of capability, seemingly the highest of the four (Craft and Halligan 2020). New Zealand has produced its own mix grounded in NPM at the beginning but is becoming more comfortably managerialist as it searches for maturity.

All systems have become politicised, in ways that challenge their traditions, but this is more pronounced in two cases. These judgements are within the Anglophone category and would change if placed within the broader canvas of the OECD and compared to heavily politicised countries in Europe (e.g. Belgium and Italy) and the United States (Pollitt and Bouckaert 2017). However, the Anglo countries have been exhibiting more of their features.

Canada has been more subject to bureaucratisation that derives from path-dependent features not fully shaped by managerialism, and a combination of pressures from external sources, central agencies and risk-averse politicians (Clarke 2019). The others all exhibit bureaucratic features, such as hierarchy and silos, but internal rules have been shown to be particularly strong in Australia.

In terms of combinations of the three components, Canada has been more systemically bureaucratised and politicised than the others. Australia has been both managerialised (with NPM featuring somewhat) and politicised, somewhat akin to Canada, but also prone to bureaucratisation. New Zealand is managerialist and politicians' influence is pervasive, but more contained than elsewhere. The United Kingdom combines all three: managerialism has been strong with NPM tendencies often central, politicisation is intense but not quite as dominant as elsewhere, while apparent bureaucratic elements are seemingly not as stifling as elsewhere.

The pathways of countries have varied over the reform era and system functionality has been in dispute in each case for several reasons: excessive political influence, excessive bureaucratisation, chronic change, over-centralisation and insufficient centralisation. In times of high-intensity NPM experiments in the UK or New Zealand, the distance between countries was greater, particularly with Canada changing more slowly and least inclined to engage with an NPM agenda. The obvious differences between the four (see Chapter 2) were apparent in their emerging reform models in the twentieth century, and over the long term included the use of instruments, level of politicisation, bureaucratisation and aspects of managerialism (e.g. degree of reliance on consultants and outsourcing) (Table 9.5).

Canada was the earliest to seek managerial devolution, but became centralised, and remained so. Britain was the early significant reformer and remained subject to constant reform. Australia sought implementation and delivery but ended up with a questionable capacity to deliver and to innovate despite (or because of) politicisation. The early radical reformer, New Zealand, spent the ensuing years trying to work around the constraints of its foundational reform principles, and to balance central capacity against that of departments. Over time it may have produced a viable if incomplete model in some respects. Similarly, centralisation and the domination of governance under Harper and Blair contrasted sharply with other leaders and governing styles (cf. Bennister 2012).

Each of the four systems is a product of its context and culture (Pollitt 2013c), but the Anglophone tradition continues to be central in that the circulation of ideas, approaches and experiments and the use of the country network remain important as a reference point.

Reform Unresolved or the Public Management System in Perpetual Crisis?

The case for reforming the public management system has been strongly promoted through programmes in all four countries during the 2010s (see Appendix 1), and by advocates at senior levels. There have been Australian calls for a royal commission on the public sector from previous heads of the public service and departmental heads, and an independent review reported in 2019 (but was not immediately published by government). New Zealand has sought to leave behind the system constraints of its public management model to move expeditiously on big issues and capability questions, and to strategic changes to the framework with a view to some reformulation (a former prime minister argued for a royal commission of inquiry into the public sector:

Palmer 2016). It has launched the most important reform in 30 years (SSC 2018a). The United Kingdom has experienced chronic reformism in the 2000s and 2010s, but the situation remains unresolved with short-term crises (Greenaway 2017). The Canadian reform agenda under one government has now morphed into that of another with different objectives.

The decade-long advocacy of major reform has been a hallmark of these countries. In Australia and New Zealand, major reviews bookend the beginning and end of the decade: Australia (AGRAGA 2010; IRAPS 2019a and b, with the final report released after this book entered production), and New Zealand (BPSAG 2011; SSC 2018a, which is planned to culminate in 2020). The need for major change has been advanced by lead agencies: 'incremental change is not the option that will best equip the APS to meet the challenges of the future. Rather change of a transformational kind is required – not just what the APS does on behalf of government but also in terms of how it manages itself' (APSC 2014, p. 16); while in New Zealand there was a call for *transformational* change at a higher level of thinking and aspiration (State Services Commission 2013). The UK reform agendas of the early 2010s (HM Government 2012), have been completely disrupted by political turmoil and the savage impact of Brexit on the operation of Whitehall. The Commons Public Administration and Constitutional Affairs Committee has been examining the future of the civil service (PACAC 2018), while its demise been a strong theme among observers (e.g. Diamond 2019b).

INTERPRETING LONG-TERM PATTERNS

In diagnosing public management systems in the 2010s, there are both internal and external issues. In terms of external issues, the environment has been changing rapidly. In a 'high-speed world' (Pollitt and Bouckaert 2011, p. 217; Fawcett 2018), the public management system has difficulties with achieving continuity and stability. Being responsive to contexts requires constant adaptation and capability development. Internally, the public management system has functioned poorly in some areas of management, and with delivering government priorities.

The limitations of politicisation and managerialism have already been reviewed. Three interpretations are used to obtain traction on what has occurred. The first revisits the contradictions that arise from the combination or juxtaposition of politicisation and managerialism in the reform era, focusing on political management. The second examines how the focus on the Anglophone administrative tradition assists with interpreting outcomes, and questions about institutional identity. The third reflects themes in public management about change and cycles and how they have been magnified in the reform era.

Political Management

The traditional executive branch combined a strong administrative system and a weak political system. In contrast, executive branches in the reform era have combined a strong political system with a management system. This results in a political management characterisation, which assumes its purest form where there is no appreciable administrative system: 'without general administrators, politics and management interact directly and produce a style which is labelled "political management"' (Self 1977, p. 180; see also Halligan and Power 1992).

Whereas the administrative system addresses the maintenance of 'structures, rules and principles' the management system focuses on directing activities and processing resources and performing a dynamic role that fits well with an instrumental agenda (Halligan and Power 1992, p. 12). Political management unites political and management elements that are both dynamic and instrumental but lacks the system maintenance role of administration.

The application of both political and managerialist paradigms can produce political management, in which the two elements co-exist as modes of operating. Adherence to two often diametrically opposed philosophies creates the preconditions for fundamental tensions. Increasing political control while pursuing managerialist objectives (e.g. empowering, decentralising) produces risk-averse behaviour (Shepherd and Stoney 2018).

Aucoin's (1990) analysis of the tension between two paradigms offers two formulas, one favouring centralisation and coordination, the other decentralisation and reducing excessive controls. The co-existence of two perceptions and prescriptions results in a significant paradox. A 'bureaucracy problem' exists because bureaucrats have to confront how to function in executive branches where both paradigms have been applied (Aucoin 1990, p. 126): 'They are caught between the proverbial rock and a hard place. They are seen simultaneously as the cause of the problem and the resolution to it.' Organizational schizophrenia has occurred in bureaucracies where enthusiasm for reform was tinged by loss of morale because of cross-pressures.

Anglophone Tradition

A central argument has been that the administrative tradition both facilitates and constrains change. It is more geared to facilitating change than other traditions and is more pragmatic about acting. At the same time, the ability to constrain change that challenges core conventions and continuity has been weakened. This has consequences for the ability of leaders to make effective use of the array of tools available.

What then became of the tradition after management displaced administration and ministers and their entourages dislodged public service roles? What had distinguished the Anglophone countries was the combination of features in their tradition – instrumentalism, pragmatism and public officials serving a government rather than the state – which enabled both major and constant change. The second attribute was that they were the first group of countries to actively and systematically implement reform that had a considerable impact, and which proved to be systemic and comprehensive. The four countries emerged as exemplars of managerialism with innovations extolled by international organisations (Pal 2012).

Political–public service relationships retained the core conception of the public service in terms of its impartiality and availability to work for successive governments, yet they have been bedevilled by tensions at the interface over the impact of responsiveness, the contested role of professionals and the institutional standing of the public service. The boundaries became more permeable, and the political executive more influential through ministers and their agents. Political actors infiltrated the preserve of the public service to an unparalleled extent. While there have been occasional reversions to more conventional modes, the systems remain vulnerable to the idiosyncratic behaviour of prime ministers and the incursions of individual ministers and political staff who disregard conventions about the role and status of the public service.

Whereas once the imbalance in the system came from the dominance of mandarins and the compliance of ministers, now the positions have been reversed. The traditional formulation of relationships envisages the minister providing the dynamic element, while the public service offers the stable dimension. With the senior public service being either less permanent or contractualised, and politicisation being pervasive, the governmental system has become vulnerable and susceptible to politicians applying levels of political control that can only apparently be acquired through expanding partisanship in the executive branch. The record shows that quite often a prime minister or individual ministers disregard the medium- and long-term consequences of their actions thereby upping the partisan ante (cases are arguably best documented in this regard by the NAO (2016a) and King and Crewe (2014).

An instrumental conception of public administration and management, long a feature of the Anglophone tradition, has remained integral along with pragmatism with regard to reforms and their efficacy. These features seem to be undiminished by coalition (or minority) governments of some form despite some initiatives being regarded as un-Westminster.

Path dependence has, however, been influential for some purposes. The pull of Westminster has continued to be apparent (Richards 2003; Richards and Smith 2006). The reversion following disaggregation and devolution was based on the strengthening of ministerial departments and the centre of government (Christensen and Lægreid 2006). Other reversals also occurred: academics argued that 'courts' displaced cabinets in Anglophone systems (Savoie 2008, 2010; Rhodes and Tiernan 2014b), although by the mid-2010s cabinets were seemingly back in vogue. The continuing influence of the Westminster tradition was attested to by observers (e.g. Rhodes 2011; Diamond 2019a).

All countries experienced fluctuations in politicising activity in the 2010s with heightened pressures for change followed by some relaxation of the pressures. There was a lull in Anglophone countries as agitation by political executives subsided, although the relationship continued to be lopsided and department heads might still be toppled at the whims of ministers or for partisan advantage. Political contexts were vexed when governments were vulnerable because of the lack of working majorities. The broader environment also continued to be turbulent.

Given the magnitude of change, to what extent have the Anglophone countries been able to accommodate it (or renew the tradition)? The administrative tradition both allows change and constrains it, and some parts are readily susceptible to modification and are not necessarily at variance, notably the relative centrality of administration and management. However, there are two ways of envisaging Westminster, and expressly the central components. The first is to see Westminster as a receptacle that is malleable and can be adaptable for different purposes. It is subject to interpretations that reflect context, the times, or the agenda of the expositor (Weller and Haddon 2016). The second focus is on whether it is necessary to regard the principles, regardless of variation with the inclusions, as setting a standard or benchmark. While some variation can be accepted, there are limits to which core principles and conventions can be flouted according to the strongest sticklers (e.g. Campbell and Wilson 1995; Diamond 2019b).[1]

In tracking changes to practice there are variations between systems (as is apparent from earlier analysis), but all have been subject to significant modifications. Everywhere there are statements about the neutrality of the public service, and recognition that it is therefore distinctive. That the public service continues across changes of government has moved into the marginal category because governments have overtly exhibited suspicion and derision for the public service, which has extended to public sacking of department heads (or turning them over covertly). The heads of the service may also be displaced with a change of government.

Anglophone countries still operate within the principles of a Westminster tradition, at least notionally. Core values, as enshrined in legislation derive from this tradition and establish parameters for action. The system has proved to be resilient in the past (Barberis 2000), although the question of how malleable the model is remains, and there have been substantial costs, including a greater divergence in the twenty-first century between rhetoric and practice and the lack of agreement among parties as to how the principles should be interpreted.

There were additional features apparent: the enhanced auditor general and the ombudsman, enlarged parliamentary committee roles, and importantly the appearance of public servants before committees.

The most explicit changes were the loss of the 'virtual' monopoly role in policy advice to ministers, the greater intrusion of ministers into all aspects of the policy roles, and the overall relegation of policy with the rise of managerialism. Apart from the expansion of ministerial roles, there was the addition of political (usually partisan) ministerial advisers, and the greater political character of public service work dictated by ministerial offices. Professional appointments were influenced much more by the political executive, which sometimes smacked of partisanship. Public servants were under much greater pressure to behave in ways that hitherto were regarded as political. The notion of behaving promiscuously has received attention despite being a long-standing element (Campbell and Wilson 1995), although the level of promiscuity was now much higher.

Finally, permanence was once registered by the titles of top officials, the career service and the understanding that the public service remained while politicians came and went. In the reform era, contract appointments became standard or permanence was tenuous, the career service was transformed and subject to staff cutbacks, turnover was often high, and a greater propensity to displace senior staff was evident. New governments were more prone to challenge the public service and its legitimacy. The long-standing convention of the professional loyalty of public servants could be challenged by replacing incumbent department heads because of new government priorities (Mulgan 2016; Varghese 2016).

How differentiated is the neo-Anglophone system from other traditions? With respect to the role of law and the conception of the state the differences remain. There are indications of some convergence with internationalisation of public management as some European countries have moved towards the Anglophones through the use of management approaches, and Anglophone countries have shifted somewhat closer to European systems with respect to the handling of relations between politicians and bureaucrats in so far as the idealised purity of the traditional system is gone and political elements are stronger.

Compared to other traditions the areas of difference have been the intensity of the focus on managerialism, the strength of performance management, flexibility in choice of instruments, the use of markets and the rate and propensity of change (cf. Pollitt and Bouckaert 2017). The Anglophone public management model as it has consistently appeared in these countries comprises several elements: management occupies centrality and permeates most areas of public sector activity, performance management has been a signature feature, and there is extensive choice available to leaders in terms of the type of instruments to employ, whether bureaucracy, markets or networks.

Politicisation has been an international phenomenon (Peters and Pierre 2004a), and the Anglophone countries followed this trend. The growth of ministerial staff and the development of other instruments have produced international responses to the challenges of modern government (OECD 2011b). Like many countries internationally, ministerial offices now play significant roles in the Anglophone systems, but they variously reject the French ministerial 'cabinet', and US-style partisans who have formed the upper level of departmental hierarchies (e.g. Halligan and Power 1992). The extent of politicisation in Anglophone countries now means that they have moved to varying extents towards other approaches that long featured what were deemed to be unacceptably high levels of politicisation. The French 'cabinet' and Germany's political appointments (who may operate not unlike Anglophone officials) no longer seem to be so alien or beyond reach. The internal/external question about the location of the partisan advisory system – either appointments to the public service or the minister's office – has not been important, simply because politicians can achieve high responsiveness with the instruments and resources acquired in the reform era.

In contrast, under the 'neo-Weberian state' model, modernisation has occurred in some respects, but the roles of the state and of administration remain significant and the public service retains distinctive qualities (Pollitt and Bouckaert 2017). However, the differentiation because of Anglophone public management reform is not as great as might be expected. The growth of bureaucratisation in Anglophone counties has meant that standard bureaucratic practices co-exist with, or are embedded in, the public management model.

What is the significance of the Anglophone approach today? The Anglophone group continues as a loose tradition, but more ambiguously. It is defined more by its differences from other traditions, if less so than before. The underlying principles remain relevant even if applications may be too protean to have meaning, functioning as artifices for another prime minister to manipulate. At worst, the tradition represents a set of countries defined by their origins in colonial relationships. The current position is borderline between an Anglophone tradition and something else.

Patterns of Change and Cycles as Explanations

The role of cycles in public management provides one type of interpretation of change dynamics (Pollitt 2008). Public organisations can experience frequent changes in being environmentally responsive. Public management systems vary in their investments in undertaking adjustments in each management cycle

(Tichy 1980, p. 165; Pollitt 2008). The several types of management addressed in Chapter 4 can be associated with separate cycles. At the organisational level it is also apparent that the attention given to management improvements can be dependent on political priorities. Political and managerial agendas operate on parallel cycles that are often in sync, but frequently are not.

Observers of government have detected medium- and long-term cycles. Kaufman (1969) distinguished a cyclical pattern in US values over time in which different branches of government dominated: congressmen, bureaucracy rose to the top, but each was in turn eventually displaced by the president, until the modern era which was too complex to manifest a dominant force. Similarly, the Anglophone senior public service was replaced by the political executive because of imbalance in the relationship. The movement towards the other end of the spectrum produced a new imbalance and eventually public reactions. Invoking this conception of cycles, it is helpful to take a long-term view (see Halligan 2003b). Historically, 'Anglophone' politicians ran nineteenth-century systems with few internal constraints, and patronage and spoils were evident, which eventually produced good governance responses that sparked the separation of a range of activities from their direct influence and moves to professionalise the public service through a central public service board. Parallels between then and the early twenty-first century have been drawn, which suggest that the UK civil service had returned to aspects of nineteenth-century governance: 'patronage was rife, and one's political views were important to one's positions, many different types of contract and remuneration existed, and wage levels were often tied to output' (Dowding 2003, p. 192).

Four decades ago, the question posed was 'Who's Master, Who's Servant?' and the answer was a reform of the bureaucracy (Hawker 1981). At the end of the 2010s, the position is reversed: the masters are the minister and partisan advisers in the minister's office and public servants are the servants (Podger 2019, pp. 5–6).

Medium-term swings have also been apparent and are part of the conventional wisdom of public administration (Spann 1981). Extreme moves beget responses because they generally fail to have traction over time. The best known is the swing between centralisation and decentralisation and the use of different organisational forms, acutely apparent in Anglophone countries during the 1990s and 2000s, or the excesses of politicians untrammelled by traditional conventions, and which prompted some form of dialectical process. Recognition of the role of pendulums, such as swings between centralisation and decentralisation, has long been familiar to observers of public administration trends (Spann 1981), and that extreme reforms that are highly centralised or decentralised, or highly politicised inevitably produce a response

(Hood 1994). The complexity of change means that both a tendency and counter-tendency may be operating (Spann 1981).

Another view of the longer term addresses the role of institutional ageing both of the political realm and managerialism. An early exploration of the middle-ageing of managerialism in the early 2000s drew on analysis of the experience of several countries and inquired whether there was movement into an age of paradox (Hood and Peters 2004). Moving from that study, largely grounded in the twentieth century, to the twenty-first century, what potential indicators are available on the condition of public management systems? There is experience of the ossification of traditional public administration and excessive bureaucratisation (see official reviews in Chapter 2, footnote 8). However, other indicators of the ageing process are also available: aversion to risk taking, rule encrustation, routinisation and burgeoning procedural rules and 'mutation-based discretion' (Garvey 1993, pp. 188–92). Regardless of an ageist judgement, the key point to note is that indications of systemic changes to the use of rules, regulation and red tape are likely to signify some broader condition of the public management system.

This study has sought to produce evidence of the impact of managerialism and bureaucratisation. In doing so it has had to confront the primary unintended consequence, bureaucratisation, and the by-product of ambivalence to collaboration. Once it was said that the civil service was the problem. Then the political executive became the main claimant to problematic status as under twenty-first-century conditions (and especially unstable and minority government, and short-termism) it became variously over-bearing and obsessed with being the leader and architect, while displaying a propensity to mishandle governance and public policy – all of which have meant problems for the operation of the public service and governance.

NOTE

1. They may be focusing on the 'Whitehall model', a concept that travels less well to other countries than Westminster, but the principles are essentially the same.

10. Postscript: directions for change

By the end of the 2010s many observers had argued that there was a crisis in governance within the Anglophone systems with far-reaching consequences for public management and governance. The identification of crises or the 'unstable state' in an 'unstable world' is not new (Parsons 2004), but in some respects had evolved and arguably been amplified by new trends such as populism (Boston 2017; Young 2018; Blick 2019). The common dimensions of the crisis have centred on the loss of trust in government, self-serving behaviour of election-fixated politicians, discreditable policy discourse and ineffective policy, and the abuse of power by political executives. Constitutional issues have come to the fore.

In late 2019, the crisis was pronounced in Australia and the United Kingdom. The Australia deterioration in governance was depicted as follows: 'Trust in all sorts of institutions, governmental and private, has been damaged or destroyed . . . . Policy ideas seem often to be framed only for partisan or sectional advantage with little articulation of how or why their implementation would contribute to the greater good' (Hayne 2019, p. 7; see also Evans et al. 2019).[1] For the United Kingdom, the multiple dimensions of the Brexit crisis have challenged the British political tradition (Hall and Marsh 2019).

The adaptability of the Anglophone tradition allows swings in how political-administrative relations are managed, stylistic preferences, and variations in how norms are respected or boundaries pushed. The experiences of Canada and New Zealand indicate some resilience: in Canada, the excesses of Harper were replaced by Trudeau's more mainstream style, although crises marred the latter's first term; and legislation in New Zealand in 2020 is expected to reaffirm the combination of traditional Westminster principles suggesting that it is most likely to uphold the Anglophone beacon. In contrast, Australia and the United Kingdom have experienced extended periods of challenges to their arrangements, which are expected to continue under prime ministers elected in 2019.

The constraining role of the administrative tradition came under challenge because new modes of operation and relationships posed questions about its viability. The internal tensions in the traditional framework have been repeatedly exposed in the twenty-first-century environment, such as the notion that the civil service can be 'both politically neutral and completely tied to "the government of the day"' (Talbot 2019, p. 65). Were these pressure points matters that could be readily accommodated or were they raising issues about the fundamentals of good governance? In other words, the constraining influence of Westminster principles has been found wanting, and the administrative tradition continued to be vulnerable in significant respects. The flexible interpretation and practice of Westminster principles has made them susceptible to stretching and abuse. There were increasing calls by those studying and working within Westminster systems that they had already passed a tipping point. Many voiced concerns about short-termism, excessive partisanship and constant campaigning, the growing use of partisan and external advisers, and a hollowed out public service which challenged the viability of Westminster (Savoie 2003, 2008, 2019c; Aucoin 2012; Diamond 2019a and b; Grube 2019).

In exploring directions for change several agendas are first considered, and then scenarios are outlined based on the relative importance of components of the executive branch and the degree of discretion accorded the public service. Finally, settings for renewed relationships are examined before concluding the study.

AGENDAS FOR CHANGE

Several agendas for public management and governance have been identified. They offer insights, but as specialised prescriptions they are incomplete for none resonates with the complexities of public management and governance.

A *bureaucratic agenda* means a reversion to either a traditional bureaucracy (Olsen 2005) or a modernised bureaucratic form. Adherents of this position advance retro solutions, such as a return to traditional public administration (Savoie 2003). A variant is to embrace neo-Weberianism, a modernised version of European bureaucracy found in countries with very different administrative traditions (Savoie 2015a). A similar position is advocacy of a return to the crafts of mandarins because the pendulum has swung too far towards the new and the fashionable. There is seen to be a need to move 'back towards bureaucracy and the traditional skills of bureaucrats as part of the repertoire of governing' (Rhodes 2015, p. 43). This option has the advantage of reducing chronic change and improving stability in the executive branch. However, bureaucratisation to varying extents has long existed, and the augmentation of bureaucratic features would reinforce existing silos and increase gridlock. There is also no evidence that political executives are willing to relinquish their power and enhanced controls, the focus on performance and outcomes, schemes for securing results through targets, and their claims on public servants. Neither is it apparent that the mandarins of a managerialist era would support a formal reversion to the features of bureaucracy, although a greater emphasis on curtailed advisory skills and stewardship would enhance capability. In addition, European bureaucracy is associated with trust as a basis for securing compliance, in contrast to Anglo-American countries (Pierre and Peters 2017).

A *politicised agenda* entails the ratcheting up of the politicisation of the reform era and encapsulates arguments advocated by politicians and their attraction to models elsewhere. Ministers would appoint their own departmental executives, possibly a tier of political senior executives, and rely more heavily on political advisers in strengthened private offices (options previously advanced in Anglophone countries). The United States has historically been seen as the most distinctive alternative with its extensive use of political appointees, but there are less extreme European options, such as the 'cabinet' where ministers' offices essentially make the decisions and mobilise action. Senior public servants can also routinely be members of political parties, which might directly determine their appointments.[2]

The experiments with 'political management' in Anglophone countries have been a mixed bag. Politicians have exploited the position, although the political system is not necessarily well-equipped for an expansive task of governing. The agenda ignores the failure of ministers to step up with more systematic and credible approaches to political leadership, management and governance. In the age of unstable and weak government, the impact on public management would be palpable.

A *managerialist agenda* had already received full expression during the reform era. This entails an unfettered emphasis on the features of managerialism that emphasise change – ranging from continuous improvement to hyper change – flexible use of internal and external instruments as required, regular deployment and turnover of senior staff (and ministers), constant machinery of government changes, and rotating indicators and targets (Pollitt 2007). An internal approach that flows from managerialist logic is to strengthen the autonomy of managers so that they can operate effectively, yet the evidence from the last 40 years is that this is difficult to accomplish in practice.

The external option is to rely on third parties much more extensively, which has benefits and issues with boundaries, the behaviour of agencies and micro-managing by principals. This could be a more refined version of NPM that is centred on outsourcing functions and services. The 'supermarket state' and the 'minimal purchasing state' are different ways of representing options (Dunleavy and Hood 1994; Olsen 1988). Externalisation in an age of refocusing government outwards and network governance offers another dimension, which is explored elsewhere (Craft and Halligan 2020). The objections to this agenda are that it is often badly done in practice where ideological objectives dominate and that it is difficult to envisage this being possible at a systemic level. The failures from relying heavily on the private sector for major delivery projects, and debates about excessive reliance on commissioned work (Pollitt 2010), bring into question a heavy commitment to a blanket approach.

However, the extent to which political executives can reconcile this with their ingrained authority and ministerial responsibility remains an imponderable.

A fourth conception is the *digital agenda*, which has a more prospective feel and significant potential implications for public management and governance. One representation is of a digital era governance covering reintegration, digitisation and needs-based holism (organising government around client groups) (Dunleavy et al. 2006; Margetts and Dunleavy 2013). Ambitious normative variants focus on digital by design and devolved architectures as a basis for reconfiguring the focus of government and external relationships (Dunleavy et al. n.d.; Andrews 2019; Clarke 2019). The case for a dominant digital future can be over-stated and reality checks raise questions. Governments' motives are often concerned with cost savings at the expense of improvements in accurate and accountable customer service and implementation difficulties.

Scenarios

There have been two foci to this study: politicisation and managerialism. The historical record indicates that unconstrained politicians can lead to system failures. The excesses of politicians under the spoils system in the nineteenth century produced dysfunctions and led to the introduction of public service boards to standardise staffing arrangements and the creation of public corporations to insulate activities from political intervention (Halligan 2003b). The public service that emerged then (but at different points in the four countries) was of a traditional bureaucratic form that emphasised permanence and process and survived for several generations. Eventually it was no longer a good fit with the environment and operated in an ossified form until the changes of the 1980s. Since then political and managerial change have been constant. A high level of politicisation and the weak performance of managerialism have been the result. Bureaucratisation has been rife. In this case, system ossification only took several decades.

A critical juncture can be argued to have been established, but what direction might the four systems take in confronting their future given the poor success rate of reform? Four options are presented in Table 10.1, which are derived from combinations of two dimensions: the relations among components of the executive branch and the degree of discretion assigned to the public service. The components are the political and managerial, one of which may have primacy (Halligan and Power 1992) and they may combine productively or negatively. An effective discretionary system depends on the bureaucracy and the political executive countering the limitations of each other. A low level of discretion for the public service occurs under two options, which differ according to whether one component dominates or a stalemate prevails. They also reflect maintenance of dysfunctional systems involving the continuance

Table 10.1   *Public management system: scenarios for the twenty-first*
century

Relationships among components	Discretion of public service	
	Weak	Strengthened
Primacy within executive branch	1. Politicised Political leader as architect model	3. Institutionalised bureaucracy Anglo variant of state model
Contending among components	2. Gridlocked Stalled innovation and performance	4. Rebalanced Mutual respect for discretions and roles

of configurations that have undermined public management, neither offering an escape from system conundrums because the preconditions do not exist for major change

The models in the left quadrants are expressions of failed systems either because of the dominance of one component of the executive branch or the mismatch of the components. The models on the right side recognise that a fundamental reformulation is required, but only one may be realistic in the Anglophone context.

1.   Politicised

The centre of governance has become unequivocally the preserve of the political executive and its agents. The public service is at best responsible for implementation (Shepherd et al. 2017) or service delivery for central government in a federal system (Morrison 2019). The dialectic of change may still allow for a review process, but the prospects are likely for a progressive increase in political influence while benefits can still be extracted. Moreover, progressive politicisation has been evident in the ascendancy of partisans and the decline of the institutional public service. This track at a minimum has public servants as implementers and service providers. A further step is moving towards partial partisanship of the public service. Without an institutionalised public service, the worst fate is the re-emergence of 'a pre-merit system that favours consultants, party insiders or hired guns' (Shepherd et al. 2017, p. 276).

2.   Gridlocked

The political and managerial components intersect in ways that impede movement forward on aspirations because of system blockages. Political leadership is risk adverse and unable to escape short termism because of the 24/7 media and internet-driven influences on the issue-attention cycle in public policy. The public service is rule-bound and bureaucratised. There are high internal and external accountability demands. The same issues keep being recycled for decades (e.g. capability) without obvious resolution. Examples of gridlocked components are evaluation as an unconnected crank (Savoie 2014), or outcomes without evaluation.

Two other scenarios are pivoted on distinctive responses to issues arising in the reform era.

3.   Public bureaucracy

This entails the reinstallation of a public bureaucracy system that would have a permanent standing as a centrepiece of government and be less vulnerable to short-term pressures and interventions. Some trappings of dysfunctional managerialism would be discarded, but the focus on results and flexibilities would be retained. Greater use would be made of quasi-autonomous agencies to reduce demands on politicians and/or re-insulate certain functions from the political cycle. The political executive would retain its authority and powers. The bureaucratic agenda advocated earlier fits here. But note that politicians under comparable systems in Europe need means for attaining leverage and this is acquired through partisan appointments to bureaucracies.

4.   Rebalanced

Under this scenario the tipping point is recognised. Political influence in the executive branch has exceeded what is acceptable for modern governance. Leaders in the twenty-first century confront the need for a shift that recalibrates the components to suit contemporary conditions and effective public management and governance. This requires addressing fundamental relationships and the discretions of politicians and bureaucrats as occurred with historical turning points mentioned earlier, as well as provision for specific management flexibilities. It would enable the redemption of elements of the Anglophone tradition as relevant and vital, and more effective government. The next section addresses several elements of rebalancing.

REVISITING SETTINGS AND ADAPTING FUNDAMENTALS FOR THE TWENTY-FIRST CENTURY

The political system has become more unpredictable, populism has been in the ascendancy and trust in government has slumped. Parties are more polarised about solutions, and there is greater volatility and swings in public policy. There are indications that the governance system is in overdrive, largely because it operates in an environment where the pace of change is high, media-driven issues surface in real time, and reliance on partisans is heightened. Policy sectors are more diffuse, complex and difficult to engage with (Craft and Halligan 2020). An era of environmental turmoil and rapid change points to the need for institutional stability, containing open-ended discretions, and a review of accountabilities. The options for resetting public management systems already exist. The core weaknesses in public management systems have often been identified: diagnoses have shown issues with regulations and red tape, the handling of risk, multiple accountabilities, excessive politicisation and various management limitations, but effective action has not been forthcoming. As official reviews have observed, the failure to confront core issues means to compound them.

Politicians need to be insulated more from disruptive external pressures through delegation of responsibilities and formal assignment of roles. Internally this entails circumscribing their discretion. Public management systems need a greater measure of insulation from partisanship, permanent electioneering and the volatile politics and leadership tossed up by stressed political systems. Enhancing the discretional role of senior public servants requires addressing incentives, boundaries, responsibilities and accountabilities. The public service role of providing a modifying effect and force for stability has been significantly eroded, producing system imbalance. The question of balance is partly about addressing the forces of stability and continuity and those of dynamism and change. Management experimentation and chronic and serial reform have costs. The turnover in senior staff has increased. Institutional memory is often poor. More credible futures entail options focusing on balancing principles, including reappraising relationships between ministers and officials.

An institutional basis entails several elements. A central public service leader is necessary who has authority to shape aspects of the public management system but operates in a power-dependent environment that requires engagement with stakeholders, in particular ministers and departments. An appointment process for heads of department that is less politically dominated is also necessary, which might take the form of an independent appointment agency for chief executives (the most influential model being the New Zealand State Services Commission). The arbitrary and perfunctory dismissal of department heads would be replaced by a formal and publicly understood process.

A stronger role for parliament is an obvious option but is dependent on that institution's capacity and its maturity in undertaking investigative and oversight roles (Halligan et al. 2007). The focus needs to be on selective targets that can contribute to public policy and governance. Simply multiplying the number of officers of parliament can contribute as much to regulatory burden as to meaningful oversight. Mandatory public reporting is another option, which might include ministerial reports on the condition of specified policy and management capabilities. The UK's audit office argues that the swing to political drivers must be countered by rebalancing permanent secretaries' incentives to ensure the effectiveness of the checks and balances required by parliament (NAO 2016a).

There is scope for greater use of trustees and stewards to counterbalance the strength of low trust principal–agent relationships. There is historical experience with using trustees. The nineteenth- and early twentieth-century solutions were independent agencies of oversight and operational autonomy. In the late twentieth century and early twenty-first century, new types of independent agency have emerged for specialised tasks, such as enhanced audit offices, productivity commissions and parliamentary budget offices (Craft and Halligan 2020).

An alternative to a strong and cavalier instrumentalist approach is stewardship, which is not incompatible with the instrumental element of the administrative tradition, except the temporal focus changes. The stewardship agenda envisages a public management system that can take advantage of management principles without a high level of constraints. This has become fairly central to the discourse in New Zealand, has some currency among public servants in Australia, and arises more narrowly in the UK and Canadian rhetoric in the specific senses of the permanent secretary's role in the stewardship of public funds (UK) and 'service stewardship' (Canada). However, stewardship is not clearly an integral element of the operations of the public management systems. Legislation can be enacted but not consistently applied in practice, nor routinely accepted by politicians. As part of the stewardship role department heads can be enabled and required to publicly report on the condition of core capabilities (and to make it part of their annual assessment), and if appropriate to parliament. Annual reports to parliament on the state of the public service can contribute to greater understanding and trust in the system (and would replace existing reports that can become overly subservient to government agendas).

CONCLUSION

This book has addressed aspects of the long-term significance of extensive public sector reform in Anglophone countries. There has been a reformation in organisation and relationships and public services to make them more streamlined in response to political, economic and social environments. At the same time, there have been renewed but tentative moves in the fourth decade of reform towards more balanced and effective public management that can avail itself of a range of options while being less subject to ideology or fashions. The verities of public administration have not been displaced through the process of learning to be effective reformers.

This study has highlighted the fundamental changes to both the roles of the political executive and appointed officials, and to public management. There has been slippage and failure, often of the type that prompted reform in the first place. The systems have been in a holding pattern in some respects with public management being subject to the pressures of unrealistic expectations (Gregory 2000), and unfulfilled potential. The differences between the four countries illuminate the condition of public management systems and the ways in which an Anglophone tradition is vulnerable. The systems continue to wrestle with the imbalances that promoted reform in the first place: politicians are still trying to achieve results, and innovation remains prized. Public policy failures still occur, although now they can be attributed to both management and political shortcomings.

The reform era began in part because of excessive constraints on politicians but has morphed into one of insufficient constraints on them. In the end, this extended period of reform has provided salutary reminders of how much the changing context matters and of how political executives need effective governing systems for delivering priorities and facing other challenges. Tensions continue to arise from core relationships and the paradoxes inherent in contradictory agenda. The need for further improvement to public management systems remains a continuing challenge for Anglophone countries. Inevitably, unintended consequences will arise again, and both bureaucratisation and politicisation will continue to have negative effects. The demands and complexities of government have been compounded. The combination of errant politicians and environmental issues at times threatens to derail the performance of the public management system.

In conclusion, this examination of the long-term results arrives at five conclusions. First, the assertion of the political executive was right and proper but unbounded expansion and capricious interventions have debased the meaning and role of the public service, affected the quality of governance, and produced variable consequences for public policy. None of the countries has achieved an appropriate balance, although the asymmetry has been greater in two of them.

Secondly, the adoption of managerialism provided a modernising solution that freed the system from the shackles of an ossified traditional bureaucracy. However, the promise of managerialism in practice failed to materialise properly. In part this was a result of limitations that contributed to generating the 'new bureaucratisation' and left it unable to readily confront other fundamental issues that made its predecessor dysfunctional. In many respects, managerialism has become as operationally ossified as its public administration predecessor.

The third conclusion concerns the implications of the Anglophone approach. The public management model with its instrumentalist character remains distinctive and elements have been highly influential, but ultimately it has served less as a model internationally and continues to falter within Anglophone countries. The sum of the public management system does not reflect the creativity of the parts.

Fourthly, despite the administrative tradition and generalised public management reform mode shared by the four countries, there remain differences in terms of scale, structure, levels of bureaucratisation, and degrees and forms of politicisation. The Anglophone countries are ailing but at different levels of dysfunction and points in the cycle of assessment of fundamentals. Canada has swung from a directive style of government – and a superficial reform agenda – to a more facilitative approach, but without evincing much beyond business as usual or a willingness to scrutinise and act on what are deemed to be weaknesses (Clarke 2019; Savoie 2019c). The UK has been particularly affected by chronic reformism with government turnovers and the impact of nonroutine events: austerity and more latterly the distorting effects of Brexit in late 2019. Rampant political executives have become the norm at times. The other two have unresolved reform programmes. Unstable and erratic government in Australia has undermined the effectiveness of reform; a 2019 reform agenda has raised system weaknesses, but expectations of much of an impact are low when the prime minister has already declared his agenda. New Zealand has been working through a decade-long reform agenda that partly reflects an extended process of correcting long-term weaknesses, but which has still to reach a conclusion. Of the four countries it has demonstrated the most sustained commitment to achieving a better-balanced system and is therefore best positioned.

More generally, the lack of appropriate balance – or poor counterposing of elements – has meant ongoing problems and seemingly intractable tensions. Perennial dilemmas remain: the balance between centre and line (or modes of centralisation and decentralisation), roles of politicians and officials (or political responsiveness versus public service capacity and expertise), internal and external, horizontal versus the vertical, and change and stability within the system of government. Addressing those problems is the subject for other books (and there already exist perceptive studies that reflect on what makes for good governance based on experience (e.g. Zussman 2013; King and Crewe 2014; Clarke 2019; Wanna 2019).

The failure of fundamental reforms and weaknesses in public management and governance in the twenty-first century have produced pressures for renewing reform programmes in all four countries. There is an argument for significant reform of the public management system that takes into account institutional contexts, the political executive and the web of accountability and rules that cramp its operation. This study points to the need to address the settings and balance. The tenability of the Anglophone approach depends on reconciling pragmatic use of instruments and creative management of constraints and having this reflected in sustainable effective relationships. Of the central dimensions of this book, the management experienced constraints on its development and public servants' contracted spheres of influence; while the political sphere, despite unbounded opportunities, often found it difficult to deliver on effective policy and results. A new settlement and balance are required for the system of public management and governance.

NOTES

1. Kenneth Hayne is a former Justice of the High Court and chair of the Royal Commission into Misconduct in the Banking, Superannuation and Financial Services Industry (2017–19).
2. There are also precedents at the state government level in Australia where politicisation has been routinely practised, except they are less a product of an articulated model and more a reflection of political regimes allowing politicising activity to occur (see Di Francesco 2012b, pp. 91–5).

Appendix 1   Reform programmes and judgements in the 2010s

LIST OF MAJOR OFFICIAL REVIEWS

Australia

AGRAGA/Advisory Group on the Reform of Australian Government Administration (2010), *Ahead of the Game: Blueprint for the Reform of Australian Government Administration*, Canberra: Commonwealth of Australia.
Department of Finance and Deregulation (2012b), *Sharpening the Focus: A Framework for Improving Commonwealth Performance*, Canberra: Commonwealth of Australia.
Commission of Audit: NCA/National Commission of Audit (2014), *Towards Responsible Government: The Report of the National Commission of Audit Phase One*, Canberra: Commonwealth of Australia.
IRAPS/Independent Review of the APS (2019a), *Independent Review of the APS: Priorities for Change*, Canberra: Commonwealth of Australia, 19 March.
IRAPS/Independent Review of the Australian Public Service (2019b), *Our Public Service Our Future*, Canberra: Commonwealth of Australia (final report submitted September and publicly released December too late for discussion in this book).

Canada

Government of Canada (2013), *Blueprint 2020: Building Tomorrow's Public Service Together*, Ottawa: Government of Canada.
Government of Canada (2014), *Destination 2020*, Ottawa: Government of Canada.

New Zealand

BPSAG/Better Public Services Advisory Group (2011), *Better Public Services Advisory Group Report*, Wellington: New Zealand Government.
State Services Commission (2018), *Reform of the State Sector Act 1988: Directions and Options for Change*, Wellington: State Services Commission. Available at https://www.havemysay.govt.nz/assets/PDFS/Folder-1/FINAL -SSA-LONG-FORM.pdf.

United Kingdom

HM Government (2012), *The Civil Service Reform Plan*, London: HM Government.
HM Government (2014), The Civil Service Reform Plan: Progress Report, London: HM Government.

EXCERPTS FROM REVIEWS

Australia

The APS lags behind international peers . . . in incorporating external advice into the policy development and service design process (AGRAGA 2010, p. 38).

There is a perceived lack of strategy and innovation across the APS. Employees do not feel equipped to develop strategic policy and delivery advice, collaboration is not a routine way of working, and the immediacy of day-to-day activities prevents employees from focusing on emerging issues and producing forward looking policy analysis (AGRAGA 2010, p. 41).

The APS is often too risk averse to be innovative and truly frank and fearless (AGRAGA 2010, p. 45).
Capability gaps across the APS have been exacerbated by sporadic workforce planning and a lack of clarity about capability requirements (AGRAGA 2010, p. 57).

Delivery and implementation of government programs and policies require specific skills and capabilities. Australian is behind other public services in this regard (AGRAGA 2010, p. 63).

The Financial Improvement Program, launched in 1984 . . . focused on the purposes of programs and the cost-effectiveness of outcomes, rather than simply on inputs and processes. The program was based on the following simple cycle [Planning–Budgeting–Implementing and Monitoring–Reporting and Evaluation]. Some of the clarity provided by this simple conception has been lost over time. Moreover, the financial framework does not currently draw links to planning, budgeting or evaluation activities (DFD 2012b, p. 15).

In a contested, low-trust environment, politics will likely continue to be conducted as a 'permanent campaign', in turn influencing the priorities of government and the risk appetite of the public service (IRAPS 2019a, p. 12). There are strong concerns that the APS's underlying capability has been weakened over time (IRAPS 2019a, p. 14).

Departmental secretaries have vital roles at the apex of the APS . . . It is therefore important that all Australians have confidence in the appointment, performance management and termination processes for secretaries (IRAPS 2019a, p. 29).

It is important that measures of outcomes and performance in the APS are not exclusively based on agency silos, reflect a robust evidence base, and address project or cross-portfolio outcomes that matter most to Australians (IRAPS 2019a, p. 30).

The APS's capability has diminished over time . . . specific skills gaps have emerged, and that the APS's bench strength is not what it once was (IRAPS 2019a, p. 36).

   Successful leadership is more often concerned with responsiveness, and upward management (IRAPS 2019a, p. 36).

It is important that APS managers are incentivised to deliver outcomes in the long-term interests of Australia (IRAPS 2019a, p. 39).

The APS is not best-placed to meet growing expectations for government services to be delivered in an integrated and individualised fashion. Technological advances and a renewed focus on outcomes and impacts rather than inputs and process, present an opportunity to rethink how the APS designs and delivers government services (IRAPS 2019a, p. 45).

The APS is too often perceived by stakeholders to be a closed book, reflecting a risk-averse culture (IRAPS 2019a, p. 46).

The APS's critical relationship with the executive and the Parliament has evolved, but without a corresponding evolution in some of the conventions and practices surrounding this relationship (IRAPS 2019a, p. 58).

Canada

Many rules and processes are overly complex, top-down, siloed, and lack coherence and consistency . . . rules become internal red tape when they are perceived as unjustified, overly burdensome, and a hinderance to action or decisions (Government of Canada 2014, p. 14).

Many employees noted they have few occasions to work directly with senior leaders . . . They have also expressed frustration that their work is often filtered through many layers of approval (Government of Canada 2014, p. 14).
[Public servants] want to strengthen understanding, internally and externally, of the fundamental roles of the public service in serving the government of the day and working in the public interest (Government of Canada 2014, p. 24).

New Zealand

The system has not been . . . effective in delivering improved social, environmental and economic outcomes (BPSAG 2011, p. 3).
Lack of coordination (BPSAG 2011, p. 9).
Slow pace and little innovation (BPSAG 2011, p. 20).
Some of the most critical leadership capabilities are weak (BPSAG 2011, p. 21).

There is concern that a previously unified Public Service was fragmented by the [1988] Act, that too little was done to ensure a strong 'centre' of the system, and that a range of issues arise from this. Overall, the issues . . . tend to fall into three broad groups:

- Matters of fragmentation including the narrowing of each department's focus to its own particular outputs and a short-term horizon . . . the 'Silo Effect'.
- Effects on the capability, in particular the senior leadership capability, of the Public Service.
- Concerns about the ethical foundations of the Public Service including the conventions around political neutrality and the provision of free and frank advice (SSC 2018, pp. 8–9).

United Kingdom

Leadership of change needs to be much stronger and more consistent; performance management is too rarely rigorous; and the culture is too often slow and resistant to change (HM Government 2012, p. 8).
The quality of policy-making is inconsistent and needs to be improved – too often policy advice draws from too narrow a range of views and evidence, and does not ensure that policy is capable of practical implementation (HM Government 2012, p. 9).

The Civil Service does not always have the right capabilities (HM Government 2012, p. 9).

[The Civil Service] culture can be cautious and slow-moving, focused on process not outcomes, bureaucratic, hierarchical and resistant to change (HM Government 2012, p. 9).

There are too few incentives (HM Government 2012, p. 9).

Policy resources should be focused on ministerial priorities (HM Government 2012, p. 14).

Whitehall has a virtual monopoly on policy development, which means that policy is often drawn up based on too narrow a range of inputs and is not subject to rigorous external challenge prior to announcement (HM Government 2012, p. 14).

Too often, overly complex processes hinder effective implementation and create inefficiency (HM Government 2012, p. 18).

There are significant gaps in capability and skills which need to be filled if the Civil Service is to be able to meet today's and tomorrow's challenges (HM Government 2012, p. 22).

A less hierarchical and more flexible culture (HM Government 2012, p. 28).

Appendix 2 Country chronologies

Sources include King 2007; Bouckaert and Halligan 2008; Weigrich 2009; Aucoin 2010; Fawcett and Gay 2010; Boston and Halligan 2012; and Pollitt and Bouckaert 2017 (which also provides complementary information about the country contexts).

Reforming public management and governance

Table A2.1   *Timeline Australia*

Year	Government	Managerialism	Politicisation and other reforms
1970s	1972–5 Whitlam Labor.	1976 Royal Commission on Australian Government Administration report	Task Forces, advisers, outsider appointments
	1975–83 Fraser Coalition.		1976 Ombudsman
1980s	1983–91 Hawke Labor.	1983 Review of Commonwealth Administration	1982 Freedom of Information Act
		1983 Reforming the Public Service report	1984 Public Service Reform Act
		1984 Financial Management Improvement Program	Ministerial consultants; Ministers' role in appointing secretaries; 'permanent' secretaries abolished; SES established
		1984 Budget Reform paper	1986 Decentralised ministerial control, strengthened cabinet committees, new departmental structure
		1986 Block Review (efficiency)	1987 Two-tier ministry created, central agencies restructuring, and mega departments established
		1987 Efficiency Scrutiny Unit	1987 Public Service Commission replaced Public Service Board
		1988 Dept of Finance, FMIP Report	
1990s	1991–6 Keating Labor.	1990 Initial privatisation	1996 Dismissal of six secretaries
		1992 Task Force evaluation of a decade of management reform	1997 Centrelink established
		1994 Public Service Act Review Group report	1999 Public Service Act
	1996–2007 Howard Coalition.	1996 report of National Commission of Audit, recommends more limited role for government	
		1996 Towards a Best Practice Australian Public Service report	
		1997 Financial Management and Accountability Act	
		IT Initiative: Whole of government outsourcing	

Year	Government	Managerialism	Politicisation and other reforms
2000s		2000 Audit Office report Implementation of IT Infrastructure Outsourcing: Market testing of activities and services 2001 Public Service Commissioner *State of the Service Report*	2003 Uhrig report on corporate governance 2004 Department of Human Services created (Centrelink later absorbed) Management Advisory Committee reports: Performance Management 2001; Connecting Government 2004
	2007–10 Rudd Labor.	2008 report Operation Sunlight: Enhancing Budget Transparency 2010 Advisory Group on Reform of Australian Govt. Administration Blueprint for reform	
2010s	2010–13 Gillard Labor. 2013 Rudd Labor.	2013 Public Governance, Performance and Accountability Act	2013 Public Service Act amendment, specification of departmental secretaries' roles 2013 Replacement of heads of central agencies
	2013–15 Abbott Coalition.	2014 report National Commission of Audit Contestability program	
	2015–18 Turnbull Coalition. 2018–19 Morrison Coalition. 2019– Morrison Coalition.	2017 Independent Review of the PGPA Act 2013 2018 Independent Review of APS, 2019 report (final report published after this book went into production)	2015 Independent Review of Internal Regulation

Table A2.2   *Timeline Canada*

Year	Government	Managerialism	Politicisation and other reforms
1980s	1980–84 Trudeau Liberal (and earlier). 1984 Turner.		Pink slips for officials. Political staff increase. Prime Minister's Office developed
	1984–93 Mulroney Progressive Conservative.	Privatisation and implementation of managerial measures 1986 Shared Management Agenda Program 1989 Public Service 2000	1986 Increased Ministerial Authority and Accountability 1992 Public Service Reform Act
1990s	1993 Campbell Progressive Conservative.		460 exempt staff, including 99 in PMO Political staff election issue.
	1993–2003 Chrétien Liberal.	1994 Expenditure Management System 1994–6 Program Review	Policy agenda, Red Book (after ten years in opposition) Abolished chief of staff position. Reduced political staff, including PMO 1994 Program Review curtailing public spending
		1996 Planning, Reporting, Accountability Structure (PRAS) 1999 Performance management for federal executives	1996 Improved Reporting to Parliament 1996 Task Force on Managing Horizontal Policy Issues
2000s	2003–06 Martin Liberal.	2000 Exempt staff increased under Chrétien 2003 Management and Accountability Framework (MAF) 2003 Public Service Modernization Act	2004–06 Gomery Commission of Inquiry into the Sponsorship Program 2004 Office Comptroller General re-established 2005 Public Service Employment Act Deputy heads undertake recruitment

Year	Government	Managerialism	Politicisation and other reforms
2010s	2006–11 Harper minority Conservative.	2005 Management, Resources and Results Structure replaces PRAS	2006 Federal Accountability Act; Created independent oversight offices
	2011–15 Harper Conservative majority.	2013 Blueprint 2020; 2014 Destination 2020	Directive leadership style of PM
	2015–19 Trudeau Liberal.		Results and delivery agenda
	2019– Trudeau Liberal minority.		2019 Resignation of two cabinet ministers, clerk of Privy Council Office and senior PM adviser over handling of SNC-Lavalin issue

Table A2.3   *Timeline New Zealand*

Government	Managerialism	Politicisation and other reforms
1980s	Pre-reform	
1975–84 Muldoon National.		
1984–9 Lange Labour.	1986 State Owned Enterprises Act	1988 State Sector Act
	1987 Government Management: Brief to Incoming Government, Treasury	Chief executives on contract, new ministerial roles
	1989 Public Finance Act	
1990s		
1989–90 Palmer.	1991 Steering Group Review of State Sector Reforms	1990 Public Service Code of Conduct issued by SSC
1990 Moore Labour.		1994 Fiscal Responsibility Act
1990–97 Bolger National.	1996 Schick Report for the State Services Commission and the Treasury	1996 Mixed-Member Proportional replaced first past the post as the electoral system
1997–9 Shipley Coalition.		
1999–2002 Clark Labour Coalition.	2001 Ministerial Advisory Group, Report on Review of the Centre	
2000s		
2002–05 Clark Labour Coalition.		2004 State Services Amendment Act attempts to strengthen coordination and SSC
2005–08 Clark Labour minority.		2008 Purchase advisers: Six short-termers to reduce public expenditure
2008–11 Key National minority.	2009 Performance Improvement Framework (PIF)	2010 Improving the Quality and Value of Policy Advice

	Government	Managerialism	Politicisation and other reforms
2010s	2011–14 Key National minority.	2012 Functional leadership established: cross-agency/system	2011 Social investment approach
		2013 Public Finance Amendment Act: introduced multi-category appropriation	2013 State Sector Amendment Act More flexible funding, outcomes focus, improved reporting, and whole of government
	2014–16 Key National minority		2012–17 Better Public Services reform agenda: ministries collaborate on priorities and horizontal connections
			2014 Directions re whole of govt.
	2016–17 English National minority.		2016–17 Social Investment Unit/Agency
	2017– Ardern Labour Coalition Minority.	2018 Reform of State Sector 1988: Directions and Options for Change: Discussion document	2018 BPS programme terminated
			2019 First well-being budget

Table A2.4   Timeline United Kingdom

	Government	Managerialism	Politicisation and other reforms
1980s	1979–90 Thatcher Conservative.	1982 Financial Management Initiative: Define objectives, output measures for all departments Delegate responsibility on finance and personnel to line management 1988 Next steps initiative to establish executive agencies Privatisation of state-owned enterprises 1987 Performance-related pay 1988 Next Steps Programme	Less concerned with special advisers initially, but use of external advisers (e.g. Rayner) Efficiency scrutinies Savings and administrative simplification through efficiency scrutiny program
1990s	1990–97 Major Conservative.	Senior Civil Service: Fixed term personalised contracts 1991 Citizen's Charter 1994 Public Finance Initiative 1994 Resource Accounting and Budgeting	1994 White Paper, Civil Service Continuity and Change 1995 White Paper, Taking Forward Continuity and Change 1996 Creation of senior civil service
	1997–2007 Blair Labour.	1998 Next Steps report 1998 Comprehensive Spending Review, Public Service Agreements 1999 White Paper Modernising Government	Major jump in numbers of advisers, particularly in No 10. Policy tsars
2000s		2004 Gershon Review of efficiency of civil service 2006 Capability Reviews launched	
	2007–10 Brown Labour.		2007 Termination of executive powers of special advisers 2010 Constitutional Reform and Governance Act. Covers status of and recruitment of civil service

	Government	Managerialism	Politicisation and other reforms
2010s	2010–15 Cameron Coalition.	2007 Functional areas and professions	2011 Open Public Service White Paper
		2010 Comprehensive Spending Review. Major cuts to civil service.	2012 Civil Service Reform Plan
		2010 PSAs abolished. DBPs introduced	
		2014 Appointment of CEO of civil service (Manzoni)	
		2015 SDPs introduced	
	2016 Cameron Conservative.		2016 Referendum. Majority vote to leave EU
	2016–19 May Conservative.		2016 May restructures departments
	2019– Johnson Conservative.		

Appendix 3   Dynamic of change: centring and decentring

Three main processes of change occurred between the 1980s and the 2010s in moving away from the inherited traditional hierarchical type: decentring entailed a reduction in central capacity and authority; recentring meant augmenting central capacity and of departments where agencies were incorporated; and neo-centralising through multiple agendas under hybrid public management and governance.

DECENTRING

Decentring covered three elements: devolving functions to departments (corporate services including transactions), disaggregation by breaking down organisations into separate units organised around a function (notably executive agencies), and third-party advice and delivery by assignment of responsibilities to organisations outside the public sector (which is not covered in this study). The summary patterns for the four countries are distinctive.

The most celebrated was New Zealand because its radical pursuit of change ranked high on all elements. The upshot of the reforms in the late 1980s and 1990s was the reduction in the role of the State Services Commission, and eventually the clipping of the powers of Treasury. The breakup of departments into smaller units also occurred (Boston et al. 1996; Scott 2001).

The intensity of the Australian shift to devolution resulted from system shortcomings as perceived by a neo-liberal government, and environmental uncertainty and threats favouring either a weaker (or stronger) centre. The result was the disestablishment of monolithic multifunctional departments, reliance on third parties for expertise and service provision, and an increasingly fragmented system. Under devolved public management, enhanced responsibilities meant the department was the focus and a disaggregated public service was the result. The impact on central agencies of management and market principles was resounding: the old Public Service Board was reduced to a shadow of its former self (Campbell and Halligan 1992). The Department of Finance acquired a 'strategic' focus (Wanna and Bartos 2003) but was diminished by the pursuit of a minimalist agenda, and so heavily purged in the second wave of market reform (the second half of the 1990s) prompting a debate about whether it would survive. The Department of the Prime Minister and Cabinet withdrew from active intervention except where required and no longer provided leadership for the public service. In Lindquist's (2001) terms, Australia moved from a strong to a smaller centre with a corresponding reduction in capacity and control of coordination; this devolved end of the spectrum was more comparable with New Zealand's arrangements.

Management reform in the United Kingdom 'altered the dominant conception of the centre of government. The Next Steps programme and 'market' mechanisms fragmented the near-unified service, threatening the cohesiveness of Whitehall; by 1995 functions considered a 'central' responsibility for nearly a century had been devolved downwards and outwards' (Lee et al. 1998, p. 5). As a consequence of organisational disaggregation, management was devolved to departments and agencies, and 'the residual functions and civil service management . . . located within the Cabinet Office' (Lee at al. 1998, p. 247). A major effect of Next Steps and management delegation was the weakening of the unified civil service. The uniform pay structure and grading, and civil service work were changed with a two-tier system based on a distinction between policy-making and implementation. There were a few delegations to departments (e.g. pay and grading for non-senior staff) (Dowding 2003).

Canada followed its own pattern. The 1990s public service cutbacks reduced senior executives, consolidated departments and agencies, modestly reformed central agencies and made large reductions in public service numbers (Aucoin and Savoie 1998). The diminution of the power of the Privy Council Office occurred under Mulroney (Aucoin and Bakvis 1988; Campbell 1988b); however, this did not represent a gain for departments but for the political sphere. The Public Service Commission had by 1985 delegated staffing authority for around 98 per cent of public service appointments (excluding the 'management category' that included the most senior executives) (Kernaghan and Siegel 1991), but this never reached the level of devolution of other countries (according to the OECD 2011a). In practice, much of this delegation was illusionary because the Commission retained oversight and departmental staff continued to function in a regulated fashion; and debate about responsibilities continued for another two decades (Juillet and Rasmussen 2008).

The injunctions to disaggregate and devolve under the influence of managerialist maxims had major implications for systemic governance. Because of decentring and the proliferation of non-departmental agencies, public sectors became characterised by fragmentation, lack of coherence and attenuated central control. The expansion of agencies under the more flexible regimes and fashions of NPM are well documented (Pollitt et al. 2004). However, there were wide variations in the propensity to agencify with some countries adopting a systemic approach, while others followed a more selective strategy. Australia choose not to agencify systemically like New Zealand and the United

Kingdom, but did create Centrelink as a one-stop-shop, multi-purpose delivery agency to provide services to several purchasing departments (Halligan 2008). The head of the public service proclaimed the dangers of 'bureaucratic prolif-eration' with departments of state employing only 22 per cent of public sector employees – most working in approximately 180 agencies (Shergold 2004).

In New Zealand, arguably the system most disaggregated vertically and horizontally following NPM reform, the results of fragmentation were stark (Duncan and Chapman 2010). Apart from the proliferation of public organ-isations the implications for the public management system overall were competition among departments for staff; feedback disconnects on policy implementation because policy advisers and delivery were in separate depart-ments; and the need for a strong centre in a fragmented system (Boston and Eichbaum 2007, p. 152).

There are continuing debates about how much power is relinquished by allowing delivery to go down and out of the public service. Certainly, for Anglophone countries the centre of government could remain relatively strong (Richards 2008); but 'hollowing out' raised questions of capacity, coherence, control and performance.

DYNAMICS OF RECENTRING: CENTRALISING AND INTEGRATION

Post-NPM there was a counter-movement towards reintegrating the frag-mented state by focusing on government as a whole and joining up the parts through horizontal (and vertical) coordination. Two readjustment processes were at work: countering the limitations of NPM and the search for balance between decentralised modes of operating and central needs for direction and control. The tendencies have been strong across a spectrum of relationships, which in summary involved rebalancing centre and line departments; a focus on performance around outcomes and improved delivery; a rationalisation of public bodies; and a commitment to whole-of-government and integrating agendas at agency and delivery levels. While the strongest movements were in the 2000s (Halligan 2006; Christensen and Lægreid 2006), several continued into the 2010s (Table A3.1).

Resurrection of the Central Agency in Coordination, Integration and Oversight

The reassertion of the centre was a prominent element in several countries as central agency weaknesses were addressed by strengthening their capacity for leadership and direction. Adjustments were made to the overall system to correct misalignments, conflicts and low effectiveness. There was significant

A3.1   *Recentring and centralising in the twenty-first century*

	Reactions to decentering	New and renewed initiatives
2000s	Central agency renaissance	Horizontal governance and management
	Re-aggregation; agency rationalising	(Chapter 9)
	Ministerial department strengthening	Political centralising through PMO (Chapters
	Whole-of-government	3 and 8)
	Reactions to austerity	**Other initiatives**
2010s	Efficiency centralising (post-GFC)	Central management (also meta)
	Functional and efficiency reviews	Central agency roles (unfinished business)
	Centralising: e.g. procurement	Central policy making; digital, etc.
	Rationalising: shared services	

rebalancing of the centre, new horizontal relationships, reform correction (even a U-turn in some cases) and realignments of different components. An overriding trend of the reform era – devolution of responsibilities to departments – remained a feature of the systems to varying extents, but was partly modified through horizontal management, and a more prominent role for central agencies in espousing and enforcing principles, monitoring performance and providing guidance.

Diminished central agencies (e.g. the Australian Public Service Commission and Department of Finance and the New Zealand State Services Commission) were reconstituted with stronger roles. The prime ministers' departments were also enhanced – quite clearly in Australia where the department drove the whole-of-government agenda – but less so when the prime minister's office was more assertive.

To counter the devolved Australian environment greater public accountability was sought through an annual report by the Australian Public Service Commissioner on the state of the public service. A much more demanding instrument was Canada's Management Accountability Framework, which represented a distinctive extension to the Treasury Board Secretariat's oversight role, including evaluation of departments and chief executives.

The Australian Department of Finance's shrunken role and capacity to oversee financial management and information was enhanced, with a greater focus on departmental programmes, and an expansion of staff capacity to provide necessary advice to government. Its role was extended again with government-driven austerity and cutback programmes in the 2010s, and even performance management (see Chapter 6). The Public Service Commission was also enabled to take on an enhanced role in capability building (APSC 2006; AGRAGA 2010).

Unlike the domination of New Zealand's Treasury in the first generation of reform, the State Services Commission began to articulate perspectives on public management towards the end of the 1990s (e.g. SSC 1999), and then acquired broader responsibilities from central agency strengthening. The outcome of the Central Agencies Review (2006) was to require a coordinated approach to the state services with the three central agencies jointly responsible for leading on the development goals (State Services Commission 2007). The State Services Commission acquired a new systemic focus across the state services and a wider role for the state services commissioner in enabling whole-of-government and central agency analysis of services. Legislation established a framework to encourage coherence, to improve overall performance, and to strengthen integration (Rennie 2008). However, it was not until 2013 that some traction was achieved (Morrison 2014), but even this was regarded as insufficient, hence the continuing reform agendas for rebalancing the centre and departments.

Re-Aggregation and Rationalising Public Agencies

A second element was system balancing of core and the broader public sector. The reversal of the agencification trend is apparent internationally, but not as explicitly as the 're-aggregation' prevalent in Britain. 'From the large-scale disaggregation of the early 1990s policy seems to have almost completely reversed itself, in practice if not in rhetoric' (Talbot and Johnson 2007, pp. 55–6). The merger of big agencies left numerous small agencies that accounted for a minority of civil servants and ministerial control was greater (Elston 2014; Dommett and MacCarthaigh 2016; Dommett et al. 2016).

Yet broadly similar movements were underway reflecting a desire to review and tighten oversight through some restructuring and considerable rationalisation of public bodies in the broader public sector. It is not at all clear that these were necessarily responses to fragmentation. The Canadian government's response to the Gomery inquiry into the 'sponsorship scandal' was to address accountability in general and control over crown corporations (Aucoin 2007).

Both Australia and New Zealand had foresworn the chronic restructuring apparent at early stages of reform. The centre in New Zealand moved to employ more effective instruments for controlling crown entities within the state services (Gregory 2006). In response to confusing arrangements for governance and problematic legislation, the Crown Entities Act 2004 established a framework for establishing and operating crown entities (of which there were over 3,000) and clarified governance including accountability relationships between entities, board members, ministers and parliament. The movement towards creating arms-length bodies stalled, and there was restructuring and consolidation (Gill 2008a).

New Zealand was always the country with the most potential for a roll back of the multiplicity of specialised agencies. For more than a decade it was standard practice to critique the fragmented state sector. Yet the changes were relatively modest and confined to restructuring within policy sectors (Gregory 2006; Boston and Eichbaum 2007). The disaggregation tendency of the 1980s and 1990s was succeeded by consolidation after 2008 (Duncan and Chapman 2010; Norman and Gill 2011). There was a steady reduction in the number of New Zealand ministries and departments in response to fragmentation and new policy agendas. Public service departments dropped in numbers (38 in 2000 to 35 in 2008 to 30 in the mid-2010s).

Australia targeted the broader public sector by commissioning a review into the corporate governance of statutory authorities and office holders (Uhrig 2003; Wettenhall 2005). Australia had no comparable experience of agencification to New Zealand and the United Kingdom because it already had a range of longstanding devolved agencies of different types (Aulich and Wettenhall 2012). Several agencies were merged within departments as part of the clarification of corporate governance templates (the Uhrig report), the most significant being the creation of a Department of Human Services (see below), which incorporated six agencies under its umbrella (Halligan 2008a, 2015a). The post-Uhrig agenda was for ministerial departments to have tighter and more direct control over public agencies because of two issues: the extent of non-departmental organisations, and their governance. The long-term result was a reduction in the number of agencies in the outer public sector (114 to 87 between 2003 and 2011) and an expansion in the number in the core public service (84 to 105).

Consolidation and Reinforcement of the Ministerial Department

An important strand of the model involved the swing back to a more comprehensive ministerial department (cf. Pollitt 2005), and ministerial steering of portfolios, a review of corporate governance of statutory authorities and office holders, and an agenda for ministerial departments to have tighter and more direct control over public agencies. Departmentalisation was expressed through absorbing statutory authorities and reclaiming control of agencies with hybrid boards that did not accord with corporate (and therefore private sector) governance prescriptions.

In Australia's case, several agencies were pulled in as part of the clarification of corporate governance templates. The most significant was the creation of a Department of Human Services to strategically direct, coordinate and broker improvements to the delivery of services provided by several agencies, including Centrelink, and their eventual merging into the department (Halligan 2015a). Agendas for rationalising non-departmental organisations were also apparent in other Anglophone systems (Christensen and Lægreid 2006).

Central Monitoring and Driving of Programme Delivery and Implementation

Implementation has often been the neglected end of the policy spectrum. Under the market agenda, outsourcing, agents and specialised agencies were favoured for service delivery. Governments reviewed internal constraints on implementation in response to public perceptions of the performance of delivery agencies. One solution was to extend central control to reduce blockages and delays. The Canadian Results and Delivery Unit has been highly ambitious (Gold 2017).

The UK's prime minister's delivery unit (PMDU) under Prime Minister Blair, established clear goals, delivery maps and reports, trajectories, league tables, stock-take sessions with the prime minister, and a working relationship with Treasury to align spending with desired outcomes (Barber 2007).

Following the UK's experiment, an Australian Cabinet Implementation Unit was established in the Department of the Prime Minister and Cabinet to ensure programme delivery was timely and responsive.[1] It was depicted as a partnership with agencies in systematically reforming the implementation of government policies and ensuring effective delivery. The authority of cabinet was drawn on both as a 'gateway' and a 'checkpoint'. Adopted policy proposals required formal, detailed implementation plans. Progress was reported to the prime minister and cabinet against milestones. Reporting to the prime minister and cabinet was regarded as a powerful incentive for organisational learning (Shergold 2004; Wanna 2006).

New Zealand's approach provided a contrast because central monitoring through a delivery unit was not a feature. Single-purpose departments with specified outputs were accepted as producing efficient service delivery. Nevertheless, there was a strong agenda around delivery and results and addressing solutions to silos through integrated service delivery, and this was reinforced through an approach focused on state sector development goals and the use of indicators to measure and monitor progress. The concern was with unifying the state services 'to consider how the operation of the whole can be greater than the sum of its parts'. This legislative basis was designed to establish a framework that encouraged coherence, improved overall performance, and strengthened integration (SSC 2007).

Neo-Centralisation

The later forms of centralising need to be distinguished from early readjustment, hence neo-centralisation where these changes reflected new managerial and political agenda for leading and steering from the centre (Halligan 2011a); twenty-first-century austerity and efficiency programmes; the recrudescence of centralised standardisation; and extending new digital technology across departments.

Centrally driven management initiatives covered whole-of-government approaches to the fragmented and siloed handling of procurement and other functions, and a more considered, even reflective revivalism of corporate approaches. The adoption of a central focus for policy making is a standard approach to departmental silos (e.g. a chief technology officer for digital policy in New Zealand: McBeth 2018, and elsewhere) or departmental corporate planning and performance management (see Chapter 6 on Australia).

A return to austerity prompted governments to make reducing deficits a priority (Pollitt and Bouckaert 2017), particularly in the United Kingdom where the Cabinet Office's Efficiency and Reform Group integrated several central functions for assisting departments with cost reductions and steering improvements in service provision (Haddon 2016).

Technological change was expressed most strongly through digital agendas (Margetts and Dunleavy 2013; Brown et al. 2017). The UK Efficiency and Reform Group took on new central responsibilities including the centralised procurement of goods and services. Shared services programmes in Australia, Canada and the United Kingdom revived the centralised provision of corporate services in a modern form. Provisional failures did not deter the relentless drive by conservative governments in this direction. Such retro-centralisation suggested that the cycle of change had returned to the pre-reform starting point.

NOTE

1. In contrast to the UK Delivery Unit, the Implementation Unit employed public servants rather than political advisers and was integrated into the Department of the Prime Minister and Cabinet.

Bibliography

Aberbach, J.D., R.D. Putnam and B.A. Rockman (1981), *Bureaucrats and Politicians in Western Democracies*, Cambridge, MA: Harvard University Press.

Accenture (2008), *An International Comparison of the United Kingdom's Public Administration*, London: National Audit Office.

Adie, R. and P. Thomas (1987), *Canadian Public Administration: Problematic Perspectives*, Scarborough, ON: Prentice-Hall.

AGRAGA/Advisory Group on the Reform of Australian Government Administration (2010), *Ahead of the Game: Blueprint for the Reform of Australian Government Administration*, Canberra: Commonwealth of Australia.

Alexander, E. and D. Thodey (2018), *Independent Review into the Operation of the Public Governance, Performance and Accountability Act 2013 and Rule*, Canberra: Commonwealth of Australia.

Allen, B. and E. Eppel (2017), The New Zealand Performance Improvement Framework – Strategic Conversation, Organisational Learning or Compliance Tool? Paper presented at IRSPM Conference 19–21 April, Budapest.

Allen, B., E. Eppel and E. Lindquist (2019), From Measuring Government Performance to Assessing Organizational Capacity: Lessons from Canada and New Zealand, IRSPM Conference, Wellington, 14 April.

ANAO/Australian National Audit Office (2003), *Public Sector Governance, Volume 1: Better Practice Guide*, Canberra: ANAO.

ANAO/Australian National Audit Office (2010a), *Building the Education Revolution— Primary Schools for the 21st Century*, Audit Report No. 33, 2009–10: Performance Audit, Canberra: ANAO.

ANAO/Australian National Audit Office (2010b), *Effective Cross-Agency Agreements*, Audit Report No. 41 2009–10, Canberra: ANAO.

ANAO/Australian National Audit Office (2011), *Development and Implementation of Key Performance Indicators to Support the Outcomes and Programs Framework*, Audit Report No. 5, 2011–12, Canberra: Commonwealth of Australia.

ANAO/Australian National Audit Office (2012a), *Development and Implementation of Key Performance Indicators to Support the Outcomes and Programs Framework*, Report No. 5, Canberra: ANAO.

ANAO/Australian National Audit Office (2012b), *Administration of Project Wickenby*, Audit Report No. 25 2011–12, Canberra: ANAO.

ANAO/Australian National Audit Office (2013a), *The Australian Government Performance Measurement and Reporting Framework: Pilot Project to Audit Key Performance Indicators*, Report No. 28, 2012–13, Canberra: Commonwealth of Australia.

ANAO/Australian National Audit Office (2013b), *Cross-Agency Coordination of Employment Programs: Department of Education, Employment and Workplace Relations*, Department of Human Services, Audit Report No. 45 2012–13, Canberra: Commonwealth of Australia.

ANAO/Australian National Audit Office (2014), *Pilot Project to Audit Key Performance Indicators*, Canberra: ANAO.

ANAO/Australian National Audit Office (2016), *Administration of the VET FEE-HELP Scheme*, Report No. 31, 2016–17, Canberra: Commonwealth of Australia.

ANAO/Australian National Audit Office (2017a), *The Shared Services Centre*, Report No. 25 2016–17, Canberra: Commonwealth of Australia.

ANAO/Australian National Audit Office (2017b), *Australian Government Procurement Contract Reporting*, Report No. 19, 2017–18, *Information Report*, Canberra: Commonwealth of Australia.

ANAO/Australian National Audit Office (2018), *Efficiency through Contestability Program*, Report No. 41, 2017–18, Canberra: Commonwealth of Australia.

Andrews, P. (2019), Transforming public services for digital society and economy, Policy Lab, digital.NSW, NSW Government. Available at https://www.digital.nsw .gov.au/digital-transformation/the-policy-lab#what (accessed 11 May 2019).

APSC/Australian Public Service Commission (2006), *State of the Service Report 2005–06*, Canberra: APSC.

APSC/Australian Public Service Commission (2007), *State of the Service Report 2006–07*, Canberra: APSC.

APSC/Australian Public Service Commission (2009), *Delivering Performance and Accountability*, Canberra: APSC.

APSC/Australian Public Service Commission (2010), *State of the Service Report 2009–10*, Canberra: APSC.

APSC/Australian Public Service Commission (2012a), *Capability Review: Department of Immigration and Citizenship*, Canberra: APSC.

APSC/Australian Public Service Commission (2012b), *State of the Service Report 2011–12*, Canberra: APSC.

APSC/Australian Public Service Commission (2013), *State of the Service Report 2012–13*, Canberra: APSC.

APSC/Australian Public Service Commission (2014), *State of the Service Report 2013–14*, Canberra: APSC.

APSC/Australian Public Service Commission (2018), *State of the Service Report 2017–18*, Canberra: APSC.

Ardern, J., Rt Hon (2019), 'Why does good government matter?', Prime Minister's speech hosted by the Melbourne City Council and the Australia and New Zealand School of Government, 18 July.

Argyris, C. (1990), *Overcoming Organizational Defenses*, Upper Saddle River, NJ: Prentice-Hall.

Aucoin, P. (1988), 'The Mulroney Government, 1984–1988: Priorities, Positional Policy and Power', in A.B. Gollner and D. Salee (eds), *Canada Under Mulroney: An End-of-Term-Report*, Montreal: Vehicule Press, pp. 335–56.

Aucoin, P. (1990), 'Administrative Reform in Public Management: Paradigms, Principles, Paradoxes and Pendulums', *Governance*, **3** (2), 115–37.

Aucoin, P. (1995), *The New Public Management: Canada in Comparative Perspective*, Montreal: Institute for Research on Public Policy.

Aucoin, P. (2002), 'Beyond the "New" in Public Management', in C. Dunn (ed.), *A Handbook of Canadian Public Administration*, Don Mills, ON: Oxford University Press, part 1, chapter 3.

Aucoin, P. (2006), 'The New Public Governance and the Public Service Commission', *Optimum Online: The Journal of Public Sector Management*, **36** (1).

Aucoin, P. (2007), 'Public Governance and Accountability of Canadian Crown Corporations: Reformation or Transformation', paper presented to Canadian Political Science Association, 2007 Annual Conference, University of Saskatchewan, 31 May.

Aucoin, P. (2008), 'New Public Management and the Quality of Government: Coping with the New Political Governance in Canada', Conference on 'New Public Management and the Quality of Government', SOG and the Quality of Government Institute, University of Gothenburg, 13–15 November 2008.

Aucoin, P. (2010), 'Canada', in C. Eichbaum and R. Shaw (eds), *Partisan Appointees and Public Servants: An International Analysis of the Role of the Political Adviser*, Cheltenham: Edward Elgar, pp. 64–93.

Aucoin, P. (2011), The Political-Administrative Design of NPM', in T. Christensen and P. Lægreid (eds), *The Ashgate Research Companion to New Public Management*, Farnham: Ashgate, pp. 33–46.

Aucoin, P. (2012), 'New Political Governance in Westminster Systems: Impartial Public Administration and Management Performance at Risk', *Governance*, **25** (2), 177–99.

Aucoin, P. and H. Bakvis (1988), *The Centralization-Decentralization Conundrum: Organization and Management in the Canadian Government*, Halifax: Institute for Research on Public Policy.

Aucoin, P. and M.D. Jarvis (2005), *Modernizing Government Accountability: A Framework for Reform*, Ottawa: Canada School of Public Service.

Aucoin, P. and D.J. Savoie (eds) (1998), *Managing Strategic Change: Learning from Program Review*, Ottawa: Canadian Centre for Management Development.

Aucoin, P., H. Bakvis and M.D. Jarvis (2013), 'Constraining Executive Power in the Era of New Political Governance', in J. Bickerton and B.G. Peters (eds), *Governing: Essays in Honour of Donald J. Savoie*, Montreal and Kingston: McGill-Queen's University Press, pp. 32–52.

Aucoin, P., M. Jarvis and L. Turnbull (2011), *Democratizing the Constitution: Reforming Responsible Government*, Toronto: Emond Publishing.

Aucoin, P., J. Smith and G. Dinsdale (2004), *Responsible Government: Clarifying Essentials, Dispelling Myths and Exploring Change*, Ottawa: Canadian Centre for Management Development.

Auditor General of Canada (2003), 2003 Status Report of the Auditor General of Canada, May, Ottawa.

Auditor General of Canada (2005), 'Managing Horizontal Initiatives', Chapter 4 in *Report of the Auditor General of Canada to the House of Commons*, November, Ottawa: Minister of Public Works and Government Services Canada.

Auditor General of Canada (2016), 'The Beyond the Border Action Plan', Report 1, *2016 Fall Reports of the Auditor General of Canada*, November, Ottawa.

Aulich, C. and R. Wettenhall (2012), 'Australia', in G. Bouckaert, P. Laegreid, S. van Thiel and K. Verhoest (eds), *Government Agencies: Practices and Lessons from 30 Countries*, Basingstoke: Palgrave Macmillan.

Bagnall, J. (2016), 'Built to fail: Politics sabotaged Shared Services before the department got off the ground', *Ottawa Citizen*, 28 December.

Bagshaw, E. (2018), 'Fraser resigns as Treasury secretary, Gaetjens gets nod', *The Canberra Times* 13 July, 4.

Baker, R.J.S. (1972), *Administrative Theory and Public Administration*, London: Hutchinson University Library.

Bakvis, H. (1997), 'Advising the Executive: Think Tanks, Consultants, Political Staff and Kitchen Cabinets', in P. Weller, H. Bakvis and R.A.W. Rhodes (eds), *The Hollow Crown: Countervailing Trends in Core Executives*, Basingstoke: Macmillan, pp. 84–125.

Bakvis, H. (2000), 'Rebuilding Policy Capacity in the Era of the Fiscal Dividend', *Governance*, **13** (1), 71–103.

Bakvis, H. and M. Jarvis (eds) (2012), *From New Public Management to the New Political Governance*, Montreal and Kingston: McGill-Queen's University Press.

Bakvis, H. and L. Juillet (2004), *The Horizontal Challenge: Line Departments, Central Agencies and Leadership*, Ottawa: Canada School of Public Service.

Barber, M. (2007), *Instruction to Deliver: Tony Blair, Public Services and the Challenge of Achieving Targets*, London: Politico's.

Barber, M. (2015), *How to Run a Government so that Citizens Benefit and Taxpayers don't go Crazy*, London: Allen Lane.

Barber, M. (2017), *Delivering Better Outcomes for Citizens: Practical Steps for Unlocking Public Value*, London: OGL.

Barberis, P. (2000), 'Prime Minister and Cabinet', in R. Pyper and L. Robins (eds), *United Kingdom Governance*, Basingstoke: Macmillan, pp. 14–38.

Barrett, P. (1996), *Managing Risk as Part of Good Management – an ANAO Perspective*, Launch of MAB/MIAC Report 22: Guidelines for Managing Risk in the Australian Public Service, Canberra.

Barzelay, M. (1992), *Breaking Through Bureaucracy: A New Vision for Managing in Government*, Berkeley: University of California Press.

Barzelay, M. (2001), *The New Public Management: Improving Research and Policy Dialogue*, Berkeley: University of California Press.

Barzelay, M. (2002), 'Origins of the New Public Management: An International View from Public Administration/Political Science', in K. McLaughlin, S.P. Osborne and E. Ferlie (eds), *The New Public Management: Current Trends and Future Prospects*, London: Routledge, pp. 15–33.

Beale, R. (2011), *Review of the Senior Executive Service: Report to the Special Minister of State for the Public Service and Integrity*, Canberra: PwC and Public Service Commission.

Behm, A. (2015), *No, Minister: So You Want to be Chief of Staff?* Melbourne: Melbourne University Press.

Behn, R. (2003), 'Why Measure Performance? Different Purposes Require Different Measures', *Public Administration Review*, **63** (5), 586–606.

Belcher, B. (2015a), *Independent Review of Whole-of-Government Internal Regulation: Report to the Secretaries Committee on Transformation, Volume 1, Recommendations*, Canberra: Department of Finance.

Belcher, B. (2015b), *Independent Review of Whole-of-Government Internal Regulation: Report to the Secretaries Committee on Transformation, Volume 2, Assessment of Key Regulatory Areas*, Canberra: Department of Finance.

Bell, S. and A. Hindmoor (2009), *Rethinking Governance: The Centrality of the State in Modern Society*, Cambridge: Cambridge University Press.

Bennister, M. (2012), *Prime Minister in Power: Political Leadership in Britain and Australia*, Basingstoke: Palgrave Macmillan.

Berlinksi, S., T. Dewan and K. Dowding (2012), *Accounting for Ministers: Scandal and Survival in British Government 1945–2007*, Cambridge: Cambridge University Press.

Beuselinck, E. (2010), 'Coordination in the United Kingdom (1980–2005)', in G. Bouckaert, B.G. Peters and K. Verhoest (eds), *The Coordination of Public Sector Organizations: Shifting Patterns of Public Management*, Basingstoke: Palgrave Macmillan, pp. 114–31.

Bevir, M. and R.A.W. Rhodes (2003), *Interpreting British Governance*, London: Routledge.

Bezes, P. (2007), 'The "Steering State" Model: The Emergence of a New Organizational Form in the French Public Administration', *Sociologie du Travail*, **49S**, 67–89.

Blick, A. (2019). *Populism and the UK Constitution*, London: Constitution Society. Available at https://consoc.org.uk/publications/populism-and-the-uk-constitution/.

Blick, A. and G. Jones (2010), *Premiership: The Development, Nature and Power of the Office of the British Prime Minister*, Charlottesville, VA: Societas.

Bogdanor, V. (ed.) (2005), *Joined-Up Government*, Oxford: Oxford University Press.

Bonner, S. (2014), 'Performance Management in the New Zealand Public Sector', Business Research Project for Masters of Business Administration, Victoria: University of Wellington.

Boston, J. (1995a), 'Inherently Governmental Functions and the Limits to Contracting Out', in J. Boston (ed.), *The State under Contract*, Wellington: Bridget Williams Books, pp.78–111.

Boston, J. (ed.) (1995b), *The State Under Contract*, Wellington: Bridget Williams Books.

Boston, J. (2016), *Governing for the Future: Designing Democratic Institutions for a Better Tomorrow*, Bingley: Emerald.

Boston, J. (2017), *Safeguarding Your Future: Governing in an Uncertain World*, Wellington: BWB Texts.

Boston, J. and C. Eichbaum (2007), 'State Sector Reform and Renewal in New Zealand: Lessons for Governance', in G.E. Caiden and T. Su (eds), *The Repositioning of Public Governance: Global Experience and Challenges*, Taipei: Taiwan National University, pp. 127–79.

Boston, J. and C. Eichbaum (2014), 'New Zealand's Neoliberal Reforms: Half a Revolution', *Governance: An International Journal of Policy, Administration, and Institutions*, **27** (3), 373–76.

Boston, J. and D. Gill (2011), 'Working Across Organizational Boundaries: The Challenge for Accountability', in J. Boston and D. Gill (eds), *Future State: Directions for Public Management in New Zealand*, Wellington: Victoria University Press, 213–47.

Boston, J. and D. Gill (eds) (2017), 'Overview – Key Issues and Themes', *Social Investment: A New Zealand Policy Experiment*, Wellington: Bridget Williams Books, pp. 11–34.

Boston, J. and J. Halligan (2012), 'Political Management and the New Political Governance: Reconciling Political Responsiveness and Neutral Competence', in H. Bakvis and M.D. Jarvis (eds), *From New Public Management to the New Political Governance*, Kingston and Montreal: McGill-Queen's University Press, pp. 204–41.

Boston, J., D. Bagnall and A. Barry (2019), *Foresight, Insight and Oversight: Enhancing Long-Term Government through Better Parliamentary Scrutiny*, Wellington: Institute for Governance and Policy Studies.

Boston, J., J. Martin, J. Pallot and P. Walsh (1996), *Public Management: The New Zealand Model*, Auckland: Oxford University Press.

Bouchal, P. and J. McCrae (2013), *Financial Leadership for Government*, London: Institute for Government.

Bouckaert, G. and J. Halligan (2008), *Managing Performance: International Comparisons*, London: Routledge.

Bouckaert, G., B.G. Peters and K. Verhoest (2010), *The Coordination of Public Sector Organizations: Shifting Patterns of Public Management*, Basingstoke: Palgrave Macmillan.

Bourgault, J. (2014), 'Federal Deputy Ministers: Serial Servers Looking for Influence', in J. Bourgault and C. Dunn (eds) (2014), *Deputy Ministers in Canada: Comparative and Jurisdictional Perspectives*, Toronto: University of Toronto Press, pp. 364–400.

Bourgault, J. (2018), 'Governance Issues for the Government of Canada Deputy Ministers in 2015', October 5, unpublished manuscript.

Bourgault, J. and C. Dunn (eds) (2014a), 'Conclusion: Deputy Ministers in Canada – Evolution of Deputy Ministers as Archetypal Figures', in J. Bourgault, and C. Dunn (eds), *Deputy Ministers in Canada: Comparative and Jurisdictional Perspectives*, Toronto: University of Toronto Press, pp. 429–50.

Bourgault, J. and C. Dunn (eds) (2014b), *Deputy Ministers in Canada: Comparative and Jurisdictional Perspectives*, Toronto: University of Toronto Press.

Bourgon, J. (2009), 'Public Purpose, Government Authority and Collective Power', Conference Paper, XIV International Congress of CLAD, Salvador de Bahia, Brazil, 27–30 October.

Bourgon, J. (2011), *A New Synthesis of Public Administration: Serving in the 21st Century*, Montreal and Kingston: McGill-Queen's University Press.

Bousted, M. (2017), 'The consequences of Gove's ideological reforms are now being felt everywhere', *TES*, 4 August.

Bowen, G.A. (2009), 'Document Analysis as a Qualitative Research Method', *Qualitative Research Journal*, 9 (2), 27–40.

Bowrey, G., C. Smark and T. Watts (2015), 'Financial Accountability: The Contribution of Senate Estimates', *Australian Journal of Public Administration*, 75 (1), 28–38.

Bozeman, B. and M.F Feeney (2011), *Rules and Red Tape: A Prism for Public Administration Theory and Research*, New York: M.E. Sharpe.

Bozeman, B. and G. Kingsley (1998), 'Risk Culture in Public and Private Organizations', *Public Administration Review*, 58 (2), 109–18.

BPSAG/Better Public Services Advisory Group (2011), *Better Public Services Advisory Group Report*, Wellington: New Zealand Government.

Brady, K. (2009), *What is the State of Public Sector Reporting, and What is it Saying About Public Sector Management?* Wellington: Office of the Auditor General. Available at https://oag.govt.nz/reports/speeches-and-papers/state-of-public-sector -reporting.

Brecknell, S. (2016), John Manzoni interview: 'Guiding people through change always takes longer than you think; it's always harder than you think', *Civil Service World*, 25 February.

Brecknell, S. (2017), 'Bernard Jenkin: now is the time to improve government – ministers and all', *Civil Service World*, 20 March.

Brown, A., J. Fishenden, M. Thompson and W. Venters (2017), 'Appraising the Impact and Role of Platform Models and Government as a Platform (GaaP) in UK Government Public Service Reform: Towards a Platform Assessment Framework (PAF)', *Government Information Quarterly*, 34 (2), 167–82.

Bryson, J.M., B.C. Crosby and L. Bloomberg (eds) (2015), *Public Value and Public Administration*, Washington, DC: Georgetown University Press.

Bull, D., J. Stephen, P. Bouchal and G. Freeguard (2013), *Whitehall Monitor: No. 41: How Departments Measure their Performance*, Institute for Government, London, August.

Burgess, K. (2019), 'APS faces "major capability issues", but staffing cap isn't one: Commissioner', *Canberra Times*, 22 October.

Burgess, V. (2017), 'APS leadership turnover set for another jolt—for better or for worse', *Mandarin*, 12 July.

Burnham, J. and S. Horton (2013), *Public Management in the United Kingdom: A New Introduction*, Basingstoke: Palgrave Macmillan.

Burnham, J. and R. Pyper (2008), *Britain's Modernised Civil Service*, Basingstoke: Palgrave Macmillan.

Cabinet Office (1999), *Professional Policy Making for the Twenty First Century*, report by the Strategic Policy Making Team, London: Cabinet Office.

Cabinet Office, Strategy Unit (2002), *Risk: Improving Government's Capability to Handle Risk and Uncertainty*, Summary Report, London: Cabinet Office.

Cabinet Office (2006), *UK Government's Approach to Public Service Reform: A Discussion Paper*, London: Cabinet Office.

Cabinet Office (2009), *Capability Reviews: An Overview of Progress and Next Steps*, London: Cabinet Office.

Cabinet Office (2013), *Enhanced Departmental Boards: Protocol*, London: Cabinet Office, available at https://www.gov.uk/government/publications/enhanced -departmental-boards-protocol.

Cabinet Office (2015a), 'The Functional Model: A Model for More Efficient and Effective Government', available at https://www.gov.uk/government/uploads/ system/uploads/attachment_data/file/418869/The_Functional_Model.pdf.

Cabinet Office (2015b), List of Cabinet Committees and their members as at 3 June 2015, available at https://www.gov.uk/government/publications/the-cabinet -committees-system-and-list-of-cabinet-committees (accessed 6 August 2015).

Cabinet Office (2017), 'Management of Risk in Government', available at https://www .gov.uk/government/publications/management-of-risk-in-government-framework.

Cabinet Office (2019), *Code of Conduct for Special Advisers*. Available at https://www .gov.uk/government/publications/special-advisers-code-of-conduct.

Cabinet Office, Government Shared Services (2019), *Shared Service Strategy of Government*, available at https://assets.publishing.service.gov.uk/government/ uploads/system/uploads/attachment_data/file/834608/Government_Shared _Services_Strategy_Refresh.pdf.

CAG NZ/Comptroller and Auditor-General (2006), *Report on Central Government: Results of the 2004–5 Audits*, Wellington: Office of the Auditor-General.

Caiden, G. (1991), *Administrative Reform Comes of Age*, New York and Berlin: de Gruyter.

Campbell, B. (2014), 'Whither Government in 2020', *Canadian Government Executive*, **20** (1), 9–10.

Campbell, C. (1983), *Governments under Stress: Political Executives and Key Bureaucrats in Washington, London and Ottawa*, Toronto: University of Toronto Press.

Campbell, C. (1988a), 'The Political Roles of Senior Government Officials in Advanced Democracies', *British Journal of Political Science*, **18** (2), 243–72.

Campbell, C. (1988b), 'The Search for Coordination and Control: When and How Are Central Agencies the Answer?' in C. Campbell and B. Guy Peters (eds), *Organizing*

Governance and Governing Organizations, Pittsburgh, PA: University of Pittsburgh Press, pp. 55–77.

Campbell, C. and J. Halligan (1992), *Political Leadership in an Age of Constraint: The Experience of Australia*, Sydney: Allen & Unwin, and Pittsburgh: University of Pittsburgh Press.

Campbell, C. and G. Szablowski (1979), *The Superbureaucrats: Structure and Behaviour in Central Agencies*, Toronto: Macmillan.

Campbell, C. and G.K. Wilson (1995), *The End of Whitehall: Death of a Paradigm?* Oxford and Cambridge: Blackwell.

Canada, Clerk of the Privy Council (2013), Blueprint 2020: Getting Started – Getting Your Views. Ottawa, June. Available at http://publications.gc.ca/collections/ collection_2015/bcp-pco/CP22-101-2013-eng.pdf.

Canada Government (2018), Cabinet Committee Mandate and Membership, available at https://pm.gc.ca/sites/pm/files/documents/cab_committee-comite.pdf.

Canada Treasury Board (2005), *Management in the Government of Canada: A Commitment to Continuous Improvement*, submitted by the President of the Treasury Board, Ottawa: Treasury Board Secretariat.

Canada Treasury Board (2007), Speech by the President of the Treasury Board of Canada to the APEX National Symposium, 9 May.

Cangiano, M., T. Curristine and M. Lazare (eds) (2013), *Public Financial Management and Its Emerging Architecture*, Washington, DC: International Monetary Fund.

Carey, G. and B. Crammond (2015), 'What Works in Joined-Up Government? An Evidence Thesis', *International Journal of Public Administration*, **38** (13–14), 1020–29.

Carroll, B.W. (1990), 'Politics and Administration: A Trichotomy?', *Governance*, **3** (4), 345–66.

Carroll, P. (2006), 'Historical Trends in Policy Transfer in Australia', presented to the Australian Political Studies Association Conference, University of Newcastle, 25–7 September.

Castles, F. (1989), 'Big Government in Weak States: The Paradox of State Size in the English-Speaking Nations of Advanced Capitalism', *Journal of Commonwealth and Comparative Politics*, **27** (3), 267–93.

Central Agencies Review 2006 (2006), *Review of Central Agencies' Role in Promoting and Assuring State Sector Performance*, NZ Treasury, available at http://www .treasury.govt.nz/publications/informationreleases/exgreviews/ca.

Chapman, R. (1996), 'The End of the Civil Service?', in P. Barberis (ed.), *The Whitehall Reader: The UK's Administrative Machine in Action*, Buckingham: Open University Press, pp. 187–91.

Charko, P. (2013), 'Management Improvement in the Canadian Public Service, 1999–2010', *Canadian Public Administration*, **56** (1), 91–201.

Christensen, T. and P. Lægreid (eds) (2006), *Autonomy and Regulation: Coping with Agencies in the Modern State*, Cheltenham: Edward Elgar.

Christensen, T. and P. Lægreid (2007), 'The Whole of Government Approach to Public Sector Reform', *Public Administration Review*, **67** (6), 1057–64.

Christensen, T. and P. Lægreid (eds) (2011a), *The Ashgate Research Companion to New Public Management*, Farnham: Ashgate.

Christensen, T. and P. Lægreid (2011b), 'Post-NPM: Whole of Government Approaches as a New Trend', in S. Groeneveld and S. Van de Walle (eds), *New Steering Concepts in Public Management*, Bingley: Emerald, pp. 11–24.

Christensen, T. and P. Lægreid (2011c), 'Complexity and Hybrid Public Administration–Theoretical and Empirical Challenges', *Public Organization Review*, **11**, 407–23.

Christensen, T. and P. Lægreid (2012), 'Competing Principles of Organization – the Reorganization of Reform', *International Review of Administrative Sciences*, **78** (4), 579–96.

Christensen, T., P. Lægreid, P. Roness and K.A. Rovik (2007), *Organization Theory and the Public Sector: Instrument, Culture and Myth*, London and New York: Routledge.

Clark, I.D. and H. Swain (2005), 'Distinguishing the Real from the Surreal in Management Reform: Suggestions for Beleaguered Administrators in the Government of Canada', *Canadian Public Administration*, **48** (4), 453–77.

Clarke, A. (2019), *Opening the Government of Canada: The Federal Bureaucracy in the Digital Age*, Vancouver and Toronto: UBC Press.

Committee on the Civil Service (Chair: Lord Fulton) (1968), *The Civil Service: Report of the Committee 1966–68*, Volume 1, Cmnd. 3638, London: HMSO.

Commonwealth (1983), *Reforming the Australian Public Service: A Statement of the Government's Intentions*, Canberra: Australian Government Publishing Service.

Commonwealth of Australia (2017), *Budget 2017–18, Agency Resourcing, Budget Paper No. 4. 2017–18*, Canberra: Commonwealth of Australia.

Commonwealth of Australia (2019), *Budget 2019–20, Agency Resourcing, Budget Paper No. 4. 2019–20*, Canberra: Commonwealth of Australia.

Cormann, M. (Minister for Finance) (2015), *Smaller and More Rational Government 2014–15*, Ministerial Paper, Canberra: Commonwealth of Australia.

Considine, M. and M. Painter (eds) (1997), *Managerialism: The Great Debate*, Carlton, VIC: Melbourne University Press.

Cook, A.-L. (2004), *'Managing for Outcomes' in the New Zealand Public Management System*, New Zealand Treasury Working Paper 04/15, Wellington: The Treasury.

CPA/Committee of Public Accounts (2008), *Managing Financial Resources to Deliver Better Public Services*, forty–third Report of Session 2007–08, HC 519, London: The Stationery Office.

CPA/Committee of Public Accounts (2011), *Accountability for Public Money*, twenty-eighth Report of Session 2010–11, HC 740, London: The Stationery Office.

CPA/Committee of Public Accounts (2016a), *Accountability to Parliament for Taxpayers' Money*, thirty-ninth Report of Session 2015–16, HC 732, London: House of Commons.

CPA/Committee of Public Accounts (2016b), *Oral Evidence: Accountability to Parliament for Taxpayers' Money*, HC 732, London: House of Commons.

CPA/Committee of Public Accounts (2016c), *Managing Government Spending and Expenditure*, twenty-seventh Report of Session 2016–17, HC 710, London: House of Commons.

CPA/Committee of Public Accounts (2016d), *Use of Consultants and Temporary Staff*, thirty-sixth Report of Session 2015–16, HC 726, London: House of Commons.

CPA/Committee of Public Accounts (2018), *Driving Value in Public Spending: Oral Evidence*, HC 1596, London: House of Commons.

Craft, J. (2015), 'Revisiting the Gospel: Appointed Political Staffs and Core Executive Policy Coordination', *International Journal of Public Administration*, **38** (1), 56–65.

Craft, J. (2016), *Backrooms and Beyond: Partisan Advisers and the Politics of Policy Work in Canada*, Toronto: University of Toronto Press.

Craft, J. (2018a), 'Out from the Shadows: Political Staff as Public Administrators', in C. Dunn (ed.), *Canadian Handbook of Public Administration*, 3rd edn, Don Mills, ON: Oxford University Press, pp. 440–54.

Craft, J. (2018b), 'Canada: Flexing the Political Arm of Government', in R. Shaw and C. Eichbaum (eds), *Ministers, Minders and Mandarins: An International Study of Relationships at the Executive Summit of Parliamentary Democracies*, Cheltenham: Edward Elgar, pp. 34–52.

Craft, J. and J. Halligan (2017), 'Assessing 30 years of Westminster Policy Advisory System Experience', *Policy Sciences*, **50** (1), 47–62.

Craft, J. and J. Halligan (2020), *Advising Governments in the Westminster Tradition: Policy Advisory Systems in Australia, Britain, Canada and New Zealand*, Cambridge: Cambridge University Press (in press).

Creve, C., P. Lægreid and L.H. Rykkja (2016), 'The Nordic Model Revisited: Active Reformers and High Performing Public Administrations', in C. Creve, P. Lægreid and L.H. Rykkja (eds), *Nordic Administrative Reforms: Lessons for Public Management*, London: Palgrave Macmillan, pp. 189–212.

CSC/Civil Service Commission (2014), Recruitment Principles, available at http:// civilservicecommission.independent.gov.uk/wp-content/uploads/2014/04/ Recruitment- Principles-April-2014.pdf.

Dahlström, C. and J. Pierre (2011), 'Steering the Swedish State: Politicization as a Coordination Strategy', in C. Dahlström, B.G. Peters, and J. Pierre (eds), *Steering from the Centre: Strengthening Political Control in Western Democracies*, Toronto: University of Toronto Press, pp. 193–211.

Dahlström, C., B.G. Peters and J. Pierre (eds) (2011a), *Steering from the Centre: Strengthening Political Control in Western Democracies*, Toronto: University of Toronto Press.

Dahlström, C., B.G. Peters and J. Pierre (2011b), 'Steering Strategies in Western Democracies', in C. Dahlström, B.G. Peters, and J. Pierre (eds), *Steering from the Centre: Strengthening Political Control in Western Democracies*, Toronto: University of Toronto Press, pp. 263–75.

Dash, K. (2012), *Permanent Secretaries?* Blog, Institute for Government, 20 November, available at http://www.instituteforgovernment.org.uk/blog/5204/permanent -secretaries/ (accessed 14 July 2014).

Davis, G. (1995), *A Government of Routines: Executive Coordination in an Australia State*, South Melbourne: Macmillan Education.

Davis, J.H., F.D. Schoorman and L. Donaldson (1997), 'Towards a Stewardship Theory of Management', *Academy of Management Review*, **22** (1), 20–47.

Davison, N. (2015), *Lifting the Policy Game across the System: The Case of 'The Policy Project'*, London: Institute for Government; and Wellington: Policy Project.

Davison, N. (2016), *Whole of Government Reforms in New Zealand: The Case of the Policy Project*, London: Institute for Government.

Dean, T. (2009), *UK Public Service Reforms: A Canadian Perspective*, Toronto: Institute of Public Administration of Canada.

De Brouwer (2017), Secretary Valedictory, Transcript of Proceedings, Canberra: Institute of Public Administration.

Delacourt, S. (2016), 'Permanent Marketing and the Conduct of Politics', in J. Ditchburn and G. Fox (eds), *The Harper Factor: Assessing a Prime Minister's Policy Legacy*, Montreal and Kingston: McGill-Queen's University Press, pp. 80–94.

Desautels, D. (Auditor General) (1997), Opening Remarks Panel Discussion, Association of Professional Executives of the Public Service of Canada Symposium, available at http://www.oag-bvg.gc.ca/internet/English/meth_gde_e_26997.html (accessed 1 January 2018).

DFD/Department of Finance and Deregulation (2012a), *Is Less More? Towards Better Commonwealth Performance*, Discussion Paper, Commonwealth Financial Accountability Review, Canberra: Commonwealth of Australia.

DFD/Department of Finance and Deregulation (2012b), *Sharpening the Focus: A Framework for Improving Commonwealth Performance*, Canberra: Commonwealth of Australia.

Di Francesco, M. (1998), 'The Measure of Policy? Evaluating the Evaluation Strategy as an Instrument for Budgetary Control', *Australian Journal of Public Administration*, **57** (1), 33–48.

Di Francesco, M. (2001), 'Process not Outcomes in New Public Management? Policy Coherence in Australian Government', *Australian Review of Public Affairs*, **1** (3), 103–16.

Di Francesco, M. (2012a), 'Grand Designs? The 'Managerial' Role of Ministers Within Westminster-Based Public Management Policy', *Australian Journal of Public Administration*, **71** (3), 257–68.

Di Francesco, M. (2012b), 'The Public Service', in D. Clune and R. Smith (eds), *From Carr to Keneally: Labor in Office in NSW 1995–2011*, Sydney: Allen & Unwin, pp. 85–99.

Di Francesco, M. (2016), 'Rules and Flexibility in Public Budgeting: The Case of Budget Modernisation in Australia', *Australian Journal of Public Administration*, **75** (2), 236–48.

Di Francesco, M. and J. Alford (2016), *Balancing Control and Flexibility in Public Budgeting: A New Role for Rule Variability*, Basingstoke: Palgrave Macmillan.

Di Francesco, M. and E. Eppel (2011), 'A Public Management Heresy? Exploring the "Managerial" Role of Ministers within Public Management Policy Design', in B. Ryan and D. Gill (eds), *Future State: Directions for Public Management in New Zealand*, Wellington: Victoria University Press, pp. 123–58.

Diamond, P. (2014), *Governing Britain: Power, Politics and the Prime Minister*, London: I.B. Tauris.

Diamond, P. (2019a), *The End of Whitehall? Government by Permanent Campaign*, Basingstoke: Palgrave Macmillan.

Diamond, P. (2019b), 'The Westminster System under the Cameron Coalition: "Promiscuous Partisanship" or Institutional Resilience?' *Public Policy and Administration*, **34** (3), 241–61.

Dobuzinskis, L., M. Howlett and D. Laycock (eds) (2007), *Policy Analysis in Canada*, Toronto: University of Toronto Press.

Doern, G.B., M.J. Prince and R.J. Schultz (2014), *Rules and Unruliness; Canadian Regulatory Democracy, Governance, Capitalism, and Welfarism*, Montreal and Kingston: McGill-Queen's University Press.

DoF/Department of Finance (2014), *Enhanced Commonwealth Performance Framework: Discussion Paper*, Canberra: Commonwealth of Australia.

DoF/Department of Finance (2015), Findings Report on the July PGPA Benefits Realisation Survey, Canberra: Commonwealth of Australia.

DoF/Department of Finance (2018), Submission to the Joint Committee of Public Accounts and Audit: Part A, Canberra: Australian Government.

Dommett, K. and M. MacCarthaigh (2016), 'Quango Reform: The Next Steps?' *Public Money and Management*, **36** (4), 249–56.

Dommett, K., M. MacCarthaigh and N. Hardman (2016), 'Reforming the Westminster Model of Agency Governance: Britain and Ireland after the Crisis', *Governance*, **29** (4), 535–52.

Donaldson, D. (2018), '"Urgent" former secretaries assess public service capability', *The Mandarin*, 12 February.

Dormer, R. and D. Gill (2010), 'Managing for Performance in New Zealand's Public Service – A Loosely Coupled Framework?', *Measuring Business Excellence*, **14** (1), 43–59.

Dowding, K. (1995), *Civil Service*, London: Routledge.

Dowding, K. (2003), 'The Civil Service', in J. Hollowell (ed.), *Britain Since 1945*, Malden, MA: Wiley-Blackwell Publishing, pp. 179–93.

Dowding, K. (2017), 'Australian Exceptionalism Reconsidered', *Australian Journal of Political Science*, **52** (2), 165–82.

DPMC/Department of the Prime Minister and Cabinet (2014), *The Policy Project – Responsive Today, Shaping Tomorrow*, Wellington: DPMC.

DPMC/Department of the Prime Minister and Cabinet (2019), *APS Policy Capability Roadmap: A Practical Plan to Lift Policy Capability across the APS*, Canberra: Australian Government.

DPMC/Department of the Prime Minister and Cabinet (2020), *Data Integration Partnership for Australia*, available at https://www.pmc.gov.au/public-data/data-integration-partnership-australia (accessed 16 January 2020).

Drewry, G. and T. Butcher (1991), *The Civil Service Today*, 2nd edn, Oxford: Basil Blackwell.

DTA/Digital Transformation Agency (2019), *Corporate Plan 2019–23*, Canberra: DTA, available at https://www.dta.gov.au/about-us/reporting-and-plans/corporate-plans/corporate-plan-2019-23.

Duncan, G. and J. Chapman (2010), 'New Millennium, New Public Management and the New Zealand Model', *Australian Journal of Public Administration*, **69** (3), 301–13.

Dunleavy, P. (2010a), *The Future of Joined-Up Services*, London: 2020 Public Services Trust.

Dunleavy, P. (2010b), 'What is the Cameron–Clegg governance strategy? Zombie "new public management" cannot work in the face of massive public expenditure cutbacks', LSE Public Services Blogs, 7 October.

Dunleavy, P. and L. Carrera (2013), *Growing the Productivity of Government Services*, Cheltenham: Edward Elgar.

Dunleavy, P. and C. Hood (1994), 'From Old Public Administration to New Public Management', *Public Money and Management*, July–September, 9–16.

Dunleavy, P. and H. Margetts (2010), The Second Wave of Digital-Era Governance, LSE Online.

Dunleavy P., M. Evans and C. McGregor (n.d.), *'Connected Government' Towards Digital-Era Governance*, Canberra: Institute for Governance and Policy Analysis and Telstra.

Dunleavy P., H. Margetts, S. Bastow and J. Tinkler (2005), 'New Public Management is Dead–Long Live Digital-Era Governance', *JPART*, **16**, 467–94.

Dunleavy P., H. Margetts, S. Bastow and J. Tinkler (2006), *Digital Era Governance: IT Corporations, the State and e-Government*, Oxford: Oxford University Press.

Dunleavy, P., A. Park and R. Taylor (2018), *The UK's Changing Democracy: The 2018 Democratic Audit*, London: LSE Press. DOI: https://doi.org/10.31389/book1.

Dutil, P., C. Howard, J. Langford and J. Roy (2010), *The Service State: Rhetoric, Reality and Promise*, Ottawa: University of Ottawa Press.

Dwivedi, O.P. and J.I. Gow (1999), *From Bureaucracy to Public Management: The Administrative Culture of the Government of Canada*, Toronto: Broadview Press.

Dwivedi, O.P. and J. Halligan (2003), 'The Canadian Public Service: Balancing Values and Management', in J. Halligan (ed.), *Civil Service Systems in Anglo-American Countries*, Cheltenham: Edward Elgar, pp. 148–73.

Easton, S. (2018), 'Australian Public Service to start running citizen-satisfaction surveys', *The Mandarin*, 4 July, available at https://www.themandarin.com.au/ 95214-australian-public-service-to-start-running-citizen-satisfaction-surveys/.

Editorial (2019), Advice just as important as service, *Canberra Times*, 29 May, p. 18.

Edwards, L. (2009), 'Testing the Discourse of Declining Policy Capacity: Rail Policy and the Department of Transport', *Australian Journal of Public Administration*, **68** (3), 288–302.

Edwards, M., J. Halligan, B. Horrigan and G. Nicoll (2012), *Public Sector Governance in Australia*, Canberra: ANU Press.

Edwards, N. (2019), The John Deeble Lecture 2019, Deeble Institute for Health Policy Research Canberra: Australian Parliament House, 18 October.

Egan, J. (2009), *Review of Work Value for the Office of Secretary: Australian Government Departments of State*, prepared for the Commonwealth Remuneration Tribunal, Sydney.

Eichbaum, C. (2017), 'Free and frank advice fast disappearing', *The Dominion Post*, 8 August.

Eichbaum, C. and R. Shaw (2007a), 'Ministerial Advisers, Politicisation and the Retreat from Westminster: The Case of New Zealand', *Public Administration*, **85** (3), 1–32.

Eichbaum, C. and R. Shaw (2007b), 'Ministerial Advisers and the Politics of Policy-Making: Bureaucratic Permanence and Popular Control', *Australian Journal of Public Administration*, **66** (4), 453–67.

Eichbaum, C. and R. Shaw (2008), 'Revisiting Politicization: Political Advisers and Public Servants in Westminster Systems', *Governance*, **21** (3), 337–63.

Eichbaum, C. and R. Shaw (2010), 'New Zealand', in C. Eichbaum and R. Shaw (eds), *Partisan Appointees and Public Servants: An International Analysis of the Role of the Political Adviser*, Cheltenham: Edward Elgar, pp. 114–50.

Eichbaum, C. and R. Shaw (2011), 'Political Staff in Executive Government: Conceptualising and Mapping Roles within the Core Executive', *Australian Journal of Political Science*, **46** (4), 583–600.

Elston, T. (2012), 'Developments in UK Executive Agencies: Re-Examining the "Disaggregation-Reaggregation" Thesis', *Public Policy and Administration*, **28** (1), 66–89.

Elston, T. (2014), 'Not so "Arm's Length": Reinterpreting Agencies in UK Central Government', *Public Administration*, **92** (2), 458–76.

Elston, T. and M. MacCarthaigh (2013), Shared Services in Ireland and the UK: Unpicking the (latest) Public Sector Panacea, paper presented to the 35th Annual Conference of the European Group of Public Administration, Edinburgh, 11–13 September.

Elston, T. and M. MacCarthaigh (2016), 'Sharing Services, Saving Money? Five Risks to Cost- Saving when Organizations Share Services', *Public Money and Management*, **36** (5), 349–56.

Emy, H. and O. Hughes (1991), *Australian Politics: Realities in Conflict*, 2nd edn, Melbourne: Macmillan.

Encel, S. (1960), 'The Concept of the State in Australian Politics', *Australian Journal of Politics and History*, **61** (1), 62–76.

Eppel, E. (2013), *Collaborative Governance: Framing New Zealand Practice*, Working Paper 13/02, Wellington: Institute for Governance and Policy Studies.

Eppel, E. and A. Wolf (2012), 'Implementing Better Public Services', *Policy Quarterly*, **8** (3), 41–8.

Eppel, E., D. Gill, A.M.B. Lips and B. Ryan (2013), 'The Cross-Organization Solution? Conditions, Roles and Dynamics in New Zealand', in J. O'Flynn, D. Blackman and J. Halligan (eds), *Crossing Boundaries in Public Management and Policy: The International Experience*, London and New York: Routledge.

Esselment, A.L., J. Lees-Marshment and A. Marland (2014), 'The Nature of Political Advising to Prime Ministers in Australia, Canada, New Zealand and the UK', *Commonwealth & Comparative Politics*, **52** (3), 358–75.

Etzioni-Halevy, E. (1983), *Bureaucracy and Democracy: A Political Dilemma*, London: Routledge and Kegan Paul.

Evans, M. and J. Davies (1999), 'Understanding Policy Transfer: A Multi-Level, Multi-Disciplinary Perspective', *Public Administration*, **77** (2), 361–86.

Evans, M., M. Grattan and B. McCaffrie (eds) (2019), *From Turnbull to Morrison: Australian Commonwealth Administration 2016–2019 – Understanding the Trust Divide*, Melbourne: Melbourne University Press.

Fawcett, P. (2010), Metagovernance and the Treasury's Evolving Role within the British Core Executive, Political Studies Association conference paper.

Fawcett, P. (2018), 'Doing Democracy and Governance in the Fast Lane? Towards a "Politics of Time" in an Accelerated Polity', *Australian Journal of Political Science*, **53** (4), 548–64.

Fawcett, P. and O. Gay (2010), 'The United Kingdom', in C. Eichbaum and R. Shaw (eds), *Partisan Appointees and Public Servants: An International Analysis of the Role of the Political Adviser*, Cheltenham: Edward Elgar, pp. 24–63.

Fellegi, I. (1996), *Strengthening our Policy Capacity*, Report of the Deputy Ministers Task Force, Ottawa: Supply and Service Canada.

Fielding, F.M. (2016), 'Letting Go and Holding On: The Politics of Performance Management in the United Kingdom', *Public Policy and Administration*, **31** (4), 303–23.

Fleury, J.-G. (2002), 'Governing for Performance in the Public Sector', Country Report for the Organisation for Economic Cooperation and Development Symposium.

Flynn, N. (2007), *Public Sector Management*, 6th edn, London: Sage.

Flynn, N. and A. Asquer (2017), *Public Sector Management*, 7th edn, London: Sage.

Francis, D. and M. Horn (2013), *Core Guide 3: Getting to Great; Lead Reviewer Insights from the Performance Improvement Framework*, Wellington: State Services Commission, the Treasury and the Department of the Prime Minister and Cabinet.

Freeguard, G. (2018), *Too Many Priorities Mean No Priorities*, London: Institute for Government.

Freeguard, G., R. Adam, E. Andrews and A. Boon (2017), *Whitehall Monitor 2017*, London: Institute for Government.

Freeguard, G., A. Cheung, A. Lilly, M. Shepheard, J. Lillis, L. Campbell, J. Haigh, J. Taylor and A. de Costa (2019), *Whitehall Monitor 2019*, London: Institute for Government.

Furphy, S. (ed.) (2015), *The Seven Dwarfs and the Age of the Mandarins: Australian Government Administration in the Post-War Reconstruction Era*, Canberra: ANU Press.

Garvey, G. (1993), *Facing the Bureaucracy: Living and Dying in a Public Agency*, San Francisco, CA: Jossey-Bass Publishers.

Gill, D. (2008a), 'Crown Entity Reform in Aotearoa-New Zealand – Pendulum Shift?' Paper presented at International Research Symposium for Public Management, Queensland University of Technology, Brisbane, 26–8 March.

Gill, D. (ed) (2011a), *The Iron Cage Recreated: The Performance Management of State Organisations in New Zealand*, Wellington: Institute of Policy Studies.

Gill, D. (2011b), 'Introduction', in D. Gill (ed.), *The Iron Cage Recreated: The Performance Management of State Organisations in New Zealand*, Wellington: Institute of Policy Studies, pp. 1–8.

Gill, D. and T. Schmidt (2011), 'Organisational Performance Management: Concepts and Themes', in D. Gill (ed.), *The Iron Cage Recreated: The Performance Management of State Organisation in New Zealand*, Wellington: Institute of Policy Studies, pp. 9–36.

Gleeson, D., D. Legge, D. O'Neill and M. Pfeffer (2011), 'Negotiating Tensions in Developing Organizational Policy Capacity: Comparative Lessons to be Drawn', *Journal of Comparative Policy Analysis: Research and Practice*, **13** (3), 237–63.

Gold, J. (2014), *International Delivery: Centres of Government and the Drive for Better Policy Implementation*, London: Institute for Government, and Toronto: Mowat Centre.

Gold, J. (2017), *Tracking Delivery: Global Trends and Warning Signs in Delivery Units*, London: Institute for Government.

Gomery Report (Commission of Inquiry into the Sponsorship Program and Advertising Activities: Chair J. Gomery) (2005), *Who is Responsible: Fact Finding Report*, Ottawa: Canadian Government.

Goodin, R. and P. Wilenski (1984), 'Beyond Efficiency: The Logical Underpinnings of Administrative Principles', *Public Administration Review*, **44** (6), 512–17.

Gourley, P. (2017), 'The folly of the Coalition's Home Affairs super ministry shake-up', *Canberra Times*, 1 August.

Government of Canada (2013), *Blueprint 2020: Building Tomorrow's Public Service Together*, Ottawa: Government of Canada.

Government of Canada (2014), *Destination 2020*, Ottawa: Government of Canada.

Gow, J.I. (1994), *Learning from Others: Administrative Innovation among Canadian Governments*, Toronto: Institute of Public Administration of Canada and the Canadian Centre for Management Development.

Gow, J.I. (2004), *A Canadian Model of Public Administration?* Ottawa: Canadian School of Public Service.

Grattan, M. (2019), 'PM attempts to calm the circus', *The Canberra Times*, 27 July, 36.

Greenaway, A. (2017), 'The civil service is in crisis', *Civil Service World*, 17 October.

Greenwood, J., R. Pyper and D. Wilson (2002), *New Public Administration in Britain*, London: Routledge.

Gregory, R. (2000), 'Getting Better but Feeling Worse? Public Sector Reform in New Zealand', *International Public Management Journal*, **3**, 107–23.

Gregory, R. (2001), 'Transforming Governmental Culture: A Sceptical View of New Public Management in New Zealand', in T. Christensen and P. Lægreid (eds), *New Public Management: The Transformation of Ideas and Practices*, Aldershot: Ashgate Publishing.

Gregory, R. (2002), 'Political Responsibility for Bureaucratic Incompetence: Tragedy at Cave Creek', *Public Administration*, **76** (3), 519–38.

Gregory, R. (2006), 'Theoretical Faith and Practical Works: De-Autonomizing and Joining-Up in the New Zealand State Sector', in T. Christensen and P. Lægreid (eds), *Autonomy and Regulation: Coping with Agencies in the Modern State*, Cheltenham: Edward Elgar, pp. 137–61.

Gregory, R. (2007), 'New Public Management and the Ghost of Max Weber: Exorcised or Still Haunting?' in T. Christensen and P. Lægreid (eds), *Transcending New Public Management: Transformation of Public Sector Reforms*, Aldershot: Ashgate, pp. 221–43.

Greve, C., P. Lægreid and L.H. Rykkja (2016), 'The Nordic Model Revisited: Active Reformers and High Performing Public Administrations', in C. Creve, P. Lægreid and L.H. Rykkja (eds), *Nordic Administrative Reforms: Lessons for Public Management*, London: Palgrave Macmillan, pp. 189–212.

Grimshaw, D. and J. Rubery (2013), 'Reinforcing Neoliberalism: Crisis and Austerity in the UK', in S. Lehndorff (ed.), *A Triumph of Failed Ideas: European Models of Capitalism in the Crisis*, Brussels: ETUI, pp. 41–57.

Grube, D. (2014), 'Responsibility to be Enthusiastic? Public Servants and the Public Face of "Promiscuous Partisanship"', *Governance*, **28** (3), 305–20.

Grube, D. (2019), *Megaphone Bureaucracy: Speaking Truth to Power in the Age of the New Normal*, Princeton: Princeton University Press.

Grube, D. and C. Howard (2016a), 'Is the Westminster System Broken Beyond Repair?' *Governance*, **29** (4), 467–81.

Grube, D. and C. Howard (2016b), 'Promiscuously Partisan? Public Service Impartiality and Responsiveness in Westminster Systems', *Governance*, **29** (4), 517–33.

Haddon, C. (2016), 'Developments in the Civil Service', in R. Heffernan, C. Hay, M. Russell and P. Cowley (eds), *Developments in British Politics Ten*, 10th edn, London: Palgrave Macmillan, pp. 161–82.

Hall, M. and D. Marsh (2019), Brexit shows both the importance of the British Political Tradition and the extent to which it is under threat, LSE Blogs, September.

Halligan, J. (1987), 'Reorganising Australian Government Departments, 1987', *Canberra Bulletin of Public Administration*, **52**, September, 40–47.

Halligan, J. (1996a), 'Learning from Experience in Australian Reform: Balancing Principle and Pragmatism', in J.P. Olsen and B.G. Peters (eds), *Learning from Reform*, Oslo: Scandinavia University Press, pp. 71–112.

Halligan, J. (1996b), 'The Diffusion of Civil Service Reform', in H. Bekke, J.L. Perry and T.A.J. Toonen (eds), *Civil Services in Comparative Perspective*, Bloomington: Indiana University Press, pp. 288–317.

Halligan, J. (1997), 'Departmental Secretaries in Canada and the United Kingdom', *Australian Journal of Public Administration*, **56** (4), 26–31.

Halligan, J. (2001), 'Politicians, Bureaucrats and Public Sector Reform in Australia and New Zealand', in B.G. Peters and J. Pierre (eds), *Politicians, Bureaucrats and Administrative Reform*, London: Routledge, pp. 157–68.

Halligan, J. (2003a), 'Anglo-American Civil Service Systems: An Overview', in J. Halligan (ed.), *Civil Service Systems in Anglo-American Countries*, Cheltenham: Edward Elgar, pp. 1–9.

Halligan, J. (2003b), 'Anglo-American Civil Service Systems: Comparative Perspectives', in J. Halligan (ed.), *Civil Service Systems in Anglo-American Countries*, Cheltenham: Edward Elgar, pp. 195–213.

Halligan, J. (2006), 'The Reassertion of the Centre in a First Generation NPM System', in T. Christensen and P. Lægreid (eds), *Autonomy and Regulation: Coping with Agencies in the Modern State*, Cheltenham: Edward Elgar, pp. 162–80.

Halligan, J. (2007a), 'Anglo-American Systems: Easy Diffusion', in J.C.N. Raadschelders, T.A.J. Toonen and F.M. Van der Meer (eds), *Comparative Civil Service Systems in the 21st Century*, Basingstoke: Palgrave Macmillan, pp. 50–64.

Halligan, J. (2007b), 'Reintegrating Government in Third Generation Reforms of Australia and New Zealand', *Public Policy and Administration*, **22** (2), 217–38.

Halligan, J. (2007c), 'Performance Management and Budgeting in Australia and New Zealand', in P. de Lancer Julnes, F. Berry, M. Aristigueta and K. Yang (eds), *International Handbook of Practice-Based Performance Management*, Thousand Oaks, CA: Sage, pp. 341–59.

Halligan, J. (2007d), 'Accountability in Australia: Control, Paradox and Complexity', *Public Administration Quarterly*, **31** (4), pp. 462–89.

Halligan, J. (2008a), *The Centrelink Experiment: An Innovation in Service Delivery*, Canberra: Australian National University Press.

Halligan, J. (2008b), 'Australian Public Service: Combining the Search for Balance and Effectiveness with Deviations on Fundamentals', in C. Aulich and R. Wettenhall (eds), *Howard's Fourth Government*, Sydney: University of New South Wales Press, pp. 13–30.

Halligan, J. (2009), 'A Comparative Perspective on Canadian Public Administration within an Anglophone Tradition', in O.P Dwivedi, T.A. Mau and B. Sheldrick (eds), *The Evolving Physiology of Government: Canadian Public Administration in Transition: From Administration to Management to Governance*, Ottawa: University of Ottawa Press, pp. 292–311.

Halligan, J. (2010a), 'Post-NPM Responses to Disaggregation through Coordinating Horizontally and Integrating Governance', in P. Lægreid and K. Verhoest (eds), *Governance of Public Sector Organizations – Autonomy, Control and Performance*, Basingstoke: Palgrave Macmillan, pp. 235–54.

Halligan, J. (2010b), 'The Fate of Administrative Tradition in Anglophone Countries during the Reform Era', in M. Painter and B.G. Peters (eds), *Tradition and Public Administration*, London and Basingstoke: Palgrave Macmillan, pp. 129–42.

Halligan, J. (2011a), 'Central Steering in Australia', in C. Dahlström, B.G. Peters and J. Pierre (eds), *Steering from the Centre: Strengthening Political Control in Western Democracies*, Toronto: University of Toronto Press, pp. 99–122.

Halligan, J. (2011b), 'NPM in Anglo-Saxon Countries', in T. Christensen and P. Lægreid, (eds), *The Ashgate Research Companion to New Public Management*, Farnham: Ashgate, pp. 83–96.

Halligan, J. (2012), 'Leadership and the Senior Service from a Comparative Perspective', in B.G Peters and J. Pierre (eds), *The Sage Handbook of Public Administration*, 2nd edn, London: Sage, pp. 115–29.

Halligan, J. (2013a), 'The Evolution of Public Service Bargains of Australian Senior Public Servants', *International Review of Administrative Sciences*, **79** (1), 111–29.

Halligan, J. (2013b), 'The Role and Significance of Context in Comparing Country Systems', in C. Pollitt (ed.), *Context in Public Policy and Management*, Cheltenham: Edward Elgar, pp. 356–73.

Halligan, J. (2015a), 'Coordination of Welfare through a Large Integrated Organisation: The Australian Department of Human Services', *Public Management Review*, **17** (7), 1002–20.

Halligan, J. (2015b), 'Capacity, Complexity and Public Sector Reform in Australia', in A. Massey and K. Miller (eds), *The International Handbook of Public Administration and Governance*, Cheltenham: Edward Elgar, pp. 323–40.

Halligan, J. (2015c), 'Anglophone Systems: Diffusion and Policy Transfer within an Administrative Tradition', in F. van der Meer, J. Raadschelders and T. Toonen (eds), *The Civil Service in the 21st Century*, 2nd edn, Basingstoke: Palgrave Macmillan, pp. 57–76.

Halligan, J. (2016), Policy Capability in Australia, Greater China Australia Dialogue on Public Administration 2016 Workshop, Centre for Chinese Public Administration Research, Sun Yat-sen University, Guangzhou, 30–31 October.

Halligan, J. (2019), 'Nadir or Renaissance for the Australian Public Service?', in M. Evans, M. Grattan and B. McCaffrie (eds), *From Turnbull to Morrison: Australian Commonwealth Administration 2016–2019 – Understanding the Trust Divide*, Melbourne: Melbourne University Press, pp. 144–59.

Halligan, J. and O. James (2012), 'Comparing Agencification in Anglo-American Countries', in K. Verhoest, S. Van Thiel, G. Bouckaert and P. Lægreid (eds), *Government Agencies: Practices and Lessons from 30 Countries*, Basingstoke: Palgrave Macmillan, pp. 77–82.

Halligan, J. and Power, J. (1992), *Political Management in the 1990s*, Melbourne: Oxford University Press.

Halligan, J. and G. Smith (2019), Intensity of collaboration between Australian government agencies and the effect on program success, paper for the annual conference of the International Research Society of Public Management, Wellington: Victoria University of Wellington, 16–18 April.

Halligan, J., F. Buick and J. O'Flynn (2011), 'Experiments with Joined-Up, Horizontal and Whole-of-Government in Anglophone Countries', in A. Massey (ed.), *International Handbook on Civil Service Systems*, Cheltenham: Edward Elgar, pp. 74–99.

Halligan, J., R. Miller and J. Power (2007), *Parliament in the 21st Century: Institutional Reform and Emerging Roles*, Melbourne: Melbourne University Press.

Hallsworth, M. (2011), *System Stewardship: The Future of Policy Making?* Working Paper, London: Institute for Government.

Hallsworth, M. and J. Rutter (2011), *Making Policy Better: Improving Core Business*, London: Institute for Government.

Hallsworth, M., S. Parker and J. Rutter (2011), *Policymaking in the Real World: Evidence and Analysis*, London: Institute for Government.

Halton, J. (Secretary, Department of Finance) (2015), 'Public Governance, Performance and Accountability Reforms', speech for 2015 Senate Occasional Lecture Series, Canberra: Parliament House.

Hamburger, P. (2007), 'Coordination and Leadership at the Centre of the Australian Public Service', in R. Koch and J. Dixon (eds), *Public Governance and Leadership*, Wiesbaden: Deutscher Universitäts-Verlag, pp. 207–31.

Hamburger, P. and P. Weller (2012), 'Policy Advice and a Central Agency: The Department of the Prime Minister and the Cabinet', *Australian Journal of Political Science*, **47** (3), 363–76.

Hamburger, P, B. Stevens and P. Weller (2011), 'A Capacity for Central Coordination: The Case of the Department of the Prime Minister and Cabinet', *Australian Journal of Public Administration*, **70** (4), 377–90.

Hammerschmid, G., S. Van de Walle, R. Andrews and P. Bezes (2016), *Public Administration in Europe: The View from the Top*, Cheltenham: Edward Elgar.

Hanger, I. (2014), *Report of the Royal Commission into the Home Insulation Program*, Canberra: Commonwealth of Australia.

Harries, R. and K. Sawyer (2014), *How to Run a Country: The Burden of Regulation*, London: Reform, available at http://www.reform.uk/wp-content/uploads/2014/12/The_burden_of_regulation_WEB.pdf.

Hasluck, P. (1995), *Light that Time has Made*, Canberra: National Library of Australia.

Hawke, L. (2012), 'Australian Public Sector Performance Management: Success or Stagnation', *International Journal of Productivity and Performance Management*, **61** (3), 310–28.

Hawke, L. (2016), 'Australia', in D. Moynihan and I. Beazley (eds), *Towards Next-Generation Performance Budgeting: Lessons from the Experience of Seven Reforming Countries*, Washington, DC: The World Bank, pp. 41–54.

Hawke, L. and J. Wanna (2010), Australia after Budgetary Reform: A Lapsed Pioneer or Decorative Architect?' in J. Wanna, L. Jensen and J. de Vires (eds), *The Reality of Budgetary Reform in OECD Countries: Trajectories and Consequences*, Cheltenham: Edward Elgar, pp. 65–90.

Hawker, G. (1981), *Who's Master, Who's Servant: Reforming Bureaucracy*, Sydney: George Allen & Unwin.

Hayne, K.M. (2019), 'On Royal Commissions', Address to Centre for Comparative Constitutional Studies Conference, Melbourne: Melbourne Law School, 26 July.

Hazell, R., A. Cogbill, D. Owen, H. Webber and L. Chebib (2018), *Critical Friends? The Role of Non Executives on Whitehall Boards*, London: Constitution Unit, University College London.

Head, B. (2015), 'Policy Analysis and Public Sector Capacity', in B. Head and K. Crowley (eds), *Policy Analysis in Australia*, Bristol: Policy Press, pp. 53–67.

Head, B. and M. Di Francesco (2019), 'Using Evidence in Australia and New Zealand', in A. Boaz, H. Davis, A. Fraser and S. Nutley (eds), *What Works Now? Evidence-Informed Policy and Practice*, Bristol: Policy Press, pp. 303–20.

Heady, B. (1974), *British Cabinet Ministers*, London: Allen & Unwin.

Heclo, H. and A. Wildavsky (1974), *Private Government of Public Money: Community and Policy inside British Politics*, London and Basingstoke: Macmillan Press.

Heinrich, C. and G. Marschke (2010), 'Incentives and their Dynamics in Public Sector Performance Management Systems', *Journal of Policy Analysis and Management*, **29** (1), 183–208.

Heintzman, R. (1997), 'Canada and Public Administration', in J. Bourgault, M. Demers and C. Williams (eds), *Public Administration and Public Management Experiences in Canada*, Sainte-Foy: Les Publications du Quebec.

Heintzman, R. (2013), 'Establishing the Boundaries of the Public Service: Toward a New Moral Contract', in J. Bickerton and B.G Peters (eds), *Governing: Essays in Honour of Donald J. Savoie*, Montreal and Kingston: McGill-Queen's University Press, pp. 85–138.

Heintzman, R. (2014), *Renewal of the Federal Public Service: Towards a Charter of Public Service*, Ottawa: Canada 2020.

Heintzman, R. (2015), 'Creeping politicization in the public service', *Ottawa Citizen*, 6 April.

Heintzman, R. (2016), Border-Crossing: The PBO, PCO and the Boundary of the Public Service, *Canadian Public Administration*, **59** (3), 357–81.

Henderson, P. (2014), 'Holistic, Transparent and Comparative Reporting in Large NZ Public Sector Organisations?' Research Report for Executive MBA Degree, Massey University.

Hennessy, P. (1989), *Whitehall*, London: Secker and Warburg.

Hitchiner, S. and D. Gill (2011), 'The Formal System as it Evolved', in D. Gill (ed.), *The Iron Cage Recreated: The Performance Management of State Organisations in New Zealand*, Wellington: Institute of Policy Studies, pp. 81–118.

HM Government (2012), *The Civil Service Reform Plan*, June, London: HM Government.

HM Government (2014), *The Civil Service Reform Plan: Progress Report*, London: HM Government.

HM Treasury (2004), *The Orange Book: Management of Risk – Principles and Concepts*, London: HM Treasury.

HM Treasury (2005), *Corporate Governance in Central Government Departments: Code of Good Practice*, London: HMSO.

HM Treasury (2013), *Review of Financial Management in Government*, London: HM Treasury.

HM Treasury (2015), *Managing Public Money*, London: HM Treasury.

HM Treasury and Cabinet Office (2011), *Corporate Governance in Central Government Departments: Code of Good Practice*. HM Treasury, London, available at https://www.gov.uk/government/publications/corporate-governance-code-for-central-government-departments.

HMT and OPSR/HM Treasury and Office of Public Services Reform (2002), *Better Government Services: Executive Agencies in the 21st Century*, London: Cabinet Office.

Hodgetts, J.E. (1983), 'Implicit Values in the Administration of Public Affairs', in K. Kernaghan (ed.), *Canadian Public Administration: Discipline and Profession*, Toronto: Butterworths.

Hodgetts, J.E., W. McClosky, R. Whitaker and V.S. Wilson (1972), *The Biography of an Institution: The Civil Service Commission of Canada*, Montreal and London: McGill-Queen's University Press.

Hoggett, P. (1997), 'New Modes of Control in the Public Service', *Public Administration*, **74** (1), 9–32.

Holliday, I. (2000), 'Executives and Administrations', in P. Dunleavy, A. Gamble, I. Holliday and G. Peele (eds), *Developments in British Politics 6*, London: Palgrave Macmillan, pp. 88–107.

Holmes, M. (1989), 'Corporate Management: A View from the Centre', in G. Davis, P. Weller and C. Lewis (eds), *Corporate Management in Australian Government*, Melbourne: Macmillan, pp. 29–47.

Hood, C. (1990), 'De-Sir Humphreyfying the Westminster Model of Bureaucracy: A New Style of Governance?', *Governance*, **3** (2), 205–14.

Hood, C. (1991), 'A Public Management for All Seasons?', *Public Administration*, **69** (1), 3–19.

Hood, C. (1994), *Explaining Economic Policy Reversals*, Buckingham: Open University Press.

Hood, C. (1996), 'Exploring Variations in 1980s Public Management Reform', in H. Bekke, J.L. Perry and T.A.J. Toonen (eds), *Civil Services in Comparative Perspective*, Bloomington: Indiana University Press, pp. 268–87.

Hood, C. (1998), *The Art of the State: Culture, Rhetoric and Public Management*, Oxford: Clarendon Press.

Hood, C. (2000), 'Paradoxes of Public-Sector Managerialism, Old Management and Public Service Bargains', *International Public Management Journal*, **3**, 1–22.

Hood, C. (2005), 'The Idea of Joined-up Government: A Historical Perspective', in V. Bogdanor (ed.), *Joined-Up Government*, Oxford: Oxford University Press.

Hood, C. (2011), *The Blame Game: Spin, Bureaucracy, and Self-Preservation in Government*, Princeton, NJ and Oxford: Princeton University Press.

Hood, C. and R. Dixon (2015), *A Government that Worked Better and Cost Less? Evaluating Three Decades of Reform and Change in UK Central Government*, Oxford: Oxford University Press.

Hood, C. and M. Lodge (2006), *The Politics of Public Service Bargains: Reward, Competency, Loyalty – and Blame*, Oxford: Oxford University Press.

Hood, C. and G. Peters (2004), 'The Middle Aging of New Public Management: Into the Age of Paradox?', *Journal of Public Administration Research and Theory*, **14** (3), 267–82.

Hood, C., H. Rothstein and R. Baldwin (2004), *The Government of Risk: Understanding Risk Regulation Regimes*, Oxford: Oxford University Press.

Hood, C., C. Scott, O. James, G. Jones and T. Travers (1999), *Regulation Inside Government: Waste Watchers, Quality Police, and Sleaze-Busters*, New York: Oxford University Press.

Howard, C. and S. Phillips (2012), 'Moving Away from Hierarchy: Do Horizontality, Partnership and Distributed Governance Really Signify the End of Accountability', in H. Bakvis and M. Jarvis (eds), *From New Public Management to the New Political Governance*, Montreal and Kingston: McGill-Queen's University Press, pp. 314–41.

Howlett, M. and A. Migone (2013), 'Searching for Substance: Externalization, Politicization and the Work of Canadian Policy Consultants 2006–2013', *Central European Journal of Public Policy*, **7** (1), 112–33.

Howlett, M. and A. Migone (2017), 'Policy Advice through the Market: The Role of External Consultants in Contemporary Policy Advisory Systems', *Policy and Society*, **32** (3), 241–54.

Howlett, M. and A.M. Wellstead (2011), 'Policy Analysts in the Bureaucracy Revisited: The Nature of Professional Policy Work in Contemporary Government', *Politics and Policy*, **39** (4), 613–33.

Howlett, M., S. Tan, A. Migone, A. Wellstead and B. Evans (2014), 'The Distribution of Analytical Techniques in Policy Advisory Systems: Policy Formulation and the Tools of Policy Appraisal', Public Policy and Administration, **29** (4), 271–91.

Hughes, P. (2019), Stewardship, Innovation and the Spirit of Service', speech by the State Services Commissioner, IRSPM Conference, Wellington, 16 April.

Hughes, P. and J. Smart (2012), 'You Say You Want a Revolution . . . The Next Stage of Public Sector Reform in New Zealand', *Policy Quarterly*, **8** (1), 3–16.

Hyndman, N. and M. Liguori (2016), 'Public Sector Reforms: Changing Contours on an NPM Landscape', *Financial Accountability and Management*, **32** (1), 5–32.

Institute for Government (2011a), Business plans: a long way to go, 11 July, available at https://www.instituteforgovernment.org.uk/news/latest/business-plans-long-way-go.

Institute for Government (2011b), Whitehall misses one in four deadlines set out in departmental business plans, 25 November, available at https://www.instituteforgovernment.org.uk/news/latest/whitehall-misses-one-four-deadlines-set-out-departmental-business-plans.

Institute for Government (2012), Government business plans fail to live up to expectations, 20 November, available at http://www.instituteforgovernment.org.uk/news/latest/government-business-plans- fail-live-expectations.

IPPR/Institute for Public Policy Research (2013), *Accountability and Responsiveness in the Senior Civil Service: Lessons from Overseas*, London: Cabinet Office.

IRAPS/Independent Review of the APS (2019a), *Independent Review of the APS: Priorities for Change*, Canberra: Commonwealth of Australia, 19 March.

IRAPS/Independent Review of the APS (2019b), *Our Public Service Our Future*, Canberra: Commonwealth of Australia.

Jabes, J., N. Jans, J. Frazer-Jans and D. Zussman (1992), 'Managing the Canadian and Australian Public Sectors: A Comparative Study of the Vertical Solitude', *International Review of Administrative Sciences*, **58** (1), 5–21.

James, C. (2002), *The Tie that Binds: The Relationship between Ministers and Chief Executives*, Wellington: Institute of Policy Studies and New Zealand Centre for Public Law, Victoria University of Wellington.

James, C. (2019), '"Wellbeing" facet points to different way of governing', *Otago Daily Times*, 31 May, 8.

James, O. (2003), *The Executive Agency Revolution in Whitehall*, Basingstoke: Palgrave Macmillan.

James, O. (2004), 'The UK Core Executive's Use of Public Service Agreements as a Tool of Governance', *Public Administration*, **82** (2), 397–419.

James, O. and A. Nakamura (2013), 'Public Service Agreements as a Tool of Coordination in UK Central Government: The Case of Employment', COCOPS Paper, available at http://www.cocops.eu/wp-content/uploads/2013/06/UK _Employment_Public-Service-Agreements.pdf (accessed 17 August 2019).

James, O. and A. Nakamura (2014), 'Coordination in UK Central Government', in P. Lægreid K. Sarapuu, L. Rykkja and T. Randma-Liiv (eds), *Organizing for Coordination in the Public Sector: Practices and Lessons from 12 European Countries*, Basingstoke: Palgrave Macmillan, pp. 91–102.

James, O., A. Moseley, N. Petrovsky and G. Boyne (2012), 'United Kingdom', in K. Verhoest, S. Van Thiel, G. Bouckaert and P. Lægreid (eds), *Government Agencies: Practices and Lessons from 30 Countries*, Basingstoke: Palgrave Macmillan, pp. 57–68.

JCPAA/Joint Committee of Public Accounts and Audit (2012), *Report 432 APS – Fit for Service: Australian Public Service Annual Update*, Canberra: House of Representatives.

Jennings, W., M. Lodge and M. Ryan (2018), 'Comparing Blunders in Government', *European Journal of Political Research*, **57** (1), 238–58.

Jensen, K., R. Scott, L. Slocombe, R. Body and L. Cowey (2014), *The Management and Organisational Challenges of More Joined-up Government: New Zealand's Better Public Services Reforms*, State Sector Performance Hub, Working Paper, 2014-1, Wellington: New Zealand Government.

Johnson, D. (2017), *Thinking Government: Public Administration and Politics in Canada*, 4th edn, Toronto: University of Toronto Press.

Johnstone, R. (2018a), 'Windrush generation/Home Office officials "lost sight of people" in immigration policy, claims Rudd', *Civil Service World*, 17 April.

Johnstone, R. (2018b), 'DfE perm sec gets ministerial direction to press ahead with technical education reforms', *Civil Service World*, 25 May.

Jones, G. (2016), *The Power of the Prime Minister: 50 Years On*, Research Paper, London: The Constitution Society.

Joyce, M. (2011), 'Performance Information and Innovation in the Canadian Government', in A. Graham (ed.), *Innovations in Public Expenditure Management: Country Cases from the Commonwealth*, London: Commonwealth Secretariat and The Institute of Public Administration of Canada, pp. 13–27.

Juillet, L. and K. Rasmussen (2008), *Defending a Contested Idea: Merit and the PSC of Canada*, Ottawa: University of Ottawa Press.

Karp, P. (2019), Deputy Nationals leader rejected more than 600 grants recommended by Sports Australia, *The Guardian*, 25 October.

Kaufman, H. (1969), 'Administrative Centralization and Political Power', *Public Administration Review*, **29** (1), 3–15.

Kaufmann, W., R. Hooghiemstra and M.K. Feeney (2018), 'Formal Institutions, Informal Institutions, and Red Tape: A Comparative Study', *Public Administration*, **96** (2), 386–403.

Keast, R. (2011), 'Joined-Up Governance in Australia: How the Past can Inform the Future', *International Journal of Public Administration*, **34** (4), 221–31.

Keast, R. and M. Mandell (2014), 'The Collaborative Push: Moving Beyond Rhetoric and Gaining Evidence', *Journal of Management and Governance*, **18** (1), 9–28.

Keating, M. (2003), 'In the Wake of "A Certain Maritime Incident": Ministerial Advisers, Departments and Accountability', *Australian Journal of Public Administration*, **62** (3), 92–7.

Keating, M. and M. Holmes (1990), 'Australia's Budgetary and Financial Management Reforms', *Governance*, **3** (2), 168–85.

Kelemen, R.D. (2015), 'Introduction: Why Look to Europe for Lessons?' in R.D. Kelemen, (ed.), *Lessons from Europe? What Americans Can Learn from European Public Policies*, Los Angeles, CA: Sage.

Kellner, P. and Lord Crowther-Hunt (1980), *The Civil Servants: An Inquiry into Britain's Ruling Class*, London: Macdonald.

Kelly, J. (2009), *Shaping a Strategic Centre*, Canberra: Commonwealth of Australia.

Kemp, D. (1986), 'The Recent Evolution of Central Policy Control Mechanisms in Parliamentary Systems', *International Political Science Review*, **7** (1), 56–66.

Kernaghan, K. and D. Siegel (1991), *Public Administration in Canada: A Text*, 2nd edn, Scarborough: NelsonCanada, available at http://lareleve.pwgsc.gc.ca/rediscover/rediscover_e.html.

Kerslake, Lord (2017), *Rethinking the Treasury: Kerslake Review of the Treasury*, commissioned by the Shadow Chancellor of the Exchequer, available at http://www.kerslakereview.co.uk/wp-content/uploads/2015/11/9076_17-Kerslake-Review-of-the-Treasury-_-final_v2.pdf.

Key, J. (2017), The 2017 Garran Oration, Institute of Public Administration Australia, Australian Parliament House, Canberra, 15 November.

Kibblewhite, A. (2018a), 'The New Zealand Policy Project: Reflections on the First Three Years', *Civil Service Quarterly*, available at https://quarterly.blog.gov.uk/2018/03/28/reflections-on-the-first-three-years-of-the-new-zealand-policy-project/.

Kibblewhite, A. (2018b), 'The Future of the Policy Profession', speech at Policy Managers Forum, Wellington, 18 December.

Kibblewhite, A. and P. Boshier (2018), 'Free and Frank Advice and the Official Information Act: Balancing Competing Principles of Good Government', *Policy Quarterly*, **14** (2), 3–9.

Kibblewhite, A. and C. Ussher (2002), 'Outcome-Focused Management in New Zealand', *Journal of Budgeting*, **1** (4), 85–109.

King, A. (2007), *The British Constitution*, Oxford: Oxford University Press.

King, A. and I. Crewe (2014), *The Blunders of our Governments*, London: Oneworld.

Knill, C. (1999), 'Explaining Cross-National Variance in Administrative Reform: Autonomous versus Instrumental Bureaucracies', *Journal of Public Policy*, **19** (2), 113–39.

Knott, J.H. and G.J. Miller (2008), 'When Ambition Checks Ambition: Bureaucratic Trustees and the Separation of Powers,' *American Review of Public Administration*, **38** (4), 387–411.

Korac-Kakabadse, A. and N. Korac-Kakabadse (1998), *Leadership in Government: A Study of the Australian Public Service*, Aldershot: Ashgate.

Koziol, M. (2018), 'Shorten says Treasury Appointment shows Liberals "addicted to stacking" government with their mates', *The Canberra Times*, 13 July, 4.

KPMG (2009), *Benchmarking Australian Government Administrative Performance*, Canberra: KPMG.

Kuhlmann, S. and H. Wollmann (2019), *Introduction to Comparative Public Administration: Administrative Systems and Reforms in Europe*, 2nd edn, Cheltenham: Edward Elgar.

Lægreid, P. and L.H. Rykkja (2015), 'Administrative Reform in the Nordic Countries – Processes, Trends and Content', paper prepared for the Permanent Study Group on 'Governance of Public Sector Organizations' at the EGPA Annual Conference, Toulouse, 26–8 August.

Lægreid, P., A.D. Nordø and L. Rykkja (2013), *The Quality of Coordination in Norwegian Central Government: The Importance of Coordination Arrangements and Structural, Cultural and Demographic Factors*, COCOPS Working Paper No. 14.

Lægreid, P., T. Randma-Liiv, L.H. Rykkja and K. Sarapuu (2014), 'Introduction: Emerging Coordination Practices in European Public Management', in P. Lægreid, T. Randma-Liiv, L. Rykkja and K. Sarapuu (eds), *Organizing for Coordination in the Public Sector: Practices and Lessons from 12 European Countries*, Basingstoke: Palgrave Macmillan.

Lægreid, P., T. Randma-Liiv, L.H. Rykkja and K. Sarapuu, (2016), 'Coordination Challenges and Administrative Reforms', in G. Hammerschmid, S. Van de Walle, R. Andrews and P. Bezes (eds), *Public Administration in Europe: The View from the Top*, Cheltenham: Edward Elgar, pp. 244–58.

Laffin, M. (1997), 'Understanding Minister-Bureaucrat Relations: Applying Multi-Theoretic Approaches in Public Management', *Australian Journal of Public Administration*, **56** (1), 45–58.

Laking, R. (2011), 'Conclusions: How Public Organisations are Controlled and Governed', in D. Gill (ed.), *The Iron Cage Recreated: The Performance Management of State Organisations in New Zealand*, Wellington: Institute of Policy Studies, pp. 405–46.

Lane, J.-E. (2000), *New Public Management*, London: Routledge.

Lasater, Z. (2011), 'Beyond the Silos: Joined-Up Government and Community Building Policies as a Source of Institutional Change Within New Governance', PhD thesis, School of Social and Political Sciences, University of Melbourne.

Lee, I. and P. Cross (2016), 'Reforms to the Federal Public Service in the Harper Years, 2006–2015', in C. Stoney and G.B. Doern (eds), *How Ottawa Spends: The Liberal Rise and the Tory Demise 2015–2016*, available at https://carleton.ca/sppa/wp-content/uploads/HOW-OTTAWA-SPENDS-2015-2016.pdf.

Lee, J.M., G.W. Jones and J. Burnham (1998), *At the Centre of Whitehall: Advising the Prime Minister and Cabinet*, Basingstoke: Palgrave Macmillan.

Legault, S. (2016), 'A Brief Retrospective', presented to the Canadian Bar Association, Annual Access to Information and Privacy Law Symposium, Ottawa: Office of the Information Commissioner of Canada, available at http://www.oic-ci.gc.ca/eng/media-room-salle-media_speeches-discours_2016_12.aspx.

Legrand, T. (2015), 'Transgovernmental Policy Networks in the Anglosphere', *Public Administration*, **93** (4), 973–91.

Lépine, G. (2007), *The Web of Rules: A Study of the Relationship between Regulation of Public Servants and Past Public Service Reform Initiatives*, Public Policy Forum, Ottawa, available at https://www.ppforum.ca/sites/default/files/web_of _rules_reportfn.pdf.

Levitt, R. and W. Solesbury (2012), *Policy Tsars: Here to Stay but More Transparency Needed: Final Report*, London, Kings College.

Lijphart, A. (1984), *Democracies: Patterns of Majoritarian and Consensus Government in Twenty-One Countries*, New Haven, CT and London: Yale University Press.

Lindquist, E. (2001), 'Reconceiving the Centre: Leadership, Strategic Review and Coherence in Public Sector Reform', in OECD, *Government of the Future,* Paris: OECD.

Lindquist, E. (2006), *A Critical Moment: Capturing and Conveying the Evolution of the Canadian Public Service*, Ottawa: Canadian School of Public Service.

Lindquist, E. (2009), 'How Ottawa Assesses Department/Agency Performance: Treasury Board's Management Accountability Framework', in A.M. Maslove (ed.), *How Ottawa Spends 2009–2010: Economic Upheaval and Political Dysfunction*, Montreal and Kingston: McGill-Queen's University Press, pp. 47–88.

Lindquist, E. (2014), 'The Responsiveness Solution? Embedding Horizontal Governance in Canada', in J. O'Flynn, D. Blackman and J. Halligan (eds), *Crossing Boundaries in Public Management and Policy: The International Experience*, London and New York: Routledge, pp. 190–210.

Lindquist, E. (2016), 'Performance Monitoring and the Management Accountability Framework: Recent Developments, Perspective, and Insights from the Literature', 30 October, unpublished paper.

Lindquist, E. (2017), 'Rethinking the Management Accountability Framework for the Open Government Era', in K. Graham and A. Maslove (eds), *How Ottawa Spends 2017–2018*, School of Public Policy and Administration, Ottawa: Carleton University, pp. 132–43.

Lipson, L. (1948), *The Politics of Equality: New Zealand's Adventures in Democracy*, Chicago, IL: University of Chicago Press.

Lodge, M. and D. Gill (2011), 'Toward a New Era of Administrative Reform? The Myth of Post-NPM in New Zealand', *Governance*, **24** (1), 141–66.

Lodge, M. and Wegrich, K. (eds) (2012), *Executive Politics in Times of Crisis*, Basingstoke: Palgrave Macmillan.

Lonti, Z. and R. Gregory (2007), 'Accountability or Countability? Performance Measurement in the New Zealand Public Service', *Australian Journal of Public Administration*, **66** (4), 468–84.

MAC/Management Advisory Committee (2001), *Performance Management in the Australian Public Service: A Strategic Framework*, Canberra: Commonwealth of Australia.

MAC/Management Advisory Committee (2004), *Connecting Government: Whole of Government Responses to Australia's Priority Challenges*, Canberra: Commonwealth of Australia.

MAC/Management Advisory Committee (2007), *Reducing Red Tape in the Australian Public Service*, Canberra: Commonwealth of Australia.

MAC/Management Advisory Committee (2010), *Empowering Change: Fostering Innovation in the Australian Public Service*, Canberra: Commonwealth of Australia.

McBeth, P. (2018), 'Comms Minister Curran keen to tear down silo approach to digital policy', *National Business Review*, 25 January, available at https://www.nbr.co .nz/article/comms-minister-curran-keen-tear-down-silo-approach-digital-policy-b -211929 (accessed 29 January 2018).

McBride, D. (2013), *Power Trip: A Decade of Policy, Plots and Spin*, London: Biteback Publishing.

McCrae, J. and J. Gold (2017), *Professionalising Whitehall*, London: Institute for Government.

McCrae, J., A. Boon, J. Harris and G. Miller (2016), *Getting to the Heart of Decision Making: Whitehall's Financial Management Reform*, London: Institute for Government, December.

McCrae, J., J. Harris and E. Andrews (2015), *All in it together: Cross-Departmental Responsibilities for Improving Whitehall*, London: Institute for Government.

McCrae, J., J. Stephen, R. Mehta and T. Guermellou (2012), *Improving Decision Making in Whitehall: Effective Use of Management Information*, London: Institute for Government.

MacDermott, K. (2008), *Whatever Happened to 'Frank' and 'Fearless'? The Impact of New Public Management on the Public Service*, Canberra: ANU E Press.

Mackay, K. (2004), Two Generations of Performance Evaluation and Management Systems in Australia, ECD Working Paper Series 11, World Bank, Washington DC.

Mackay, K. (2011), 'The Performance Framework of the Australian Government, 1987 to 2011', *OECD Journal on Budgeting*, **11** (3), 75–122.

McLeay, E. (1995), *The Cabinet and Political Power in New Zealand*, Auckland: Oxford University Press.

McPhee, Ian (2005), 'Outcomes and Outputs: Are We Managing Better as a Result?' CPA National Public Sector Convention, 20 May.

Maer, L. and G. Ryan-White (2018), *Civil Service Recruitment: Heads of Department*, Briefing Paper No. 06697, House of Commons Library, 8 February.

MAG/Ministerial Advisory Group (2001), *Report of the Advisory Group of the Review of the Centre*, Wellington: State Services Commission.

Mahoney, J. and K. Thelen (2010), 'A Theory of Gradual Institutional Change', in J. Mahoney and K. Thelen (eds), *Explaining Institutional Change: Ambiguity, Agency and Power*, Cambridge: Cambridge University Press, pp. 1–37.

Maley, M. (2000), 'Too Many or Too Few? The Increase in Federal Ministerial Advisers 1972–1999', *Australian Journal of Public Administration*, **59** (4), 48–53.

Maley, M. (2010), 'Australia', in C. Eichbaum and R. Shaw (eds), *Partisan Appointees and Public Servants: An International Analysis of the Role of the Political Adviser*, Cheltenham: Edward Elgar, pp. 94–113.

Maley, M. (2011), 'Strategic Links in a Cut-Throat World: Rethinking the Role and Relationships of Australian Ministerial Staff', *Public Administration*, **89** (4), 1469–88.

Maley, M. (2015), 'The Policy Work of Australian Political Staff', *International Journal of Public Administration*, **38** (1), 46–55.

Maley, M. (2019), 'Border Crossings: The Employment of Public Servants in Ministers' Offices in Australia', International Conference on Public Policy, Montreal 26–8 June 2019.

Maley, M. and J. Stewart (2007), 'The Howard Government and Political Management: The Challenge of Policy Activism', *Australian Journal of Political Science*, **42** (2), 277–93.

Malpess, L. (2019), 'What exactly is NZ's wellbeing budget?' *Australian Financial Review*, 3 June, 36–7.

Manzoni, J. (2018), 'A civil service fit for the future', presentation to the Institute for Government, London, video, 1 May, available at https://www.instituteforgovernment .org.uk/events/civil-service-fit-future.

Manzoni, J. (2019), Making the Civil Service a great place to work, Blog, Civil Service Quarterly, 4 July, available at https://quarterly.blog.gov.uk/2019/07/04/making-the -civil-service-a-great-place-to-work/.

Maor, M. (1999), 'The Paradox of Managerialism', *Public Administration Review*, **59** (1), 5–18.

March, J. and J. Olsen (1989), *Rediscovering Institutions: The Organizational Basis of Politics*, Glencoe: Free Press.

March, J. and J. Olsen (2003), 'Organizing Political Life: What Administrative Reorganization Tells us about Government', *American Political Science Review*, **77** (2), 281–96.

March, J. and J. Olsen (2006), 'The Logic of Appropriateness', in M. Moran, M. Rein and R.E. Goodin (eds), *The Oxford Handbook of Public Policy*, Oxford: Oxford University Press, pp. 689–708.

Margetts, H. and P. Dunleavy (2013), 'The Second Wave of Digital-era Governance: A Quasi-paradigm for Government on the Web', *Philosophical Transactions of the Royal Society A*, 371: 20120382, http://dx.doi.org/10.1098/rsta.2012.0382.

Marsden, D. (2010), 'The Paradox of Performance-Related Pay System', in H. Margetts, Perri 6 and C. Hood (eds), *Paradoxes of Modernisation: Unintended Consequences of Public Policy Reform*, Oxford Scholarship Online.

Marsh, D. (2011), 'The New Orthodoxy: The Differentiated Polity Model', *Public Administration*, **89** (1), 32–48.

Marsh, D. and Fawcett, P. (2011), 'Branding and Franchising a Public Policy: The Case of the Gateway Review Process 2001–2010', *Australian Journal of Public Administration*, **70** (3), 246–58.

Marsh, D., D. Richards and M.J. Smith (2001), *Changing Patterns of Governance in the United Kingdom: Reinventing Whitehall?*, Basingstoke: Palgrave Macmillan.

Martin, J.R. (2015), 'An Age of the Mandarins? Government in New Zealand, 1940–51', in S. Furphy (ed.), *The Seven Dwarfs and the Age of the Mandarins: Australian Government Administration in the Post-War Reconstruction Era*, Canberra: ANU Press, pp. 81–110.

Matthews, F. (2013), *Complexity, Fragmentation, and Uncertainty: Government Capacity in an Evolving State*, Oxford: Oxford University Press.

Matthews, F.M. (2016), 'Letting Go and Holding On: The Politics of Performance Management in the United Kingdom', *Public Policy and Administration*, **31** (4), 303–23.

Maude, F. (Minister of the Cabinet Office) (2013), 'Ministers and Mandarins: speaking truth unto power', Leonard Steinberg lecture about civil service reform, 4 June, available at https://www.gov.uk/government/speeches/ministers-and-mandarins -speaking-truth-unto-power.

Metcalfe, L. (1994), 'International Policy Co-ordination and Public Management Reform', *International Review of Administrative Sciences*, **60** (2), 271–90.

Metcalfe, L. and S. Richards (1987), *Improving Public Management*, London: Sage.

Micheli, P. and A. Neely (2010), 'Performance Measurement in the Public Sector in England: Searching for the Golden Thread', *Public Administration Review*, July/ August, 591–600.

Miller, G.J. and A.B. Whitford (2016), *Above Politics: Bureaucratic Discretion and Credible Commitment*, Cambridge: Cambridge University Press.

Mitchell, D. and R. Conway (2011), 'From the Deputy Shuffle to the Deputy Churn: Keeping the Best and Brightest in Ottawa', *Policy Options*, May, 60–64.

Moran, T. (2011), The John Paterson Oration 2011, Australia and New Zealand School of Government Annual Conference, 28 July.

Moreton, L. (2018), 'Opinion: unfair criticism of Home Office staff over Windrush deflects blame from cuts', *Civil Service World*, 23 April.

Morrison, A. (2014), 'Picking up the Pace in Public Services', *Policy Quarterly*, **10** (2), 43–8.

Morrison, S. (2019), Prime Minister's speech to Institute of Public Administration, Canberra: Parliament House, 19 August.

Mulgan, R. (1997), *Politics in New Zealand*, 2nd edn, Auckland: Auckland University Press.

Mulgan, R. (1998), 'Politicisation of Senior Appointments in the Australian Public Service', *Australian Journal of Public Administration*, **57** (3), 3–14.

Mulgan, R. (2003), *Holding Power to Account: Accountability in Modern Democracies*, Basingstoke: Palgrave Macmillan.

Mulgan, R. (2007), 'Truth in Government and the Politicization of Public Service Advice', *Public Administration*, **85** (3), 569–86.

Mulgan, R. (2008), 'The Accountability Priorities of Australian Parliamentarians', *Australian Journal of Public Administration*, **67** (4), 457–69.

Mulgan, R. (2016), 'Goodbye, Westminster: Is Our Political System Dying or Just Evolving?' *Public Sector Informant, Canberra Times*, 30 July.

NAO/National Audit Office (2004), *Managing Risk in Public Services*, London: National Audit Office.

NAO/National Audit Office (2006), *Achieving Innovation in Government*, London: National Audit Office.

NAO/National Audit Office (2009), *Innovation across Central Government*, Session 2008–09, HC 12, London: National Audit Office.

NAO/National Audit Office (2010), *Evaluation in Government*, London: National Audit Office.

NAO/National Audit Office (2011a), *Managing Risks in Government*, London: National Audit Office.

NAO/National Audit Office (2011b), *Progress in Improving Financial Management in Government*, Session 2010–11, HC 487, London: National Audit Office.

NAO/National Audit Office (2013a), *Integration across Government*, Session 2012–13, HC1041, London: National Audit Office.

NAO/National Audit Office (2013b), *Integration across Government and Whole-Place Community Budgets*, HC472, Session 2013–14, London: National Audit Office.

NAO/National Audit Office (2013c), *Financial Management in Government*, HC 131, London: National Audit Office.

NAO/National Audit Office (2014), *The Centre of Government*, Session 2014–15, HC 171, London: National Audit Office.

NAO/National Audit Office (2015), *The Centre of Government: An Update*, Session 2014–15, HC 1031, London: National Audit Office.

NAO/National Audit Office (2016a), *Accountability to Parliament for Taxpayers' Money*, HC 849, Session 2015–16, London: National Audit Office.

NAO/National Audit Office (2016b), *Government's Management of its Performance: Progress with Single Department Plans*, HC 872, Session 2016–17, London: National Audit Office.

NAO/National Audit Office (2016c), *Spending Review 2015*, HC 571, 21 July, London: National Audit Office.

NAO/National Audit Office (2016d), *Shared Service Centres*, HC 16 Session 2016–17, London: National Audit Office.

NAO/National Audit Office (2018a), *Digital Transformation in Government*, London: National Audit Office.

NAO/National Audit Office (2018b), *PF1 and PF2*, HC 718, Session 2017–18, London: National Audit Office.

NAO/National Audit Office (2018c), *Improving Government's Planning and Spending Framework*, HC 1679, Session 2017–19, London: National Audit Office.

NCA/National Commission of Audit (2014), *Towards Responsible Government: The Report of the National Commission of Audit Phase One*, Canberra: Commonwealth of Australia.

Newman, J. (2002), 'The New Public Management, Modernization and Institutional Change', in K. McLaughlin, S.P. Osborne, and E. Ferlie (eds), *New Public Management: Current Trends and Future Prospects*, London: Routledge.

Ng, Y.-F. (2016), *Ministerial Advisers in Australia: The Modern Legal Context*, Alexandria: Federation Press.

Ng, Y.-F. (2018), *The Rise of Political Advisors in the Westminster System*, New York: Routledge.

Norman, R. (2003), *Obedient Servants? Management Freedoms and Accountabilities in New Zealand*, Wellington: Victoria University Press.

Norman, R. (2006), 'Managing for Outcomes while Accounting for Outputs: Defining "Public Value" in New Zealand's Performance Management System', a Performing Public Sector: The Second Transatlantic Dialogue, EGPA/ASPA, Public Management Institute, Catholic University of Leuven, 1–3 June.

Norman, R. (2008), 'At the Centre or in Control? Central Agencies in Search of New Identities', *Policy Quarterly*, **4** (2), 33–8.

Norman, R. and D. Gill (2011), 'Restructuring: An Over-used Lever for Change in New Zealand's State Sector?', in B. Ryan and D. Gill (eds), *Future State: Directions for Public Management in New Zealand*, Wellington: Victoria University Press, pp. 262–77.

Norman, R. and R. Gregory (2003), 'Paradoxes and Pendulum Swings: Performance Management in New Zealand's Public Sector', *Australian Journal of Public Administration*, **62** (4), 35–49.

Nutley, S., J. Downe, S. Martin and C. Grace (2013), 'Policy Transfers and Local Government Performance Improvement Regimes', in P. Carroll and R. Common (eds), *Policy Transfer and Learning in Public Policy and Management: International Contexts, Content and Learning*, London: Routledge, pp. 30–49.

NZPC/New Zealand Productivity Commission (2014), *Regulatory institutions and Practices*, Wellington: New Zealand Productivity Commission.

NZPC/New Zealand Productivity Commission (2018), *Improving State Sector Productivity: Final Report of the Measuring and Improving State Sector Productivity Inquiry, Vol. 1*, Wellington: New Zealand Productivity Commission.

OAG/Office of the Auditor General of Canada (2001), *Public Sector Management Reform: Progress, Setbacks and Challenges*, Ottawa: OAG.

OAG/Office of the Auditor General (2015), *Reports of the Auditor General of Canada Report: 4, Information Technology Shared Services*, Autumn, Ottawa: Auditor General of Canada.

OAG/Office of the Auditor General (2017), *Report 1 – Phoenix Pay Problems, 2017 Fall Reports*. Ottawa: Auditor General of Canada.

OAG/Office of the Auditor General (2018), *Building and Implementing the Phoenix Pay System*, spring reports, Ottawa: Auditor General of Canada.

Oberg, S.A. and H. Wockelberg (2016), 'Nordic Administrative Heritages and Contemporary Institutional Design', in C. Creve, P. Lægreid and L.H. Rykka (eds), *Nordic Administrative Reforms: Lessons for Public Management*, Basingstoke: Palgrave Macmillan, pp. 57–78.

O'Donnell, G. (2013), 'Better Government', *The Political Quarterly*, **84** (3), 380–87.

OECD (Organisation for Economic Co-operation and Development) (1995), *Governance in Transition: Public Management Reforms in OECD Countries*, Paris: OECD.

OECD (Organisation for Economic Co-operation and Development) (2005), *Modernising Government: The Way Forward*, Paris: OECD.

OECD (Organisation for Economic Co-operation and Development) (2011a), *Government at a Glance*, Paris: OECD.

OECD (Organisation for Economic Co-operation and Development) (2011b), *Ministerial Advisors: Role, Influence and Management*, Paris: OECD.

OECD (Organisation for Economic Co-operation and Development) (2015), *National Performance Frameworks and Key Indicators across Organisation for Economic Co-operation and Development Countries*, Paris: OECD.

OECD (Organisation for Economic Co-operation and Development) (2017a), *Policy Advisory Systems: Supporting Good Governance and Sound Public Decision Making*, Paris: OECD.

OECD (Organisation for Economic Co-operation and Development) (2017b), *Government at a Glance – 2017*, OECD, available at https://stats.oecd.org/Index .aspx?QueryId=78411.

OECD (Organisation for Economic Co-operation and Development) (2017c), *Delegation in Human Resources Management*, OECD, available at https://www .oecd-ilibrary.org/docserver/gov_glance-2017-45-en.pdf?expires=1554414451&id =id&accname=guest&checksum= A8F5A065C82E4A50F6EC638748758D4B.

Office of the Auditor General of Canada (1999), 'Innovation in the Federal Government: The Risk Not Taken', *The Innovation Journal: The Public Sector Innovation Journal*, **4** (2), available at https://www.innovation.cc/discussion-papers/1999_4_2 _4_risk2.htm.

O'Flynn, J. (2009), 'The Cult of Collaboration in Public Policy', *Australian Journal of Public Administration*, **68** (1), 112–16.

O'Flynn, J., D. Blackman and J. Halligan (eds) (2014), *Crossing Boundaries in Public Management and Policy: The International Experience*, London and New York: Routledge.

O'Leary, R. (2014), *Collaborative Governance in New Zealand: Important Choices Ahead*, Wellington: Fulbright New Zealand.

Olsen, J.P. (1988), 'Administrative Reforms and Theories of Organization', in C. Campbell and B.G. Peters (eds), *Organizing Governance & Governing Organizations*, Pittsburgh, PA: University of Pittsburgh Press, pp. 233–54.

Olsen, J.P. (2005), 'Maybe it is Time to Rediscover Bureaucracy', *Journal of Public Administration Research and Theory*, **16**, 1–24.

Ongaro, E. (2009), *Public Management Reform and Modernization: Trajectories of Administrative Change in Italy, France, Greece, Portugal and Spain*, Cheltenham: Edward Elgar.

OPSR (Office of Public Service Reform) (2010), *Reforming our Public Services: Principles into Practice*, London: OPSR.

Orton, T. (n.d., circa 2018), 'Landmark review of public sector offers great potential for change', available at https://www.nousgroup.com/insights/landmark-review-of -public-sector-offers-great-potential-for-change/.

Osbaldeston, G.F. (1989), *Keeping Deputy Ministers Accountable*, Toronto: McGraw-Hill Ryerson.

Osborne, S. (2010), 'The (New) Public Governance: A Suitable Case for Treatment?' in S. Osborne (ed.), *The New Public Governance*, Abingdon: Routledge, pp. 1–16.

PAC/House of Commons Public Administration Committee (2009), *Good Government*, Eighth Report of Session 2008–09, London.

PACAC/House of Commons Public Administration and Constitutional Affairs Committee (2018), *The Minister and the Official: The Fulcrum of Whitehall Effectiveness*, Fifth Report of Session 2017–19, HC 497, London.

Page, E. (2010), 'Has the Whitehall Model survived?', *International Review of Administrative Sciences*, **76** (3), 407–23.

Page, E. and B. Jenkins (2005), *Policy Bureaucracy: Government with a Cast of Thousands*, Oxford: Oxford University Press.

Page, J., J. Pearson, N. Panchamia, P. Thomas and J. Traficante (2014), *Leading Change in the Civil Service*, London: Institute for Government.

Page, K. (2015), *Unaccountable: Truth and Lies on Parliament Hill*, Toronto: Penguin.

Painter, C. (2006), 'The Dysfunctionalities of Public Service Reform', *Public Money and Management*, June, 143–4.

Painter, M. (1990), 'Values in the History of Public Administration', in J. Power (ed.), *Public Administration in Australia: A Watershed*, Sydney: Hale & Iremonger, pp. 73–93.

Painter, M. (2011), 'Managerialism and Models of Management', in T. Christensen and P. Lægreid (eds), *The Ashgate Research Companion to New Public Management*, Farnham: Ashgate, pp. 237–50.

Painter, M. and B.G. Peters (2010a), 'The Analysis of Administrative Tradition', in M. Painter and B.G. Peters (eds), *Tradition and Public Administration*, Basingstoke: Palgrave Macmillan, pp. 3–16.

Painter, M. and B. G. Peters (eds) (2010b), *Tradition and Public Administration*, Basingstoke: Palgrave Macmillan.

Pal, L.A. (2012), *Frontiers of Government: The OECD and Global Public Management Reform*, Basingstoke: Palgrave Macmillan.

Palmer, A. (2015), *The Return of Political Patronage: How Special Advisers Are Taking Over from Civil Servants and Why We Need to Worry About It*, London: CIVITAS.

Palmer, G. (2016), 'The Constitution and the Public Service', speech to the Public Service Association introducing *A Constitution for Aotearoa New Zealand*, Wellington, 28 November.

Palmer, G. (2017), 'Transparency, Governance and Constitutions', speech notes, address to Transparency International New Zealand, Chapman Tripp, Wellington, 22 May.

Palmer, G. and A. Butler (2018), *Towards Democratic Renewal: Ideas for Constitutional Change in New Zealand*, Wellington: Victoria University Press.

Palmer, G. and M. Palmer (2004), *Bridled Power: New Zealand's Constitution and Government*, 4th edn, South Melbourne: Oxford University Press.

Panchamia, N. and P. Thomas (2014), *Civil Service Reform in the Real World: Patterns of Success in UK Civil Service Reform*, London: Institute for Government.

Parker, R. and L. Bradley (2004), 'Bureaucracy or Post-Bureaucracy? Public Sector Organisations in a Changing Context', *Asia Pacific Journal of Public Administration*, **26** (2), 197–215.

Parker, S., A. Paun, J. McClory and K. Blatchford (2010), *Shaping Up: A Whitehall for the Future*, London: Institute for Government.

Parkinson, M. (2018a), 'Dr Martin Parkinson: Brexit, multilateralism and how the media impacts policy work', *The Mandarin,* 19 October, available at https://www.themandarin.com.au/100211-dr-martin-parkinson-brexit-multilateralism-and-how-the-media-impacts-policy-work/?utm_campaign=TheJuice&utm_medium=email&utm_.

Parkinson, M. (2018b), '2018 Address to the Australian Public Service', in *IPAA Speeches 2018*, Canberra: Institute of Public Administration, pp. 149–59.

Parris, H. (1968), 'The Origins of the Permanent Civil Service, 1780–1830', *Public Administration*, **46** (2), 143–66.

Parsons, W. (2004), 'Not Just Steering but Weaving: Relevant Knowledge and the Craft of Building Policy Capacity and Coherence', *Australian Journal of Public Administration*, **63** (1), 43–57.

Pastré, A. and T. Cain (2012), *The Role of Independent Guardians: Description and Synthesis*, a background paper for a discussion forum on achieving balance in accountability and oversight, Ottawa: Institute on Governance.

Patapan, H., J. Wanna and P. Weller (2005), *Westminster Legacies: Democracy and Responsible Government in Asia and the Pacific*, Sydney: UNSW Press.

Patrick, A. (2016), *Credlin & Co: How the Abbott Government Destroyed itself*, Carlton: Black Inc.

Paun, A. (2013), *Supporting Ministers to Lead: Rethinking the Ministerial Private Office*, London: Institute for Government.

Paun, A. and K. Blatchford (2014), 'The Performance Target Solution? Cross-Cutting Public Service Agreements in the United Kingdom', in J. O'Flynn, D. Blackman and J. Halligan (eds), *Crossing Boundaries in Public Management and Policy: The International Experience*, London and New York: Routledge.

Paun, A., J. Harris with I. Magee (2013), *Permanent Secretary Appointments and the Role of Ministers*, London: Institute for Government.

PCO/Privy Council Office (2019), Deputy Minister Committee and Task Force Mandates and Memberships, September, available at https://www.canada.ca/en/privy-council/programs/appointments/senior-public-service/deputy-minister-committees.html.

Per Capita (2019), *Evidence Based Policy Analysis: 20 Case Studies*, Report Commissioned by the Evidence Based Policy Research Project and facilitated by the newDemocracy Foundation, available at https://percapita.org.au/our_work/evidence-based-policy-analysis-2019/.

Percival, S. (2018), 'A Policy Community for the Federal Public Service and Beyond', *Policy Options*, 29 March.

Perrow, C. (1977), 'The Bureaucratic Paradox: The Efficient Organization Centralizes in Order to Decentralize', *Organizational Dynamics*, **5** (4), 3–14.

Peters, B.G. (1987), 'Politicians and Bureaucrats in the Politics of Policy-Making', in J. Lane (ed.), *Bureaucracy and Public Choice*, London: Sage.

Peters, B.G. (1996), *The Policy Capacity of Government*, Research Paper No. 18, Ottawa: Canadian Centre for Management Development.

Peters, B.G. (1997), 'Policy Transfers between Governments: The Case of Administrative Reform', *West European Politics*, **20** (4), 71–88.

Peters, B.G. (1998a), *Comparative Politics: Theory and Methods*, Basingstoke: Macmillan.

Peters, B.G. (1998b), 'Managing Horizontal Government: The Politics of Coordination', *Public Administration*, **76** (2), 295–311.

Peters, B.G. (2003), 'Administrative Traditions and the Anglo-American Democracies', in J. Halligan (ed.), *Civil Service Systems in Anglo-American Countries*, Cheltenham: Edward Elgar, pp. 10–26.

Peters, B.G. (2013), 'The Future of Public Administration', in J. Bickerton and B.G. Peters (eds), *Governing: Essays in Honour of Donald J. Savoie*, Montreal and Kingston: McGill-Queen's University Press, pp. 203–21.

Peters, B.G. (2015), *Pursuing Horizontal Coordination: The Politics of Public Sector Coordination*, Lawrence: University of Kansas Press.

Peters, B.G. (2018), 'The Challenge of Coordination', *Policy Design and Practice*, **1** (1), 1–11.

Peters, B.G. and J. Pierre (eds) (2001), *Politicians, Bureaucrats and Administrative Reform*, London: Routledge.

Peters, B.G. and J. Pierre (2004a), 'Politicization of the Civil Service: Concepts, Causes, Consequences', in B.G. Peters and J. Pierre (eds) *Politicization of the Civil Service in Comparative Perspective: The Quest for Control*, London: Routledge, pp. 1–13.

Peters, B.G. and J. Pierre (eds) (2004b), *Politicization of the Civil Service in Comparative Perspective: The Quest for Control*, London: Routledge.

Peters, B.G. and J. Pierre (2004c), 'Conclusion: Political Control in a Managerialist World', in B.G. Peters and J. Pierre (eds), *Politicization of the Civil Service in Comparative Perspective: The Quest for Control*, London: Routledge, pp. 283–90.

Pierre, J. (1995), 'Conclusions: A Framework of Comparative Public Administration', in J. Pierre (ed.), *Bureaucracy in the Modern State: An Introduction to Comparative Public Administration*, Aldershot: Edward Elgar, pp. 205–18.

Pierre, J. and B.G. Peters (2017), 'The Shirking Bureaucrat: A Theory in Search of Evidence?', *Policy & Politics*, **45** (2), 157–72.

Plimmer, G. and G. Parker (2018), 'Chancellor poised to announce PFI review', *Financial Times*, 29 October.

Plowden, W. (1994), *Ministers and Mandarins*, London: IPPR.

Podger, A. (2007), 'What Really Happens: Departmental Secretary Appointments, Contracts and Performance Pay in the Australian Public Service', *Australian Journal of Public Administration*, **66** (2), 131–47.

Podger, A. (2009), *The Role of Departmental Secretaries: Personal Reflections on the Breadth of Responsibilities Today*, Canberra: ANU E Press.

Podger, A. (2015), 'Further Development of Australia's Performance Management System: Emphasising "How" And "Why" As Well As "What"', paper for 2015 AGPA Conference, Seoul, September.

Podger, A. (2019), 'Protecting and nurturing the role and capability of the Australian Public Service', Parliamentary Library Lecture, 10 September.

Policy Profession Board (2019), 'Looking Back to Look Forward: From "Twelve Actions" to "Policy Profession 2025"', London: Policy Profession, UK Government, available at https://assets.publishing.service.gov.uk/government/uploads/system/uploads/attachment_data/file/805985/Policy_Profession_12_Actions_Revised.pdf.

Pollitt, C. (1990), *Managerialism and the Public Services: The Anglo-American Experience*, Oxford: Basil Blackwell.

Pollitt, C. (1993), *Managerialism and the Public Services*, 2nd edn, Oxford: Basil Blackwell.

Pollitt, C. (2005), 'Ministries and Agencies: Steering, Meddling, Neglect and Dependency', in M. Painter and J. Pierre (eds), *Challenges to State Policy Capacity*, Basingstoke: Palgrave Macmillan.

Pollitt, C. (2006), 'Performance Information for Democracy: The Missing Link?', *Evaluation*, **12** (1), 38–55.

Pollitt, C. (2007), 'New Labour's Re-Disorganisation: Hyper-Modernism and the Costs of Reform – a Cautionary Tale', *Public Management Review*, **9** (4), 529–43.

Pollitt, C. (2008), *Time, Policy, Management: Governing with the Past*, Oxford: Oxford University Press.

Pollitt, C. (2010), *Public Management Reform during Financial Austerity*, Statskontoret, Stockholm, available at http://www.statskontoret.se/globalassets/publikationer/om-offentlig-sektor-1-11/om-offentlig-sektor-2.pdf.

Pollitt, C. (2011), 30 years of public management reforms: Has there been a pattern? Blog, The World Bank, available at https://blogs.worldbank.org/governance/30-years-of-public-management-reforms-has-there-been-a-pattern.

Pollitt, C. (2012), 'The Evolving Narratives of Public Management Reform', *Public Management Review*, **15** (6), 899–922.

Pollitt, C. (2013a), 'The Logics of Performance Management'. *Evaluation*, **19** (4), 346–63.

Pollitt, C. (2013b), '40 Years of Public Management Reform in UK Central Government – Promises, Promises . . .', *Policy and Politics*, **41** (4), 465–80.

Pollitt, C. (ed.) (2013c), *Context in Public Policy and Management: The Missing Link*, Cheltenham: Edward Elgar.

Pollitt, C. (2016), 'Managerialism Redux?', *Financial Accountability and Management*, **32** (4), 429–47.

Pollitt, C. and G. Bouckaert (2011), *Public Management Reform: A Comparative Analysis: New Public Management, Governance and the Neo-Weberian State*, 3rd edn, Oxford: Oxford University Press.

Pollitt, C. and G. Bouckaert (2017), *Public Management Reform: A Comparative Analysis – Into the Age of Austerity*, 4th edn, Oxford: Oxford University Press.

Pollitt, C., C. Talbot, J. Caulfield and A. Smullen (2004), *Agencies: How Governments do Things Through Semi-Autonomous Organizations*, Basingstoke: Palgrave Macmillan.

Power, M. (2005), 'The Theory of the Audit Explosion', in E. Ferlie, L. Lynn and C. Pollitt (eds), *The Oxford Handbook of Public Management*, Oxford: Oxford University Press, pp. 326–44.

Prebble, M. (2005), 'Annual Report of the State Services Commissioner', in *Annual Report of the State Services Commission for year ended 30 June 2005*.

Prime Minister (1999), *Modernising Government White Paper*, Command Paper 4310 Session 1998–9, London.

Prince, M.J. (2018), 'Trends and Directions in Canadian Policy Analysis and Advice', in L. Dobuzinskis and M. Howlett (eds), *Policy Analysis in Canada*, Bristol: Policy Press, pp. 449–65.

Privy Council Office (2015), Performance Management Program Guidelines for Deputy Ministers, Associate Deputy Ministers and Individuals Paid in the GX Salary Range, available at https://www.canada.ca/en/privy-council/programs/ appointments/governor-council-appointments/performance-management/senior -public-servants.html.

Productivity Commission (2017), *Shifting the Dial: 5 Year Productivity Review*, Inquiry Report No. 84, Commonwealth of Australia, Canberra: Australian Government Publishing Service.

PSC (Public Service Commission of Canada) (2011), *Merit and Non-Partisanship under the Public Service Employment Act (2003)*, Ottawa: Public Service Commission of Canada.

Public Policy Forum (2016), *Optimizing Government: A White Paper on Public Sector Modernization*, Ottawa: Canada's Policy Forum.

Public Service Act Review Group (1995), *Report*, Commonwealth of Australia, Canberra: Australian Government Publishing Service.

Public Service Commission of Canada (2011), *Merit and Non-Partisanship under the Public Service Employment Act (2003): A Special Report to Parliament by the Public Service Commission of Canada*, Ottawa: Public Service Commission of Canada.

Raadschelders, J.C.N. and M. Bemelmans-Videc (2015), 'Political (Systems Reform): Can Administrative Reform Succeed Without?', in F.M. van der Meer, J.C.N Raadschelders and T.A.J. Toonen (eds), *Comparative Civil Service Systems in the 21st Century*, 2nd edn, Basingstoke: Palgrave Macmillan, pp. 334–53.

Radin, B.A. (2006), *Challenging the Performance Movement: Accountability, Complexity and Democratic Values*, Washington, DC: Georgetown University Press.

Radwanski, A. (2016), 'All Pearson, no Pierre: Inside Trudeau's inner circle', *The Globe and Mail*, 9 January.

Raudla, R. (2012), The Use of Performance Information in Budgetary Decision-Making by Legislators, *Public Administration*, **90** (4), 1000–1015.

RCAGA (Royal Commission on Australian Government Administration) (Chair: H.C. Coombs) (1976), *Report*, Canberra: Australian Government Publishing Service.

RCGO (Royal Commission on Government Organization) (Chair: J.G. Glassco) (1962), *Management of the Public Service, Vol. 1*, Ottawa: Privy Council Office.

Read, M. (2013), *Practical Steps to Improve Management Information in Government*, An Independent Report Commissioned by the Minister for the Cabinet Office and Chief Secretary to the Treasury, London, available at https://assets.publishing .service.gov.uk/government/uploads/system/uploads/attachment_data/file/206869/ Read_Review_2013-06-12.pdf.

Rennie, I. (2008), 'Annual Report of the State Services Commissioner', in *Annual Report of the State Services Commission for year ended 30 June 2008*.

Results and Delivery Unit, Privy Council Office (2016), *Results and Delivery in Canada: Building the Culture and the Systems*, Ottawa: Government of Canada.

Rhodes, R., J. Wanna and P. Weller (2009), *Comparing Westminster*, Oxford: Oxford University Press.

Rhodes, R.A.W. (2011), *Everyday Life in British Government*, Oxford: Oxford University Press.

Rhodes, R.A.W. (2015), 'Recovering the "Craft" . . . of Public Administration in Network Governance' [online], *Public Administration Today*, No. 41 (January– March), 42–5, available at http://search.informit.com.au/documentSummary;dn= 864598315491942;res=IELBUS> ISSN: 1832-0066 (accessed 8 July 2017).

Rhodes, R.A.W. and A. Tiernan (2014a), *The Gate Keepers: Lessons from Prime Ministers' Chiefs of Staff*, Carlton, VIC: Melbourne University Press.

Rhodes, R.A.W. and A. Tiernan (2014b), *Lessons in Governing: A Profile of Prime Ministers' Chiefs of Staff*, Carlton, VIC: Melbourne University Press.

Richards, D. (1997), *The Civil Service under the Conservatives 1979–1997: Whitehall's Political Poodles*, Brighton: Sussex Academic Press.

Richards, D. (2003), 'The Civil Service in Britain: A Case-Study in Path Dependency', in J. Halligan (ed.), *Civil Service Systems in Anglo-American Countries*, Cheltenham: Edward Elgar, pp. 27–69.

Richards, D. (2008), *New Labour and the Civil Service: Reconstituting the Westminster Model*, Basingstoke: Palgrave Macmillan.

Richards, D. and M. Smith (2002), *Governance and Public Policy in the United Kingdom*, Oxford: Oxford University Press.

Richards, D. and M. Smith (2004), 'The "Hybrid State": Labour's Response to the Challenge of Governance', in S. Ludlam and M.J. Smith (eds), *Governing as New Labour: Policy and Politics under Blair*, Basingstoke: Palgrave Macmillan, pp. 106–25.

Richards, D. and M. Smith (2006), 'The Tensions of Political Control and Administrative Autonomy: From NPM to a Reconstituted Westminster Model', in T. Christensen and P. Lægreid (eds), *Autonomy and Regulation: Coping with Agencies in the Modern State*, Cheltenham: Edward Elgar, pp. 181–200.

Richards, D. and M. Smith (2016), 'The Westminster Model and the "Indivisibility of the Political and Administrative Elite": A Convenient Myth Whose Time is Up?', *Governance*, **29** (4), 499–516.

Richardson, J. (2018), *British Policy-Making and the Need for a Post-Brexit Policy Style*, London: Palgrave Macmillan.

Riddell, P. (2019), *15 Minutes of Power: The Uncertain Life of British Ministers*, London: Profile Books.

Riddell, P., Z. Gruhn and L. Carolan (2011), *The Challenge of being a Minister: Defining and Developing Ministerial Effectiveness*, London: Institute for Government.

Ritchie, F. (2014), *Resistance to Change in Government: Risk, Inertia and Incentives*, Economics Working Paper Series 1412, Bristol: University of the West of England.

Roberts, A. (1996), *So-Called Experts: How American Consultants Remade the Canadian Civil Service, 1918–21*, Monographs on Canadian Public Administration No. 18, Toronto: The Institute of Public Administration of Canada.

Roberts, J. (1987), *Politicians, Public Servants and Public Enterprise*, Wellington: Victoria University Press for the Institute of Policy Studies.

Robertson, G. (2018), Minister of Finance, speech to the Institute of Public Administration New Zealand, 15 February.

Robson, S. (2016), 'Policy, Operations and Outcomes in the New Zealand Employment Jurisdiction 1990–2008', PhD thesis, Faculty of Law, University of Otago.

Ross, M. (2018), 'Global Government Summit 2018; Part 2', Global Government Forum, 1 May, available at https://www.globalgovernmentforum.com/global -government-summit-2018-part-2/.

Rouban, L. (2004), 'Politicization of the Civil Service in France: From Structural to Strategic Politicization', in B.G. Peters and J. Pierre (eds), *Politicization of the Civil Service in Comparative Perspective: The Quest for Control*, London: Routledge, pp. 81–100.

Rouban, L. (2012), 'Politicization of the Civil Service', in B.G. Peters and J. Pierre (eds), *Handbook of Public Administration*, London: Sage, pp. 380–91.

Rouban, L. (2014), 'Political–Administrative Relations: Evolving Models of Politicization', in F.M. van der Meer, J.C.N. Raadschelders and T.A.J. Toonen (eds), *Comparative Civil Service Systems in the 21st Century: Comparative Perspectives*, Basingstoke: Palgrave Macmillan, pp. 317–33.

Rutter, J. (2015a), David Cameron's Implementation Taskforces could be good for Whitehall, *The Guardian*, Institute for Government, 9 June.

Rutter, J. (2015b), No contest – the time has come to ditch or reboot the Ministerial Contestable Policy Fund, 15 June, available at https://www.instituteforgovernment .org.uk/blog/no-contest---time-has-come-ditch-or-reboot-ministerial-contestable -policy-fund.

Rutter, T. (2018), Unions: Ministerial code 'tinkering' not enough to protect civil servants from harassment, *Civil Service World*, 10 January.

Ryan, B. (2011a), 'The Signs are Everywhere: Community Approaches to Public Management', in B. Ryan and D. Gill (eds), *Future State: Directions for Public Management in New Zealand*, Wellington: Victoria University Press, pp. 85 122.

Ryan, B. (2011b), 'Getting in the Road: Why Outcome-Oriented Performance Monitoring is Underdeveloped in New Zealand', in D. Gill (ed.), *The Iron Cage Recreated: The Performance Management of State Organisations in New Zealand*, Wellington: Institute of Policy Studies, pp. 447–69.

Ryan, B. and D. Gill (eds) (2011), *Future State: Directions for Public Management in New Zealand*, Wellington: Victoria University Press.

Ryan, B., D. Gill and R. Dormer (2011), 'Case Study – Department of Corrections: How the Department Defines and Assesses Performance and how its Operational Arms Regard Performance Information', in D. Gill (ed.), *The Iron Cage Recreated: The Performance Management of State Organisations in New Zealand*, Wellington: Institute of Policy Studies, pp. 255–94.

Saint-Martin, D. (2004), *Building the New Managerialist State: Consultants and the Politics of Public Sector Reform in Comparative Perspective*, Oxford: Oxford University Press.

Salamon, L. (1981), 'The Question of Goals', in P. Szanton (ed.), *Federal Reorganization: What Have We Learned?*, Chatham, NJ: Chatham House.

Sarapuu, K., P. Lægreid, T. Randma-Liiv and L.H. Rykkja (2014), 'Lessons Learned and Policy Implications', in P. Lægreid, T. Randma-Liiv, L.H. Rykkja and K. Sarapuu (eds), *Organizing for Coordination in the Public Sector: Practices and Lessons from 12 European Countries*, Basingstoke: Palgrave Macmillan, pp. 263–78.

Sasse, T. and E. Norris (2019), *Moving On: The Costs of High Staff Turnover in the Civil Service*, London: Institute for Government.

Savoie, D.J. (1994), *Thatcher, Reagan, Mulroney: In Search of a New Bureaucracy*, Pittsburgh, PA: University of Pittsburgh Press.

Savoie, D.J. (1999), *Governing from the Centre: The Concentration of Power in Canadian Politics*, Toronto: University of Toronto Press.

Savoie, D.J. (2003), *Breaking the Bargain: Public Servants, Ministers, and Parliament*, Toronto: University of Toronto Press.

Savoie, D.J. (2004), 'The Search for a Responsive Bureaucracy in Canada', in B.G. Peters and J. Pierre (eds), *Politicization of the Civil Service in Comparative Perspective: The Quest for Control*, London and New York: Routledge, pp. 139–58.

Savoie, D.J. (2008), *Court Government and the Collapse of Accountability in Canada and the United Kingdom*, Toronto: University of Toronto Press.

Savoie, D.J. (2010), *Power: Where is it?*, Montreal and Kingston: McGill-Queen's University Press.

Savoie, D.J. (2011), 'Steering from the Centre: The Canadian Way', in K. Dahlström, B.G. Peters, and J. Pierre (eds), *Steering from the Centre: Strengthening Political Control in Western Democracies*, Toronto: University of Toronto Press, pp. 147–65.

Savoie, D.J. (2014), *Whatever Happened to the Music Teacher? How Government Decides and Why*, Montreal and Kingston: McGill-Queen's University Press.

Savoie, D.J. (2015a), *What is Government Good At? A Canadian Answer*, Montreal and Kingston: McGill-Queen's University Press.

Savoie, D.J. (2015b), 'The Canadian Public Service: In Search of a New Equilibrium', in A. Massey and K. Miller (eds), *The International Handbook of Public Administration and Governance*, Cheltenham: Edward Elgar, pp. 182–98.

Savoie, D.J. (2019a), 'Our top public servant should not be wearing so many hats', *Globe and Mail*, 4 March.

Savoie, D.J. (2019b), 'In trying to adapt, public service blurs some lines', *The Guardian*, 21 March.

Savoie, D.J. (2019c), *Democracy in Canada: The Disintegration of Our Institutions*, Montreal/Kingston: McGill-Queen's University Press.

Scharpf, F.W. (1997), *Games Real Actors Play: Actor Centered Institutionalism in Policy Research*, Boulder, CO: Westview.

Schick, A. (1996), *The Spirit of Reform: Managing the New Zealand State Sector in a Time of Change*, a report prepared for the State Services Commission and the Treasury, Wellington.

Schick, A. (2001), *Reflections on the New Zealand Model*, based on a lecture at New Zealand Treasury, August.

School of Government (2017), *Independent Review of the Performance Improvement Framework*, commissioned by the State Services Commission, Wellington: Victoria University of Wellington.

Scott, C. and K. Baehler (2010), *Adding Value to Policy Analysis and Advice*, Sydney: UNSW Press.

Scott, G. (1997), 'Continuity and Change in Public Management: Second Generation Issues', in *Roles, Responsibilities and Relationships, State Services Commission: Future Issues in Public Management*, Wellington: SSC, pp. 15–26.

Scott, G. (2001), *Public Management in New Zealand: Lessons and Challenges*, Wellington: New Zealand Business Roundtable.

Scott, G. (2017), 'Governance, Public Policy and Public Management', in J. Boston and D. Gill (eds), *Social Investment: A New Zealand Policy Experiment*, Wellington: Bridget Williams Books, pp. 419–36.

Scott, G., P. Faulkner and P. Duignan (2010), *Improving the Quality and Value of Policy Advice*, Review of Expenditure on Policy Advice, Wellington: Government of New Zealand, available at https://treasury.govt.nz/sites/default/files/2011-04/report-repa-dec10.pdf.

Scott, G. and L. McKenzie (2001), New Zealand, World Bank, available at http://www1.worldbank.org/publicsector/civilservice/rsNewZealand.pdf.

Scott, R. (2016), 'Theoretical Foundations of Department Chief Executive Performance Appraisals', State Sector Performance Hub Working Paper 2016-4, Wellington.

Scott, R. and R. Boyd (2016a), *Collective Impact in the Public Sector: The New Zealand Results Approach*, Working Paper 2016-1, State Sector Performance Hub, Wellington.

Scott, R. and R. Boyd (2016b), 'Results, Targets and Measures to Drive Collaboration: Lessons from the New Zealand Better Public Services Reforms', in D.J. Gilchrist and J.R. Butcher (eds), *The Three Sector Solution: Delivering Public Policy in Collaboration with Not-for-profits and Business*, Canberra: ANU Press, pp. 235–57.

Scott, R. and R. Boyd (2017a), 'Joined-Up for What? Response to Carey and Harris on Adaptive Collaboration', *Australian Journal of Public Administration*, **76** (1), 138–44.

Scott, R. and R. Boyd (2017b), *Interagency Performance Targets: A Case Study of New Zealand's Results Programme*, Washington, DC: IBM Centre for the Business of Government.

Selden, S.C., J.E. Sowa and J. Sandfort (2006), 'The Impact of Nonprofit Collaboration in Early Child Care and Education on Management and Program Outcomes', *Public Administration Review*, **66** (3), 412–25.

Self, P. (1977), *Administrative Theories and Politics*, 2nd edn, London: George Allen & Unwin.

Self, P. (1978), 'The Coombs Commission: An Overview', in R.F.I Smith and P. Weller (eds), *Public Service Inquiries in Australia*, St Lucia: University of Queensland Press, pp. 310–33.

Sepuloni, C. (2018), *Investing for Social Wellbeing*, Office of the Minister for Social Development Office of the Chair of the Social Wellbeing Committee, Wellington.

SFPAC/Senate Finance and Public Administration Committee (2018), *Digital Delivery of Government Services*, Canberra: Commonwealth of Australia.

Shand, D. and R. Norman (2005), 'Performance Budgeting in New Zealand', paper prepared for IMF Fiscal Affairs Department seminar on Performance Budgeting, Washington DC, 5–7 December.

Shaw, R. and C. Eichbaum (eds) (2018), *Ministers, Minders and Mandarins: An International Study of Relationships at the Executive Summit of Parliamentary Democracies*, Cheltenham: Edward Elgar.

Shepherd, R. and C. Stoney (2018), 'Policy Analysis in the Federal Government: Conditions and Renewal Initiatives in the Trudeau Era', in L. Dobuzinskis and M. Howlett (eds), *Policy Analysis in Canada: An Introduction*, Bristol: Policy Press, pp. 71–96.

Shepherd, R., C. Stoney and L. Turnbull (2017), 'The Changing Roles of Politicians and Public Servants', in T.R. Klassenn, D. Cepiku and T.J. Lah (eds), *Routledge Handbook of Global Public Policy and Administration*, London and New York: Routledge, pp. 271–9.

Shepherd, R.P. (2016), 'The Program Evaluation Function: Uncertain Governance and Effects', in T. Klassen, D. Cepiku and T.J. Lah (eds), *Handbook of Global Public Policy and Administration*, New York: Routledge, pp. 335–46.

Shergold, P. (2003), 'A Foundation of Ruined Hopes?' Address to Public Service Commission, Canberra, 15 October.

Shergold, P. (2004), 'Plan and Deliver: Avoiding Bureaucratic Hold-Up', presentation to the Australian Graduate School of Management/Harvard Club of Australia, Canberra, 17 November. Archived, National Library of Australia.

Shergold, P. (2013), 'My Hopes for a Public Service for the Future', *Australian Journal of Public Administration*, **72** (1), 7–13.

Shergold, P. (2015), *Learning from failure: what large government policy initiatives have gone so badly wrong in the past and how the chances of success in the future can be improved.* An independent review of government processes for implementing large programs and projects, Canberra: Commonwealth of Australia.

Shipman, T. (2017), *Fall Out: A Year of Political Mayhem*, London: William Collins.

Smith, A. (2009), *Roles and Responsibilities of Central Agencies*, Ottawa: Library of Parliament.

Smith, G. (2015), 'The Influence of Political Support on the Robustness of Performance Measurement Systems in Australia', paper for Mapping the Purple Zone Panel B101, IRSPM Conference 2015, Birmingham.

Smith, H. (2018), *Doing Policy Differently: Challenges and Insights*, in *IPAA Speeches 2018*, Canberra: Institute of Public Administration, pp. 35–43.

Smith, M. and D. Richards (2006), 'Central Control and Policy Implementation in the UK: A Case Study of the Prime Minister's Delivery Unit', *Journal of Comparative Policy*, **8** (4), 325–45.

Smith, M.J. (2011a), 'Tsars, Leadership and Innovation in the Public Sector', *Policy and Politics*, **39** (3), 343–59.

Smith, M.J. (2011b), 'The Paradoxes of Britain's Strong Centre: Delegating Decisions and Re-Claiming Control', in C. Dahlström, B.G. Peters and J. Pierre (eds), *Steering from the Centre: Strengthening Political Control in Western Democracies*, Toronto: University of Toronto Press, pp. 166–90.

Spann, R.N. (1979), *Government Administration in Australia*, Sydney: George Allen & Unwin Australia.

Spann, R.N. (1981), 'Fashions and Fantasies in Public Administration', *Australian Journal of Public Administration*, **40** (1), 12–25.

SSC (State Services Commission) (1999), *Improving Accountability: Setting the Scene*, Occasional Paper No. 10, Wellington: SSC.

SSC (State Services Commission) (2006), Role of State Service Commissioner and Public Service Chief Executive Performance, SSC website.

SSC (State Services Commission) (2007), Transforming the State Services: State of the Development Goals Report 2007, SSC, Wellington.

SSC (State Services Commission) (2013), Transforming the State Sector, available at https://ssc.govt.nz/our-work/transforming-the-state-sector/.

SSC (State Services Commission) (2014), *State Services Commission Statement of Intent 2014–18, available at* http://www.ssc.govt.nz/resources/9516/all-pages.

SSC (State Services Commission) (2016), Strategic Intentions – Part 1 of the Four-Year Plan 2016–20, available at https://ssc.govt.nz/resources/strategic-intentions-four -year-plan-2016-20?e969=action_viewall#.

SSC (State Services Commission) (2017), Strengthening Functional Leadership – increasing value and reducing the costs of government business functions, 6 April, available at http://www.ssc.govt.nz/bps-functional-leadership.

SSC (State Services Commission) (2018a), *Reform of the State Sector Act 1988: Directions and Options for Change*, discussion document for public feedback, September.

SSC (State Services Commission) (2018b), *State Sector Act Reform Factsheet: Organisations of the Public Service, available at* https://ssc.govt.nz/assets/Legacy/ resources/Factsheet-6-Organisations-of-the-Public-Service.pdf.

SSCNF (Standing Senate Committee on National Finance) (2018), *Issue No. 70*, Evidence, Ottawa, 12 June.

Stephen, J., R. Martin and D. Atkinson (2011), *See-Through Whitehall: Departmental Business Plans One Year On*, London: Institute for Government.

Stoker, G. and M. Evans (2016), 'Evidence-Based Policy Making and Social Science', in G. Stoker and M. Evans (eds), *Evidence-Based Policy Making in the Social Sciences: Methods that Matter*, Bristol: Policy Press, pp. 15–27.

Stone, J. (2011), 'The Degradation of the Public Service', *Quadrant*, July–August, 36–43.

Sutherland, S. (1993), 'The Public Service and Policy Development', in M.M. Atkinson (ed.), *Governing Canada: Institutions and Public Policy*, Toronto: Harcourt Brace and Jovanovich Canada.

Talbot, C. (2001), *Performance Models*, presentation to the Public Administration Committee Conference (PACC).

Talbot, C. (2008), 'Performance Regimes – The Institutional Context of Performance Policies', *International Journal of Public Administration*, **31** (14), 1569–91.

Talbot, C. (2010), *Performance in Government: The Evolving System of Performance and Evaluation Measurement, Monitoring, and Management in the United Kingdom*, ECD Working Paper Series No. 24, Washington, DC: World Bank.

Talbot, C. (2017), Performance measurement: the history and future of Whitehall's target culture, CSW, 23 June, available at https://www.civilserviceworld.com/articles/feature/performance-measurement-history-and-future-whitehall's-target-culture.

Talbot, C. (2019), An Impartial Civil Service – Myth and Reality, in S. Barwick (ed.), *Impartiality Matters: Perspectives on the Importance of Impartiality in the Civil Service in a 'Post Truth' World*, London: Smith Institute, pp. 63–71.

Talbot, C. and C. Johnson (2007), 'Seasonal Cycles in Public Management: Disaggregation and Re-Aggregation', *Public Money and Management*, **27** (1), 53–60.

Talbot, C. and C. Talbot (2014), 'The Structure Solution? Public Sector Mergers in the United Kingdom', in J. O'Flynn, D. Blackman and J. Halligan (eds), *Crossing Boundaries in Public Management and Policy: The International Experience*, London and New York: Routledge.

Talbot, C. and C. Talbot (2019), 'One step forward, two steps back? The rise and fall of government's Next Steps agencies', *Civil Service World*, 23 September.

Talbot, C., L. Daunton and C. Morgan (2001), *Measuring Performance of Government Departments – International Developments: Report to the UK National Audit Office*, Abergavenny: Public Futures Ltd.

Tanner, Lindsay (Minister for Finance and Deregulation) (2008), *Operation Sunlight: Enhancing Budget Transparency*, December.

Taylor, J. (2009), 'Strengthening the Link between Performance Measurement and Decision Making', *Public Administration*, **87** (4), 853–71.

Taylor, J. (2010), *Building Capability in the Commonwealth of Australia*, Leuven: Public Management Institute, Catholic University of Leuven.

Taylor, J. (2011), 'Factors Influencing the Use of Performance Information for Decision Making in Australian State Agencies', *Public Administration*, **89** (4), 1316–34.

Taylor, L. (2008), Mix and match the new market design, *Australian*, 11 October.

Taylor, M. (2015), 'The critical fault line damaging departmental effectiveness? The relationship between politicians and senior officials', *Civil Service World*, 4 November.

TBS/Treasury Board of Canada Secretariat (2002), *Assessment of 2001 Departmental Performance Reports*, Ottawa: Treasury Board Secretariat.

TBS/Treasury Board of Canada Secretariat (2003), *Review and Assessment of 2002 Departmental Performance Reports*, Ottawa: Treasury Board Secretariat.

TBS/Treasury Board of Canada Secretariat (2006), *From Red Tape to Clear Results: The Report of the Independent Blue Ribbon Panel on Grant and Contribution Program*, Ottawa: Treasury Board Secretariat.

TBS/Treasury Board of Canada Secretariat (2009a), 'Tackling the Web of Rules', available at https://www.tbs-sct.gc.ca/reports-rapports/wr-lr/index-eng.asp (accessed 20 March 2017).

TBS/Treasury Board of Canada Secretariat (2009b), *2009-09 Departmental Performance Report*, Ottawa: Treasury Board Secretariat.

TBS/Treasury Board of Canada Secretariat (2009c), *Towards Effective Government: Untangling the Web of Rules: Report on the Web of Rules Initiative Results for 2008–09 and Directions for 2009–10*, Ottawa: Treasury Board Secretariat.

TBS/Treasury Board of Canada Secretariat (2016a), *Cutting Internal Red Tape: Building a Service Culture*, Final Report by the Blueprint 2020 Internal Red Tape Reduction Tiger Team, September.

TBS/Treasury Board of Canada (2016b), Policy on Results, available at https://www.tbs-sct.gc.ca/pol/doc-eng.aspx?id=31300.

TBS/Treasury Board of Canada Secretariat (2017a), *Evaluation of the Management Accountability Framework*, Ottawa: TBS, available at https://www.canada.ca/en/treasury-board-secretariat/corporate/reports/evaluation-management-accountability-framework.html.

TBS/Treasury Board of Canada Secretariat (2017b), *2016–17 Management Accountability Framework government-wide report*, available at https://www.canada.ca/en/treasury-board-secretariat/services/management-accountability-framework/2016-17-management-accountability-framework-government-wide-report.html.

Te Kawa, D. and K. Guerin (2012), 'Provoking Debate and Learning Lessons: It is Early Days but what does the Performance Improvement Framework Challenge us to Think About?', *Policy Quarterly*, **8** (4), 28–36.

TFMHPI (Task Force on Managing Horizontal Policy Issues) (1996) *Managing Horizontal Policy Issues*, Privy Council Office and Canadian Centre for Management Development, available at http://publications.gc.ca/collections/Collection/SC93-8-1996-3E.pdf.

TFMI (Task Force on Management Improvement) (1993), *The Australian Public Service Reformed: An Evaluation of a Decade of Management Reform*, Australian Government Publishing Service, Canberra/Management Advisory Board, Commonwealth of Australia.

Thain, C. (2010), 'Budget Reform in the United Kingdom: The Rocky Road to "Controlled Discretion"', in J. Wanna, L. Jensen and J. de Vires (eds), *The Reality of Budgetary Reform in OECD Countries: Trajectories and Consequences*, Cheltenham: Edward Elgar, pp. 35–64.

't Hart, P. (2010), 'Lifting its Game to Get Ahead: The Canberra Bureaucracy's Reform by Stealth', *Australian Review of Public Affairs*, July.

Thomas, P.G. (1998), 'The Changing Nature of Accountability', in B.G. Peters and D.J. Savoie (eds), *Taking Stock: Assessing Public Sector Reform*, Montreal: McGill-Queen's University Press, 348–93.

Thomas, P.G. (2004), *Performance Measurement, Reporting and Accountability: Recent Trends and Future Directions*, Public Policy Paper 23, Regina: The Saskatchewan Institute of Public Policy.

Thomas, P.G. (2009), 'Parliament Scrutiny of Government Performance in Australia', *Australian Journal of Public Administration*, **68** (4), 373–98.

Thomas, P.G. (2013), Communications and Prime Ministerial Power', in J. Bickerton and B.G. Peters (eds), *Governing: Essays in Honour of Donald J. Savoie*, Montreal and Kingston: McGill-Queen's University Press, pp. 53–84.

Thomas, P. (2014), 'Two Cheers for Bureaucracy: Canada's Public Service', in J. Bickerton and A.-G. Gagnon (eds), *Canadian Politics*, 6th edn, Toronto: University of Toronto Press, pp. 177–97.

Tichy, N.M. (1980), 'Problem Cycles on Organizations and the Management of Change', in J.R. Kimberly, R.H. Miles and Associates (eds), *The Organizational Life Cycle: Issues in the Creation, Transformation and Decline of Organizations*, San Francisco, CA: Jossey-Bass, pp. 164–183.

Tiernan, A. (2007a), 'Building Capacity for Policy Implementation', in J. Wanna (ed.), *Improving Implementation: Organisational Change and Project Management*, Canberra: ANU E Press, pp. 113–20.

Tiernan, A. (2007b), *Power without Responsibility: Ministerial Staffers in Australian Governments from Whitlam to Howard*, Sydney: UNSW Press.

Tiernan, A. (2011), 'Advising Australian Federal Governments: Assessing the Evolving Capacity and Role of the Australian Public Service', Australian Journal of Public Administration, **70** (4), 335–46.

Tilley, P. (2019), *Changing Fortunes: A History of the Australian Treasury*, Melbourne: Melbourne University Press.

Tingle, L. (2015), 'Political Amnesia: How we Forgot How to Govern', *Quarterly Essay*, **60**, available at https://www.quarterlyessay.com.au/essay/2015/11/political -amnesia/extract.

Travers, M. (2007), *The New Bureaucracy: Quality Assurance and its Critics*, Bristol: Policy Press.

Uhrig, J. (2003), *Review of the Corporate Governance of Statutory Authorities and Office Holders Report*, Canberra: Commonwealth of Australia.

Urban, M.C. (2018), *Abandoning Silos: How innovative Governments are Collaborating Horizontally to Solve Complex Problems*, Toronto: Mowat Centre, University of Toronto.

van der Meer, F., T. Steen and A. Wille (2015), 'Civil Service Systems in Western Europe: A Comparative Analysis', in F. van der Meer, J.C.N Raadschelders and T.A.J Toonen (eds), *Comparative Civil Service Systems in the 21st Century*, 2nd edn, Basingstoke: Palgrave Macmillan, pp. 38–56.

Van Dooren, W. and C. Hoffmann (2017), 'Performance Management in Europe: An Idea Whose Time has Come and Gone?', in S. van Thiel and E. Ongaro (eds), *Palgrave Handbook of Public Administration and Management in Europe*, Basingstoke: Palgrave Macmillan, pp. 207–26.

Van Dooren, W., G. Bouckaert and J. Halligan (2015), *Performance Management in the Public Sector*, 2nd edn, London: Routledge.

van Thiel, S. and F.L. Leeuw (2002), 'The Performance Paradox in the Public Sector', *Public Performance and Management Review*, **5** (3), 267–81.

Varghese, P. (2016), 'Parting Reflections', Secretary's speech to IPAA, 9 June.

Veggeland, N. (2007), *Paths of Public Innovation in the Global Age*, Cheltenham: Edward Elgar.

Veilleux, G. and D.J. Savoie (1988), 'Kafka's Castle: The Treasury Board of Canada Revisited', *Canadian Public Administration*, **31** (4), 517–38.

Vromen, A. and P. Hurley (2015), 'Consultants, Think Tanks and Public Policy', in B. Head and K. Crowley (eds), *Policy Analysis in Australia*, Bristol: Policy Press, pp. 167–82.

Wakem, B. (2015), *Not a Game of Hide and Seek*, Wellington: Office of the Ombudsman.

Walker, R.M. and G.A. Brewer (2009), 'Can Public Managers Reduce Red Tape? The Role of Internal Management in Overcoming External Constraints', *Policy and Politics*, **37** (2), 255–72.

Waller, P. (2014), *Understanding Whitehall: A Short Introduction for Special Advisers*, London: Constitution Unit, University of London.

Walter, J. (1986), *The Ministers Minders: Personal Advisers in National Government*, Melbourne: Oxford University Press.

Wanna, J. (2005), 'New Zealand's Westminster Trajectory: Archetypal Transplant to Maverick Outlier', in H. Patapan, J. Wanna and P. Weller (eds), Westminster Legacies: Democracy and Responsible Government in Asia and the Pacific, Sydney: UNSW Press, pp. 153–85.

Wanna, J. (2006), 'From Afterthought to Afterburner: Australia's Cabinet Implementation Unit', *Journal of Comparative Policy Analysis*, **8** (4), 347–69.

Wanna, J. (2019), The Annual Allan Barton Memorial Research Lecture, Certified Practising Accountants Congress, Canberra 17–18 October.

Wanna, J. and S. Bartos (2003), '"Good Practice": Does it Work in Theory? Australia's Quest for Better Outcomes', in J. Wanna, L. Jensen, and J. de Vries (eds), *Controlling Public Expenditure: The Changing Role of Central Budget Agencies – Better Guardians?*, Cheltenham: Edward Elgar, pp. 1–29.

Wanna, J. and P. Weller (2003), 'Traditions of Australian Governance', *Public Administration*, **81** (1), 63–94.

Wanna, J., J. Kelly and J. Forster (2000), *Managing Public Expenditure in Australia*, Sydney: Allen & Unwin.

Washington, S. (2016), 'New Zealand's Reforms to Improve Policy', Institute for Government, London, 5 October.

Washington, S. and M. Mintrom (2018), 'Strengthening Policy Capability: New Zealand's Policy Project, *Policy Design and Practice*, **1** (1), 30–46, doi:https//10 .1080/25741292.2018.1425086.

Waterford, J. (2009), 'On a West Wing and a Prayer', *The Canberra Times*, 16 May, 8.

Weigrich, K. (2009), 'Public Management Reform in the United Kingdom: Great Leaps, Small Steps and Policies as their Own Cause', in S.F Goldfinch and J.L Wallis (eds), *International Handbook of Public Management Reform*, Cheltenham: Edward Elgar, pp. 137–54.

Weller, P. (2001), *Australia's Mandarins: The Frank and Fearless?*, Sydney: Allen & Unwin.

Weller, P. (2007), *Cabinet Government in Australia, 1901–2006: Practice, Principles, Performance*, Sydney: UNSW Press.

Weller, P. (2010), *Cabinet Government in Australia, 1901–2006: Practice, Principles, Performance*, Sydney: UNSW Press.

Weller, P. (2018), *The Prime Ministers' Craft: Why Some Succeed and Others Fail in Westminster Systems*, Oxford: Oxford University Press.

Weller, P. and C. Haddon (2016), 'Westminster Traditions: Continuity and Change', *Governance*, **29** (4), 483–98.

Wellstead, A.M. (2019), 'From Fellegi to Fonberg: Canada's Policy Capacity Groundhog Day? Policy Capacity Reflections', *Canadian Public Administration*, **2** (1), 166–72.

Wettenhall, R. (2005), 'Statutory Authorities, the Uhrig Report, and the Trouble with Internal Inquiries', *Public Administration Today*, Issue 2 (December 2004–February 2005).

Wettenhall, R. (2006), 'The "State Tradition" in Australia: Reassessing an Earlier View', *Journal of Contemporary Issues in Business and Government*, **12** (2), 15–46.

Wettenhall, R. (2010), 'Mixes and Partnerships through Time', in G.A. Hodge, C. Greve and A.E. Boardman (eds), *International Handbook on Public–Private Relationships*, Cheltenham: Edward Elgar, pp. 17–42.

Wheatley, M. (2018), Government should publish real Single Departmental Plans, London: Institute for Government, available at https://www.instituteforgovernment .org.uk/blog/government-should-publish-real-single-departmental-plans.

White, A. and P. Dunleavy (2010), *Making and Breaking Whitehall Departments: A Guide to Machinery of Government Changes*, London: Institute for Government/ LSE Public Policy Group.

Whitehead, J. (2006), 'The Imperative for Performance in the Public Sector', paper presented to Public Sector Governance Seminar, APEC 2006 Vietnam–New Zealand Seminars, Da Nang, available at http://www.treasury.govt.nz/speeches/ipps.

Whitehead, M. (2003), '"In the Shadow of Hierarchy": Meta-Governance, Policy Reform and Urban Regeneration in the West Midlands', *Area*, **35** (1), 6–14.

Whyte, S. (2019), 'New APS head of HR profession', *Canberra Times*, 29 October, 5.

Wilby, P. (2017), 'David Laws: "The quality of education policymaking is poor"', *The Guardian*, 1 August.

Wilenski, P. (1986), *Public Power and Public Administration*, Sydney: Hale and Iremonger.

Wilks, S. (2007), 'Boardization and Corporate Governance in the UK as a Response to Depoliticization and Failing Accountability', *Public Policy and Administration*, **22** (4), 443–60.

Wilks, S. (2013), *The Political Power of the Business Corporation*, Cheltenham: Edward Elgar.

Williams, H. (1998), 'Authority and Accountability – Management of the APS', *Canberra Bulletin of Public Administration*, **88**, 10–17.

Williams, P. (2002), 'The Competent Boundary Spanner', *Public Administration*, **80** (1), 103–24.

Wilson, G.K. (1991), 'Prospects for the Public Service in Britain: Major to the Rescue', *International Review of Administrative Sciences*, **57** (3), 327–44.

Wilson, G.K. (1998), *Only in America: The Politics of the United States in Comparative Perspective*, Chatham, NJ: Chatham House.

Wilson, J.Q. (1994), 'Can the Bureaucracy be Regulated? Lessons from Government Agencies', in J. Dilulio Jr (ed.), *Deregulating the Public Service: Can Government be Improved?*, Washington: The Brookings Institution, pp. 37–61.

Wilson, R.P. (2016a), 'Trust but Verify: Ministerial Policy Advisors and Public Servants in the Government of Canada', *Canadian Public Administration*, **59** (3), 337–56.

Wilson, R.P. (2016b), 'The Inter-Executive Activity of Ministerial Policy Advisers in the Government of Canada', in G.B. Doern and C. Stoney (eds), *How Ottawa Spends 2016–2017: The Trudeau Liberals in Power*, School of Public Policy and Administration, Ottawa: Carleton University, pp. 191–215.

Wintringham, M. (2001), 'Annual Report of the State Services Commissioner', in *Annual Report of the State Services Commission for year ended 30 June 2001*.

Wintringham, M. (2003), 'Annual Report of the State Services Commissioner', in *Annual Report of the State Services Commission for year ended 30 June 2003*.

Woolcott, P. (2019), Opening Keynote by the Australian Public Service Commissioner, HR Professional Stream Strategy Launch, 28 October.

Yong, B. and R. Hazell (2014), *Special Advisers: Who They Are, What They Do and Why They Matter*, Oxford: Hart Publishing.

Young, A. (2018), 'Populism and the UK Constitution', *Current Legal Problems*, **71**(1), 17–52.

Zifcak, S. (1994), *New Managerialism: Administrative Reform in Whitehall and Canberra*, Buckingham: Open University Press.

Zussman, D. (1986), 'Walking the Tightrope: The Mulroney Government and the Public Service', in M.J. Prince (ed.), *How Ottawa Spends: 1986–87: Tracking the Tories*, Toronto: Methuen, pp. 250–82.

Zussman, D. (2008), *The New Governing Balance: Politicians and Public Servants in Canada*, The Tansley Lecture, Regina, 13 March.

Zussman, D. (2012), 'Setting Boundaries for Political Advisors', *Canadian Government Executive*, **18** (3), 30.

Zussman, D. (2013), *Off and Running: The Prospects and Pitfalls of Government Transitions in Canada*, Toronto: University of Toronto Press.

Zussman, D. (2015), 'Public Policy Analysis in Canada a 40-Year Overview', in E. Parson (ed.), *A Subtle Balance: Expertise, Evidence, and Democracy in Public Policy and Governance, 1970–2010*, Montreal and Kingston: McGill-Queen's University Press, pp. 11–36.

Zussman, D. (2016), 'Stephen Harper and the Federal Public Service: An Uneasy and Unresolved Relationship', in J. Ditchburn and G. Fox (eds), *The Harper Factor: Assessing a Prime Minister's Policy Legacy*, Montreal and Kingston: McGill-Queen's University Press, pp. 44–61.

Index

Abbott, Tony 57, 69, 86
accountability
    layering 146–7
    paradox 146
    types 146
accounting officer 35, 58, 59, 82–3, 151
administrative coordination 158, 163–8
administrative traditions
    differentiating features 22–3
agencification 11, 35, 46, 96–7, 107, 240
agency theory 10, 67
Anglo-American tradition 21n1
Anglophone countries
    British Commonwealth 31, 32
    diffusion and policy transfers 32–3
    disconnects and the role of context
        35–6
    identity 26–7
    reform transfers in public
        management 33–5
    reinforcement of group
        distinctiveness 30–36
    variations between 27–30
Anglophone administrative tradition 27
    adaptability 211
    core principles and constraints 23–4
    features 22–3
    impact of politicisation and
        managerialism 204–8
    instrumentalism 6, 24
    instrumentalist conception 67–8,
        205
    pragmatism 24, 25, 27, 29
    role and continuing significance 5–8
    and Westminster model 23–4,
        211–12
Anglo-Saxon tradition see Anglophone
    administrative tradition
appointment systems for department
    heads 66
    in Australia 69, 73–4, 75, 85–6
    in Canada 74, 85–6

evolution of 70–71
informal processes 76
management of appointments 75–6
in New Zealand 71–3
'political' appointment systems
    73–4
politicising effects on behaviour
    76–83
professional appointment systems
    71–3
recruitment process 70
source of appointments 70
in United Kingdom 69, 72–3, 75, 86
variations between countries 85–7
Ardern government (NZ) 130, 162
austerity 109–10, 166, 180, 183
Australia
    and Anglophone reform model 5
    Cabinet Implementation Unit 47,
        165
    efficiency scrutiny model 34
    instrumentalism 37n4
    Member of Parliament (Staff) Act
        1984 (Cth) 53
    ministerial offices 53, 54, 55
    minister/public servant relationship
        81–2, 192, 193, 194
    new public management (NPM) 27,
        201
    policy failure 62–3, 65n12
    political advisers 59, 63, 173
    pragmatism 25
    prime minister's department 164
    prime minister's office (PMO) 51–2,
        65n6, 162
    Public Governance, Performance
        and Accountability Act 2013
        (Cth) 102, 118
    public service see Australian public
        service (APS)
    Public Service Board 73

reforms of public management 106,
   228–9
reviews of public management
   106–7, 203, 222, 223–4
Australian public service (APS)
accountability system 146
agencification 35, 96–7
appointment of department heads
   69, 73–4, 75, 78, 85–6
Data Integration Partnership for
   Australia 171
bureaucratisation 201
capabilities 110
capability reviews 167
collaboration 178, 182
consultants 62, 111
decentring 236–7
delegation 95
devolution 93, 94, 144
digital transformation strategy 169
Efficiency through Contestability
   Programme 166
financial management 33–4, 98,
   144, 145
Financial Management Improvement
   Program (FMIP) 33–4, 98,
   117
Functional and Efficiency Reviews
   135n9
horizontal coordination 171, 172
human resource management
   99–100, 109
impact of job insecurity and
   turnover on senior public
   servants 76–7
inter-agency agreements 171
internal regulation and red tape 139,
   143, 145
mandarins 68
managerialism 34, 201, 228–9
networks 177
outcomes and outputs 126–7
performance management 117–8,
   123, 126, 127, 130, 132
policy capability 103, 104
politicisation 42, 189, 201, 228–9
Priorities and Delivery Unit 165
Public Service Amendment Act
   2013 (Cth) 82
Public Service Commissioner 75

Red Tape Reduction Framework
   143
removal of department heads 73–4
risk aversion 141, 142, 144
risk management 102
Secretaries Board 168
shared services 167
status of department heads 69
system failures 200
task forces 174

Blair government (UK)
centralisation 57, 202
and civil service reform 193
control of civil service 54, 85
delivery culture 63, 151
joined-up agenda 183
managerialism 234
ministerial offices 53–4
No. 10 and Cabinet Office 52, 55,
   79, 164
performance regime and targetism
   29, 128
permanent secretary appointments
   and turnover 69, 76
policy tsars 47, 60
Prime Minister's Delivery Unit
   (PMDU) 46–7, 165, 242
public–private partnerships 34
role of No. 10 staff 52
Strategy Unit 164, 165
Brown government (UK)
bureaucracy
regulation construction 143–5
relationship with democracy 7, 15,
   21n4
bureaucratisation
accountability layering 146–7
control, risk and culture 137–8
demands and responses 147–9
entrenchment of 136
implications for incentive structures
   150–52
implications for management 150
implications for public management
   systems 149–50
multiple demands and
   accountabilities 145–9
and politicisation 152–4
under public management 153–4

rules and regulations *see* rules and
regulations

Cabinet and its committees 160–61
Cameron government (UK) 45, 57, 69,
76, 85, 122, 138, 161, 165, 188,
193
Canada
Blueprint 2020 140
cabinet committees and political
coordination 161
Coordinating Committee of Deputy
Ministers 168
Federal Accountability Act 2006 35
incrementalism 29
influence of United States and
Britain 28–9, 37n5
lead ministers and political
coordination 161–2
Management, Resources and Results
Structure (MRRS) (CA)
118–9
Management and Accountability
Framework (MAF) 118, 119,
123, 124–5, 147, 167–8
managerialism 27, 201, 230–31
ministerial offices 53, 54
ministerial policy-related roles 48
minister/public servant relationship
193–4
new public management (NPM) 202
number of ministers 65n8
Policy on Results 119
political advisers as policy actors
45–6, 49
pragmatism 25, 29
prime minister's office (PMO) 51,
162, 163, 173–4
reforms of public management 106,
230–31
reviews of public management 222,
224–5
Canadian public service
accountability system 147
agencification 35, 96–7
appointment of department heads
74, 85–6
bureaucratisation 201
decentralisation 93, 94, 237
delegation 95

deliverology 21n4, 34
digital coordination 169
executive performance 123
financial management 99
horizontal coordination 171
horizontal management 182–3
human resource management 100
internal regulation and red tape 139,
140, 143–4, 145
leadership bodies 168
mandarins 68
networks 177
performance management 118–9,
123, 124–5, 126, 127, 128,
130, 132
policy capability 103–4
politicisation 42, 189, 201, 230–31
Privy Council Office 74, 75, 83,
123, 165
programme evaluation 126
Public Service Employment Act
2003 144
quality of performance information
127
Results and Delivery Unit 165
risk aversion 141, 142, 144–5, 150
risk management 102
shared services 167
stewardship 83
system failures 200
Web of Rules Action Plan 140
capability reviews 34–5, 167–8
capacity of the state 16
central capacity 41
central coordination 160
Centrelink (AU) 96, 172
change
'change continuity' 84
and cycles in public management 17
provision for 16
Chrétien government 57, 86
Clark government 63
collaboration
austerity and 183
definition 158, 170
explanations for rise, decline and
plateauing of 181–3
nature of 170–71
patterns of 179–83
politicisation and 183

reform cycle and 182–3
searching for 177–9
vertically centred financial
arrangements and 182
collaborative governance 158
coordination *see also* political
coordination
administrative coordination 158,
163–5
central coordination 160
horizontal coordination 157,
169–72, 180, 181
instruments 157–8, 180
management coordination 180–81
modes of 157–9
paradox of 184
patterns of 179–83
political coordination 158, 160–63
vertical coordination 157, 159–60,
179
corporate performance assessment 125
court government 160

debureaucratisation 136, 139, 197–8
decentralisation 197
delegation and centralisation within
departments 95–6
devolution to departments 93–4, 197
disaggregation to agencies through
agencification 96–7
modes of 92–7
decentring 236–8
deliverology 21n4, 34
democracy, relationship with
bureaucracy 7, 15, 21n4
departments, integration and mergers 172
deregulation 197–8
devolution 93–4, 95, 143, 197
digital coordination 169

efficiency 166
exceptionalism 27, 29, 30

financial management 33–4, 48, 98–9,
108

Gateway Review process 34
Gove, Michael 45, 103

Harper government (CA) 45, 51, 57, 80,
151, 162, 182, 202, 211
Hawke government (AU) 53
Heseltine, Michael 48
Heywood, Jeremy 47, 72, 89n4
Hodge, Margaret 83
horizontal coordination 157, 180, 181
instruments 169–71, 183
integration and mergers 172
programme delivery and
inter-agency cooperation 171
horizontal management 170, 179, 182
Howard government (AU) 52, 56–7, 79,
82, 86, 151, 162
human resource management 99–100,
108

incentive structures 150–52
incrementalism 29
innovation and risk 149–50
interdepartmental committees (IDCs)
174–5, 179
interest groups, role in policy process 62

Keating government (AU) 73

leadership instruments 168

management control 91–2
management coordination 180–81
managerialism 10–13
in Australia 228–9
and bureaucratisation 136, 153–4
in Canada 230–31
combined with politicisation 14
decentralisation 197
deregulation and debureaucratisation
197–8
financial management and 98–9
impact on reform of public
management 108
impact on role of senior public
servants 102, 103
long-term results 195, 196
management improvement 195–7
management paradox 111
and modern reform era 31–2
in New Zealand 46, 232–3
performance and 113

performance and results 198
rise of 3
system design, reform and change
    199
system failures 200
in United Kingdom 234–5
mandarins 68
Maude, Francis 57–8, 61, 65n5, 69
May government (UK) 45, 52, 55, 161
ministerial advisers *see* political advisers
ministerial departments, consolidation
    and reinforcement 241
ministerial resources
    ministerial offices 52–6, 79
    and politicisation of executive
        branch 50–56
    prime ministers' offices (PMOs)
        50–52
minister/public servant relationship 3
    agency-like relationship 67–8,
        69–70
    impact of job insecurity and
        turnover on 76–7
    modernised and rebalanced 191–2
    oscillating 192–3
    politically skewed 193–4
    stewardship 15, 68, 81–3, 89n2
    tension in reformulated relationships
        59
    traditional configuration 191
    trustee relationship 67, 68
    types of relationship 189–94
    Westminster model 8, 25
ministers
    contradictions in empowering
        ministers 60–61
    instruments for expanding influence
        of 10*t*
    lead ministers 161–2
    management roles 48–50, 58
    micromanagement by 50
    ministerial discretion 77, 94
    ministerial responsibility 60
    performance 60
    policy implementation roles 44,
        46–8, 56–7, 58
    policy initiation and development
        roles 44–5, 56–7, 58
Mulroney government (CA) 41, 42, 45,
    53, 57, 74

neo-centralisation 242–3
neo-Taylorism 90
'network governance' 12
networks 170
    functional and professional networks
        175–7
    IDCs, forums, task forces and
        working parties 174–5
    political networks 173–4
    task forces 174
    working parties 174
new political governance (NPG) 3, 9, 13,
    43, 80, 86
new public governance 12
new public management (NPM) 3, 10,
    12, 21n3, 27, 32, 109–10, 201
new right ideas, influence of 41–2
New Zealand
    and Anglophone reform model 5
    Administrative and Support Services
        Benchmarking (BASS) 125
    Better Public Services (BPS) agenda
        47, 126, 179, 198
    Better Public Services Advisory
        Group 120
    Better Public Services (BPS) review
        161–2
    cabinet committees and political
        coordination 161
    exceptionalism 30
    Fiscal Responsibility Act 1994 120
    lead ministers and political
        coordination 161–2
    Managing for Outcomes 120
    ministerial offices 53, 54, 56
    ministerial policy-related roles 45,
        47
    ministerial responsibilities 60
    minister/public servant relationship
        81, 191–2
    new public management (NPM) 27,
        202
    prime minister's department 164
    Public Finance Act 1989 119, 120
    reforms of public management 106,
        202–3, 232–3
    reviews of public management 203,
        222–3, 225
    State Sector Act 1988 71

State Sector Amendment Act 2013
81
State Services Commission 71, 81,
119, 123–4
State Service Commissioner 71, 75,
123, 192
New Zealand public service
accountability system 147
agencification 35
appointment of department heads
71–3
bureaucratisation 201
capabilities 110
capability reviews 167
collaboration 178–9, 182
corporate performance assessment
125
decentring 236, 238
delegation 95
devolution 93–4
executive performance 123–4
functional networks 175–6
horizontal coordination 171, 172
human resource management 100
impact of job insecurity and
turnover on senior public
servants 77
internal regulation and red tape 139
management control and discretion
108
managerialism 46, 201, 232–3
outcomes and outputs 126–7
performance management 119–20,
123–4, 125, 126, 128, 130,
132–3
policy capability 104, 105
politicisation 42, 85, 189, 201,
232–3
programme evaluation 125
Public Service Leaders Group 168
risk aversion 142, 149
risk management 102
State Services Leadership Team 168
stewardship culture 81
system failures 200

O'Donnell, Gus 89n4

Parkinson, Martin 62

path dependence 117–8, 181, 205
Pearson government (CA) 50, 51
performance management 101
Anglophone countries commitment
to 114
Australian frameworks 117–8, 130
British frameworks 121–2, 130
Canadian framework 118–9, 124–5,
130
corporate performance assessment
125
cross-cutting programme
performance 126
decoupling of functions from
operational practice 127–8
executive performance 123–4
frameworks 116–26, 129–30
implementation/delivery and results
123
New Zealand framework 119–20,
130
outcomes and outputs 126–7
ownership of performance
instruments 132–3
paradox of performance 113
performance instruments and
systems 115–6
performance management systems
34, 130–33
performance movement 113
Planning, Reporting and
Accountability Structure
(PRAS) 118
political coordination and 166
programme evaluation 125–6
purposes of performance
information 114–5
quality of performance information
127
renewal through planning and
priorities 129–31
specialised instruments 122–6
targetism 128
use of performance information
128–9
weaknesses of 115, 126–9
whole-of-government framework
113–4
policy capability 102–5
policy formulation

initiation and development by
        ministers 44–6, 56–7
    separation from implementation 35
policy implementation
    policy failure 62–3, 142
    role of ministers 46–8, 56–7
    separation from policy formation 35
policy process
    consequences of politicising 61–3
    externalising advice 61–2, 111
    impact on public policy 63
    policy advice and analysis 61
    policy-based evidence 62, 103, 109
    role of interest groups 62
policy tsars 47, 56, 58, 59, 163
political advisers
    accountability and capability 55,
        59, 63
    in ministers' offices 52–6
    as policy actors 45–6
    political networks 173–4
political advisory system 164
political control 152–3
political coordination 158
    cabinet and its committees 160–61
    lead ministers 161–2
    and performance management 166
    policy tsars 163
    political advisory system 163
    politicisation and 160
    prime minister's office 162–3
    whole-of-government frameworks,
        programmes and instruments
        143, 165–8
political management 204
politicisation
    in Australia 42, 189, 201, 228–9
    and bureaucratisation 152–4
    in Canada 42, 189, 201, 230–31
    collaboration and 183
    combined with managerialism 14
    consequences for public service
        194–5
    consequences of politicising policy
        process 61–3
    contradictions in empowering
        ministers 60–61
    definition 38–9
    dynamic and dialectics of 87–8
    functions affected by 188

impact on reform of public
        management 108, 187–95
impacts on senior public servant
        behaviour 77–80
instruments and levers 39–40, 84–8,
        188–9
ministerial performance 60
ministerial policy and management
        roles 43–50
nature of 8–10
new political governance and 43
in New Zealand 42, 189, 201, 232–3
policy tsars as political appointees
        47
political executive dynamics over
        reform era 40–43
responding to new public
        management and new
        environments 42
responsiveness and new right ideas
        41–2
shifts and swings between roles
        56–61
strengthening of central capacity
        and 41
tension in reformulated relationships
        59
unbounded and ambiguous spheres
        of operation 58–9
in United Kingdom 41–2, 189, 201,
        234–5
prime minister's department (PMD)
        164–5
prime ministers' offices (PMO) 50–52,
        84, 163–4, 188–9
principal-agent theory 9, 15, 59, 67
private sector, distinguished from public
        sector 26
programme delivery and implementation
    central monitoring and driving of
        242
    deliverology 21n4, 34
    delivery failure 21n4
programme evaluation 125–6
public choice paradigm 15
public management and governance
    agendas for change 212–16
    bureaucratic agenda 212–13
    contemporary crisis in 211–12
    cycles in 17

digital agenda 214
managerialist agenda 213–14
politicised agenda 213
reform *see* reform of public
    management and governance
revisiting settings and adapting
    fundamentals 216–18
scenarios for twenty-first century
    214–16
public management systems
administrative traditions 22–3
Anglophone tradition *see*
    Anglophone tradition
bureaucratic discretion 15
comparison of 200–202
control and autonomy within 14–15
control and discretion 107–11
core capabilities constrained by
    contexts 97–102
decentralisation 92–7
delegation and centralisation within
    departments 95–6
design and development 7–8
devolution to departments 93–4, 95
dilemmas 90–91, 107
disaggregation to agencies through
    agencification 96–7
evolution of 10–11
financial management 98–9, 108
human resource management
    99–100, 108
implications of bureaucratisation
    149–50
incentive structures 150–52
innovation and risk 149–50
internal regulation and red tape
    138–40
long-term patterns 203–10
management attrition, marking time,
    and reversals 107–11
patterns of change and cycles as
    explanations 208–10
policy capability 102–5
political management 204
processes and capabilities 108–9,
    110
propensity to change 109–11
reform *see* reform of public
    management and governance

reform unresolved or perpetual crisis
    202–3
risk aversion 140–43
risk management 101–2
rules and regulations *see* rules and
    regulations
public policy, impact of policy process
    on 63
public sector, distinguished from private
    sector 26
public service
department heads/permanent
    secretaries *see* senior public
    servants
erosion of policy capacity 61
management *see* public management
    systems
policy advice 57
roles in governing 57
secondments to ministers' offices 79
use of consultants 62
public service/political executives
    relationship *see* minister/public
    servant relationship
public value governance 12

rational choice theory 7
re-aggregation, and rationalising public
    agencies 240–41
recentring 238–40
red tape 137, 138–40
reform of public management and
    governance
in 1980s 186
analysis of 6–8
Anglophone approach *see*
    Anglophone tradition
changes over last forty years 3–4
cycles of reform 182
disrupters to 1–2
disruptive steering 110
dysfunctional trends 186–7
instigation of modern era of reform
    2–3, 31–2
key ideas behind 6–7
lack of progress 1
major official reviews 222–6
managerialism *see* managerialism
politicisation of executive branch
    see politicisation

propensity for 105–7, 109–11
questions about long-term reform
        2–6
reform transfers as endogenous
        process 33–5
results and consequences of
        sustained reform 4–5, 136
types of initiatives 106, 107
types of reforms 186
regulation
    factors affecting nature of 137
    internal regulation and red tape
        138–40
risk aversion 138, 140–41
    blaming of public servants and 142
    fear of audit and 142–3
    implementation failures and 142
    public scrutiny and 141–2
    sources 141
risk culture 137
risk management 101–2
Rudd government (AU) 52, 73, 164
rules and regulations
    deregulation 143, 197–8
    factors affecting nature of 137
    internal regulation and red tape
        138–43
    'over-control' 137
    risk aversion and 140–43
    'rule-evolution red tape' 137–8
    'rule-inception red tape' 137
    self-infliction of regulatory burdens
        143–5

senior public servants
    appointment *see* appointment
        systems for department heads
    careers 76–7
    categories 78
    managerialism's impact on role of
        102, 103
    mandarins 68
    performance management 123–4
    politicisation impacts on behaviour
        77–80
    politicising of central agency
        positions 75
    promiscuous partisanship 80–81

relationship with ministers *see*
        minister/public servant
        relationship
    removal of 73–4, 75–6
    status 66, 69
shared services 35–6, 166–7
social services 172
special advisers (spads) *see* political
        advisers
stability, provision for 16
stewardship 15, 68, 81–3, 89n2, 218

Taylorism 27, 28
Thatcher government (UK) 2, 31, 32, 41,
        45, 56, 65n1, 69, 72, 85, 86
the state, expanding role 41
traditional public administration (TPA)
        7, 179
Trudeau, Justin government (CA) 47, 51,
        79, 161, 211
Trudeau, Pierre government (CA) 9, 41,
        51, 53, 75
trust crisis 211, 216
trustee theory 15, 67, 68

United Kingdom
    and Anglophone reform model 5
    cabinet committees and political
        coordination 161
    chronic reformism 29
    civil service *see* UK civil service
    Civil Service Commission (CSC)
        72, 85
    Constitutional Reform and
        Governance Act 2010 72
    exceptionalism 29–30
    influence during reform era 33, 35,
        36
    influence of new right ideas 41–2
    Ministerial Contestability Policy
        Fund 61–2
    ministerial discretion 94
    ministerial management
        responsibilities 48, 49–50, 58
    ministerial offices 53–4
    ministerial performance 60
    ministerial policy-related roles 45,
        47, 58

minister/senior public servant relationship 82–3, 193
National Audit Office (NAO) 99, 143
new public management (NPM) 27, 201, 202
No. 10 Downing St 52, 55, 162, 164, 180
policy tsars 47, 56, 58, 59
Prime Minister's Delivery Unit (PMDU) 46–7, 164
Public Accounts Committee 143
public–private partnerships (PPP) 34
reforms of public management 106, 202–3, 234–5
reviews of public management 203, 223, 225–6
special advisers (spads) 173
UK civil service
accountability system 147
agencification 35, 96, 97
appointment of permanent secretaries 69, 72–3, 75, 86
bureaucratisation 201
Cabinet Office 52, 55, 164, 180
capabilities 110–11
capability reviews 167
Civil Service Reform Plan 72, 138–9
Civil Service Steering Board 168
departmental boards 49–50, 65n4
departmental business plans (DBPs) 122
decentring 237
digital coordination 169
Efficiency and Reform Group 166
executive performance 124
externalising policy advice 61–2
Financial Management Initiative (FMI) 33–4, 48, 98, 117–8, 121
financial management 33–4, 48, 98–9, 108–9
financial stewardship 81
functional networks 175
horizontal coordination 171
human resource management 100, 109

impact of job insecurity and turnover on senior civil servants 76, 77
incentive structures 151
internal regulation and red tape 138–9
joined-up government 177–8, 180, 182
management control and discretion 108
managerialism 34, 201, 234–5
mandarins 68
Next Steps reform programme 35, 97, 110
outcomes and outputs 127
Output Performance Analyses (OPAs) 121
performance management 101, 121–2, 124, 127, 128, 130, 132
Permanent Secretaries Management Group 168
policy capability 103, 105
politicisation 45, 85, 189, 201, 234–5
professional networks 176
programme evaluation 125
Public Finance Initiative (PFI) 34
Public Service Agreements (PSAs) 121–2, 128, 151, 177
quality of performance information 127
removal of permanent secretaries 76
risk aversion 143, 145, 149
risk management 101
shared services 166–7
single departmental plans (SDPs) 122, 130–31, 182
system failures 200
targetism 128
Upton, Simon 48

vertical coordination 157, 159–60, 179

Westminster model 21n1, 37n2
relations between politicians and bureaucrats 8, 25–6
role in Anglophone tradition 23

as source of core principles and
  constraints 23–4
Westminster democracies 26
Whitlam government (AU) 53, 73
whole-of-government frameworks,
  programmes and instruments
  165–8
  capability reviews 167–8
  digital coordination 169

efficiency 166
governing and leadership bodies 168
internal regulation and red tape 140,
  143
performance management 113, 114,
  115, 119, 122, 127, 130
political coordination 143
shared services 35–6, 166–7
Wilson government (UK) 50